Luigi Maruotti - Carmine Volpe
Vincenzo Neri - Marina Perrelli
Roberta Ravasio

# THE ITALIAN COUNCIL OF STATE IN EUROPE

## Dialogue with the other Supreme Administrative Courts

Compendium of the proceedings
of the two-year term of the Italian Presidency
of the ACA-Europe (2021-2023)

ISBN: 9791281851184 (Merita edizioni)
ISBN: 9791370108458 (Tirant Lo Blanch)
ISBN: 9783748962540 (Nomos Verlag)

Graphic design and layout: Catia De Bacco
Editorial coordination: Giusy Bravetti


Piazza Teresa Noce, 17/D – 10155 Torino, Italy
www.meritaeditore.com

Published in co-edition with:

Nomos Verlagsgesellschaft mbH & Co. KG Waldseestr. 3–5 76530 Baden-Baden
Tirant lo Blanch - Artes gráficas 14, Bajo dcha. 46010 Valencia

# EDITED BY

LUIGI MARUOTTI, President of the Council of State

CARMINE VOLPE, Adjunct President of the Council of State and Director of the Study and Training Office of Administrative Justice

VINCENZO NERI, President of Section of the Council of State and Vice Coordinator of the Study and Training Office of the Administrative Justice

MARINA PERRELLI, Councillor of State and member of the the Massimario Office of the Administrative Justice

ROBERTA RAVASIO, Councillor of State and member of the Study and Training Office of the Administrative Justice

# INDEX

# PREFACE

During Italy's two-year presidency of the ACA-Europe, from 2021 to 2023, the Italian Council of State has gained important experience, such as the meeting of the Association's delegates with the President of the Republic, Mr Sergio Mattarella, in the Quirinale on 23 May 2022.

The Head of State recalled how «valuable is the task of every association leading to rediscover the reasons of European culture and law» and how, through constant dialogue, exchange of information and good practices, ACA-Europe «contributes to defining the living law of the European Union and of its Member States, strengthening cohesion while respecting their different identities».

This publication stems from the idea of bringing together in a single volume the result of the efforts of the Council of State during the two years of the Italian Presidency, consisting in the general reports of the six events held in Fiesole, Paris, Rome, Madrid, Riga, and Naples, the contents of the glossary created to explain the one hundred and fifty definitions shared by the Courts, as well as a report on the dissemination activities carried out in collaboration with the universities.

The dialogue and the cooperation within all the members of ACA-Europe represent the DNA of this Association.

The "horizontal dialogue" among Supreme administrative courts and Councils of State was the topic chosen by those who preceded me as President of the Council of State – I am referring to Filippo Patroni Griffi and to the late Franco Frattini.

During my Presidency, particular attention has been paid to issues relating to common standards of judicial protection in cases involving the exercise of public powers by administrative judges, aiming to share a "common judicial culture", while respecting the national legal systems: in the European judicial area, the most effective and timely protection of citizens and companies is a fundamental building block in the realisation of an effective European citizenship.

With this in mind, as Vice-President of ACA-Europe, at the meeting in Versailles in November 2024, I made a suggestion that our Jurifast database should be enhanced in order to gather in a more systematic way the judgments of the Supreme Administrative Courts which have ruled on the scope and interpretation of European provisions applicable in the territory of all Member States. Awareness of these decisions should then be disseminated more widely through an easily accessible and searchable *newsletter*.

This initiative is in line with what the Court of Justice of the European Union decided in its judgment of 6 October 2021, C-561/2019 – the so-called new CILFIT – where it stated that, in order to decide whether or not to refer a question under Article 267 TFEU, the national court must examine the actual or presumed position of other interpreters in the different Member States, also in light of the multiple language versions of EU rules.

In other words, the Court of Justice has drawn attention to the desirability of developing the 'horizontal dialogue' among national courts, which is all the more useful when EU law may lend itself to divergent interpretations within the different systems.

Still as part of the dialogue among the courts, another initiative was promoted during the Italian Presidency: the creation of a glossary.

Thanks to the work of the Glossary Group, coordinated by the Italian Council of State, one hundred and fifty terms and expressions were identified and, after being submitted for approval to all the Member States, make up the first group of a "vocabulary" of shared definitions of substantive and procedural administrative law, published on the website of the Aca-Europe.

The initiative is an instrument for dialogue not only among the Supreme Administrative Courts and the supranational Courts, but also among the public administrations of the different Member States, as already exists for civil and criminal law. This concept has also been reiterated by the European Court of Justice, which, in a letter of September 2023, underlined how this glossary would contribute to a better understanding and dissemination of the concepts of administrative law and litigation in Europe.

A further initiative cultivated during the Italian Presidency involved the "dissemination" activity, strongly promoted and encouraged by the European Commission, in order to spread awareness of ACA-Europe beyond its specialist field.

At the end of each seminar held in Italy (in Florence, Rome and Naples), a meeting was organised at the law faculties of the local universities involving the President of ACA-Europe, a representative of a European Supreme

Administrative Court and students, professors and scholars of administrative law, in order to explain the nature, aims, and activities of the Association.

This publication is also meant to serve as a tool for the further dissemination of knowledge about the ACA-Europe.

We are living through years of extraordinary complexity, both nationally and internationally: after the critical phase of the pandemic, there are still wars that also affect Europe's borders, climate change, financial and energy crises, and social problems related to all of the above.

The rapid and radical change in society demands an equally accelerated pace from public authorities to understand the problems and find solutions.

The same accelerated pace is also imposed on the administrative judge, who is the natural judge of the exercise of public power and who plays a central role in the system of safeguards, as an institution close to and necessary for the citizens, and at the same time as an instrument for the stability and strengthening of the European project.

I am therefore convinced that dialogue, constructive debate and the sharing of our decisions and experiences in the common house of the Aca-Europe are a fundamental tool for giving substance to the principles of the rule of law: among these, first and foremost, those of the responsibility and equality of each person before the law, and for trying to counteract the phenomena that undermine its fundamental rules.

The democratic fabric of each Member State is based not only on individual national constitutions, but also on European principles, which are now a unifying element.

Luigi Maruotti

Rome, May 2025

# INTRODUCTION

The idea behind this publication is twofold.

Firstly, the need to bring together in a single volume – for a more immediate consultation – the result of the choral effort made by the Italian Council of State during its presidency of the ACA-Europe.

Secondly, the conviction that the information on the legal and procedural systems of the Member States, gathered thanks to the answers to the questionnaires drafted on the topics selected for the six seminars held between 2021 and 2023 – Fiesole, Paris, Rome, Madrid, Riga and Naples – is a useful tool for developing a standardised method of control of public administrations and for improving the sense of European citizenship, which is even more effective if it is guaranteed by a consistent level of protection.

This publication is in line with the mission of the Office for Studies and Training in Administrative Justice and is functional for its implementation, for the following reasons:

- it is a means of introducing administrative judges, also with training to newly appointed judges and in service training, with the ACA-Europe and its objectives, as well as familiarising them with the substantive and procedural legal systems of other Member States, highlighting their similarities and differences and sharing their "best practices";

- it is a useful and valuable tool for the in-depth study of issues of remarkable importance to administrative justice, such as social rights, the limits of the administrative judge's review and the means of protecting individuals and companies in the exercise of discretion, in a key that is not only comparative and doctrinal but also correlated with case law;

- it provides an additional channel for dialogue with international institutions and, in particular, with supranational courts, as it contributes to a better understanding and dissemination of concepts related to administrative cases, also through the glossary of 150 terms in English and French. In such a way it facilitates the dissemination and mutual knowledge of the various national jurisprudences, which constitute a valuable resource for the progressive reduction of legitimate doubts with reference to the correct interpretation of the European Law.

In my capacity as Director of the Office for Studies and Training in Administrative Justice, I hope that this publication will be useful to the European Administrative Courts, which have contributed to it with their answers to the questionnaires.

As a matter of fact, I truly believe in their fundamental role as institutions close to the citizens and necessary in the process of integration of Europe and in the spirit of the rule of law, as a tool to tackle those phenomena which increasingly attack its rules of peaceful coexistence.

In addition, I believe that the publication can be of help to the Italian administrative judges, enabling them to enhance their ability to use the tools for the protection of the rights and interests, targeted by the exercise of public power, for the construction of a true European administrative law, made up of common principles and rules and consistency in their case law.

Carmine Volpe

Rome, May 2025

# PHOTOS

**ACA-Europe Naples, 26 June 2023** - Colloquium "Services to citizens and social rights", Mr Luigi Maruotti, President of the Council of State of Italy, handing over the Presidency of ACA-Europe to Mr Kari Kuusiniemi, President of the Supreme Administrative Court of Finland, who exercises the Presidency in close collaboration with Ms Helena Jäderblom, President of the Supreme Administrative Court of Sweden

**Fiesole, 4 October 2021** - Seminar "Law, Courts and guidelines for the public administration"

**Paris, 6 December 2021** - Seminar "The judicial review of regulatory authorities"

**Rome, 23 May 2022** - Seminar "Techniques for the protection of private subjects in contrast with public authorities: actions and remedies – liability and compliance"

**ROME, 23 MAY 2022 -** Meeting of ACA-Europe delegates with the President of the Republic of Italy Sergio Mattarella, "Presidency of the Republic Press Office"

**ROME, 23 MAY 2022 -** Meeting of ACA-Europe delegates with the President of the Republic of Italy Sergio Mattarella, "Presidency of the Republic Press Office"

**Rome, 23 May 2022** - Meeting of ACA-Europe delegates with the President of the Republic of Italy Sergio Mattarella, "Presidency of the Republic Press Office"

**Rome, 23 May 2022** - General Assembly of ACA-Europe

**Madrid 21 November 2022** - Seminar "The application of general principles and clauses in the case law of contentious-administrative courts"

**Riga, 27 April 2023** - Seminar "The judge and inert administration. Administrative discretionary power"

| **Naples, 26 June 2023** - Colloquium "Services to citizens and social rights"

| **Naples, 26 June 2023** - Colloquium "Services to citizens and social rights"

**Naples, 26 June 2023 -** Colloquium "Services to citizens and social rights"

# ACA-Europe Seminar
# “Law, Courts and guidelines for the public administration”

**Fiesole, Italy**
**4 October 2021**
**General Report by the Italian Council of State**

# Summary of the General Report of the Seminar "Law, Courts and guidelines for public administration" held in Fiesole, Italy, 4 October 2021

The Fiesole seminar was the first event of the Italian Presidency of the ACA-Europe and its aim was to explore the potential of the "horizontal dialogue" between Supreme Administrative Courts.

The report summarises, organising them in aggregate manner, the main indications that can be deduced from the answers given to the questionnaire in order to:

1) outline the rules governing the interpretation and application of the law in each State, with particular regard to the instruments available to the judge;

2) investigate what institutions exist in the various States to ensure the uniformity and homogeneity of case law with an in-depth study of the complying effect of the decisions of the Supreme Courts in relation to the case decided and the enucleation of principles and/or guidelines to direct the future action of the public administration;

3) identify the procedural institutes through which the effective enforcement of the decision can be achieved, investigating the different forms of protection granted by each legal system;

4) investigate the advisory functions of the Supreme Courts, where they exist, towards the government and public administrations in general.

An examination of the replies to the questionnaire reveals that in almost all the Member States there are general rules for the interpretation of the law, most of which are positively regulated, as they are provided for by the Civil Code, the Constitution, the Code of Administrative Justice.

There are a few cases in which the rules of interpretation are based exclusively on case law (Germany, the European Union, Greece and Luxembourg).

Usually, the Supreme Administrative Courts together with the other high courts, *i.e.* the Constitutional Court and the Supreme Court of Cassation, contribute to the definition and clarification of the general rules of interpretation, sometimes even through the elaboration of interpretative guidelines, with the notable exceptions of Finland and France, where the administrative court of last instance determines the general rules and methods of interpretation of the law.

The interpretative criteria, used uniformly by almost all countries, are the literal criterion and the *ratio legis*, which is interpreted in relation to the coherence of the legal system and deduced from the preparatory works of legislative texts and the opinions rendered by the Supreme Courts themselves in their consultative capacity. In the event of gaps in the legislative text, the analogical criterion is used.

Common to many Courts is the use as interpretative parameters of both European Union law and the clauses of proportionality and reasonableness, while recourse to custom and professional usage is residual. Sometimes alone as in Germany, more frequently together with the general principles of the national legal system, European law and general clauses such as reasonableness and proportionality.

The case of the Estonian legal system, which admits the possibility of filling the gaps for which the legislature was responsible to be unconstitutional, is quite original.

In most countries, the Courts use internally created bodies for the collection and publication of judgments. These bodies are generally composed of judges or civil servants, rarely university professors, who also provide information support through the preparation of reports on decisions of the European courts, periodic updates on new case law or new legislation, the preparation of statistical analyses, training of judges and the preparation and study of individual cases.

In most countries, there are freely accessible databases for searching the judgments of administrative courts, although some countries provide criteria for the selection of decisions, excluding judgments on manifestly inadmissible or unfounded cases (the Netherlands), or on specific areas of interest (such as immigration for the Netherlands or aliens legislation for Belgium), or on less important disputes (Finland).

In most countries, the Supreme Court's ruling does not have a binding value in itself, but the consistency and uniformity of case law is ensured through the system of precedents, the possibility of raising preliminary questions in the interest of law, informal meetings between Supreme Court judges prior to the discussion of the case and, above all, the authority of the function exercised by the SAC.

In this respect, there are many Supreme Courts operating in special or extended composition when they are called upon to resolve conflicts of interpretation and to whose pronouncements specific procedural rules attribute enhanced effectiveness, e.g. through the exclusion of dissenting opinions of individual judges or individual chambers or through the provision of special mechanisms to stimulate possible reconsideration.

It deserves to be emphasised that both in systems where the decisions of the Supreme Administrative Courts are binding on the lower courts and in those where this is not the case, the consistency and predictability of decisions reaches a very high level, ranging between 75% and 100% for most countries and between 50% and 75% for a small minority.

As regards the dissenting opinion, in some countries (Estonia, Finland, Latvia, Norway, Portugal, Romania), the individual judge of the Supreme Court may formally dissent, while in other (Italy, Belgium, Finland, Greece, Lithuania, Czech Republic) a section of the Supreme Court may dissent from the principle upheld in a special composition and refer the case back to the Court.

As regards the relationship between the different jurisdictions, it is common to set up working groups between the representatives of the different courts or informal mechanisms for regular consultation between the different jurisdictions. In some Member States, consistency in the interpretation guidelines between the different jurisdictions is ensured by the adoption of special interpretative measures adopted jointly by the judges of the General Assembly of judges of the Court of Cassation and the Supreme Administrative Court, or by the possibility of referring the matter to a panel composed of representatives of the different jurisdictions, or by promoting appeal or cassation in the interest of the law or in a preventive function.

In dual systems, the resolution of conflicts of jurisdiction is entrusted to a special judicial body composed of representatives of the various jurisdictions or to the Court of Cassation, whereas in a few countries the issue is resolved individually by each judicial order, without centralised coordinating powers.

As regards to the impact of Supreme Courts decisions on the activity of the public administration, in most countries, the judgment annulling an administrative act binds the public administration in the subsequent exercise of power, with only two exceptions (in limited cases, such as the factual circumstances – Estonia – and rare cases such as requirements of fiscal nature that induce the Ministry of Finance not to enforce the decision – Germany).
The extent of the obligation considerably varies across the different countries, as do the consequences of non-compliance with the ruling.
A common fact that emerges from the experience of almost all States is the tendency of the public administration to take into account the guidelines expressed by the Supreme Administrative Courts and to follow them in its own activity, even in the absence of a specific legal constraint, in application of the principles of legal certainty and equality.
With regard to the proper and timely execution of judgments, the situation that emerges from the answers is extremely varied.
In most countries, there is a judicial procedure before the administrative judge or the ordinary judge to ensure the full and complete execution of rulings, also through the direct substitution of the administration by the judge or the appointment of a commissioner *ad acta*; in others, there are alternative procedures, mostly of administrative nature, and/or the provision of sanctions for delay which guarantee the execution of judicial rulings (Bulgaria, Norway and the Czech Republic).
A further disincentive in almost all legal systems is the liability of the public administration and the official for damage caused by the inexact or non-execution of judicial decisions, although the forms of liability are formulated very differently, as are the criteria for allocating jurisdiction for actions for damages.
The replies show that, on average, the percentage of judgments whose implementation is incorrect or incomplete is extremely low, less than 2%, and that this eventuality is defined as 'extremely rare' by the majority of States, with the exception of a few special cases.
Only in a few Member States (Belgium, Finland, France, Greece, Italy, Norway, the Netherlands and the EU) do the Supreme Administrative Courts also have advisory functions for the government and the public administration, although they these are formulated differently:
- as to the type of acts submitted for an opinion, government and parliamentary initiative bills, draft primary legislation, government and ministerial regulations, codification projects and single texts;
- as to who may request an opinion, Government, Parliament, Regions, independent administrative authorities;
- as to the possibility of issuing an opinion upon request or *ex officio*;
- as to the mandatory but non-binding nature for certain types of acts (Belgium, Greece, Italy) or optional (in Finland and Norway).

The rules governing the forms of cooperation between administrative judges and the Government or the public administration vary considerably from one country to another. In some countries, judges may be seconded to the administration (Belgium, France, Italy, Greece), in others only to the Ministry of Justice (Slovenia), in others they may hold university teaching posts, participate in study commissions, competition commissions, with or without suspension from judicial functions.

# Index

# General Report
# Fiesole, 4 October 2021

## Introduction

Dear Colleagues,

It is a pleasure and an honour for me to present this General Report as an introduction to the first seminar of the Italian Presidency of ACA, which, if the health emergency had not occurred, would have taken place last autumn.

Let me briefly recall what I said at the General Assembly held in Berlin in May 2019 when I presented our programme for the upcoming two-year period 2020/2022.

Our intention is to continue along the path undertaken during the German Presidency and to reinforce the potentiality of horizontal dialogue among the Supreme Administrative Courts, a theme perfectly in line with the DNA of ACA, that is to say, of promoting the exchange of mutual knowledge and continuing constructive dialogue.

In particular, the goal we have set ourselves, and which we aim to achieve, is to use horizontal dialogue to render the protection of the rights and interests of individuals and companies as homogeneous as possible, while continuing to respect the individual specifics of each internal system, with a particular focus on those sectors which are not directly subject to European legislation.

The ultimate aim of horizontal dialogue is to achieve the maximum standardisation of the means by which the rights of individuals and companies are protected when dealing with public authorities and this is a fundamental element for the construction of true European citizenship. This serves to avoid that by merely activating legal safeguards in one Member State as opposed to another could result in a diversity of protection levels of the same legal situations.

The pandemic gave us the opportunity to intensify comparisons with what was happening across all European countries, whose judges had to deal with new cases dictated by the emergency laws and the need to reorganise working methods in order to be able to continue their activities and to ensure the protection of rights, precisely at a moment when the health emergency had given the administrative authorities powers that would affect fundamental rights and freedoms, such as freedom of movement, freedom of association and freedom of economic initiatives.

The health emergency has shown how crisis factors tend to be transnational and how they must be dealt with by means of multilateral collaboration at all levels, without reserve.

The intense dialogue developed over the months of the health crisis among the European Administrative Courts has also shown that the administrative court, in its role as the authority competent to fully understand the legitimacy of the acts adopted by the Government and by the different territorial authorities to deal with the health emergency, has taken on the role of guarantor in this difficult balance between the requirements of safety and health protection and the relevant limitations and subsequent limitation of fundamental individual rights.

Clear evidence of the intensification of dialogue and confrontation among the Courts has been the creation on JuriFast of a special section dedicated to Covid-related cases which allows all judges to find out, in real time, how their European colleagues and counterparts have dealt with similar situations, and the creation of a questionnaire "The Supreme Administrative Courts in times of COVID-19 crisis – a lesson learned", whose declared purpose is to understand how the different administrative Courts have organized themselves in order to facilitate the continuance of jurisdictional activity even during the emergency phase in compliance with the fundamental principles of administrative trial, such as public hearings and the full contradictory hearing between the parties, and to share the "best practice" previously adopted to deal with the difficulties and solve the problems encountered.

I believe, therefore, that this General Report and the seminar that will follow constitute yet another important contribution towards guaranteeing the continuity of the experience of horizontal dialogue, a topic that has taken on even more significance during the global health crisis.

Thanks to the replies you all provided in the questionnaire, in fact, it has been possible:

a) to outline what the rules governing the interpretation and the enforcement of the law in each State are, with particular emphasis on the tools available to the judge;

b) to investigate which existing institutes in the different States are in place to ensure the uniformity and homogeneity of jurisprudence together with an in-depth examination of the conforming effect of the decisions of the Supreme Courts, in relation to the decided case and to the elaboration of principles and/or guidelines which will serve to direct the future actions of the public administration;
c) to identify the procedural institutes through which it is possible to effectively enforce the decisions, by analysing the different forms of protection provided by each individual legal system;
d) to analyse in-depth the issue of the advisory functions of the Supreme Courts, where they exist, for the Government public administrations in general.

According to authoritative doctrine, the law as a technique and style of regulation of the inter-subjective relations of a given group (the State) represents one of the strongest and most characteristic identifying elements in the process of integration of the State as part of a superior entity, which is undoubtedly the European Union.

Faced with the changing historical and political frameworks of reference, legal institutions inherently have a long-term stability that allows them to represent a strong identifying element of the human pool within which they operate.

If the judges of the different Member States were able to consult, one with the other, the Courts will therefore be able to make a valid contribution to an ever closer union among European countries, which is the objective of the Treaties of Rome, and make the European judicial and legal area the most effective instrument for the construction of a common constitutional patrimony, a multiple and identifiable common heritage which will allow us to transition “From judge-made law to judge-made Europe”.

In conclusion, I can assure you that this Report would not have seen the light of day without the extraordinary and diligent work coordinated by the Professor of Administrative Law in the Faculty of Law at the Sapienza University of Rome, Avv. Marcello Clarich, and his collaborators, Prof. Giuliano Fonderico, Prof. Alfredo Moliterni and Avv. Gianlorenzo Ioannides.

They contributed to the first draft of the General Report with great enthusiasm and competence. My warmest thanks go to them and to the magistrates who collaborate on a daily basis within the International Sector of the

Council of State and who have also provided invaluable help in the organisation of this first Seminar of the Italian Presidency of Aca-Europe.

Finally, I would like to thank the ACA-Europe Secretariat which has constantly and consistently provided timely, efficient assistance in the various organizational tasks throughout the preparatory phase preceding our Presidency, together with the President of the German Federal Administrative Court, Klaus Rennert, for the extraordinary work accomplished by and under the German presidency. This presidency was extended by one year, and amply demonstrated his exceptionally high standards of dialogue and equilibrium that I have come to appreciate over the years.

## FIRST SESSION:

## THE METHOD OF INTERPRETATION OF THE LAW AND ITS APPLICATION BY THE COURTS

### 1. The role of the Supreme Administrative Courts in the interpretation of the law

A first profile that is of central importance for reconstructing the interpretative function of the Supreme Administrative Courts (SACs) is that of the potential presence and efficiency of the general rules on interpretation within the individual legal systems. There are general rules for the interpretation of the law in all countries which were invited to complete the questionnaire. One of the few exceptions is The Netherlands, whose legal system, beyond the provisions of European law, does not have a clear hierarchy in interpretative criteria, nor an explicit prohibition to use certain interpretative methods[1].

---

[1] With the exception of the provisions contained in the master plan for which the intention of the regulatory body – the city council – can only be used if the written provisions or the overall planning system cannot provide a clear answer [«In the Dutch national legal system, apart from EU law, there are no general rules on how to interpret laws. There is no hierarchy of interpretation methods and no general prohibition on the use of certain interpretation methods. There is one exception, namely regulations in a zoning plan. According to case law of the Administrative Judicial Division of the Council of State (AJD), the intention of the regulator (usually the council of a municipality) can only be used in the interpretation of a regulation if the text of the regulation or the system of the zoning plan do not provide a clear answer»].

As for the legal source that regulates these interpretative criteria, in most cases it is ordinary law (Bulgaria, Latvia, Norway and Serbia) and, especially, the Civil Code (the Czech Republic, Estonia, France, Hungary, Italy, Romania, Spain and Switzerland), the Criminal Code (Belgium and France), or the Code of Administrative Justice itself (Lithuania, Portugal and Slovakia).

In some countries, however, the interpretation criteria are based on the text of the Constitution (Belgium, Finland, Hungary, Ireland, Romania and Slovenia). Only in limited cases may these criteria be provided for by regulatory acts (as in the case of Portugal, where administrations may intervene with secondary acts in order to further clarify and specify the law) or by soft law acts (as in the case of Croatia where the criteria are regulated by guidelines).

On the contrary, there are very few cases in which the rules of interpretation are based only on jurisprudence and not on positive law: this is the case, for example, of Germany (where the Constitutional Court and the higher courts play a decisive role), but it is also the case of the European Union, Greece and Luxembourg.

Generally speaking, however, the Supreme Courts contribute, together with the law, to the definition and clarification of the general rules of interpretation (Belgium, Ireland, Norway, Poland, Portugal, Serbia and Switzerland), sometimes also by means of drawing-up interpretative guidelines (Estonia).

Finally, in several countries, doctrine also plays a key role in the definition of interpretation criteria (the Czech Republic, Finland, Germany, Latvia, Lithuania, Poland and Switzerland).

As for the individual interpretative reference criteria, in almost all countries the literal criterion and the *ratio legis* are applied. Several countries also refer to the criterion of the consistency of the legal system (Belgium, Bulgaria, Croatia, Estonia, Finland, Ireland and Italy).

It is also very frequently possible to refer to the preparatory work of the same normative texts to be interpreted (Belgium, Bulgaria, Croatia, Estonia, EU, Finland, Italy, Latvia, Luxembourg, The Netherlands, Norway, Poland, Romania, Serbia, Spain and Switzerland). Finally, in some countries. it is also possible to refer, by interpretation, to the same opinions issued by the SAC in the context of the process of adoption of the law (Belgium, Bulgaria, Croatia, Finland, Italy and Portugal).

Where gaps in the regulatory text emerge, the analogical criterion is taken into account in almost all countries. Sometimes this criterion is the only one that can fill the gaps in positive law – such as in Germany – while in many cases it can also refer to the general principles of the legal system (Belgium, Bulgaria, Croatia, Estonia, Finland, Italy, Latvia, The Netherlands and Norway).

In the Swiss legal system, for example, gaps can also be filled by the Federal Court by referring to constitutional rules and principles (as was the case of the general principle of equality, which made it possible, before the passing of a federal law, to introduce, by interpretation, the rule of equal pay for both women and men).

Moreover, in some countries, the SAC itself may intervene to fill legislative gaps by applying the general principles of the legal system, including, in particular, that of the coherence of the legal system (Luxembourg). Sometimes, as has been the case with France, gaps in the legislative text can also be filled by referring back to European law; while, in other cases, it is also possible to refer to professional practice and customs (Romania). Finally, it is uniquely the case of the Estonian legal system that it is possible to declare as unconstitutional the omission for which the legislator is ultimately responsible.

As for the specific role played by the SAC, in most cases it contributes to the creation of criteria and methods of interpretation, although, generally, this role is jointly covered by the highest jurisdictions, such as the Constitutional Court or the Court of Cassation (Belgium and Bulgaria).

Indeed, it is a rare occurrence that only the SAC provides the general criteria of interpretation, as is the case of Finland or France (where the Council of State determines the general rules and methods of interpretation of the law based, among others, on the principles set out in Articles 4 and 5 of the Civil Code and Article 111-4 of the Criminal Code).

A final consideration, countries where the SAC is not directly involved in the process of the creation of the interpretation criteria are in a minority (as is the case of Greece, Italy, Norway, Spain, Slovenia and Portugal, where, however, the Administrative Justice Code provides the relative SAC with a series of instruments to ensure overall uniformity of interpretation).

In the decision of individual cases, there is frequent reference to European Union law (Bulgaria, Croatia, Estonia, Finland, France, Germany,

Greece, Ireland and Italy), although there are also countries where this reference operates in a more restricted way (Belgium, Hungary, Norway and Serbia). However, the extent of the reference to European law depends entirely on the individual subject matter: as highlighted by The Netherlands, for example, the openness is greater when dealing with topics such as immigration or the environment.

Moreover, in most of the countries under consideration, the reference to the European Convention on Human Rights is less frequent, on an interpretative level, than the reference to European Union law, (although there are cases in which the references to such supranational systems are substantially equivalent, such as for Croatia, Finland, France, Greece, Norway and Switzerland).

Conversely, the reference to the general clauses of proportionality and rationality is absolutely predominant, except in isolated cases where these clauses operate in a more limited way (Hungary and Slovakia). Equally frequent is the importance attributed – within the interpretative process – to the relevance and weight of the interests concretely at stake (Belgium, Bulgaria, Estonia, EU, Finland, France, Germany, Italy and Poland); only in a few cases does this reference operate in a more restricted way (Croatia, Greece, Ireland, Latvia and Lithuania).

One of the most consistent trends is the limited predisposition to make reference, in an interpretative way, to the jurisprudence of foreign courts in similar cases (Belgium, Bulgaria, Croatia, Estonia, Finland, France, Germany, Greece, Ireland, Italy, Latvia, Lithuania, Norway, Romania and Serbia). Cases of greater openness to the law of other Countries are reported – beyond the case of the Court of Justice of the European Union – with regard to Luxembourg, Portugal and The Netherlands, where, in particular, there have been open attitudes to German case law on religious beliefs, or to British case law on the sexual orientation of refugees.

Another prevailing trend is the infrequent reference to regulatory impact analysis, which is completely absent in many countries (Croatia, Finland, Hungary, The Netherlands, Portugal, Slovenia and Switzerland). The exception is Italy, where sometimes reference is made to this instrument, especially in the consultative session.

In some countries, attention to the possible impact and effects of the decision is more frequent (as in the case of Luxembourg, Norway or The Netherlands, where, for example, the financial impact of the decision is taken into consideration, especially with regard to the interpretation of laws). At times, consideration of the overall impact of the decision can even be significant (Estonia, France, Germany, Ireland, Italy and Switzerland).

Finally, among the additional and specific benchmarks, France highlights how the Council of State takes highly into consideration the Constitution and the other elements of the "*bloc de constitutionnalité*" (Declaration of the Rights of Man and the Citizen of 1789, Preamble of the Constitution of 27 October 1946, 2004 Environment Charter, objectives of constitutional value), as well as the interpretative reservations with which the *Conseil constitutionnel* accompanied the declaration of constitutionality of a legislative provision[2].

## 2. Tools supporting judicial activity

As for the instruments used to support the interpretation process by the SAC, some countries do not have specific bodies for the classification of judgments and the elaboration of the abstracts of jurisprudence (Bulgaria, Croatia, Finland and Slovakia). Sometimes, although there is no specific office within the SAC, this function is performed by the same sections responsible for issuing opinions on proposed legislation (Belgium), or by the judges themselves (as in the case of Luxembourg, where each judge prepares a summary of the judgment).

Most countries, however, have specific support bodies for the classification and collection of the main judgements, which are periodically sent to judges, (the Czech Republic, Estonia, European Union, France, Germany, Greece, Hungary, Italy, Lithuania, the Netherlands, Norway, Poland, Portugal, Romania, Serbia, Slovenia and Switzerland).

Sometimes, these bodies consist of members of the different jurisdictions present in the legal system (as in the case of Ireland); on the contra-

---

[2] Council of State, 5th July 2018, n. 401157, Langer. [«Le Conseil d'Etat prend également souvent en compte la Constitution et les autres composantes du bloc de constitutionnalité (Déclaration des droits de l'homme et du citoyen de 1789, Préambule de la Constitution du 27 octobre 1946, Charte de l'environnement de 2004, objectifs de valeur constitutionnelle), ainsi que les réserves d'interprétation dont le Conseil constitutionnel a assorti la déclaration de constitutionnalité d'une disposition législative (CE, 5 juillet 2018, n°401157, M. Langer)»].

ry, however, in a few cases, they also are made up of university professors (Spain).

In addition to the collection and classification of rulings, in most cases these bodies – or other specific bodies responsible for study and research activities (Ireland and Portugal) – provide the Courts with expert and informative support, also by means of the provision of comparative law studies (as recently occurred in France in reference to the measures adopted in European countries for dealing with the pandemic crisis), the drafting of reports on international courts (especially European courts), periodic updates on the existence of new legal guidelines or new regulatory interventions.

In some countries, these support bodies not only draw up the abstracts of rulings and enter them in special databases, but they also update *ad hoc* operating manuals in different areas of interest which are made available to judges (Ireland and The Netherlands). In other cases, these bodies may be called upon to prepare statistical analyses of the activities of the SAC (Estonia).

Tasks relating to the training of judges are more infrequently assigned to the same bodies (as is the case in Estonia, Hungary, Ireland, Italy, Lithuania, Poland, Serbia, and Slovenia); in some cases, these training tasks are assigned to specific bodies within the SAC (Belgium and France).

Sometimes, these bodies – or rather, specific professionals appointed within the Courts (Belgium) – can also offer support in the preparation and study of individual cases (Italy), sometimes directly at the request of the judges (Ireland).

Moreover, such bodies may also offer support for the preliminary assessment of the case, while the assessment generally remains at an abstract level which does not go into the details of the specific dispute (Norway). Finally, at times, such support bodies may decide to submit the most important cases to informal groups within the Court and may provide support to the Advocate General (The Netherlands).

In most countries there are freely accessible databases available for the retrieval of previous rulings by the administrative courts (Belgium, Bulgaria, the Czech Republic, Croatia, Estonia, EU, Finland, France, Germany, Greece, Hungary, Ireland, Italy, Latvia, Lithuania, Luxembourg, Norway, Poland, Portugal, Romania, Serbia, Slovakia, Slovenia, Spain and Switzerland), although sometimes rulings on manifestly inadmissible or unfounded cases (The Netherlands) or on specific areas of interest (such as immigration for The Netherlands or legislation on foreigners for Belgium) are not published. Furthermore, in some countries, restrictions are placed on the publication of minor disputes (Finland).

As for the tools available to judges, the latter often consult the aforementioned public databases in the execution of their activities, as well as private databases developed by other bodies (Belgium, Bulgaria, the Czech Republic, Croatia, Estonia, EU, Finland, France, Germany, Greece, Hungary, Ireland, Italy, Lithuania, Luxembourg, the Netherlands, Norway, Poland, Portugal, Serbia, Slovakia, Slovenia, Spain and Switzerland). There are very few cases of judges who consult public databases only (Lithuania and Romania).

In almost all countries, there are currently no projects entailing the use of artificial intelligence systems for the elaboration or preparation of jurisprudential decisions (Belgium, Bulgaria, Estonia, EU, Finland, Germany, Greece, Hungary, Ireland, Latvia, Lithuania, Norway, Poland, Portugal, Romania, Serbia, Slovakia, Slovenia, Spain and Switzerland). At times, support to judges is limited simply to the processing of damages or expenses for witnesses and lawyers (Croatia and Italy).

In a few countries, projects have been set up to test machine learning and natural language in order to facilitate rendering judgements anonymous (The Netherlands). Finally, in France, where there is an explicit legal prohibition to take jurisdictional decisions on the basis of automated systems – unless it is to support the reasoning of the judge – there is, however, a project underway that uses artificial intelligence to identify cases with similarities with a view to dealing with them as a priority within a type of "pilot jurisdiction".

## 3. The application of law: the *νομοφυλακία* (nomophilachia) function in the system of administrative jurisdiction

The binding effect of SAC rulings on the lower courts is recognised only in certain countries (Belgium, the Czech Republic, EU, Hungary, Ireland, Latvia, Norway, Portugal, Romania, Serbia, Slovenia and Switzerland).

Sometimes, this binding effect operates only when the SAC pronounces when reunited in a certain specific panel (Bulgaria and Poland), or when it pronounces on matters of jurisdiction or on certain specific issues (The Netherlands). In other countries – even though the decision is not formally binding outside the parties of the same judgement – the law identifies a series of cases in which, due to hierarchical superiority or specific competence, the decision may still remain binding (Estonia).

In many other countries, on the other hand, the SAC's pronouncement is not, in itself, binding although it may be relevant in terms of interpretation and its power of persuasion (Croatia, Finland, France, Germany, Greece and Italy). In cases where the decision is not binding, the consistency and uniformity of the case law are guaranteed by the history of precedent, through the possibility of raising preliminary questions (Greece), through the possibility of calling informal meetings among the SAC judges before the case is actually discussed (Luxembourg) and, above all, through the authority of the role played by the SAC (France and Italy).

Moreover, in some countries, in the event of differences in interpretation, the SAC may decide on the format of an extended panel (Finland, Italy and Poland), or it may convene panels with a greater number of members (Latvia and Slovakia) or even special administrative sections within the Supreme Court (Spain).

There are also some countries (The Netherlands) where uniformity of interpretation is ensured through a variety of instruments (including the Commission for the Unity of the Law in Administrative Law, the mechanisms for appointing administrative judges as substitutes in other Administrative Courts, the creation of panels with more members in each Administrative Court of last resort). Finally, in other countries (Romania) uniformity of interpretation is ensured by the possibility of activating the instruments of appeal in the interest of the law and preliminary rulings for the determination of a matter of law.

Thanks to all these instruments, even in countries where the SAC decision is not binding, the consistency and predictability of decisions is very high: in some countries this percentage is between 50% and 75% (Italy, Lithuania, Romania and Slovakia); while in the majority of countries the percentage is between 75% and 100% (Croatia, the Czech Republic, Estonia, Finland, France, Greece, Latvia, Luxembourg, The Netherlands, Portugal, Serbia and Spain).

Generally speaking, SACs that intervene to resolve certain interpretative conflicts operate as a special panel which can be plenary or simply have more members (Belgium, Bulgaria, the Czech Republic EU, France, Finland, Greece, Hungary, Ireland, Italy, Latvia, Lithuania, The Netherlands, Norway,

Poland, Portugal, Slovakia, Slovenia, Spain and Switzerland). In other cases, the special panel of the SAC operates in the limited cases provided for by the law (Estonia).

In Romania the special panel operates in an administrative section set up within the High Court of Cassation. However, in some countries there is no special panel for the resolution of conflicts of interpretation in the SAC (Germany, Luxembourg and Serbia).

In most cases, special rules are in place to promote the involvement of the SAC operating in special panels (Belgium, Bulgaria, Estonia, EU, Finland, France, Greece, Italy, Latvia, Lithuania, Norway, Poland, Portugal, Czech Republic, Romania, Slovakia, Slovenia, Spain and Switzerland).

With regard to the possibility for the individual SAC judge to disagree with the orientation of the SAC in a special panel, it must be borne in mind that in many countries the individual SAC judge has the right to not adhere to a principle affirmed by the SAC in a special panel, by formally expressing his dissenting opinion (Bulgaria, Estonia, Finland, Latvia, Norway, Portugal and Romania).

In Italy and in the EU Court of Justice, however, it is not possible to express a single dissenting opinion. In Lithuania, any dissenting position may be attached to the file, but may not be made public. Furthermore, in Norway, Portugal and Italy, the dissenting judge is exempted from drafting the judgement.

Finally, in some countries special provision has been made, the result of which, is that the administrative judge may not disagree with the principle established by a special panel (France and The Netherlands).

With regard to the possibility for a Chamber of the SAC to disagree with the orientation of the SAC in special panel, in some countries, if a Chamber of the SAC decides not to follow the orientation of the SAC in a special panel, it is obliged to refer the matter once more to the same authority in a special panel (Belgium, the Czech Republic, Estonia, Finland, Greece, Italy, Latvia, Lithuania, Poland, and Slovakia).

In Italy, in particular, a Chamber of the SAC cannot adopt a decision contrary to a decision of the Plenary Meeting without making a preliminary referral, with the exception of application of EU law. In this case, the Chamber may directly refer the matter to the EU Court of Justice (see the Puligenica case).

The choices of the SAC as a collegial panel are binding and can only be modified by the SAC as a special panel, by means of a jurisprudential *revirement* (EU, Slovenia and Switzerland).

In Spain, having established the independence of the individual Chambers as being separate from the Assembly in Plenary Meeting, it is possible that the individual Chamber may deviate from the orientation of the Plenary Assembly, but by giving reasons for so doing.

In order to ensure uniformity and consistency of case law within the SAC – but also among the top bodies of the various higher magistracies – there are often regular meetings or seminars within the SAC (Belgium, EU, Finland, France, Greece, Ireland, Italy, Latvia, Luxembourg, the Netherlands, Poland, Portugal, Romania, Slovenia and Spain); in some cases there are special regulatory mechanisms in place to ensure uniformity of jurisprudence among the different Chambers (Lithuania, Slovakia and Germany).

In consideration of the relationship among the different jurisdictions, the formation of working groups among the representatives of the various Courts (France) occurs fairly frequently or, sometimes, there are informal mechanisms in place for regular consultation among the judges from different jurisdictions (Croatia, Estonia, Hungary, Italy, Latvia, Poland, Serbia and Switzerland); at times, such meetings are primarily aimed at sharing good practices (Lithuania).

In other cases, in contrast, consistency in the interpretative guidelines among the different jurisdictions is ensured by means of implementing specific interpretative measures which are adopted jointly by the judges of the General Assembly and the judges of the Court of Cassation and the SAC, as in the case of Bulgaria.

Finally, in some countries, consistency and uniformity are ensured by the possibility of referring the matter to an extended panel, consisting of representatives of the various jurisdictions (Germany), or through the possibility of an appeal, or an appeal at Cassation level in the interest of the law (Greece), or a special appeal as a preventive measure (Portugal).

Conversely, countries in which such coordination mechanisms among the various jurisdictions are not guaranteed, are completely in the minority (the Czech Republic and Luxembourg).

Finally, with regard to conflicts of jurisdiction in countries with a different administrative jurisdiction to the ordinary one, in many cases the resolution of such conflicts is allocated to a special jurisdictional body consisting of the representatives of the various different jurisdictions (Bulgaria, the Czech Republic, Estonia, France, Greece, Lithuania, Portugal and Spain); but special meetings among the representatives of the different jurisdictions (Latvia) may also be appointed for this purpose.

In some cases, however, the resolution of conflicts is allocated to the ordinary Supreme Court (Belgium, Croatia, Italy, Luxembourg, Serbia, Slovenia and Switzerland).

In other cases, cooperative mechanisms have only recently been made available, while the question of jurisdiction continues to be formally resolved autonomously by each individual court (Finland). Finally, in some countries the matter is resolved on a case-by-case basis by each court (Germany, The Netherlands and Poland), without the provisions of centralised coordination competencies.

## SECOND SESSION

## THE IMPACT OF THE DECISIONS OF THE SUPREME ADMINISTRATIVE COURT ON FUTURE DEVELOPMENTS OF ADMINISTRATIVE ACTIVITY

### 1. The effects of the administrative judge's ruling on the subsequent activity of the public administration (the so-called conforming effect)

The ruling of the administrative judge annulling an administrative act binds the public administration in the subsequent exercise of power in all countries under investigation. CJEU decisions are also binding, both for the European institutions and for the public administrations of the Member States. A minor exception to this principle exists in Estonia, where the binding effect of a court decision may be nullified if it is based on factual circumstances that change after it has been issued. In Germany, in some rare cases, mainly in fiscal matters, ministers may order the administration not to apply a particular judgement. However, such an order would most likely result in an immediate appeal.

The extent of the obligation changes considerably across the different countries, as are the differing consequences of not respecting a SAC pronunciation. A first distinction, in practice in many countries (Croatia, Finland, Greece, Italy, Lithuania, Luxembourg and Spain), derives from the defect identified by the administrative court: in the case of a purely formal defect, the administration may again adopt the annulled act, with the formal defect highlighted by the court having been amended.

Where the defect found is significant, the administration shall once again exercise its power within the limits indicated by the judge and within the margins of discretion that will persist following the ruling. In European law, the administrations of the Member States are obliged to apply European legislation, as interpreted by the Court of Justice, even if this entails non-application of any potentially conflicting national legislation. If the Court finds that a national law conflicts with European law, the Member State is obliged to take all necessary measures to ensure that it is amended and the conflict identified by the CJEU, subsequently eliminated.

The judgment annulling an administrative act can provide the administration with indications on how power should once again be exercised (Bulgaria, Croatia, France, Greece, Hungary and Italy); indications and clarifications on how to correctly enforce a judgment can also be requested later, by initiating the appropriate procedure (France and Italy).

The administrative judge may replace the public administration subsequent to the annulment of an act, in some cases indicated by law, (Belgium, Bulgaria, Estonia, Hungary, Italy, Luxembourg and The Netherlands), or in the event that the administration does not execute the sentence within the prescribed terms (Italy and Slovenia). This may occur in the judgement annulling the act or in the enforcement phase.

The consequences that may arise from failure to comply with a ruling of the administrative judge, or from the incorrect or untimely execution of the same, are similarly varied. In Portugal and Italy, failure to comply with a judgement, in addition to determining the nullity of any act adopted in violation of the same, may be a source of civil, criminal and disciplinary responsibility for the official and of compensation for damages for the administration (Italy). In the Slovak Republic, if the administrative judge annuls an administrative act a second time for the same reasons for which it was previously annulled, the administration may be obliged to pay a penalty.

## 2. The effects of the decision of the administrative judge *ultra partes* and in similar cases

As a rule, the court decision has only *inter partes* effects. However, it may, in some cases, affect the activity of the administration even beyond the objective and subjective perimeter of the case decided. This may depend, in the first instance, on the nature of the contested act: in the case of the annulment of regulatory acts, town planning plans, indivisible administrative acts, the judge's decision will produce *erga omnes* effects in Bulgaria, Estonia, Lithuania, Hungary, Italy, the Netherlands, Poland, Romania and Spain.

It is also possible that the SAC, when pronouncing on a specific case, may express general principles which serve to guide the activity of the administration (Ireland and Italy). In France, jurisprudential rulings not only interpret laws and regulations, but also fill any potential regulatory gaps, establishing rules and principles to which all administrative activity must adapt. The administration is required to apply the principles expressed in a decision in all subsequent similar cases it may have to deal with, in application of the principle of fairness and impartiality.

The guidelines expressed by the administrative judge, and in particular by the SAC, are generally implemented by public administrations, even in the absence of a specific regulatory obligation, in application of the principles of legal certainty and fairness and this is to avoid acts which potentially may not conform to jurisprudence and become the object of numerous disputes and subsequent annulments. (Belgium, the Czech Republic, Croatia, Estonia, Finland, Germany, Greece, Hungary, Italy, Latvia, Lithuania, Luxembourg, The Netherlands, Norway, Portugal, Romania, Slovak Republic, Slovenia and Switzerland). To further facilitate compliance with case law, in some cases the SAC prepares reports on its own decisions which are to serve as guidelines for administrations on the topic of the correct application of the law (Latvia).

To guarantee legal certainty and to comply with the principle of fairness, the administration may orientate its future activity by changing its practices to conform with case law and, in some cases, even extend the effects of a judgment to similar cases.

Modification of administrative practices to align them with the principles expressed by case law in decisions on similar cases is frequent in Belgium, Estonia, Finland, France, Greece, Hungary, Luxembourg, the Netherlands, Norway, Serbia, Spain and Switzerland.

The effects of a judgement can be extended to similar cases in Bulgaria – although this does not occur frequently – Croatia, Estonia, Latvia and Portugal. In Italy, this decision is left to the discretion of the public administration, with the exception of civil service litigation, where the extension of the effects of judgements favourable to third parties is excluded for reasons of public expenditure restraints.

In some countries, the interested party may request that the administration review its decision if the administrative judge has declared similar measures illegitimate (this is always possible in Greece, and, only in some cases, in Spain).

However, it is not possible to extend the effects of the court's decision beyond the case decided in the Czech Republic, Ireland, Lithuania, Poland, Romania and Slovenia.

## THIRD SESSION
## ENFORCEMENT OF DECISIONS

### 1. The measures to ensure the enforcement of decisions with regard to the public administration

The principle of effectiveness of protection requires that court decisions are effectively and promptly enforced by the administration. To this end, most of the countries surveyed (Croatia, France, Germany, Greece, Hungary, Italy, Ireland, Latvia, Luxembourg, Poland, Portugal, the Slovak Republic, Serbia, Slovenia, Spain and Switzerland) provide for judicial proceedings to monitor and ensure the full and complete enforcement of court decisions.

In addition to these, there are also countries in which, in order to enforce decisions made by the administrative judge, or in any event made with regard to the public administration, the same ways and methods which are applied in the process of the execution of the sentences of ordinary judges, are implemented.

This is the case, in particular, of Lithuania, where, if the administration or the person obliged to enforce a decision of the administrative judge does not execute it within fifteen days, or within the different time limit set by the

Court, the latter shall issue a letter of execution at the request of the claimant or, in some cases, even *ex officio*.

With this letter, the claimant can initiate the executive procedure, conducted by judicial officers, provided for by the Code of Civil Procedure. Even in Romania, where there is no separate administrative jurisdiction from the ordinary one, sentences handed down to the administration are enforced through the procedure provided for by the Civil Procedure Code for the enforcement of all jurisdictional measures.

In Italy, with regard to convictions in which the public administration is ordered to pay sums of money, it is possible to apply both the specific remedy for the enforcement of sentences before the administrative court (compliance judgement) and the executive procedures before the ordinary court.

Even among countries that do not provide for judicial proceedings, alternative procedures and/or sanctions are frequently provided for to ensure the correct enforcement of decisions.

Finland is an emblematic case from the point of view of the first aspect, where any measures necessary to ensure the enforcement by the administrative authority of the judge's decisions can be taken, *ex officio* or on request, within the ordinary system of checking the legality of administrative action (the Parliamentary Ombudsman and the Chancellor of Justice).

Sanctions, which indirectly guarantee the full, timely and correct enforcement of court decisions, are provided for in the legislation of The Netherlands and Estonia. In the first case, the administration which does not execute the judge's decision within the prescribed terms is automatically required to pay a penalty for each day of delay. In Estonia and in Italy, on the contrary, the application of penalties for the indirect enforcement of sentences (*astreintes*) is the remit of the administrative judge.

In order to encourage the spontaneous enforcement of the decision by the administration, thus avoiding litigation, French law stipulates that the jurisdictional procedure for enforcement be preceded by an administrative phase, overseen by the President of the competent court. This administrative phase, in 2019, made having to resort to the jurisdictional phase for the majority of legal proceedings possible.

Conversely, there is no provision for any type of procedure aimed at monitoring and ensuring the full and complete execution of the judge's decisions in Bulgaria, the Czech Republic and Norway.

The percentage of decisions whose implementation is incorrect or incomplete and which therefore requires the activation of the procedure for enforcement, is very low, less than 2%, or is defined as "extremely rare" in Croatia, Estonia, France, Germany, Greece, Hungary, Ireland, Luxembourg, Portugal and Slovenia. In Italy, the percentage of recourse to enforcement proceedings is around 15%. The other countries that do provide for enforcement proceedings have no quantitative data available.

In order to initiate the procedure required to ensure the full and complete enforcement of the judgement, it is necessary for it to become *res judicata* in Croatia, Estonia, Hungary, Latvia, Luxembourg, Poland, Romani, Serbia, the Slovak Republic, Slovenia and Spain. A few countries allow the enforcement procedure to be activated even before the decision becomes final, in the event of typified situations, and this is generally directly linked to the risk that the delay in enforcement may render enforcement impossible or cause serious damage. (Estonia, Italy, Latvia and Spain).

In Italy, in particular, initiating proceedings is generally allowed before the first instance enforceable judgement becomes *res judicata*, unless the judgement is temporarily suspended by the Council of State.

The transition of the decision into *res judicata* is also required for the activation of the substitute mechanisms provided for in Finland.

## 2. The exercise of substitute powers by the administrative court

One of the ways of ensuring the correct execution of the judge's decisions is the option that, in the event of inertia on the part of the administration, or incorrect execution, the Court may take the place of the administration, either directly or by appointing an *ad acta* commissioner.

The Court may directly replace the administration, and thus take the measures necessary for the proper enforcement of its decisions, in Belgium, Croatia, Italy, Portugal, Serbia, Slovenia and Spain. A similar power of direct replacement, but limited to specific cases expressly indicated by law, is provided for in The Netherlands and Poland. In Luxembourg and in Italy, the authority to replace may be exerted by appointing an *ad acta* commissioner.

A few countries provide for forms of guaranteed enforcement which are different to the mere recognition of a substitute power by the Court. In

Greece, a judge may be appointed to instruct the administration on the correct way to enforce judgements.

In Hungary, in addition to the option of imposing a financial penalty on the administration which does not enforce the decision, the administrative judge may order that the judgement be enforced by another administration, different to the one that has been obligated, while still retaining the same powers, or be enforced by the supervisory body responsible for the non-complying administration.

Only if both solutions are impossible, can the judge adopt temporary executive measures which lose effectiveness when the administration executes the judgement. Indirect methods of ensuring enforcement, by imposing sanctions, are provided for in Estonia, Italy and Latvia.

The judge cannot replace the administration in order to enforce judgements, nor are alternative mechanisms available in Bulgaria, EU, Finland, France, Germany, Hungary, Ireland, Lithuania, Romania, the Slovak Republic and Switzerland.

## 3. The responsibility of the public administration and public officials in the event of non-execution or incorrect execution of decisions

The public administration and the official who acted are responsible for the damage caused by the inaccurate or non-execution of the judge's decisions in all the countries under investigation, with the sole exception of the Slovak Republic. However, this responsibility comes in different forms in different countries. In Estonia, the responsibility for damage lies only with the public administration, while in Greece the responsibility of the official arises only if disciplinary responsibility has been previously ascertained. In Portugal, in addition to the civil responsibility of the official, there are also certain kinds of criminal responsibilities, as well as financial penalties.

Jurisdiction over legal actions seeking damages is attributed in some cases to the administrative court, in others to the ordinary judge, and the solutions can be extremely varied. Specifically, the administrative judge has jurisdiction over actions seeking damages in Bulgaria, France, Hungary and Spain. In Hungary, the administrative court can order the administration to pay a penalty in addition to compensation for damages, although this occurs very rarely.

The ordinary judge is competent in Croatia, Germany, Greece, Ireland, Lithuania, Luxembourg, Norway, Poland and Romania. A particular case of subdivision of jurisdiction is that provided for in The Netherlands where jurisdiction over actions regarding sentencing is determined and based on the extent of the claim: the administrative judge deals with claims for an amount lower than € 25,000, while the civil judge with claims for a higher amount.

In Slovenia, the administrative court has jurisdiction if the action for damage compensation is proposed at the same time as the proceedings for enforcement of the decision, whereas the ordinary court has jurisdiction when it is brought independently. In Belgium, the administrative court may order the payment of compensation, but actions for damages are dealt with by the ordinary judge.

In Italy, the administrative judge is competent for actions seeking damages caused by the administration in the exercise of public office while the ordinary judge deals with the civil liability of the public administration in all other cases and the liability of individual officials towards third parties.

Damages resulting from the non-execution or incorrect execution of judgements sent down from the Court of Justice, on the part of an individual Member State, may be sought in the ordinary courts of the Member States themselves. If a Member State fails to comply with the decisions of the CJEU, the European Commission, by taking the necessary measures, may refer the non-compliant State to the Court of Justice pursuant to Article 258 TFEU.

# FOURTH SESSION
# THE ADVISORY FUNCTION OF THE SUPREME ADMINISTRATIVE COURT AND SUBSEQUENT IMPACT ON ADMINISTRATIVE ACTIVITY

## 1. The advisory functions of SACs

The SAC has an ordinary advisory role towards the administration only in some of the countries surveyed (Belgium, EU, Finland, France, Greece, Italy, The Netherlands and Norway). This role varies extensively from one country to another.

In Belgium, the Council of State includes a consultative section which expresses an opinion on all significant legislative acts and government regulations.

In Finland, the SAC may be asked to give its opinion on draft rules of primary rank or regulations, and may propose amendments to existing legislation.

In France, the opinion of the Council of State is mandatory for all bills and draft ordinances drawn up by the Government while it remains optional for bills submitted by parliamentarians.

In addition, government regulations schemes and certain individual administrative decisions of particular importance (for example, the declaration of public utility, revocation of citizenship) must be submitted to the Council of State for prior opinion and the Government may consult the Council on administrative matters, or to identify the correct interpretation of a rule, or on matters of subdivision of competence between the State and certain overseas communities. At the request of the Government, or on its own initiative, the Council of State may carry out studies on the management of public policies and prepare an annual report on the reforms which it deems necessary.

In Greece, the Council of State issues an opinion on the legitimacy of regulations adopted by presidential decree, as well as on issues of general interest and organisational matters relating to the Council itself and the proper administration of justice.

In Italy, the advisory function of the Council of State may deal with primary and secondary sources, governmental and ministerial regulations, codification projects and consolidated texts. The opinion of the Council of State may also be requested by the President of the Council of Ministers on bills, especially those regarding the implementation of EU law. Finally, the Council of State may be consulted by the Regions or Independent Authorities.

In Norway, the SAC may participate in the preparation of bills in normal hearing procedures in which any interested party whatsoever may submit their opinion to Parliament. In addition to this, there is a distinctive role provided for in the Constitution, according to which Parliament may request an opinion on a point of law (this right, however, has not been exercised since 1945).

In The Netherlands, the advisory division of the Council of State expresses opinions on many acts of Parliament and Government indicated by law (acts of approval of treaties or withdrawal from treaties; government regulations; the annual budget of the Government, even those dealing with European constraints; expropriation decisions), as well as on various other issues (compliance with the European Stability and Growth Pact and climate policy; some conflicts between the Dutch Government and the governments of The Dutch Antilles).The Government and Parliament can then request opinions on legislation and public administration even outwith the cases expressly provided for by law, and the Council of State can advise the Government *ex officio*.

The Court of Justice of the European Union also has an advisory role. The European Parliament, the Council, the Commission and a Member State may request an opinion on the compatibility with the Treaties of an international agreement which would be binding for the European Union before it enters into force.

The SACs of Bulgaria, Croatia, the Czech Republic, Estonia, Germany, Hungary, Ireland, Latvia, Lithuania, Luxembourg, Poland, Portugal, Romania, Serbia, the Slovak Republic, Slovenia, Spain and Switzerland, ordinarily, do not perform advisory functions. In Spain, the SAC only performs jurisdictional functions and there is a Council of State which only performs advisory functions. In some of these countries, however, the SAC may perform advisory functions exclusively in specific matters, or on an occasional basis and as a matter of practice.

This is the case of Poland, where the SAC may be consulted by Parliament, like any other public body, in the context of the law-making process and may express its opinion in relation to bills regarding the status and organisation of the magistracy and of procedure.

Similarly, in Estonia, the SAC may be only consulted on the compatibility between provisions of the Constitution and European law.

In Switzerland, the SAC submits suggestions to Parliament annually to resolve any critical issues which have come up in cases decided on during the year.

In Lithuania, it is possible that the Government or Parliament may ask for the opinion of the SAC on bills, especially when they relate to issues concerning the administration of justice; this opinion is informal and non-binding.

In the Czech Republic, the SAC must give a mandatory, but non-binding, opinion on bills or regulations relating to jurisdiction.

Finally, in Ireland, the SAC expresses a preventive constitutionality judgement on bills.

## 2. The nature of the opinions given by the SAC (mandatory or optional, binding or not)

The nature of the opinion given by the SACs, which ordinarily perform advisory functions, differs widely among the various countries. The opinion of the Council of State in Belgium is mandatory for all draft legislative acts, or their amendments, which are proposed by governments; for all draft legislative acts, or their amendments, when required by a minimum number of members of the Legislative Assembly required to approve them; for draft regulations drawn up by the governments of the various components of the country.

Similarly, in France, the opinion is mandatory but only for certain types of acts, indicated by law, and is not binding, although it is generally observed. On the other hand, it is binding for certain individual decisions (for example declarations of public utility).

In Greece, the SAC opinion on presidential decrees is mandatory but not binding, although, as a rule, the President of the Republic does not issue decrees that would conflict with this opinion.

In Italy, the opinion of the Council of State is mandatory but not binding on Government or Ministerial regulations, on acts of Parliament, if it is required by law.

In The Netherlands, as mentioned previously, the law requires the acquisition of an opinion of the Council of State in relation to numerous acts and issues. This opinion is not binding.

In Finland and Norway, the opinion of the SAC is optional and non-binding.

Finally, the opinion requested from the CJEU on the compatibility of an international treaty which is about to be signed with the European Treaties is optional, however, where the opinion is negative, the treaty cannot come into force unless it has been amended in line with the Court's observations.

In some cases, the SAC, when performing advisory functions, may seek the opinion of experts. This is the case of Belgium, where the Council of State may ask experts for an opinion on the legitimacy of major regulatory reform projects of entire sectors of the law, or on reform projects regarding highly technical matters. In Italy, this occurs when drafting consolidated texts. Also in France, the Council of State frequently convenes hearings of experts before giving its opinions, or for conducting its own research. In The Netherlands, there are members of the advisory division of the Council of State who have specialist experience in economic and financial matters.

The option of seeking the advice of experts is not available in Finland, Norway and the CJEU.

## 3. The forms of collaboration between administrative judges and the Government or public administration

The framework for the creation of forms of collaboration between administrative judges and the government or public administration varies greatly among the different countries.

In Belgium it is possible that magistrates of the Council of State, or more frequently in the case of hearing officers – for example the section of the Council responsible for the preparation of cases to be dealt with – may be seconded to the administration.

In France, the magistrates of the Council of State may be appointed, at the request of the Government, to carry out inspections, or to assist in the elaboration of a bill; they may also be seconded to public institutions, public companies or public administrations and participate in competition and administrative boards.

In Italy, administrative judges may take leave in order to take up top positions in the cabinets and legislative offices of ministries or independent authorities, for a maximum limit of 10 years. They may also hold university teaching positions, participate in study groups, competition panels, or work as magistrates in the Constitutional Court, as researchers, while continuing to remain in service.

In Ireland, magistrates may preside over public enquiries on matters of public interest or over *ad hoc* courts established for a limited period of time to decide on specific compensation claims. Magistrates may also be appointed to publish reports on matters of public interest and may preside over referendum commissions, *i.e.* independent bodies whose main role is to explain to the public the subject matter of the referendum to validate amendments to the Constitution, and to encourage the electorate to vote.

In Slovenia, judges may be seconded to the Ministry of Justice for a limited period, or be involved in the preparation of bills. In both cases, a decision of the Judicial Council is required.

In Estonia, where the SAC does not have advisory functions, and in Luxembourg, magistrates may be called upon to take over administrative or university teaching positions but they cannot perform the functions of a judge during this time.

Finnish law and CJEU law do not provide for forms of cooperation. This is also the case in The Netherlands where, however, it is possible that a member of the Council of State may be called upon to cover a role for which particular professionalism and expertise is required, on condition that this does not adversely affect the independence and impartiality of the judicial function.

In Greece, magistrates cannot perform governmental or administrative functions. However, the law provides for the presence of members of the judicial order on committees that prepare bills, monitor the financial situation of parliamentarians and magistrates, in study commissions, and to evaluate the quality of regulation.

## 4. The recourse to the advisory function of the SAC as an alternative dispute resolution tool

The advisory function cannot serve as an alternative dispute resolution mechanism in any of the countries under investigation, with the exception of Italy, in the terms that will be detailed below, and of the European Union.

Member States may in fact refer the resolution of conflicts arising among them regarding matters regulated by the Treaties, to the CJEU. So far, this has happened only once.

In Italy, there is an alternative remedy to the jurisdictional appeal, called "extraordinary recourse to the Head of State", in which the Council of State is required to give a mandatory and binding "opinion", which is then implemented in a decree issued by the Head of State. This "opinion" is binding because it essentially puts an end to the dispute. It is promoted by a private party for the annulment of an administrative measure.

In Luxembourg, although an alternative dispute resolution function is not provided for, the administrative judge may act as mediator in certain conflicts between the administration and another party, provided that the subject-matter is not in the category of those issues which, if they were to result in a dispute, would come under the remit of the administrative jurisdiction.

# ACA-Europe Seminar
# "The judicial review of regulatory authorities"

**Paris, France**
**6 December 2021**
**General Report by the French Council of State**

# Summary of the General Report of the Seminar "The judicial review of regulatory authorities" held in Paris, France, 6 December 2021

The ACA seminar dealing with judicial review of the acts of regulatory authorities was organized in the face of the observation that these authorities have gradually emerged as a new form of state intervention. Their scope of action covers a wide range of administrative activities, and in a broad sense the notion of regulatory authorities can refer both to authorities responsible for compliance with competition law and to authorities responsible for compliance in specific sectors, such as electronic communications, transportation, energy, or personal data protection.

The seminar was organized with the idea that it might be an opportunity to examine the specific problems to which litigation over the acts of regulatory authorities gives rise, problems related to three particular characteristics of these authorities: first, the wide variety of tools they use to intervene, tools ranging from soft law, codes of conduct, to more traditional regulations, sanctions, and communication through the media; second, the fact that the relevant decisions require great technical expertise in the area of their respective competence; and lastly, the fact that these authorities and their decisions are embedded in complex social and economic systems, often of European or international significance.

In order to bring into focus the most important problems that arise in judicial litigation involving the acts of regulatory authorities, the ACA administered a questionnaire, to which the administrative courts of 24 countries responded.

The questionnaire sought, first of all, to ascertain whether the notion of "regulatory authorities" is interpreted homogeneously in the various states: the responses show that a common datum is that of the autonomous legal personality of these entities and, in addition, the fact that their respective activities are linked to a specific market that needs to be regulated; in some cases, authorities that operate in a "decentralized" manner, or that are, structurally or financially, separate from other institutions, are also defined. Portugal specifies that they are subject to a specific body of rules, and that they have the status of independent administrative authorities, responsible for regulating economic activities, defending general interests, protecting consumers, or protecting competition in various sectors.

With regard to the courts with jurisdiction over the litigation in question, it was found that the administrative judge mostly does not have exclusive and absolute jurisdiction: in some cases, jurisdiction is determined by the sector involved, or by the type of regulatory authority; in Cyprus, the administrative court only knows about acts directed at individual persons, and not also about general regulatory acts, which can be challenged only by way of exception; for the most part, the administrative court shares jurisdiction with the civil court; in Latvia the Constitutional Court has jurisdiction to rule on whether the acts of the Public Utilities Authority and the Market Authority conform to the "highest standards," *i.e.*, to compliance with hierarchically superior norms; in Austria for appellate judgments, jurisdiction is divided between the Supreme Administrative Court and the Constitutional Court, which alone is responsible for ruling on the validity of acts of general regulatory acts. It also emerged that in some cases states litigation is single-degree, and takes place before the Supreme Administrative Court, in other cases it is double-degree, of which the second may be limited to questions of legitimacy only. In Finland, where litigation is single-degree before the Supreme Administrative Court, there is also a procedure-filter deputed to assess the admissibility of the application. In any case, the model in which the Supreme Administrative Court serves as the court of first and sole instance in this matter is a minority one, as is the model that completely excludes the jurisdiction of the civil courts. In Norway the entire litigation is devolved to the civil courts due to the fact that there are no administrative courts. Where jurisdiction is reserved for the civil court, these may be specialized sections. The reason for such jurisdiction is sometimes related to the fact that these are disputes subject to civil law but involving a regulatory authority as a party; generally, the jurisdiction, of the administrative and civil courts is determined by the regulated sector or the regulatory authority.

In the majority of states, actions allowed against acts of regulatory authorities do not differ from those allowed with acts of other administrative authorities; the procedural law is generally determined by the competent court.

In the majority of states, the admissibility of appeals against binding, and therefore injurious, regulatory acts does not present particular problems, compared to appeals against other administrative acts. In some states, the admissibility of appeals concerning decisions by regulatory authorities to dismiss proceedings against economic operators suspected of engaging in illegal activities has been an issue.

Conversely, in the majority of states, judicial challenge of so-called soft-law acts (opinions, recommendations, notices, position papers, press releases) is not considered possible, since these are acts that are not binding. In fact, in some states this is equally possible when in fact they are likely to affect the rights of the plaintiff (Germany), or have significant effects of an economic nature or on the behavior of the recipients of the act (France). In Lithuania, too, the Supreme Administrative Court has ruled that soft-law acts cannot be completely excluded from judicial review if effects are likely to result from them. In Portugal, soft-law acts are always considered appealable when they are interpretative of binding regulatory acts or when they are a preparatory act to the adoption of binding acts.

Regarding the subject of standing to appeal, it should be noted, first of all, that in none of the states is popular action allowed to appeal against the acts of regulatory authorities. In a significant number of states, standing to appeal exists where it is inferred that the challenged act is likely to affect legitimate or legally protected interests of the plaintiff: in some cases it has been specified that the injured interest must be personal, direct and actual (Greece), or otherwise specifically and certainly (France), moral or financial (Cyprus); in Latvia, standing to appeal against acts directed at a specific person is vested in the latter, obviously if possible consequential damage is attached, while in appeals against general regulatory acts standing is vested in those who infer d resent from the act a violation to constitutionally guaranteed rights, and in this case jurisdiction to decide is in the Constitutional Court. In other states, standing to appeal against the acts of regulatory authorities is recognized only when there is an allegation of an injury to subjective rights, and when constitutional rights are involved, jurisdiction is sometimes devolved to the Constitutional Court.

The possibility of challenging the unlawfulness of the general regulatory act as an exception exists in the majority of states, and in some cases (Estonia, Cyprus, Austria, Slovakia and Sweden), it is the only way to challenge a general regulatory act. In that case several consequences arise against the general act if it is found to be unlawful. In Estonia, any judge may raise before the Supreme Court, *ex officio* or at the request of a party, a question of the legality of a general regulatory act with respect to the Constitution, which, if it finds the question well-founded, may annul the general act *erga omnes*, either *ex tunc* or *ex nunc*, while with respect to the plaintiff the annulment is always effective *ex tunc*. In Greece, France, Lithuania, Sweden, and Slovakia, annulment of the general act, even if it is deemed unlawful, is not permitted, but only of the challenged individual act. In Austria, the general regulatory act may be challenged by way of exception, which, however, must be referred by the judge in the case to the Constitutional Court, which has sole jurisdiction over the validity of general regulatory acts: in such a case, the Constitutional Court's decision may lead to the annulment of both the individual act and the underlying general regulatory act. Relative to some states, including Belgium, Croatia, Latvia, Luxembourg, Hungary and Poland and Norway, the opposite answer was given, to the effect that the possibility of challenging a general regulatory act by way of exception is precluded; however, the scope of this assertion needs to be detailed: Belgium answered in the negative on the grounds that the relevant regulatory authorities do not have the power to adopt acts of general scope; Croatia actually admits that the illegality of a general act can be invoked to challenge an act directed to a specific addressee, if that general act is a prerequisite to it: the ruling of the Supreme Administrative Court, in that case has the effect of invalidating the general act from the day of publication. In Latvia, since general regulatory acts can be challenged only if they infringe on fundamental rights, the administrative court before which an individual act has been challenged must stay the proceedings and refer the matter to the Constitutional Court (which, as noted above, has jurisdiction to decide on the legality of general regulatory acts). In Luxembourg, it is accepted that the general regulatory act can be made the subject of a plea of illegality only when the latter arises from non-compliance with European law. In Hungary, the illegitimacy of general regulatory acts can only be invoked as an exception, together with a challenge to the individual act, if the general act is soft-law: general "hard-law," *i.e.*, binding, acts adopted by regulatory authorities are in fact considered to have legislative status, and as such are removed from the review of the administrative court.

In all states it appears possible to bring liability actions against regulatory authorities or against the state to obtain compensation for damages resulting from the adoption of illegitimate acts by regulatory authorities: the circumstance that in some cases the addressee of the claim may not be the regulatory authority is explained by the fact that not in all states and not in all cases do regulatory authorities have an autonomous legal personality: in France, for example, some authorities do not have the status of independent authorities, nor do they have legal personality, which is why claims for compensation must be directed against the state.

The Courts that participated in the interview were asked by what criteria appeals involving acts of regulatory authorities are assigned. In about half of the states, the technicality and complexity inherent in these litigations is taken into account, and thus they are assigned to chambers that deal with the subject matter systematically to enable the assigned magistrates to acquire special expertise in the subject matter. That being said, it remains the case that the composition of the internal chambers and the criteria for assigning matters to the individual internal chambers of judicial bodies must be predetermined and published. In 10 of the states, however, the assignment of appeals involving the acts of regulatory authorities are not assigned to "specialized" judges in the sense specified above.

In ten of the states (including Italy), it appears that the relevant courts do not have specific internal resources available to assist magistrates in the technical aspects that are relevant in individual cases. In the other 14 states, however, the courts have various types of internal resources available to strengthen their expertise in the regulatory areas of their respective jurisdiction. These resources include, for example: internship periods for assigned magistrates, organization of seminars and exchanges with professionals in the field, the legal and technical qualities of individual magistrates themselves, acquired through their experience in litigation or in the exercise of other professional functions performed externally, the use of judicial assistants, the creation and updating of databases containing precedents, and the implementation in the courts of entities dedicated to legal research.

With regard to the judicial inquiry and means of investigation, almost all states have reported summarizing in the oral hearing and the acquisition of reports from experts, and in many cases also the intervention of an *amicus curiae*; in Estonia, Spain, France and Lithuania the administrative judge also makes use of technical advice; other means of investigation allowed are testimony (Czech Republic, Latvia, Lithuania), search of offices, premises, premises (France), assistance of experts (Turkey). With regard to what should be desirable reforms on the point, there is a convergence of views on the possibility of the judge in the case having his own autonomous and independent experts who can be of help in understanding technical problems, of the market concerned, possibly even supplementing the panel of judges.

In the vast majority of states, administrations and stakeholders who are not directly affected are not technically considered parties to the case. In some cases, however, they may intervene in the judgment, and in some countries it is possible for the judge in the case to request opinions/views/opinions from other administrations, unrelated to the judgment, as part of the trial inquiry.

In almost all countries, the court proceedings are based on written documents, so oral argument is limited to the issues that the court submits to the parties and to the adversarial discussion between the parties, which should have the function of allowing the confrontation of the most technically sensitive issues, to ask the parties for clarifications and explanations, but also to protect the public interest in all cases where the decision has a wider social impact (Slovakia). In some cases, there is provision for holding a hearing prior to the public hearing, the function of which is to enable the judge to better understand the complexity and technicality of the cases and to focus on the most relevant issues and to identify the type of decision best suited to the specific case.

Regarding the types of flaws invoked against the decisions of regulatory authorities, in many countries they are not substantially different from those that can be invoked to challenge different administrative acts. In particular, the most frequently invoked vices are: Lack of competence due to invasion of the sphere of competence of a different regulatory authority; violation of procedural rules and in particular of the rules on consultation and guarantees of defence; failure to respect privacy in the exercise of supervisory and investigative powers, by the regulatory authority; violation of the principle of impartiality, violation of the party's right to inspect the documents on which the challenged act is based; in the balancing of opposing interests, incorrect assessment of the various interests to be considered or lack of proportionality; violation of the principle of proportionality of decisions, violation of the principle of reasonableness and the principle of sustainability of the decision; erroneous exercise of discretion by the regulator (Turkey). In France, Cyprus, Lithuania, and Austria the question of impartiality, independence, and transparency of regulatory authorities often emerges in litigation involving the acts of regulatory authorities, particularly for the reason that various powers (of recommendation, regulation, authorization, control, injunction, sanction) are combined in them.

With the exception of Greece, Cyprus and Poland, it was found that in all states the administrative judge is not bound by the technical and economic evaluations made by the regulatory authority, and thus can subject them to review or investigative measures. In some states the extent of the administrative judge's review varies according to the margin of discretion given to the authority, and does not extend to the appropriateness of the decision made by the authority. In Belgium, the review of discretion is limited to manifest error. In Germany, the Federal Administrative Court generally determines the scope of its review by interpreting the referenced rules, deciding whether to exercise full review; in the area of review of the acts of regulatory authorities, it has said that many of the referenced rules give the regulatory authorities wide margins of discretion, which allow for limited review, so that the court is in practice responsible for verifying compliance with procedural rules, whether the authority has correctly understood the applicable rules, and whether it has not engaged in arbitrariness. Also in Estonia, France, Lithuania, Luxembourg, Hungary, and Norway, the extent of the administrative judge's review is limited where the challenged act was adopted in the exercise of discretionary power, which implies that it stops at a finding that the relevant rules were correctly interpreted and applied, that the competence of other authorities was not violated, that the act is not based on a manifest error.

With regard to the powers of the court, in 12 countries, if he or she ascertains the illegitimacy of the challenged act, all he or she can do is annul it, without being able to replace the authority in modifying the act, consistent with the fact that these are normally acts that are expressions of administrative discretion. It should be noted, however, that in Belgium there is a judicial body-the Market Court-that also has full jurisdiction over certain cases involving regulatory authorities, over which it can exercise full jurisdiction. In other countries, on the contrary, the administrative court has the power to modify the challenged act; however, according to reports in the questionnaire, this power of modification, linked to full jurisdiction, concerns only sanctioning acts, and translates into the possibility of annulling or reducing them.

According to the findings of the questionnaire, the views of the European Commission and that of the European regulators are taken into account by both national regulators and national administrative courts. However, there is a convergence in stating that national authorities may depart from them with reasons when necessary to adapt national characteristics that deviate from the European model. In France, the Council of State has also affirmed the possibility of invoking the invalidity of a European soft-law act in support of a challenge to a French regulatory authority's soft-law act. Litigation over the acts of regulatory authorities also appears to be, in many of the countries interviewed, fertile ground for preliminary references to the Court of Justice of the European Union, of which numerous examples were given.

In many countries there is no particular difficulty with regard to the drafting of the decision by the administrative judge. In other countries various difficulties are reported, related to the complexity, technicality, media interest in the matter. Mainly the problems associated with the drafting of the judicial decision are due to the need (a) to ensure respect for commercial secrecy and any other legally protected secrets, (b) to base the decision on sufficiently thorough legal and factual reasoning, and (c) that the decision be understandable both to the community of jurists and practitioners and to the public, without therefore betraying technical and legal accuracy. The difficulty in drafting decisions on acts of regulatory authorities implies an increase in the workload of the magistrate, which requires adjustments: in Lithuania, for example, this entails reducing the number of affairs assigned to the magistrate and bringing in a support team and legal assistants and assistant linguists to take care of the linguistic quality of the reasoning.

Judicial decisions on acts of regulatory authorities are subject to institutional communication because of the jurisprudential interest they hold, as well as the economic effects they may have. Recurring ways are the publication of the decision on the Court's website, or in the official gazette, or on the website of the regulatory authorities concerned, or even the issuance of press releases of the most important decisions.

In half of the countries participating in the questionnaire, judges dealing with litigation over acts of regulatory authorities do not participate in exchanges with officials of the sector authorities. In other states, however, this form of exchange is organized during the judges' internship; in still others, it is the court itself that organizes round tables between judges and officials or with professionals in the field, or between judges of the various courts that have jurisdiction over the acts of regulatory authorities; it may also be the participation of judges in seminars or academic meetings.

In most countries, judges who litigate over regulatory authorities are not permitted to exercise functions in one of these authorities. Such a situation is permitted, and regulated, in Belgium; in Spain it is allowed as part of the internship; in France, on the other hand, the secondment to regulatory authorities of judges who can then share experience is encouraged, and in Italy it is allowed subject to disciplinary rules.

## Summary

# General Report
# Paris, 6 December 2021

## Introduction

Regulatory authorities have gradually emerged as one of the new forms of State intervention. In addition to the Regal State or the State as a supplier of goods and services, the regulatory authorities, in the broad sense, cover a wide range of administrative activities: they may be authorities responsible, in a given sector or across the board, for correcting market imbalances in a context of opening up markets to competition, or for ensuring that free competition is reconciled with other general interest objectives; in the broadest sense, regulatory activities may refer to any administrative activity that seeks to reconcile interests that may be contradictory or to organise access to scarce resources in a manner consistent with general interest objectives. In this broadest sense, this notion can refer as much to the transversal authorities responsible for enforcing competition law (e.g. the French Competition Authority) as to sectoral authorities (electronic communications, transport, energy, etc.), including national data protection authorities or authorities responsible for the marketing or evaluation of health products.

The ACA-Europe seminar organised in Paris on 5 and 6 December 2021 should be an opportunity to examine the specific issues that disputes concerning acts taken by these regulatory authorities may raise in the administrative courts. These questions arise from certain characteristics of the acts of these authorities, characteristics over which they do not have a monopoly compared with other forms of administration, but which combine or take on a particular role. These characteristics are at least three in number: firstly, the use of a wide range of acts or intervention tools, from flexible laws and codes of conduct to more traditional regulatory acts or sanctions, via a variety of communication media (press releases, public statements, FAQs, etc.); secondly, the degree of expertise and technicality of the decisions taken in a given activity sector (energy, health, electronic communications, etc.) and/or a certain technological context (personal data protection, cyberspace, etc.); finally, integration into complex economic and social ecosystems, often with a significant European or even international dimension, and likely to have a high media profile.

In this context, from the particular object of study that is disputes concerning the acts of these regulatory authorities, the seminar will make it possible to address the important challenges that these appeals raise for the effectiveness and credibility of the court's intervention.

This report is a synthesis of information provided by ACA-Europe members and observers in response to a questionnaire on disputes arising from acts of regulatory authorities. Twenty-four courts responded: Belgium, Bulgaria, Czech Republic, Germany, Estonia, Greece, Spain, France, Croatia, Italy, Cyprus, Latvia, Lithuania, Luxembourg, Hungary, Austria, Poland, Portugal, Slovenia, Slovakia, Finland, Sweden, Turkey and Norway. A list of the institutions that submitted a report in response to the questionnaire is attached. It is not possible to give a detailed account of all the information provided by the courts, but the aim is to identify the main themes and areas of discussion, which will be addressed during the seminar, and to highlight the similarities and differences in the way in which ACA-Europe members and observers deal with disputes involving regulatory acts. The report is organised into six main sections: courts competent to hear disputes involving regulatory issues; the admissibility of appeals against regulatory acts, the internal organisation of the courts, the investigation of appeals, decision-making, the judge in the regulatory ecosystem.

## 1. Courts competent to hear disputes involving regulatory authorities

### *1.1. Presentation of the regulatory authorities of the States of the respondent courts*

Regulatory authorities with various powers, including regulatory and sanctioning powers, exist in all States of the respondent courts. The responses highlighted the diversity of entities that national legal orders group under this term and the variety of interpretations that are made of the concept of regulatory authority itself.

Belgium defines a regulatory authority as an institution under public law, with legal personality and operating in a more or less decentralised manner.

Estonia has chosen to interpret the concept of regulatory authority in a broad sense, including most of the supervisory authorities that are related to market regulation, such as tax and customs authorities.

For Cyprus, a regulatory authority is a legal body under public law, legally and functionally distinct from the State and any other public or private body.

In Hungary, the term refers to a body, established by an act of public law, structurally and financially separated, at least to a certain extent, from the regular administrative institutions, and exercising the responsibility of regulating a market.

In Portugal, regulatory authorities, governed by the Framework Law on Independent Administrative Entities (LQER), are legal persons under public law, with the status of independent administrative entities, exercising powers in relation to the regulation of an economic activity, or the defence of services of general interest, or the protection of consumer rights and interests, or the protection of competition in the private, public, cooperative and social sectors.

**Table presenting the principal regulatory authorities of the States of the respondent courts**

| | |
|---|---|
| Belgium | Financial Services and Markets Authority<br>Belgian Institute for Postal Services and Telecommunications Commission for Electricity and Gas Regulation<br>Belgian Competition Authority National Bank of Belgium<br>Vlaamse Regulator voor de Media (Flemish Regulator for the Media)<br>Federal Agency for Medicines and Health Products<br>Superior Audiovisual Council National Accounts Institute Federal Agency for Nuclear Control<br>Regulatory Commission for Energy in the Brussels-Capital Region Brussels gas electricity Health Insurance Fund Control Office<br>National Railway Company of Belgium |
| Bulgaria | Bulgarian National Bank<br>Financial Supervision Commission Communications Regulation Commission Commission for Protection of Competition Energy and Water Regulatory Commission Electronic Media Council<br>Commission for Protection against Discrimination |
| Czech Republic | Office for the Protection of Competition Czech Telecommunication Office<br>Council for Radio and Television Broadcasting Energy Regulatory Office |
| Germany | Bundeskartellamt (Federal Cartel Office)<br>Bundesnetzagentur (Federal Network Agency for Electricity, Gas, Telecommunications, Post and Railway) |
| Estonia | Tax and Customs Board Competition Authority Financial Supervision Authority<br>Agriculture and Food Board |

| | |
|---|---|
| Greece | Hellenic Competition Commission<br>Hellenic Telecommunications & Post Commission Regulatory Authority for Energy<br>Hellenic Capital Market Commission<br>Hellenic Data Protection Authority |
| Spain | Bank of Spain<br>National Securities Market Commission Spanish Data Protection Agency<br>National Markets and Competition Commission, Nuclear Safety Council<br>Institute of Accounting and Auditing |
| France | French Anti-Doping Agency<br>French Prudential Supervision and Resolution Authority French Competition Authority<br>Financial Markets Authority<br>Regulatory Authority for Electronic Communications, Post and Press Distribution National Gaming Authority<br>Transport Regulatory Authority Nuclear Safety Authority<br>French Energy Regulatory Commission Superior Audiovisual Council<br>French Data Protection Authority<br>High Authority for Transparency in Public Life<br>National Commission for the Monitoring of Security Interceptions.<br>National Agency for the Safety of Medicines and Health Products<br>Airport Noise Control Authority |
| Croatia | Croatian Competition Agency (AZTN)<br>Croatian Financial Services Supervisory Agency (HANFA) Croatian Energy Regulatory Agency (HERA)<br>Croatian Regulatory Authority for Network Industries (HAKOM)<br>Agency for Science and Higher Education (AZVO) |
| Italy | Authority for the protection of personal data Authority for Competition and the Market Authority of regulation of transports<br>Authority of regulation of the energy |
| Cyprus | Commission for the Protection of Competition<br>Office of the Commissioner of Electronic Communications and Postal Regulations Cyprus Energy Regulatory Authority<br>Cyprus Securities and Exchange Commission Cyprus RadioTelevision Authority<br>Cyprus Transmission System Operator<br>Office of the Commissioner for Personal Data Protection Cyprus Gaming and Casino Supervision Commission<br>Ombudsman |
| Latvia | Public Utilities Commission<br>Financial and Capital Market Commission<br>Competition Council |
| Luxembourg | Luxembourg Competition Council Financial Sector Supervisory Commission<br>Luxembourg Institute of Regulation |

| | |
|---|---|
| Hungary | Hungarian Energy and Public Utility Regulatory Authority National Media and Infocommunications Authority Public Procurement Authority<br>Hungarian Competition Authority<br>National Authority for Data Protection and Freedom of Information<br>National Election Office |
| Austria | Energy-Control Austria for the regulation of the electricity and gas sector Regulatory Authority for Broadcasting and Telecommunications Communications Authority Austria<br>Telecommunications Control Commission Postal Control Commission<br>Rail-Control GmbH<br>Rail Control Commission |
| Poland | Financial Supervisory Authority<br>President of the Office of Electronic Communications<br>President of the Office of Competition and Consumer Protection |
| Portugal | Authority for Mobility and Transportation National Authority for Civil Aviation<br>Authority for the Supervision of Insurances and Pension Funds Competition Authority<br>National Communications Authority Regulatory Entity for Energy Services Regulatory Entity for Health<br>Regulatory Entity for Water and Residue Services Regulatory Entity for Communication Securities Market Commission<br>Bank of Portugal |
| Slovenia | Slovenian Competition Protection Agency Securities Market Agency The Bank of Slovenia Insurance Supervision Agency Communications Networks<br>Services Agency of the Republic of Slovenia |
| Slovakia | Antimonopoly Office of the Slovak Republic Regulatory Office for Network Industries<br>Regulatory Authority for Electronic Communications and Postal Services Council for Broadcasting and Retransmission<br>Office for Personal Data Protection Health Care Surveillance Authority Transport Authority<br>Office for Public Procurement |
| Finland | Financial Supervisory Authority<br>Finnish Competition and Consumer Authority Finnish Patent and Registration Office<br>Regional Centres for Economic Development, Transport and the Environment Finnish Medicines Agency Fimea<br>National Supervisory Authority for Welfare and Health Valvira Finnish Transport and Communications Agency Traficom Finnish Transport Infrastructure Agency<br>Finnish Energy Authority<br>Regional State Administrative Agencies |

| | |
|---|---|
| Turkey | Radio and Television Supreme Council<br>Information Technologies and Communication Authority Capital Markets Board<br>Banking Regulation and Supervision Agency Energy Market Regulatory Authority<br>Public Procurement Authority Competition Authority<br>Public Oversight Accounting and Auditing Standards Authority |
| Norway | Norwegian Competition Authority Norwegian Data Protection Authority |

### *1.2. The competence of the administrative courts and, in particular, the respondent supreme administrative courts in disputes involving regulatory issues*

All 24 courts that responded to the questionnaires are competent to hear appeals against the acts of regulatory authorities.

However, it should be noted that the Supreme Court of Norway, which responded to the questionnaire as a guest, is not an administrative court. Norway states that it has no administrative jurisdiction. Like all administrative disputes, disputes involving regulatory acts are heard by the ordinary courts in accordance with the Norwegian Civil Procedure Act.

The respondent courts have varying degrees of regulatory competence, often shared with other courts.

On the one hand, it is restricted in some States to certain categories of act or sector.

For example, in Cyprus and Sweden, the administrative courts, and therefore the supreme administrative courts, are only competent to review by way of action individual decisions of regulatory authorities. The legality of regulatory acts can only be challenged by way of exception, in support of an appeal against an individual decision.

In Germany, the Federal Administrative Court (Bundesverwaltungsgericht) has limited jurisdiction over three regulatory sectors: electronic communications, post and railways.

In Portugal, the competence of the Supreme Administrative Court is exceptional, as there is in principle no double level of jurisdiction in administrative matters. It is limited to disputes of significant social importance and complexity and to questions of law (Article 150 of the Code of Administrative Court Procedure). The Supreme Administrative Court acts as '*an internal safety valve of the system*'.

On the other hand, the competence of the respondent courts is shared in some States with other courts (other than the civil courts, whose competence in regulatory matters is analysed below in 1.3).

In Greece, jurisdiction in disputes is shared between the Council of State and the Court of Appeal, which has been given jurisdiction by law to hear appeals against individual decisions of the Hellenic Telecommunications and Post Commission and the Hellenic Capital Market Commission.

In Spain, given the regional form of the State, appeals against acts of the territorial regulatory authorities, whose competence is limited to the territory of an autonomous community, are judged by the High Courts of Justice of these autonomous communities.

In Latvia, the Constitutional Court is competent to assess the conformity of regulatory acts of the Public Utilities Commission and the Financial and Capital Markets Commission with higher standards.

In Austria, competence to hear appeals against decisions of the Federal Administrative Court in disputes involving individual decisions and sanctions of regulatory authorities is shared between the Supreme Administrative Court (Verwaltungsgerichtshof) and the Constitutional Court (Verfassungsgerichtshof). In addition, the Constitutional Court is competent to assess the validity of regulatory acts of regulatory authorities.

The respondent courts in most cases exercise either appellate or cassation jurisdiction over decisions taken by the administrative courts on appeals against the acts of regulatory authorities.

For example, in Germany, disputes involving the regulation of telecommunications, post and railways are brought before the administrative courts (Verwaltungsgericht) in the first instance, on appeal to the Higher Administrative Court (Oberverwaltungsgericht) and then in the last instance before the Federal Administrative Court in Leipzig (Bundesverwaltungsgericht), which only rules on points of law.

In Estonia, the administrative courts also have three instances. The Administrative Chamber of the Supreme Court hears appeals in cassation that have been allowed after a filter procedure.

In Spain, appeals against decisions of the regulatory authorities are brought before the Administrative Chamber of the National High Court (Audiencia Nacional) and then before the Supreme Court, which acts as a court of cassation.

In Cyprus, appeals against acts, decisions and omissions of regulatory authorities, taken in the exercise of public powers, are brought before the administrative courts in the first instance and then before the Supreme Court on appeal.

In Luxembourg, the Administrative Court is competent to hear appeals against the acts of regulatory authorities.

In Hungary, appeals against the acts of regulatory authorities are brought in the first instance before the High Court of Budapest, whose judgments could initially be challenged before the Curia by the parties or persons concerned alleging a violation of the law. From now on, since a reform of the procedural rules came into force on 1 April 2020, they can only be subject to judicial review by the Curia, provided they meet strict eligibility criteria.

In Slovakia, regional courts are the basic element of administrative justice and have competence in the first and last resort. The Supreme Court has the power of cassation of decisions of the regional courts.

As a court ruling on questions of fact and of law, the Supreme Administrative Court of Finland is competent to hear, after a filter procedure (leave to appeal), decisions of the regional administrative courts as well as part of those of the Market Court in disputes involving regulatory issues.

However, a minority of the respondent courts have competence in the first and last instance in regulatory matters.

In Belgium and Greece, the Council of State is in principle the competent body to judge disputes involving acts of regulatory authorities, unless the action has been specifically assigned by law to the jurisdiction of another court.

In France, the Council of State is competent, pursuant to the Code of Administrative Justice, to rule directly, at first and last instance, on a significant part of disputes involving acts of regulatory authorities. As a court of cassation, it is also competent to hear disputes involving regulatory authorities, which do not fall within its direct jurisdiction, but within the jurisdiction of the administrative courts under ordinary law (such as, for example, disputes involving compensation).

In Croatia, the Supreme Administrative Court has competence in the first instance, specially assigned by law, in matters of public procurement procedures and the right of access to information, in case of challenges to the administrative acts of the Croatian Network Industries Regulatory Authority and the Croatian Competition Authority.

In Lithuania, the Supreme Administrative Court is competent in the first and last instance to review the legality of regulatory administrative acts of regulatory authorities. Apart from this, it is the court of appeal for decisions taken by the regional administrative courts in disputes involving regulatory issues.

In Turkey, the Council of State is competent to hear appeals directly against regulatory acts of the regulatory authorities. Appeals are first heard by the Thirteenth Chamber, whose decisions may then be appealed to the Council of Administrative Chambers of the Council of State. In addition, the Council of State is competent to hear at third instance appeals against individual decisions of regulatory authorities, with the exception of disputes arising from tendering procedures, for which it is competent at second instance.

### *1.3. The competence of the civil courts in disputes involving regulatory issues*

A minority of respondent States (Estonia, Greece, Croatia, Luxembourg, Slovenia, Slovakia and Turkey) indicate that their civil courts have no jurisdiction in relation to disputes involving regulatory issues.

In the other respondent States, the civil courts have varying degrees of competence in this area. Depending on the case, these civil courts are either ordinary courts or specialised courts such as in Belgium or Poland.

As mentioned above, since Norway does not have an administrative court, all disputes involving acts of regulatory authorities are heard by the civil courts. In Slovakia, such disputes are heard by specialised chambers of the judicial courts. However, the establishment by a constitutional revision (Constitutional Act No 422/2020 Coll.) of a separate Supreme Administrative Court as of 1 January 2021 is the first step towards the organisation of an administrative jurisdiction independent of the judicial courts.

Some respondent States (Latvia, Portugal, Czech Republic, Spain) explain that civil courts have jurisdiction over private-law disputes involving regulatory authorities. In others (Germany, Cyprus, Sweden, Hungary, Poland), they have jurisdiction over claims for compensation for damage caused by the acts of regulatory authorities.

In several respondent States, specific laws attribute to the civil courts, by derogation from the general rules of jurisdiction of the administrative courts, competence for appeals against certain administrative acts of regulatory authorities. France explains that these attributions of competence are justified by '*the interest of the proper administration of justice*', Germany by a consensus within the country's institutions that it is preferable that economic matters be decided by civil courts.

In Belgium, for example, laws have transferred to the Market Court, a section of the Brussels Court of Appeal, jurisdiction in disputes for some of the decisions of the Financial Services and Markets Authority (FSMA), for decisions of the Belgian Institute for Postal Services and Telecommunications (BIPT), of the Commission for Electricity and Gas Regulation (CREG), of the Competition Authority (ABC), for decisions of the National Bank of Belgium (NBB) imposing an administrative fine.

In Germany, the division of competence between administrative and civil courts depends on the regulatory sector. The civil courts have jurisdiction over disputes concerning the regulation of electricity and gas. They are also competent for disputes arising from decisions taken by the Federal Cartel Office (Bundeskartellamt).

In France, the Paris Court of Appeal has competence to rule in the first and last instance on part of disputes involving individual decisions of certain regulatory authorities, the Competition Authority, the Electronic Communications, Post and Press Distribution Regulatory Authority and the Financial Markets Authority.

In Italy, the civil courts are competent for appeals against acts of the Personal Data Protection Authority and against sanctions of the banking and financial markets regulatory authorities.

In Poland, a specialised civil court, the Competition and Consumer Protection Court (one of the divisions of Warsaw District Court), has been given jurisdiction to hear appeals against regulatory acts of regulatory authorities (e.g. regulatory decisions of the President of the Office for Electronic Communications by Article 206 of the Telecommunications Act).

Finally, in two respondent States (Germany and Lithuania), civil courts have jurisdiction over appeals against sanctions taken by regulatory authorities. In Germany, these appeals are heard by the criminal courts, in accordance with the Code of Criminal Procedure. In Lithuania, a change in legislation in 2011 transferred disputes involving administrative offences committed by natural persons to the civil courts.

### *1.4. The lack of specificity of remedies against acts of regulatory authorities*

The majority of respondent States consider that the remedies available against acts of regulatory authorities are of the same nature as those available against equivalent or similar acts of other administrative authorities.

Germany specifies that the civil courts adapt their procedure when judging disputes involving regulatory issues (implementation of an inquisitorial procedure).

Poland explains that the scope of the court's review varies depending on whether the appeal is heard by the administrative or civil court. The civil court, the Competition and Consumer Protection Court, applies the *de novo* procedure, while the administrative court reviews the validity of the administrative decision *ex tunc*, depending on the legal and factual circumstances at the date of the decision.

## 2. Admissibility of appeals against regulatory acts

### *2.1. The particular issues of admissibility of appeals against 'hard-law' regulatory acts*

For the vast majority of respondent countries, disputes involving 'hard-law' regulatory acts do not present particular issues of admissibility compared with appeals against other administrative acts. Belgium, Bulgaria, Germany, Spain, France, Italy, Croatia, Cyprus, Latvia, Lithuania, Luxembourg, Hungary, Austria, Poland, Slovenia, Slovakia, Finland, Sweden, Turkey and Norway thus indicate that they are governed by the general rules of admissibility of appeals against administrative acts.

Some respondent States, however, report particular questions that their courts have asked about the admissibility of appeals against 'hard-law' regulatory acts.

Estonia explains that while competing undertakings and consumers are not in principle entitled to challenge discretionary refusals by regulatory authorities to prosecute or take action against an undertaking, the Supreme Court has accepted the admissibility of the appeal where the regulatory authority's supervisory powers have been conferred on it to protect the applicant's subjective rights and these are likely to be infringed by the illegal activity of the undertaking.

In the same vein, Greece states that particular questions arise as to the legitimate interest of applicants in challenging decisions by regulatory authorities not to investigate or to reject their complaints about market distortions or their interest in challenging the duration and severity of sanctions imposed on economic actors.

In Portugal, it was debated before the Constitutional Court whether the devolutive and non-suspensive effect of appeals against regulatory authorities' sanctioning decisions violates the principle of presumption of innocence enshrined in the Constitution. A decision of the Constitutional Court ruled that the appeal against final and enforceable sanctioning decisions of the body responsible for regulating health matters has a purely devolutive effect, and can only have a suspensive effect if the applicant argues that the enforcement of the sanction is likely to cause him or her considerable harm (Constitutional Court decision, No 74/2019, 7 March).

### *2.2. The institution of appeals against 'soft-law' acts*

A majority of respondent States (Belgium, Czech Republic, Greece, Spain, Croatia, Cyprus, Luxembourg, Austria, Poland, Slovenia, Slovakia, Finland, Sweden, Norway) indicate that 'soft-law' acts (opinions, recommendations, warnings) and position papers (press release, website section, FAQ, etc.) of regulatory authorities cannot be directly challenged for annulment as they are not binding.

In the other respondent States (Germany, Estonia, France, Italy, Latvia, Lithuania, Hungary, Portugal, Turkey), the 'soft-law' acts of regulatory authorities may in some cases be subject to appeal.

In Germany, recourse to the administrative courts does not depend on the legal form of the act, but on the applicant's standing, who must show that the act has infringed his or her individual rights. 'Soft-law' acts and statements of regulatory authorities are subject to appeal if their indirect effects do not merely reflect legal regulation, but infringe the individual right of the applicant, for example, his or her freedom of enterprise under Article 12 of the Basic Law.

In Estonia, 'soft-law' acts can be challenged if they have been used as a basis for a decision, e.g. the published position of the Tax and Customs

Commission on the taxation of certain categories of share transfers, on the basis of which it taxed a group of shareholders.

In France, soft-law acts may be subject to appeal if they are likely to produce significant effects, in particular of an economic nature, or are intended to have a significant influence on the behaviour of the persons at whom they are directed (CE, Ass., 21 March 2016, *Société Fairvesta International GMBH* and others, Nos 368082, 368083, 368084 and *Société NC Numéricable*, No 390023). For example, the Council of State accepted the admissibility of an appeal against the recommendations of good professional practice issued by the French Prudential Supervision and Resolution Authority, which are intended to encourage insurance undertakings and intermediaries to modify their reciprocal relations significantly (CE, 20 June 2016, *Fédération française des sociétés d'assurance*, No 384297).

In Latvia, 'soft-law' acts cannot in principle be appealed, unless the applicant establishes that they infringe his or her legal rights or interests (e.g. violation of trade secrets).

Lithuania states that in the case law of its Supreme Administrative Court, 'soft-law' acts are interpreted in accordance with the binding 'hard-law' provisions that they supplement. Their nature as acts of 'soft law' cannot erase their legal effects or exclude them completely from judicial review. In a recent case, decided by an enlarged panel of judges, the Court held that the statutory obligation on financial institutions to follow the regulator's guidelines is not sufficiently precise to enable them to assess in advance whether disregard of these non-binding guidelines amounts to a violation of the law that may be sanctioned by a fine (Case No eA-663-822/2021).

However, Lithuania makes a distinction in the case of warnings or cautions. According to constitutional case law from 2017, a warning of a possible suspension of the validity of a licence is an act subject to judicial review.

In Portugal, courts review 'soft-law' acts of regulatory authorities. While they cannot replace the regulators, they are competent to verify the regularity of the procedure they follow and the 'reasonableness' of their actions. Article 8 of the Code of Administrative Court Procedure requires administrative authorities to reject 'manifestly unreasonable' solutions.

Portugal also stresses that 'soft-law' acts may have legal value either because they interpret binding 'hard-law' acts or because they are a preliminary step to the adoption of such acts. Thus, in decision 1233/20.9.BEPRT of 2

April 2021, the Central Administrative Court of the South assessed whether the publication on the Internet by the competent authority of a notice on an illegality committed by persons identified by name, without implementing an adversarial procedure, violates their right to be presumed innocent.

### *2.3. Persons entitled to challenge the acts of regulatory authorities*

In none of the respondent States is there an *actio popularis* against the acts of regulatory authorities. Applicants must have standing.

In some States (Greece, Spain, France, Croatia, Cyprus, Latvia, Lithuania, Luxembourg, Hungary, Poland, Sweden, Turkey, Norway) it is sufficient for the applicant to establish that the contested act affects one of his or her legitimate or legally protected interests.

Greece specifies that this legitimate interest must be personal, direct and current.

In France, persons entitled to challenge the acts of regulatory authorities are those whom they adversely affect in sufficiently special, certain and direct conditions.

Cyprus states that a claim may be brought by any aggrieved person who, as an individual or as a member of a group, has a legitimate, direct and existing interest affected by the contested act. The recognition of a legitimate interest to act does not necessarily imply the violation of a subjective right. The legitimate interest may be financial or moral.

Latvia distinguishes between individual decisions and regulatory acts of regulatory authorities. The former may be challenged before the administrative courts by individuals whose legal rights and interests they infringe or are likely to infringe. The latter, on the other hand, may be appealed to the Constitutional Court only by persons who allege violation of their constitutionally protected fundamental rights.

In Sweden, individual decisions of regulatory authorities can be challenged by any person directly concerned. Distant legal interest is not enough. The admissibility of the appeal depends on the practical (legal, economic or other) effect of the act on the applicant.

In other States (Czech Republic, Germany, Estonia, Austria, Slovakia, Finland), the applicant is only entitled to challenge the act if it affects one of his or her subjective rights.

In the Czech Republic, acts of regulatory authorities may be challenged by any person claiming an infringement of his or her rights either directly by the act itself or during its adoption procedure.

In Germany, as already mentioned above, the applicant must establish a violation of his or her subjective rights. Disregarding only political or economic interests is not sufficient to give standing. The crucial question is therefore whether regulatory acts serve to protect the rights of individuals. For example, if the Federal Network Agency (Bundesnetzagentur) imposes regulatory obligations on an undertaking with significant market power in a regulated market, a competitor is entitled to bring an action for the imposition of new regulatory obligations, since the obligations to provide access to a market, to create transparency and to keep separate accounts are also intended to protect competitors (BVerwGE 130, 39 para 14 et seq.).

In Estonia, the Code of Administrative Court Procedure provides that individuals may only apply to an administrative court for the protection of their rights.

In some States (Latvia, Lithuania, Poland, Portugal), public authorities are empowered by law to challenge the legality of regulatory acts before the courts.

In Latvia, the conformity of regulatory acts of regulatory authorities with the hierarchy of norms can be challenged before the Constitutional Court by certain authorities, including the President, the Saeima, 20 deputies of the Saeima, the Prosecutor General, the Ombudsman, etc.

In Poland, the public prosecutor, the human rights defender (Ombudsman), social organisations, within the limits of their statutory interests, and public bodies (municipalities, inter-municipal structures, districts, voivodships) are entitled to challenge the acts of regulatory authorities.

In Portugal, the public prosecutor, as the guardian of legality, and the executive are entitled to challenge the acts of regulatory authorities.

### *2.4. The exception of illegality of general acts of regulatory authorities*

The questionnaires did not reveal any particularity specific to disputes involving the acts of regulatory authorities, as the replies referred to the general rules of administrative disputes in the respondent countries.

Eight respondent States (Belgium, Croatia, Italy, Latvia, Luxembourg, Hungary, Poland, Norway) indicate that the illegality of general acts of regulatory authorities cannot be challenged by way of exception in an appeal against an individual decision. However, this statement must be qualified by the additional explanations that some of them provided.

Belgian law recognises and applies the technique of the exception of the illegality of regulatory acts. However, Belgium points out that the regulatory authorities do not have regulatory powers, so the question is not relevant for Belgium. 'Soft-law' acts of regulatory authorities (guidelines and recommendations) can be challenged in support of an appeal against an individual decision implementing them. In Belgium's view, this is not an objection to the illegality of a regulatory act, but a challenge to the individual decision on the grounds that it is based on an incorrect interpretation.

In Croatia, the applicant may, in an appeal against an individual decision of a regulatory authority, invoke the illegality of the general act on the basis of which it was taken. The Supreme Administrative Court is then competent to review the legality of the general act, at the request of the court before which the appeal against the individual decision is pending (Article 83 of the Administrative Judicial Procedure Act). The general act, which the Supreme Administrative Court has found to be illegal, ceases to be valid on the date of publication of the Court's decision in the Official Gazette.

In Latvia, the courts may stay an appeal in order to refer a question to the Constitutional Court for a preliminary ruling on the conformity with the Constitution or international law of a legal provision applicable to the dispute.

The exception of illegality is not recognised in Luxembourg administrative law. However, the Administrative Court did apply the plea of illegality mechanism in a case that gave rise to a request for a preliminary ruling from the Court of Justice of the European Union, in order to comply with European Union law. The exception of illegality has never yet been applied in disputes involving regulatory acts.

In Hungary, the plea of illegality can only be raised in support of an appeal against an individual decision if the general act is an act of 'soft law'. Indeed, because of their binding nature, general acts of 'hard law' are considered to be legislative acts falling within the scope of the 2010 Law on Legislation and are not subject to review by the administrative courts.

Fourteen respondent States (Czech Republic, Estonia, Germany, Greece, Spain, France, Cyprus, Lithuania, Austria, Portugal, Slovakia, Finland, Sweden, Turkey) apply the plea of illegality mechanism to disputes involving regulatory issues. In some States (Estonia, Cyprus, Austria, Slovakia, Sweden), the plea of illegality is the only way to challenge the legality of general acts of regulatory authorities that cannot be appealed directly.

In Estonia, all courts may refer to the Supreme Court, *ex officio* or at the request of a party, a question on the conformity with the Constitution of a regulatory act applicable to a dispute pending before them. If the Supreme Court finds the act contrary to the Constitution, it may annul it, either *ex tunc* or *ex nunc*. The annulment is always retroactive for the specific dispute in which the question of constitutionality was raised. The Supreme Court may decide to limit the retroactive effect of the annulment to disputes already pending before the courts.

In Greece, the exception of the illegality of a general act cannot lead to its annulment, but only to the annulment of the individual decision taken on the basis of it. Should the illegality of the general act result from a formal or procedural defect, the judges may not annul the individual decision if the general act has been in force for a long period of time and the consequences of its illegality on the individual decision are likely to affect legal certainty (Article 50, Section 3, paragraph (c) of Presidential Decree No 18/1989 on proceedings before the Council of State).

In France, the general acts of regulatory authorities, both 'hard law' and 'soft law', may be challenged by way of exception. If the exception of illegality is accepted by the judge, it only leads to the annulment of the individual decision that applies the general act, and not the general act itself. Similarly, in Lithuania, Slovakia and Sweden, the exception of the illegality of the general act only leads to the annulment of the individual decision.

In Austria, the legality of a regulatory act of a regulatory authority may be challenged before the Constitutional Court, on the occasion of an appeal against an individual decision implementing it, either by the court before which it is pending, or by the parties, after the appeal has been ruled on by the court of first instance. The recognition of the illegality of the regulatory act by the Constitutional Court entails its annulment as well as that of the individual decision based on this act.

Similarly, in Turkey, the plea of illegality, if upheld, leads to the retroactive annulment of the regulatory act.

### *2.5. Bringing an action for damages against regulatory authorities*

In all respondent countries, it is possible to bring a liability action either against the regulatory authorities or against the state to obtain compensation for damages caused by regulatory activity, in particular by the issuing of illegal regulatory acts.

In Lithuania in particular, the duty to remedy damage caused by unlawful actions of state authorities is a constitutional principle. Where the exercise of discretionary power by administrative authorities is at issue, Lithuanian administrative courts take into account the seriousness of the breach of the rule of law in assessing the liability of the State.

Some respondent States (Belgium, Greece, France, Latvia, Luxembourg, Hungary, Slovenia) indicate that liability claims should be directed against the regulatory authorities themselves when they have legal personality.

In France, only some of the regulatory authorities have legal personality. These have the status of independent public authorities (Article 2 of the Act of 20 January 2017 on the general status of independent administrative authorities and independent public authorities). The liability action must be directed against the State when the damage has been caused by a regulatory authority that does not have its own legal personality.

## 3. The internal organisation of the courts

### *3.1. The allocation of cases concerning regulatory authorities*

In 14 respondent States (Belgium, Bulgaria, Germany, Estonia, Spain, France, Italy, Latvia, Lithuania, Austria, Portugal, Slovenia, Finland, Turkey), cases concerning regulatory authorities are assigned to specialised judges or panels of judges to take account of their complexity and technicality.

In Germany, the Constitution provides for a constitutional right to be tried by a judge appointed by law. This right does not allow for random assignment of cases or variation in the composition of panels according to their complexity. The number of panels, their areas of jurisdiction and the assignment of judges to panels are set out for each court in its annual business plan (Geschäftsverteilungsplan), drawn up by the 'Präsidium', a council elected by the court's judges. As the composition of the chambers normally remains stable from one year to the next, the internal organisation of the courts leads to judges specialising and becoming experts in their field. Young judges benefit from the knowledge and experience of older judges. At the Federal Administrative Court, cases concerning the regulatory authorities are heard by the Sixth Chamber (or Senate).

Similarly, in Spain, the rules for assigning cases to each court are set annually and published in the official State gazette.

In Estonia, specialisation is only possible if the court and the volume of disputes are large enough. In the Supreme Court, administrative disputes are heard by five judges, each of whom has specialised areas (including disputes involving regulatory issues) as rapporteur. Cases are decided by panels of at least three judges, so it may be that only the rapporteur is an expert in the field.

In France, disputes concerning acts of regulatory authorities are divided between several chambers within the Legal Section of the Council of State. The regulatory authority that initiated the contested act or the sector in which it operates determines the chamber to which the case is assigned. The chambers have other competences, so that they are not only specialised in disputes involving regulatory issues. Similarly, in Austria, disputes involving regulatory issues are assigned to two specialised chambers of the Supreme Administrative Court, which do not deal exclusively with such disputes, but hear cases in various fields of administrative law.

In Latvia, the assignment of cases and the composition of panels take into account the specialisations of the judges. The same is true in Lithuania, which indicates that the law has become so complex and specific in certain areas of regulation that a proper examination of cases requires a high level of specialisation.

In the 10 other respondent States (Czech Republic, Greece, Croatia, Cyprus, Luxembourg, Hungary, Poland, Slovakia, Sweden, Norway), disputes involving regulatory issues are not assigned to judges or to specialised judicial panels.

Greece points out, however, that while the Council of State does not have a chamber specialising in disputes involving regulatory issues, other courts have specialised panels that only hear cases concerning a particular regulatory authority. For example, the Athens Court of Appeal has a specialised panel to hear appeals against the Greek Competition Authority.

There are two panels for administrative law cases in the Supreme Court of Cyprus. Each panel hears appeals in all branches of administrative law, and does not specialise in any one area. Moreover, due to the multitude of competences of the Supreme Court, which performs, among others, the functions of constitutional court, court of final appeal in civil and criminal matters, court of appeal in family law and electoral court, its judges cannot specialise in a particular competence or sector.

In Poland, cases concerning regulatory authorities are heard by the Commercial Chamber of the Supreme Court, but there are no panels within the Chamber dedicated exclusively to disputes involving regulatory issues.

In the Supreme Court of Norway, the composition of the panels is decided randomly and changes every week.

### *3.2. The internal resources of the courts to deal with disputes involving regulatory authorities*

Ten states (Germany, Italy, Hungary, Austria, Poland, Slovenia, Slovakia, Sweden, Turkey, Norway) replied that the courts do not have internal resources to help judges become familiar with the technical aspects of disputes involving regulatory issues.

Sweden states, however, that the procedure before the Stockholm Administrative Court of Appeal, which has final jurisdiction over disputes relating to electronic communications, makes use of the existing technical and economic expertise within the court to hear such cases.

In the 14 other respondent States (Belgium, Bulgaria, Czech Republic, Estonia, Greece, Spain, France, Croatia, Cyprus, Latvia, Lithuania, Luxembourg, Portugal, Finland), the courts have various internal resources to strengthen their expertise in the regulatory sectors they oversee.

These resources are the initial and ongoing training of judges, the organisation of seminars and exchanges with regulation professionals, the legal and technical skills of judges, acquired through their specialisation in disputes involving regulatory issues or through the exercise of other professional functions outside the courts, the use of judicial assistants, the creation and updating of case-law databases, and the establishment within the courts of entities dedicated to legal research.

For example, in Estonia, the Supreme Court, which is responsible for organising the ongoing training of judges of all courts, recently organised seminars on artificial intelligence and applied economics (on business practices in general and more specifically in the construction sector).

In Spain, the administrative courts include a category of magistrates specialised in administrative disputes, recruited through a competitive examination open to judges and prosecutors, which includes regulatory and competition law. Specialised magistrates have priority over non-specialised magistrates in the allocation of positions in the courts.

In France, a small number of members of the Council of State have expertise in regulatory matters thanks to their professional background outside the court. Consideration is currently being given to developing the court's internal resources. A series of lectures in economics by professors of economics is being organised and offered this autumn to members of the Council of State. They can also be followed remotely by all members of the administrative jurisdiction (administrative courts of appeal and administrative tribunals).

In Latvia, the Case Law and Research Division of the Supreme Court is responsible for legal studies in the fields of European Union and international law, case law of international courts and comparative law. It may conduct a study on a particular legal issue at the request of a judge. Similarly, in Lithuania, the judges of the Supreme Administrative Court are assisted by the Legal Research and Documentation Department, which consists of a multidisciplinary team of assistant judges, advisers, academics and other legal professionals. The investigation of complex cases in the field of competition law, financial market supervision and energy regulation often gives rise to the consultation of senior legal advisers in the Legal Research and Documentation Department for additional legal research and analysis.

In Finland, specialised knowledge in certain areas of law and practice is considered a major advantage in the recruitment of judges. In addition, for judging cases in certain fields (environment, intellectual property), the panels are composed of two experts in the fields concerned.

## 4. The investigation of appeals

### *4.1. Investigative techniques*

Three respondent States (Germany, Estonia, Austria) indicate that their supreme courts, as courts of cassation, only consider questions of law and are bound by the findings of fact of the courts of first instance. Therefore, unlike the latter, they do not use fact-finding or investigative techniques.

Cyprus explains that its Supreme Court makes only limited use of fact-finding and investigative techniques, as it limits itself to reviewing the legality of administrative action, to verifying that the administrative authorities have exercised their discretionary powers within the legal limits. Its competence does not extend to technical matters or to those requiring specialist knowledge.

In Poland, the Supreme Administrative Court bases its decisions on the case file compiled by the regulatory authority and does not conduct additional investigations, except in exceptional cases of serious doubt.

**Table of the main investigative measures used in the respondent countries**

| Country | Oral hearing | Expert's report | *Amicus curiae* | Solicitation of a reference expert administration | Other investigative techniques |
|---|---|---|---|---|---|
| Belgium | X | X (exceptional cases) | | | Request additional information and explanations from the parties |
| Bulgaria | | X | | | |
| Czech Republic | | X | X | | Witness testimony |
| Germany | X | X | | | |
| Estonia | X | | X | X | |
| Greece | X | X | | | |
| Spain | | | X | X | |
| France | X | X | X | X | Investigation in court or on the premises |
| Croatia | X | X | | | |
| Italy | X | X | X | | |
| Cyprus | X | | X | | |

| | | | | | |
|---|---|---|---|---|---|
| Latvia | X | X | X | | Witness testimony |
| Lithuania | X | X | X | X | Witness testimony |
| Luxembourg | X | X (exceptional cases) | | | |
| Hungary | X | X | | | |
| Austria | X | | X (only when the recourse to *amicus curiae* is based on European Union law) | | |
| Poland | | | | | |
| Portugal | X | X | | | |
| Slovenia | X | X (uncommon) | X (uncommon) | | |
| Slovak Republic | X | X | X | | |
| Finland | X | X | | | |
| Sweden | X | X | | X | |
| Turkey | X | X | | | Use of scientific work |
| Norway | X | X | X | | Use of lay judges with expertise in the field |

Six respondent States (Greece, France, Italy, Hungary, Slovakia, Portugal) consider that disputes involving regulatory issues require a specific method of investigation.

Greece believes that courts should recruit their own independent and impartial experts (economists, engineers, etc.) to assist judges in understanding complex technical issues (e.g. market analysis).

Similarly, the Slovak Republic advocates the appointment of consultants to advise judges and provide them with the expertise and technical explanations necessary for a proper understanding of cases during their investigation.

Italy goes even further by considering that the possibility of including professionals from the sector in panels of judges should be studied.

Because of the technical nature of the disputes or the economic equilibrium involved, France notes a particularly strong need to mobilise expert opinions or methods of investigation involving oral hearings and the presence of all the parties prior to the judgment hearing, in order to ensure that the court has a good understanding of the facts. These are often technical, and presented in quite different lights by the parties, without the judge having his or her own expertise enabling him or her to spontaneously disentangle the true from the false. The direct confrontation of the words of both sides is therefore sometimes essential to establish or understand the facts (for example, the actual effectiveness of the geo-blocking techniques implemented by certain Internet search engines to prevent the display, on the terminals of European users, of search results that have been the subject of a 'de-indexing' decision by a national data protection authority, under the right to be forgotten enshrined in the GDPR: CE, 27 March 2020, *Société Google Inc.*, No 399922).

Hungary explains that in case of recourse to an expert opinion, the judge should only take into account the opinions given by the expert on technical issues and decide alone on legal issues.

Portugal considers that the particular technicality of disputes involving regulatory issues would require the creation of a set of specific procedural rules, the provision of technical means for the courts to assess certain aspects of the activities of regulatory authorities and the guarantee of rapid procedures that are essential for appropriate regulation.

### *4.2. The role of administrations and other stakeholders in the investigation of appeals*

The vast majority of respondent States (Belgium, Bulgaria, Czech Republic, Germany, Estonia, Greece, Spain, Croatia, Italy, Cyprus, Lithuania, Luxembourg, Hungary, Slovenia, Slovakia, Poland, Portugal, Finland, Sweden, Turkey, Norway) indicate that the administrations and other stakeholders who are not parties to the proceedings have no place or only a very limited place in the investigation of appeals.

However, in Germany, administrative authorities may present their views in proceedings pending before the administrative courts through the representative of the public interest, and before the Federal Administrative Court through the representative of the interest of the Federation. These authorities cannot appeal, but they can intervene in all proceedings pending before the courts. In practice, they rarely intervene in proceedings to which the regulatory authorities are party, as the latter are already sufficiently representative of the administrations' views.

In Spain, the European Commission, the National Commission for Markets and Competition and the competent authorities of the Autonomous Regions may, within the scope of their competences, intervene, on their own initiative or at the request of the court, in proceedings concerning trusts and data protection, without having the status of party, in order to produce written or oral observations or transmit information.

In Greece, where the regulatory authority, as a party to the dispute, has applied a regulatory act issued by another administrative authority, the judge reporting on the case may request observations from the latter. Similarly, in Lithuania, the Minister for Energy, in his or her capacity as energy policy-maker, has been involved in disputes challenging the decisions of the National Energy Regulator on the pricing of heating production.

In addition, in some respondent States, the courts may request or use, in the context of the investigation of appeals, the opinion of administrations (Estonia, Spain, France, Croatia, Sweden), or of private persons (Spain, France, Croatia, Sweden) who are not parties to the proceedings, on the legal and technical issues in question. For example, in Sweden, the Swedish Association of Local Authorities and Regions (SKR) is often asked to comment on cases that have a significant practical impact on local authorities.

### *4.3. The role of oral proceedings in the investigation of appeals*

In the majority of the respondent States (Belgium, Bulgaria, Czech Republic, Estonia, Greece, Spain, France, Italy, Lithuania, Luxembourg, Slovenia, Slovakia, Poland, Portugal, Finland, Sweden), judicial proceedings before the supreme administrative court are generally and mainly in writing, with oral proceedings playing only a limited or subsidiary role in the investigation and judgment of appeals. However, they stress the usefulness of holding a public hearing, especially in complex regulatory cases, to gather evidence (Czech Republic, Slovakia, Spain), to question the parties (Estonia, Greece, Luxembourg) and to confront their arguments on the most sensitive technical aspects (Italy), to ask experts for clarifications and explanations of their reports (Spain), to call for the intervention of an *amicus curiae* (Estonia) or to protect the public interest when the issues at stake have a wider social impact (Slovakia).

In Germany, the Federal Administrative Court and other administrative courts are obliged to hear appeals in oral proceedings, unless the parties agree to dispense with a public hearing.

In Cyprus, judicial proceedings consist of two phases, a written preliminary phase and a trial phase with a public hearing. The arguments exchanged and the clarifications made by the parties during the hearing can be decisive for the resolution of the case.

In Hungary, the right of the parties to be heard in open court, at least in the first instance, has been recognised by the Constitutional Court. However, the Court has clarified that a case may be decided without a hearing if the parties waive their right to such a hearing and there is no public interest in holding a hearing.

In addition, some respondent States (Germany, Estonia, France, Latvia) indicate that preliminary hearings, prior to the public hearing of the case, can be organised to allow judges to better understand the complexity and technicality of the cases and to hand down more relevant decisions adapted to the situation. In France, a Decree of 18 November 2020 set up an 18-month experiment at the Council of State with oral examination proceedings and investigative hearings in technical and sensitive cases. Germany points out that these informal, non-public preliminary hearings sometimes enable judges to resolve the dispute at this stage, and in all other cases to better prepare for the public hearing.

## 5. Decision-making

### *5.1. The main categories of grounds invoked against the acts of regulatory authorities*

Several respondent States (Belgium, Bulgaria, Greece, Slovenia, Slovakia, Poland, Portugal, Finland, Norway) indicate that the grounds invoked against the acts of regulatory authorities are not original compared with those invoked against other administrative acts.

For example, in Poland, appeals in cassation before the Supreme Administrative Court are based either on the disregard of substantive law by the lower administrative court or on the violation of a procedural rule that substantially affected the outcome of the dispute.

Other respondent States identify procedural and substantive grounds that are more particularly invoked in disputes involving regulatory issues:

- respect by the regulatory authorities of their competence (France, Cyprus, Hungary);
- compliance with procedural rules (France, Croatia, Italy, Cyprus, Hungary, Turkey), and in particular with the rules on consultation, the rights of defence and the right to be heard;
- respect for privacy in the exercise by regulatory authorities of their supervisory and investigative powers (France);
- respect for the principle of impartiality (France, Cyprus);
- the right of access of citizens to the documents on which the regulatory authorities base their decisions (Luxembourg, Hungary);
- a balancing of interests by the regulator that takes account of all the interests involved, properly assesses their respective importance and does not disproportionately affect any of them (Germany);
- compliance with the principle of proportionality of the decision (Germany, Estonia, Spain, Italy, Cyprus);
- the technical reasonableness and economic sustainability of the decision (Italy);
- the erroneous exercise of discretion by the regulator (Lithuania, Turkey).

France, Cyprus, Lithuania and Austria consider that disputes involving regulatory issues raise particular problems relating to the independence of regulatory authorities and respect for the principle of impartiality, particularly because of the combination of multiple powers (recommendation, regulation, authorisation, control, injunction, sanction).

In France, the Council of State ruled that the power of a regulatory authority, vested with the power to impose sanctions, to refer to itself cases falling within its area of competence must be sufficiently circumscribed so as not to give the impression that the members of the disciplinary panel consider the facts referred to in the decision to initiate the procedure or the subsequent notification of the complaints as already established or their reprehensible nature with regard to the rules or principles to be applied as already recognised, in disregard of the principle of impartiality (CE, 22 December 2011, *Union Mutualiste Générale de Prévoyance*, No 323612).

In Cyprus, challenges to the independence and impartiality of the members of regulatory authorities, due to their possible political involvement, personal and financial interests, and connections, are frequently invoked against their decisions.

In Lithuania, there is a general principle of separation of functions, which implies that investigation and sanctioning cannot be conducted by the same persons or the same entities of the regulatory authority. However, this general principle can be challenged by special rules. Parties frequently argue that the general principle should apply despite the existence of special rules.

In Austria, the Supreme Administrative Court has ruled in two decisions on the structural independence of the regulatory authority in the energy sector. It ruled that this is not guaranteed if a member of the regulatory authority's decision-making body works in an organisation responsible for the protection of consumers' interests and entitled to challenge the regulator's decisions (decision of 15 December 2014, 2013/04/0108), and that the general right of the Federal Minister for Energy to be informed about matters dealt with by the regulatory authority does not necessarily compromise its independence, but that the regulatory authority must not respond to the Minister's requests for information in cases where this could undermine its independence (decision of 23 November 2016, 2016/04/0013).

### *5.2. The extent of the regulatory judge's review*

With the exception of Greece, Cyprus and Poland, all the respondent States indicate that their courts are not bound by the technical and economic assessments of the regulatory authority and that they are entitled to review them, by comparing them with the arguments and evidence provided by the applicants (Spain, Sweden), by taking investigative measures and, if necessary, by calling in an expert (Belgium, Czech Republic, Croatia, Slovakia).

Greece explains that the Council of State considers itself bound by the technical and economic assessments of the regulatory authority, which it does not oversee directly, and that only a limited review of the reasoning followed by the regulatory authority is allowed.

Furthermore, as mentioned above, in Cyprus the Supreme Court does not review technical matters or matters requiring specialist knowledge, and in Poland the Supreme Administrative Court in principle decides on the basis of the facts established by the administrative authority, and only conducts additional investigations, at the request of the parties or *ex officio*, if they are necessary to remove a serious doubt and do not unduly prolong the proceedings.

In the other respondent States, the extent of the regulatory judge's review varies according to the margin of discretion enjoyed by the administrative authority. Several of them indicate that the judge does not review the appropriateness of the decision taken by the regulatory authority (Lithuania, Slovakia, Finland).

In Belgium, the judge's review is restricted to manifest error when the administrative authority has a certain power of discretion, even if limited.

In Germany, the Federal Administrative Court determines the scope of its review by interpreting the relevant legal provisions and decides whether it exercises full control or accepts a margin of discretion on the part of the administrative authority. In regulatory law, it has ruled that several legal provisions (on market regulation and access, tariffs, frequency allocations) give a wide margin of discretion to the regulatory authorities, which leads to a restriction of judicial review. The judge merely checks that the authority has applied the procedural rules correctly, has based its decision on a correct understanding of the applicable legal provisions, has fully and correctly verified the relevant facts, has applied the evaluation standards in force and in particular has not disregarded the prohibition of arbitrariness.

In Estonia, judicial review is also restricted when the contested decision has been taken in the exercise of discretionary power, which is frequently the case in the field of regulation. It is limited to manifest error if the authority's margin of discretion is wide and the infringement of the applicant's rights minor. Where the administrative authority has no discretionary power, the judge may usually substitute his or her own assessment for that of the administrative authority. However, he or she limits his or her review to manifest error where the legislation is sparse, the infringement of the applicant's rights is minor and/or the assessment requires specific non-legal knowledge or experience. In all cases, the judge exercises full review of the facts on which the decision is based, as well as a review of its rationality.

Similarly, in France, the extent of the administrative judge's review varies according to the room for manoeuvre available to the authority under the law, the nature of the decisions challenged and the content of the questions asked.

In Italy, the judge exercises full review of the facts and the logical reasoning followed by the regulator. However, where the latter has given a specific answer to a technical problem under discussion, the judge may not substitute his or her own assessment, but is limited to checking that the regulatory authority's assessment is plausible, reasonable and proportionate in the light of the state of scientific knowledge.

In Lithuania, because of the principle of separation of powers, the judge cannot substitute his or her own assessments for those of the regulator. He or she merely checks that the regulator has not exceeded its powers of discretion, made a manifest error or abused its power. The judge also checks that the regulatory authority has respected the procedural rules and correctly assessed the factual circumstances.

In Luxembourg, the judge checks that the regulatory authority has not exceeded the margin of discretion granted to it by the legislator, by applying a principle of proportionality.

In Hungary, when the administrative courts review an act taken by a regulatory authority in the exercise of a discretionary power, they limit themselves to verifying that the authority has taken the decision within the limits of its competence.

Finally, in Norway, judicial control is limited when the administrative authority is endowed by law with a discretionary power. The judge checks that it has based its decision on considerations within the legal framework, has not discriminated unfairly, has not taken its decision on a purely random basis, and that the decision is not highly unreasonable.

### *5.3. The powers of the regulatory judge*

In 12 respondent States (Belgium, Germany, Estonia, Greece, Italy, Cyprus, Latvia, Hungary, Poland, Portugal, Norway, Turkey), the judge only has the power to annul the decision of the regulatory authority.

In Belgium, while the Council of State only has the power to annul, the Market Court, a judicial court with jurisdiction over some disputes involving regulatory issues, is fully competent in certain cases.

In Germany, the administrative courts can only annul binding decisions of regulatory authorities, either in whole or in part if they are divisible. They do not have injunctive powers where the administrative authorities have a margin of discretion, which is often the case in the field of regulation. They can only annul the contested decision. The authority is then obliged to decide again on the application, taking into account the legal reasoning behind the court's decision.

In Italy, acts of regulatory authorities cannot be modified directly by the judge. However, when he or she annuls an administrative act, he or she prescribes the rules that the administrative authority must follow in taking a new decision.

In Cyprus, the Supreme Court cannot change decisions of regulatory authorities or substitute its own assessment for theirs.

In Latvia, the law does not give the judge the power to modify the contested administrative act in disputes involving regulatory issues. The court is competent to set aside or declare invalid the contested act, and to order the administrative authority to issue a new act taking into account the legal and factual considerations of its decision.

In Portugal, the judge has the power to set a time limit under penalty for the administrative authority to execute its decision.

In the other respondent States (Bulgaria, Czech Republic, Spain, France, Croatia, Lithuania, Luxembourg, Slovenia, Slovakia, Finland, Sweden), the judge has the power to modify the administrative decision.

In Bulgaria, the court has jurisdiction both to repeal and reduce the sanction, but cannot increase it.

In the Czech Republic, the courts of first instance (the regional courts) may reduce the sanction, exceptionally and at the request of the applicant.

In Spain, the court can annul the act or sanction. If it finds that the sanction is disproportionate in the particular circumstances of the case, it may decide that the sanction should be reduced. According to Article 71(2) of the Administrative Jurisdiction Act, when the judge annuls an act, he or she cannot substitute himself or herself for the administrative authority in determining the terms and discretionary content of the new decision that the latter will have to take to replace the annulled one.

In France, the judge rules as a judge with full jurisdiction on the sanctions pronounced by the regulatory authorities, *i.e.* he or she has the power to annul and modify the contested sanctions, by reducing or increasing them.

The same applies to Croatia, Lithuania, Luxembourg, Slovenia, Slovakia, Finland and Sweden.

### *5.4. Taking account of European Union law*

Several respondent States (Germany, Spain, France, Estonia, Italy, Cyprus, Hungary, Austria, Sweden) indicate that national regulatory authorities and administrative courts take into account the opinions of the European Commission and the European regulatory authorities.

Germany questions the legal scope of recommendations of the European institutions, which, according to Article 288(5) of the Treaty on the Functioning of the European Union, are not binding but which, according to the case law of the Court of Justice of the European Union (Case C-322/88, 13 December 1989, *Grimaldi*), national authorities and courts are obliged to take into account, in particular when they clarify the interpretation of national provisions implementing European Union law or when they supplement Community provisions of a binding nature. It considers that the indirect legal effect of recommendations does not preclude national authorities and courts from departing from them. Thus, the Federal Network Agency carries out a 'comprehensive evaluation' to accommodate national characteristics that deviate from the European standard.

France explains that the Council of State accepted the admissibility of the plea of invalidity of an act of European soft law in support of an appeal against an act of soft law of a French regulatory authority. At issue in this case was an opinion of the French Prudential Supervision and Resolution Authority to comply with the guidelines on the governance and supervision of retail banking products issued by the European Banking Authority on the basis of Regulation (EU) No 1093/2010 of the European Parliament and of the Council of 24 November 2010 establishing a European Supervisory Authority (CE, 4 December 2019, No 415550, *Fédération bancaire française*).

Cyprus considers that regulatory authorities do not relinquish their discretionary decision-making powers when they take into account the opinions, guidelines and best practices of the European institutions, particularly in the field of personal data protection.

Hungary states that the national regulatory authorities are responsible for implementing European Union law aimed at liberalising the markets for the supply of electricity, gas, water, waste management, telecommunications, etc., and for ensuring the consistent application of the rules in the European Union. In this perspective, they take into account the opinions and decisions of the European Commission and the European regulatory authorities. National law itself imposes such an obligation, for example in the field of electronic communications.

Similarly, several respondent States (Bulgaria, Greece, Spain, France, Italy, Latvia, Lithuania, Austria, Slovakia) consider that disputes involving regulatory issues are a special field of preliminary questions to the Court of Justice of the European Union.

France stresses that European construction has played an important role in the development of state regulation. The opening up to competition of a growing number of sectors, including network services, within the framework of the internal market has contributed to the emergence and expansion of economic regulation to ensure the application of the principle of free competition and to reconcile it with other objectives of general interest. European Union law is an important source of the legality of acts of national regulatory authorities in the economic field as well as in other areas, such as data protection. In its review of regulatory acts, the Council of State is required to apply Community standards and to refer to the Court of Justice of the European Union for a preliminary ruling on the validity and interpretation of these standards. For example, it referred questions to the Court for a preliminary ruling on the interpretation of Directive 2009/73 EC of 13 July 2009 concerning common rules for the internal market in natural gas and on the material and territorial scope of the right to de-index personal data enshrined in its *Google Spain* judgment of 13 May 2014.

The respondent States give various examples of preliminary questions referred to the Court of Justice of the European Union in the context of disputes involving acts of regulatory authorities:

- questions referred for a preliminary ruling on the interpretation of the provisions of the Directive on payment services in the internal market, in connection with a challenge to the legality of a decision by the Financial and Capital Markets Commission to impose a fine for failure to execute a payment order, or on the interpretation of the Treaty on the Functioning of the European Union and the European regulations on state aid and regulated sectors, in disputes over compensation for the loss suffered by

an electricity producer due to the failure to pay for the supply of electricity to a public operator at a price higher than the market price (Latvia);
- questions referred for a preliminary ruling in relation to the food industry and competition, electronic communications, the energy sector, consumer protection, the financial sector (Lithuania);
- question referred for a preliminary ruling on the scope of the right of access of citizens to the files on which the regulatory authorities base their sanctions and its reconciliation with business secrecy (Luxembourg);
- questions referred for a preliminary ruling on competition law, regulation of the internal electricity market (Slovakia).

### *5.5. Drafting the judicial decision*

Sixteen respondent States (Belgium, Bulgaria, Czech Republic, Germany, Greece, Italy, Latvia, Luxembourg, Austria, Slovenia, Slovakia, Poland, Portugal, Finland, Sweden, Norway) consider that the drafting of judicial decisions does not present particular challenges in disputes involving acts of regulatory authorities.

The other respondent States (Estonia, Spain, France, Croatia, Cyprus, Lithuania, Hungary, Turkey) identify a variety of difficulties in drafting judicial decisions in disputes involving regulatory authorities, linked to the technicality, complexity, sensitivity and media coverage of the cases. As a result, the drafting of judicial decisions presents three main challenges.

First, the drafting must not betray business secrecy (Estonia) or any other legally protected secret.

Furthermore, the legal and factual reasoning of the decision must be sufficiently thorough to make the legal community and professionals understand the reasoning followed by the judge (France, Lithuania).

Finally, the decision must be written in a way that is accessible to the public without betraying the legal and technical accuracy of the solution (Spain).

The drafting of decisions in complex cases leads to an increase in the workload of judges, which requires adjustments. For example, in Lithuania, these take the form of a reduction in the number of cases considered by judges and the establishment of a support team comprising legal assistants and linguists to give sufficient attention to the quality of the legal reasoning of decisions.

## 6. The judge in the regulatory ecosystem

### *6.1. Communication on judicial decisions in regulatory matters*

The respondent States indicate that judicial decisions in the field of regulation are not publicised or communicated in any particular way because of the specific nature of this field, but according to their legal and jurisprudential interest, their socio-economic effects and their media impact.

The institutional communication of supreme administrative courts on important regulatory decisions takes several forms. One of them is the publication of decisions and/or summaries of them on the court's website (Greece, France, Spain, Italy, Latvia, Finland, Norway), in its activity report (France, Lithuania), in an official gazette or legal journal (Croatia, Lithuania, Hungary), or on the websites of the regulatory authorities (Croatia).

Lithuania explains that the publication by the Supreme Administrative Court of summaries of the most important decisions, written in a concise manner, is particularly important and useful in disputes involving regulatory issues, due to its complexity, to ensure a better understanding of the Court's case law by professionals and the general public.

Another form of institutional communication by courts, which is quite common, is the publication of press releases on the most important decisions. This practice exists in Belgium, in Germany, which gives as an example the press release on the decision of the Federal Administrative Court on the auction of 5G frequencies, in Estonia, which cites decisions concerning the pharmaceutical market, wind energy, taxi applications, the publication by the Financial Supervisory Authority of warnings on dubious commercial practices, in France, such as, for example, on the decisions of 19 June 2020 by which the Council of State on the one hand rejected the appeal against a 50 million euro penalty imposed on Google by the French Data Protection Authority for violation of the General Data Protection Regulation and on the other hand partially annulled the French Data Protection Authority's guidelines on cookies and other connection tracers, in Latvia, Lithuania, Luxembourg, Austria, which mentions decisions on the allocation of frequencies or on the structural independence of the energy regulator, in Slovenia, Slovakia, Finland, Sweden and Norway.

Cyprus reports that its Supreme Court does not make a practice of using press releases to communicate its decisions, even when these have a high media profile. The Court only communicates with the parties, other judges, the legal community and the general public through its decisions, which are the final products of court proceedings.

### *6.2. The participation of judges in general exchanges with professionals from the regulatory sectors*

Twelve respondent States (Belgium, Bulgaria, France, Croatia, Cyprus, Latvia, Luxembourg, Hungary, Poland, Portugal, Turkey, Norway) indicate that their judges do not participate in general exchanges with professionals in the regulatory sectors.

Cyprus and Luxembourg consider that such exchanges would be contrary to the principle of separation of powers and, for Cyprus, to the principle of the independence of judges. However, Luxembourg specifies that the Court's magistrates may participate in colloquia organised by the university on regulatory issues.

France explains that the exchanges organised in the past with the regulators (e.g. with the Electronic Communications and Post Regulatory Authority) were abandoned because they were too hampered by reciprocal ethical precautions concerning ongoing litigation, too unstructured, and without a clear vision of the respective contributions.

Spain also states that there are no regular exchanges between judges and professionals, as judges are not required to participate in conferences or meetings where issues that may be subject to litigation are discussed. However, it states that the annual training plan for judges usually includes internships for a limited number of judges in regulatory bodies to enable them to gain a better understanding of their activities.

In the other respondent States where exchanges between judges and regulatory professionals are organised, the latter are generally involved in the ongoing training of judges (Czech Republic, Spain, Estonia, Italy, Lithuania, Slovenia, Finland). In some countries, the courts themselves organise round tables or exchanges between their members and professionals (Estonia, Lithuania), or between the judges of the various courts with jurisdiction over disputes involving regulatory issues (Germany). The participation of judges in colloquia and seminars organised by the regulatory authorities or by the academic world also allows for such exchanges on regulatory law and practice (Germany, Greece, Italy, Luxembourg, Austria, Slovakia).

Finally, in Austria, judges participate in annual public events bringing together judges, lawyers, academics, regulators and representatives of the regulated sectors, such as the 'Telekom-Forum', the 'Rundfunk-Forum', etc., and in Sweden, some judges are, in addition to their judicial activity, members of groups or associations of lawyers specialised, for example, in tax law or public procurement.

### *6.3. The exercise by judges of functions in regulatory authorities*

In the majority of the respondent States, the exercise by judges of functions in regulatory authorities is not possible (Bulgaria, Czech Republic, Greece, Croatia, Cyprus, Latvia, Hungary, Austria, Slovenia, Slovakia, Poland, Portugal, Finland, Sweden, Turkey, Norway) or not very common (Germany, Estonia, Lithuania, Luxembourg).

In Belgium, the law provides in certain cases for the participation of members of the Council of State in the bodies of regulatory authorities (Vlaamse Regulator voor de Media, Sanctions Commission of the National Bank of Belgium). In Spain, as mentioned above, judges can undertake internships in regulatory bodies as part of their training. In France, the secondment of members of the Council of State and judges from administrative courts and administrative courts of appeal to regulatory authorities is possible and encouraged because it enables them to develop a regulatory competence and culture, which they can then use and share on their return to the courts. Similarly, in Italy, the secondment of judges to senior functions in regulatory authorities is allowed in accordance with the rules of professional conduct.

## Annex 1 – List of member and observer institutions that submitted a national report in response to the questionnaire

### ACA members

| Country | Institution |
|---|---|
| Belgium | Conseil d'Etat – Council of State |
| Bulgaria | Върховен административен съд – Supreme Administrative Court |

| Country | Institution |
|---|---|
| Czech Republic | Nejvyšší správní soud – Supreme Administrative Court |
| Germany | Bundesverwaltungsgericht – Federal Administrative Court |
| Estonia | Riigikohus – Supreme Court of Estonia |
| Greece | Συμβούλιο της Επικρατείας – Council of State |
| Spain | Tribunal Supremo de España – Supreme Court |
| France | Conseil d'Etat – Council of State |
| Croatia | Visoki upravni sud Republike Hrvatske – Supreme Administrative Court |
| Italy | Consiglio di Stato – Council of State |
| Cyprus | Ανώτατο Δικαστήριο της Κύπρου – Supreme Court of Cyprus |
| Latvia | Augstākā tiesa – Supreme Court |
| Lithuania | Lietuvos vyriausiasis administracinis teismas – Supreme Administrative Court of Lithuania |
| Luxembourg | Administrative Court |
| Hungary | Kúria – Curia |
| Austria | Supreme Administrative Court |
| Poland | Naczelny Sąd Administracyjny – Supreme Administrative Court |
| Portugal | Supremo Tribunal Administrativo – Supreme Administrative Court |
| Slovenia | Vrhovno sodišce Republike Slovenije – Supreme Court of the Republic of Slovenia |
| Slovak Republic | Najvyšší súd Slovenskej republiky – Supreme Court of the Slovak Republic |
| Finland | Korkein hallinto-oikeus – Supreme Administrative Court of Finland |
| Sweden | Högsta förvaltningsdomstolen – Supreme Administrative Court |

## ACA observer

| Turkey | Danıştay – Council of State |
|---|---|

## Invited court

| Norway | Norges Høyesterett – Supreme Court of Norway |
|---|---|

# Annex 2 – Quantitative data on disputes involving regulatory issues before the respondent courts for 2020

| Country | Number of cases recorded | Number of cases settled | Percentage of cases recorded | Percentage of cases settled | Percentage of cases in which the regulatory act was annulled totally or partially |
|---|---|---|---|---|---|
| Belgium | 24 | 20 | 0.90% | 0.70% | 15% |
| Bulgaria | Not available | Not available | Not available | Not available | Not available |
| Czech Republic | 70 | 74 | 1.6% | 1.8% | 46% |
| Germany | 15 | 12 | 1.3% | 1% | 0% |
| Estonia | Not available | 30 | Not available | 44% | 80% |
| Greece | 34 | 27 | 1% | 2% | 0% |
| Spain | Not available | Not available | Not available | Not available | Not available |
| France | Not available | 69 | Not available | 0.71% | 20% |
| Croatia | 147 | 188 | 2.52% | 2.98% | 7.45% |
| Italy | 567 | 396 | 5.58% | 5.5% | 26.8% |
| Cyprus | Not available | Not available | Not available | Not available | Not available |
| Latvia | 87 (18 allowed) | 12 | 5% (2% allowed) | 1.3% | Not relevant |

| **Country** | **Number of cases recorded** | **Number of cases settled** | **Percentage of cases recorded** | **Percentage of cases settled** | **Percentage of cases in which the regulatory act was annulled totally or partially** |
|---|---|---|---|---|---|
| Lithuania | Not available | Not available | Not available | Not available | Not available |
| Luxembourg | 2 | 2 | Not available | Not available | Not available |
| Hungary | 44 | 86 | 1.4% | 2.52% | 22% |
| Austria | Not available | Not available | Not available | Not available | Not available |
| Poland | 89 | 39 | 0.61% | 0.24% | Not available |
| Portugal | Not available | Not available | Not available | Not available | Not available |
| Slovenia | 13 | 23 | 2% | 2% | 32% |
| Slovak Republic | 50 | 19 | 2.78% | 2.50% | 31.6% |
| Finland | Not available | Not available | Not available | Not available | Not available |
| Sweden | 70% | 70% | Not available | Not available | 10 to 20% |
| Turkey | 2,713 | 2,400 | 67.63% | 59.15% | Not available |
| Norway | Not available | 0 | Not available | 0% | 0% |

# ACA-Europe Seminar
# “Techniques for the protection of private subjects in contrast with public authorities: actions and remedies – liability and compliance”

**Rome, Italy**
**23 May 2022**
**General Report by the Italian Council of State**

# Summary of the General Report of the Seminar "Techniques for the protection of private subjects in contrast with public authorities: actions and remedies – liability and compliance" held in Rome, Italy, 23 May 2022

The subject of the May 23, 2022, seminar follows the hope, expressed by the Court of Justice of the European Union in its judgment in Case C-561/2019, that the horizontal dialogue between national courts will be amplified, so as to allow (i) to enucleate what constitute, albeit in the specificity of national systems, the common features of systems for the protection of the rights and interests of individuals private citizens or businesses, (ii) to develop, within the various member countries of the European Union, a common method of reviewing public administrations, and (iii) to enable national courts to assess whether European Union law lends itself to different interpretations within individual member countries, so as to make the obligation to make a preliminary reference under Art. 267 TFEU.

With regard to the court competent to issue decisions in trials in which a public administration is a party, in most member states this type of litigation is reserved for specific courts, which may belong either to the plexus of ordinary jurisdiction, or to a separate plexus dedicated to administrative jurisdiction.

This type of litigation is, generally, governed by statute or, in common law states, by case law precedents, and contemplates two, if not three, levels of adjudication.

It is generally provided that before the administrative judge one may bring both an action for the annulment of an administrative act and an action against the silence of the public administration; not all, however, recognize the power of the administrative judge to adjudicate on claims for compensation. Provisional measures are also generally provided for. Most states have stated that it is not possible for the administrative judge to requalify claims *ex officio*. However, it should be noted in this regard that the question has sometimes been understood in various ways and, therefore, responses have not always been homogeneous.

Appeal of final acts is generally allowed, while appeal of endoprocedural acts and administrative acts of a general nature is recognized in many of the surveyed states, but more limitedly. On the other hand, there is a general convergence in denying the possibility of challenging acts of a political nature, which is allowed by way of exception if they are acts that affect constitutionally guaranteed fundamental rights (Spain), or limited to those parts of the measure that contain "regulated elements".

Regarding the type of flaws, which can be the basis for the annulment of an administrative act, it is generally admitted (i) the violation of law, with the specification that in various States the violation of norms of a formal/procedural nature is not, considered sufficient to lead to the annulment of the act, requiring for this purpose that the violation is expressly sanctioned by a norm, that it is expressed in a complete lack of the legal form of the act or procedure, or that it is a violation that has not been remedied in the course of the procedure; (ii) excess of power, understood as an act not fulfilling the purpose for which the law provided it; (iii) incompetence. In the United Kingdom, as it is a common law system, permissible defects are enucleated from precedent and are mostly attributable to improper use of power, violation of procedural rules, and irrationality.

Regarding the court's powers, in the event of the annulment of an administrative act, most of the countries surveyed allow both total and partial annulment of an act. The possibility that the administrative judge, in pronouncing the annulment, may, by his decision, replace the annulled party, or otherwise determine the content of the measure that is to replace the annulled one, is permitted only in relation to administrative activities with a binding content. France referred, in answering the question, to the cases of "full litigation" within the administrative court's jurisdiction.

In relation to the effects of annulment pronouncements, it can be said that in most states the annulment of a general administrative act follows the general rule, *i.e.*, that of annulment with retroactive effects, but in some cases the administrative judge is given, by a rule or precedents of case law, the power to modulate the effects differently. However, it must be acknowledged that in a significant number of states (more than ten) the administrative judge has no power in this regard.

An action for damages resulting from the illegality of an administrative act is generally allowed. In some states such a claim is subject to certain limits: for example, to the fact that the claim is brought in the same suit as the claim for annulment; or to the fact that the claim for compensation has been preceded by an express refusal of the administration concerned to recognize the damage, a refusal which thus serves as a condition of procedural feasibility. In several states such a claim is subject to limitation periods (30 days in Croatia, 2 months in Spain, 1 year in the United Kingdom), but in most states the period is the ordinary limitation period for asserting non-contractual liability.

Most states allow that compensation can be claimed for both material and non-material damages, but compensation for loss of chances and moral damage is not allowed in all cases. In most states, damages avoidable by taking the appropriate legal action are not compensable: in some cases the prior bringing of an action for annulment is a condition of admissibility of the claim. In other states, failure to bring an action for annulment does not absolutely preclude an action for damages, but may be regarded as negligent conduct capable of affecting damages.

In most states, public administration liability is considered to be strict in nature and such that the subjective element of culpability is not required.

As for the burden of proof, it is generally on the injured party to prove the constituent elements of the tort.

The responses provided by the states revealed a general tendency to differentiate procedural rules for certain matters or sectors, according to criteria reflecting the particularities of national jurisdictions; in each case, it is a functional differentiation to ensure greater protection of sensitive or particularly important interests or greater expeditiousness. The areas often affected by simplified rites are those for access to documents, against the silence of the administration, injunction and enforcement proceedings, while the need for protection is found, in the special rites relating to the subjects of immigration, urban planning, procurement, expropriation, taxes, elections and acts of independent authorities.

Often the specialty of the procedure is generally characterized by expeditiousness, as to the filing of the application, the conduct of the trial or the time limit for filing the decision. In some cases, the specialty of the rite implies limitations on the adjudicatory power of administrative courts, for example by precluding the lodging of appeals, or conversely a greater breadth of the court's powers, in terms of the possibility of assessing evidence more informally or issuing decisions drafted in a simplified form.

In most countries, the specialty of a procedure can relate either to a particular matter or to specific actions; a number of countries have specified that specialty can relate only to matters, and not to actions.

Most countries have acknowledged the existence, in their respective legal systems, of actions aimed at reacting to silence kept by the administration, but it is not always clear whether "silence" means mere inaction, that is, the omission of a due measure, or, instead, a qualified silence with the value of a favorable or unfavorable measure. In France and Belgium, for example, silence is always qualified, and thus corresponds to a measure, tacit, of favorable or unfavorable content. In Finland and Norway, protection against silence is not provided in general, but at the level of procedural remedies. In Finland, in particular, there is provision for intervention by the Minister of Justice or the Ombudsman, as a reaction in the general interest of legality, and at the jurisprudential level the administrative court has been granted the power to recall the competent administration to the duty to take action, when inaction may cause damage to individual rights. The Czech Republic has a system similar to that in place in Italy until the codification of action against silence, while in Turkey, in addition to an action against total inaction, it is also possible to challenge the inconclusive measure of a proceeding when it is considered as an unfavorable final decision.

The rules are generally contained in legislation and often include a time limit within which the action against silence must be brought.

In most states, it is possible for the administrative law judge to order a public administration to adopt a specific act if the refusal or failure to adopt a specific act is contrary to law or if the adoption of a specific act is mandatory, according to law.

The questionnaire showed that in many countries administrations almost always spontaneously execute the administrative judge's decisions, without the need to exhaust any particular remedy, while another art reported that the rate of spontaneous compliance with decisions is around 50 percent of cases. In some cases, even, there is not even a particular remedy to react to the administrations' noncompliance with the administrative judge's decisions.

In countries in which there is a remedy against noncompliance with decisions, the procedure may provide for variable measures: for example, the possibility of ordering the administration to pay a sum of money parameterized to the delay and the situation, the appointment of an extraordinary commissioner,

Some countries have reported that in their respective systems there is no specific action to obtain the enforcement of a judgment, but failure to comply notes as a cause of liability, civil or criminal, of the relevant administration.

A distinction is made between the system in force in the United Kingdom, where a distinction is made between failure to execute a decision containing a binding order, and failure to execute a decision containing a mere finding: in the former case, the situation amounts, in essence, to contempt of court and thus incorporates offenses punishable by up to two years' imprisonment, while in the latter case the person concerned has a specific action at his or her disposal; however, in the United Kingdom the percentage of spontaneous execution is such that the need to exhaust the remedy in question has never arisen.
On the point under consideration, the responses to the questionnaire revealed more than one system. One set of countries is characterized by allowing, as a general rule, the enforcement of first instance judgments, while another set of countries provides for the possibility of enforcing judgments only when they become final. In still other countries, the general rule is that first instance judgments subject to appeal are not enforceable, but with some exceptions.
With regard to the effects of the filing of the appeal, too, there is no preponderance of a particular solution: in some countries the filing of an appeal has an automatic suspensive effect on the appealed judgment, while in others the general rule is the opposite. In Cyprus, the appealed judgment can also be suspended *ex officio* by the court, but the decision can be challenged by the parties.
Most countries have reported that there are no specific mechanisms in their legal systems that result in the gradual reduction of administrative discretion as a consequence of an annulment decision.
There is a general tendency to consider the first instance decision, by means of its reasoning, suitable for guiding the administration in the redoing of the action. Some states have emphasized the link between the reduction of administrative discretion and the grounds for appeal, which have been examined and found to be well-founded in the annulment decision.
In most states, it is found that the appeal of an administrative act does not produce, automatically, the suspension of the effectiveness of the contested act. In countries where this is permitted, the suspensive effect of the appeal is, as a rule, linked to certain conditions, such as the admissibility of the appeal, or its possible merits; Among countries where the first instance appeal does not have an automatic suspensive effect, such an effect may be exceptionally provided for certain matters. In some countries, precautionary measures may be granted *ex officio* by the court.
Variety is also found with regard to the type of precautionary measures, which in many states are atypical, and in others may consist only of the suspension of the effectiveness of the contested act. In most countries, however, interim protection is a generalized remedy and thus not limited to certain situations or matters.
The necessary conditions for the granting of interim measures are generally identified by the existence of profiles of merits or urgency: the relationship between these two elements varies from state to state; more than one country has reported on the duty/power of the judge to carry out a balancing of conflicting interests or to take into account the public interest as the preeminent interest, which, however, may take second place in the face of

the manifest illegitimacy of the challenged act. As for the possibility of conditioning the granting of a protective measure on a bond, the answer was negative in most countries.
Appeal on precautionary measures is generally allowed, regardless of the monocratic or collegial nature of the measure, although with some variations: appeal is sometimes excluded limited to the review order, while in other countries it is allowed only for certain particularly important flaws or after passing an appeal "admissibility test".
Precautionary measures *ante causam* appear not to be used in many countries, while among those that do allow them there is no uniformity as to when they lose effect: some cases after a certain predetermined number of days, in other cases as a result of the failure to introduce the main trial. In France, only certain types of precautionary measures can be granted *ante causam*.
Not in all participating countries is there a rite especially dedicated to the handling of interlocutory measures, and in any case there is no uniformity of discipline. In some cases the decision is collegial, in others monocratic.
The handling of the interlocutory application may be an occasion for the settlement of the case on the merits; however, this is not provided for in the legal system of the majority of the surveyed states, due to the autonomous nature of interlocutory proceedings.
In most states, it is provided that the appellate court may rule on the stay of the appealed judgment, while in other cases such a stay is provided for directly by law. It is interesting to note that in Estonia, where enforcement of a judgment is permitted only when it has become final, it is nevertheless possible to file an application in order to paralyze any order for immediate enforcement.
In terms of the number of appealed protective orders, few countries had the availability of statistical data to report. In first place was Hungary, with 50 percent of appealed protective orders, followed by Italy, with 39 percent, Slovenia with 20 percent, Romania with 13 percent, and Greece with 10 percent. Other states provided much lower statistics: for example, in France, Germany, Poland, Lithuania the percentage is around 3-4%.

# General Report
# Rome, 23 May 2022

Dear Colleagues

Last year the Italian Presidency of ACA-Europe was inaugurated in Fiesole with the seminar entitled "*Law, Courts and guidelines for the public administration" and continued with the seminar organised in December in Paris entitled* "*The judicial review of regulatory authorities*".

Both events provided an opportunity to start exploring the potential of the "horizontal dialogue" between the various Supreme Administrative Courts – this topic represents, as you now know, the leitmotif of our Presidency and will accompany us during our next meetings.

The General Report on "*Techniques for the protection of private subjects in contrast with public authorities: actions and remedies – liability and compliance*" allows us to take a further important step towards the "ever-closer union among the peoples of Europe", a very forward-looking objective of the Treaties of Rome.

Through the analysis of the actions that can be brought before the administrative judge, through the investigation on the techniques of protection ensured, through the study on the existence of special rites, aimed at the protection of "sensitive" interests of "economic and social" impact or characterised by the speeding-up of time-limits, mutual knowledge of our respective systems is further intensified.

The foundations are laid for making the protection of the rights and interests of individuals and businesses as homogeneous as possible in the single European area, while continuing to respect "domestic" specificities.

The Court of Justice of the European Union, in its judgment of 6 October 2021 in Case C-561/2019 Consorzio Italian Management, reaffirming principles on the obligation to make a preliminary reference under Article 267 TFEU, stated that the national court of last instance, when faced with a doubt on the interpretation of EU law, must verify the actual or presumed attitude of the other interpreters in the various EU Member States.

The Court of Justice itself has, therefore, drawn attention to the desirability of widening the horizontal dialogue among national courts, which is all the more useful when EU law might lend itself to divergences in interpretation within the different legal systems.

The strengthening of the dialogue between the Court of Justice and the national courts has made and continues to make the integration of European and national law more harmonious.

The dialogue among the various national courts will subsequently be able to develop a homogeneous method of controlling public administrations and, while continuing to respect the specific features of each individual system, standardise the methods for protecting and safeguarding the rights of citizens and businesses in their relations with the public authorities.

This is a fundamental element for the achievement of effective "European citizenship."

**SESSION I**
**ACTIONS BEFORE THE ADMINISTRATIVE JUDGE**



# SESSION I

# ACTIONS BEFORE THE ADMINISTRATIVE JUDGE

## I.1. Identification of the competent jurisdiction

A first aspect, with regard to the techniques for protecting private persons against the public authorities, which is of central importance for highlighting the similarities and differences existing among the different legal systems of the Member States, is the identification of the competent court.

The replies show that, in general, both administrative courts and ordinary courts have jurisdiction in disputes involving the public administration depending on the type of dispute.

In most legal systems, administrative courts belong to a distinct jurisdictional area compared to that of the ordinary courts (e.g. Austria, France, Italy, Lithuania, Luxembourg, Portugal, Romania), but in some countries, the administrative courts operate within the ordinary courts (e.g. Ireland, Norway, Spain, United Kingdom). Some countries have provided details on the structure of their court system. While, in most countries there are at least two, if not three, levels of jurisdiction (e.g. Estonia, France): in Belgium, the Council of State is the sole administrative jurisdiction with general powers at only one level (except for the relative jurisdiction of the administrative Court of Cassation with regard to the decisions of special administrative courts set up at state or federal level to deal with specific matters).

## I.2. Actions which may be brought and the sources of the rules governing them

All the countries taking part in the questionnaire replied that their legal systems provide for the possibility of bringing different types of action before the administrative courts. In particular, in those countries where jurisdiction over disputes against the public authorities lies with the administrative judge, there are (at least) actions for the annulment of administrative acts and actions against silence. On this point, the countries concerned provided further indications in reply to question no. 4 of Session II (see below).

Not in all systems do the administrative courts have jurisdiction over actions for damages. For example, the administrative courts do not have jurisdiction in, Cyprus, the Czech Republic, Finland and Sweden. In several countries, there is an action for performance (for example, in addition to Italy, this is true for Germany, Hungary, Ireland, Portugal, Romania and the United Kingdom). In France, there is also an action to obtain the interpretation of an act whose meaning is obscure or ambiguous.

In response to the question, some countries also referred to precautionary protection: Belgium specified that the Council of State may order the suspension of the execution of an act or a regulation and may order all measures necessary to safeguard the interests of the parties or persons concerned;

Portugal referred to injunctions; Cyprus, Romania (HCCJ) and Serbia admit precautionary suspension. On this point, the States concerned provided further information in Session III (see below).

With regard to the sources governing the actions that can be brought, the replies show that the main source cited is the law.

France's reply on this point is worth noting as it specified that "*Les principes essentiels du droit du contentieux administratif sont issus de la jurisprudence du juge administratif mais ces principes trouvent de plus en plus un ancrage textuel*".

Ireland and the United Kingdom, in keeping with their tradition of *common law,* also cite jurisdictional precedent as sources. In Sweden, too, jurisdictional precedents are cited as sources.

Some countries also consider the regulations of tribunals as sources (Cyprus, Ireland).

## I.3. Action for annulment: measures against which action may be brought and defects in cancellation

### *A) Contestable acts*

The replies show that it tends to be the case that all administrative acts can be challenged, even those of a general nature, such as regulations.

Several countries, however, replied that regulatory acts cannot be annulled by administrative courts. For example, in Austria, regulations can only be annulled by the Constitutional Court. Swedish courts can only disapply regulations and not annul them.

In some countries, even general acts cannot be appealed (Cyprus, Estonia). Serbia and Slovakia also replied that only administrative acts with a specific addressee can be challenged in their systems.

In Lithuania, on the contrary, there is an *ad hoc* procedure for challenging general administrative acts and regulations. In the Netherlands, general acts and regulations can be challenged before the civil courts.

An analysis of the replies subsequently reveals that acts within the procedure cannot, as a rule, be the subject of an independent appeal. In some cases, this has been expressly stated (e.g. Austria, Germany), in others it is implicitly deduced from the characteristics of the acts that can be challenged and, in particular, from the fact that they are acts that definitively decide upon a certain issue. Some countries have specified that the challenge of acts internal to the procedure is admitted as an exception: for example, when they affect important rights or interests of the addressees or significantly impede their exercise (Latvia) or when they bring the procedure to a halt (Spain).

With regard to political acts, most countries agree that they cannot be challenged. Spain replied that control of political acts is allowed, as far as their "*regulated elements*" are concerned or when they affect fundamental rights guaranteed by the Spanish Constitution. Belgium specified that "administrative" acts of the Constitutional Court and legislative assemblies, the Court of Auditors, the Council of State and administrative courts, as well as organs of the judiciary and the High Council of Justice may be challenged before the administrative courts, unless the dispute is assigned by law to another jurisdiction.

### *B) Objectionable defects*

With reference to the defects which can lead to the annulment of administrative acts, the replies showed that all the systems consider the infringement of the law – understood as the infringement of formal and substantive rules – as a defect of the administrative act.

There are, however, differences as to the consequences of this defect.

Some countries state that administrative acts can be annulled for breach of substantive and procedural law, without anything else being specified (e.g. Austria, Bulgaria, Spain, Sweden). Several jurisdictions limit the possibility of obtaining annulment of the act on the basis of procedural defects to cases where the forms are "substantial/essential or prescribed on penalty of nullity" (Belgium, Bulgaria, Greece, Hungary, Slovakia). In Germany, breaches of procedural law result in annulment only in certain cases, as provided for in Section I of the Code of Administrative Procedure (Sec. 44-45 of the Code of Administrative Procedure-CAP). In Portugal, annulment can only be obtained if there is a total lack of legal form or a total breach of procedural rules. Hungary allows annulment for breach of procedural rules but only if the breach cannot be remedied in the course of the proceedings. In Estonia, Italy, Norway and Slovenia the breach of formal/procedural rules does not provide grounds for annulment if the final content of the act could not have been different to what was effectively adopted.

Several legal systems provide for forms of judicial review of the conformity of the act with the purpose of the law through the figures of excess or misuse of power (e.g. France, Greece, Italy). Bulgarian law provides for the defect of "non-conformity" with the purpose of the law.

In the United Kingdom, annulment can be obtained on the basis of a number of defects elaborated by *case law* such as incorrect interpretation or misuse of powers granted by Parliament ("*illegality*"), breach of procedural rules (e.g. infringements of the "*right to be heard*") or irrationality. Also in other legal systems, non-codified principles can be invoked to obtain annulment, as is the case of the Netherlands in reference to the principle of legal certainty.

Incompetence is an objectionable defect in the majority of jurisdictions interviewed and is often considered as "*species*" of the general category of infringement of the law.

### I.4. Contents of the judicial decision to annul: partial annulment, substitution of the measure and shaping of subsequent administrative action

#### *A) Partial annulment*

Most countries replied that the court may partially annul an unlawful act. Some countries specified that partial annulment is subject to the condition that the act is divisible (e.g. Austria, Cyprus, Czech Republic, France, Germany, Slovenia, Spain, United Kingdom). Finland specified that partial annulment is not allowed if it can modify the decision *in toto* in a way that is incompatible with its content.

#### *B) Replacement of the measure*

The replies showed that the administrative judge can, in theory, replace the administration, but the models differ considerably.

In several countries, the judge can replace the administration only in the case of binding activity, "in concreto" or "in abstracto" (Bulgaria, Germany, Italy and Spain). In Austria, the courts of first instance may replace the public administration if the relevant facts emerge from the case file, but they may also verify the factual findings for reasons of speed or if this leads to significant cost savings (Art. 28, para. 2 VwGVG).

Croatia replied that the court replaces the administration in the event of annulment, except when the decision is of a discretionary nature or when it is not possible due to the "nature of the issue" (Art. 58 *of the Code*). In Sweden, substitution is the rule. In Luxembourg, replacement depends on the action brought (it is allowed in case of an appeal "for reform", but not for annulment). Latvia allows the possibility in theory, in cases provided for by law, but the law does not provide for specific cases.

Other countries replied that substitution is possible for certain matters. For example, in Cyprus, Estonia and Finland, the court may substitute the administration only in tax and immigration matters. In the Czech Republic, substitution is possible in matters of sanctions, access, referendums and elections.

Substitution is generally not allowed in Ireland, Romania, Turkey and the United Kingdom. However, the United Kingdom has specified a number of cases in which substitution is exceptionally permitted.

Most countries replied in the affirmative.

Some countries replied that, in their systems such a power is always or is, as a rule, excluded (Greece, Ireland, Turkey). In the United Kingdom it is possible, but with strict limitations.

In France, if the judge of the excess of power cannot replace the administration, the judge, "*de plein contentieux*", in this case, has very broad powers, including the power to reform an administrative act and to replace the administration's decision with his own.

Germany has specified that modification is not possible when the administrative authority is authorised to exercise a discretionary power. In other cases, the court may oblige the administrative authority to perform the act requested (art. 113 para. 5 CACP). Only in this case can the judge modify an administrative act.

### *C) Conformation*

Luxembourg emphasised that, in the event of an action for annulment, the court may, by means of the reasons for its decision, outline the new decision to be implemented by the administration following the referral after the annulment of the previous decision.

## I.5. Effects of the judicial decision of annulment and its modulation

The replies showed that, in most jurisdictions, annulment has retroactive effect. In some states, however, annulment always, or for certain acts, has *ex nunc* effect. In Finland, annulment is as a rule *ex nunc* (in this regard, for example, it is specified that "*if the election of a member of a municipal board or commission by a later court judgment is declared illegal, the decisions made by the board or commission do not become void retroactively. But, e.g., if a building permit has been granted and the applicant has been afforded the right to start the work before the decision has gained legal force, the revocation of the permit by a later court judgment will make the permit void so that the works done in the meantime must be demolished*"). In Portugal, as a rule, the annulment of an administrative act takes effect from the date on which the judgment becomes final (*ex nunc*), but by decision of the administrative judge or of the administration itself, it can take effect *ex tunc*, eliminating the effects produced in the meantime by the illegitimate act. On the contrary, in Norway, annulment generally takes effect from the date of adoption of the measures (*ex tunc*), but for annulment pronouncements concerning permits or benefits, annulment takes effect from the date on which the judgment becomes final.

In Latvia, it is the judge who determines the date from which the administrative act is to be considered annulled (in most cases, from the date of its adoption).

Some countries have given specific answers for the annulment of general acts and regulatory acts. In Croatia, the annulment of general acts takes effect from the day of publication of the judgment in the Official Gazette. Luxembourg specified that while the annulment of individual acts is normally retroactive, with the possibility for the court to give it *ex nunc* effect, for regulatory acts, annulment takes effect *ex lege* only from the moment the judicial decision has become final. However, the Luxembourg Constitutional Court doubted the constitutional compatibility of such a clear-cut provision, and an amendment to the legislation is under way to introduce the possibility of modulating the effects of the annulment decision also for regulatory acts.

Lithuania specified that the annulment of regulatory acts has, as a rule, *ex nunc* effect but, taking into account the circumstances of the case, annulment may take effect as soon as the act is adopted. The Czech Republic specified that the annulment of general acts takes effect *ex nunc* or from the future date otherwise indicated by the court.

With regard to the possibility recognised by the court of modulating the effects of the annulment decision over time, it should be noted that the answers to this question overlap, in part, with the answers given to the previous one.

Several countries replied that in their respective legal systems, the judge is not allowed to vary the effects of his annulment decisions over time (Austria, Bulgaria, Croatia, Cyprus, Germany, Norway, Poland, Serbia, Slovenia, Sweden, Turkey). Others, (Belgium, Italy, Luxembourg and Portugal), on the contrary, replied that the law provides for this possibility. As for Italy, the variation over time of the annulment decisions is not provided for by law but by case law concerning specific cases.

In France, case law held that the administrative court may exceptionally order the preservation, even partial, of the effects of the annulled act, if the retroactive effect of the annulment is such that it entails consequences that are manifestly excessive in relation to the principle of legal certainty.

Spain replied that sometimes ("*in certain procedures*") the judge may vary the effects of the judgment: in this respect, it has been reported, by example, that in environmental litigation the judge may postpone the effect of annulment to allow a new ruling to come into effect.

In Lithuania, the court may modulate the effects of a judgment annulling a regulatory act by making it retroactive or it may order that the judgment be published after a certain period of time so as to postpone its effects.

In Latvia, the court always decides, on a case-by-case basis, the moment from which annulment takes effect.

In the Czech Republic it is possible to modulate the effects of the judgment in time only when the annulment concerns measures of a general nature. In Greece, temporal modulation of the effects of the judgment is permitted in the context of the review of excess of power. In Hungary, modulation is allowed only if it is justified by the public interest, legal certainty or interests which are particularly important to the parties involved. Finland replied that modulation is allowed in theory but that "*there are not specific doctrines on this issue*".

## I.6. Action for an order for damages: procedure, tortious conduct and compensable damage

The majority of countries replied that an action for damages can be brought separately from other actions (e.g. Belgium, Bulgaria, Estonia, France, Greece, Ireland, Italy, Norway, Turkey).

In some countries, an action for an order to pay money must necessarily be brought together with another action (Croatia, Serbia, Spain). Germany has specified that "*An autonomous order of payments is only possible if no administrative act is necessary to find or specify the legal claim*".

In several systems, the civil court has jurisdiction over the claim for damages and, therefore, the latter must necessarily be filed separately from the claim for annulment (Cyprus, Czech Republic, Poland). In the United Kingdom, the claim for damages cannot be dealt with in the judicial review proceedings but only in the civil tort proceedings.

Slovenia replied that, in theory, the administrative court can hear claims for compensation, but in practice it always declines to do so. Therefore, these claims are heard in civil proceedings. In Sweden, the civil courts have jurisdiction, but the Chancellor of Justice has the power to settle out-of-court claims on behalf of the State.

In Latvia and the Netherlands, a claim for compensation may be brought at the same time as another action or, after annulment, it must be submitted to the administration and only after that is it possible to challenge any refusal.

The time limits for bringing an action vary substantially among the various jurisdictions and the answers provided do not always specify the starting date of the limitation or prescription period for bringing an action. Many countries replied that the time limit for bringing an action for damages before a civil or administrative court is the ordinary limitation period for obligations arising from non-contractual wrongdoing (3-5 years on average).

In Italy, the action for compensation for damages for injury to legitimate interests, if it is brought independently, must comply with the limitation period of one hundred and twenty days starting from the day on which the event occurred or from the moment of awareness of the measure if the damage derives directly from it.

Slovakia specifies that the time limit of three years is valid from the moment of awareness of the damage or from the notification of the annulment or modification of the act if the right to compensation derives from that decision.

The United Kingdom highlighted that the time limit is one year if it regards an infringement of the *Human Rights Act*, unless the court considers that a different time limit is appropriate; in other cases, the time limit is six years.

In the Czech Republic, the time limits differ depending on whether the claim is for compensation for material or non-material damages: for material damages, the time limit is from 3 – 10 years and from 6 months to 10 years for non-material damages.

In Croatia, the action for damages must be brought together with the application for annulment, within the time limit provided for the latter (30 days).

In Spain the time limit is two months and corresponds to the time limit for challenging the act.

In Turkey, the interested parties may bring "Actions for annulment and full remedy actions" directly before the Council of State or before the administrative and fiscal courts or by "Directly filing a full remedy action". In the latter case, the law requires an application to be made to the administration before asking the court for compensation for the damage resulting from the administrative action ("full remedy action"). The prior application must be filed within one year of written notice or of the knowledge of the harmful action and, in any event, within five years from the date of the action. The provision then specifies that "*If these requests are partially or wholly rejected, an action can be filed within the time limit for the action as of the day following the notification of the procedure on this matter, or if no answer is given within thirty days about the request, from the end of such period*".

## I.7. Relationship with an action for annulment and allocation of the burden of proof of liability

### *A) Types of compensable damage*

Most countries replied that commission and omission activities unlawfully carried out by the public administration may result in compensable damages.

Some countries replied that an action for damages against the public administration is possible in all of the above-mentioned cases (Bulgaria, Croatia, Italy, Lithuania, Romania).

Ireland and the United Kingdom provide for the possibility of bringing an action for damages in certain circumstances.

The United Kingdom has specified that an action for damages may be brought in the event of a breach of a statutory duty if the person concerned can prove that the duty was imposed for the protection of a restricted group of citizens and that Parliament intended to confer on them a private right of action, or if a common law duty of care is breached, or if the administration has deliberately misused its power (misfeasance of public office). In Ireland, on the other hand, compensation may also be awarded in cases of state liability for misapplication of EU law in compliance with the *Francovich* case law; this type of damage is no longer compensable in the United Kingdom as of 2018, following the UK's withdrawal from the European Union.

In Luxembourg, the 'dysfonctionnement objectif' of the administration is a cause for compensation for material and non-material damages, including loss of opportunity, but the relative litigation falls under the jurisdiction of the ordinary courts. In Slovakia, damages for maladministration ("*maladministration*" integrated by "*breach of the duty of an administrative authority to take action or issue a decision within the time limit laid down by law, omission of an administrative authority in the exercise of public power, unnecessary delay in proceedings or other unlawful intervention in the rights and legally protected interests of natural and legal persons*") are also deemed relevant.

Belgium referred to the possibility of obtaining equitable compensation from the administrative judge for "*la réparation d'un dommage exceptionnel, moral ou matériel, causé par une autorité administrative*" In this case, the condition for the admissibility of the action to obtain this form of compensation ("indemnité") is the previous total or partial rejection of the request addressed to the public administration for this purpose or the silence – non-fulfilment of the same and results in the preclusion to claim compensation for the same prejudice in civil proceedings (preclusion which also operates in the opposite sense).

In general, countries have replied that both material and non-material damages are compensable. In some countries, such as Germany and Serbia, only material damage is compensable.

France clarified that *pretium doloris* and loss of *opportunity* are compensable only if the injury is not merely possible.

Luxembourg and the Netherlands replied that loss of opportunity was compensable under their respective laws, while Sweden stated that both material and non-material damages were compensable. Sweden pointed out that its law does not use the expression loss of opportunity, but that loss of opportunity for financial gain due to a mistake by a governmental body can be compensated as material damage.

***B) Avoidable damage and relations with actions of annulment***

The replies showed that, in most jurisdictions, damages that could have been avoided by taking appropriate legal action are not recoverable.

In some jurisdictions, the prior annulment of the act is a condition of admissibility for obtaining compensation for damage resulting directly from it (Cyprus Germany, Latvia, Portugal, Romania, Spain and Luxembourg by case law).

In the Netherlands, the rule of case-law is that a measure that is not challenged within the time limit is consolidated, so that both the administrative and civil courts will consider it legitimate, regardless of any substantial or procedural shortcomings. The administrative act assumes the status of "formele rechtskracht". However, case law itself has drawn up exceptions to this rule, for example in the case of decisions permitting the performance of activities entailing major risks for persons and property, since the damage often occurs at a later date and the persons involved cannot be expected to challenge the administrative act in order to prevent possible damage in the future.

In other jurisdictions, failure to bring an action for annulment or other action is not an obstacle and is not assessed in terms of negligent conduct (Croatia, France, Greece, Serbia, Turkey). France and Greece specified that failure to bring an action for annulment is not a condition for the admissibility of the action for damages and does not affect the total amount of damages sought.

The United Kingdom stated, in general terms, that in some specific cases, the failure to bring an action for annulment could affect the right to damages or the amount of damages, and that the bringing of a damages claim in civil proceedings may be regarded as an abuse of process in cases where the claimant could have sought *judicial review*.

### *C) Subjective element*

From the replies, it emerges that most countries consider the liability of the administration as an objective liability (without fault) and the burden of proof of the elements of the tort lies with the claimant.

Few jurisdictions require the subjective element of the tort (malice or negligence).

### *D) Burden of proof*

In France, the burden of proof is always on the injured party, but may vary depending on whether the administration is at fault or not, as in cases of objective liability ("*responsibilité sans faute*").

Germany and Latvia specify that the burden of proof is mitigated by the powers of the judge at the preliminary stage.

The United Kingdom replied that "*the claimant bears the burden of establishing that a relevant wrong has been committed in respect of which damages are recoverable and of establishing on the balance of probabilities that he has suffered loss (see R (Sturnham) v Parole Board [2013] UKSC 23 at para 82)*".

In Estonia, the burden of proof of the constituent elements of liability rests with the claimant, *i.e.* the identification of the right infringed and of the damage suffered, while there is a legal presumption in relation to non-asset damage, when, for instance, a person sues for the prejudice suffered due to the unjustified loss of personal liberty or in case of damage to personal safety and health caused by the administration, as well as in matters of "common knowledge".

Romania (HCCJ) specified that, as a rule, the burden of proof of the liability of the public administration lies with the injured party. In disputes concerning the determination of civil servants' remuneration, case law holds that the burden of proof lies with the employer who must produce all relevant documentation, while in tax disputes, the burden of proof of the legality of the act and the determination of the tax claim lies with the tax authority.

In Slovenia, the general rules of civil law apply, but there is a presumption of (relative) fault on the part of the administration.

Turkey, on the other hand, affirms that an administrative act carried out in the general interest, even if lawful, may give rise to a right to compensation when it creates an exceptional burden exclusively for certain individuals, such as risky activities. The fundamental principle of equality in the bearing of public burdens and the principle of social equity justify in these cases the liability of the administration for damage caused by its acts or actions without fault and it is for the court *ex officio* to determine the 'fault of the service'.

## I.8. Action for an order for the release of the measure

The majority of countries replied in the affirmative (Bulgaria, Czech Republic, Germany, Greece, Hungary, Italy, Latvia, Poland, Portugal, Romania, Spain).

France pointed out that "*La situation évoquée dans cette question se plie difficilement aux catégories traditionnelles du contentieux administratif français*".

Germany referred to art. 113 co. 5 CACP: "*Insofar as the rejection or omission of the administrative act is unlawful and the plaintiff's rights are violated thereby, the court shall announce the obligation incumbent on the administrative authority to effect the requested official act if the case is ripe for adjudication*".

In Portugal, the Public Administration may be ordered to adopt the unlawfully omitted administrative act if the following conditions exist: (a) absence of a decision within the statutory time limit; (b) rejection or refusal to examine the application; (c) failure to comply with the obligation to decide, irrespective of the existence of an application; (d) replacement of an administrative act with a positive content that does not fully satisfy the request of the interested party.

Greece specified that the administrative judge may order the administration to adopt an act that it has unlawfully refused, when its adoption is mandated by law.

Luxembourg stated that the administrative judge cannot order the adoption of a specific administrative act. However, in the context of the *recours en réformation*, the administrative judge may adopt a decision which replaces the one found to be unlawful. As already specified in reply 8, in the context of the action of annulment, the judge can, by means of the motivation of his decision, indicate instructions to be followed for the new decision to be adopted.

Other countries replied that this possibility is excluded, without further specification (e.g. Lithuania, Norway, Slovakia, Slovenia).

Finland replied that the courts do not have a general remedy in the event that an administrative authority persistently delays in taking a decision or even totally neglects to do so.

## I.9. Powers of the court: conversion of actions

It should be noted that the question has been interpreted in different ways, as can be seen from the fact that some answers concern the conversion of the action, while others concern the re-qualification of the application.

In Italy, the Code of the Administrative Procedure gives the judge the task of qualifying the action brought, in accordance with the principle "*iura novit curia*". The judge may, therefore, requalify the application with the consequent conversion of the action into another, only if the action originally proposed has all the prerequisites for the one into which it is converted. For example, an action to ascertain the right of a company to obtain a revision of the price of a supply contract by a public administration may be converted into an action against the silence maintained by the administration on the request for revision.

However, most countries state that conversion of the *ex officio* action is not possible in their respective jurisdictions.

In many countries, however, the re-qualification of the application by the judge is allowed.

France specified that, since '*recours pour excès de pouvoir*' do not require the services of a lawyer, unlike '*recours de plein contentieux*', the re-qualification of the action by the judge assumes particular importance ("*Si une requête, introduite sans avocat, se présente sous la forme d'un recours pour excès de pouvoir alors qu'il s'agit en fait d'un recours de plein contentieux (...), alors le juge peut prétoriennement requalifier lesdites conclusions et rejeter ladite requête pour irrecevabilité*").

Hungary replied that conversion is allowed only in cases brought by the central government against the failure of local governments to exercise their decision-making or regulatory powers.

Ireland pointed out that the Supreme Court, if it considers that it cannot convict the administration on *judicial review*, may order that the case be continued in civil proceedings.

**SESSION II**
**THE SPECIAL RITES**



# SESSION II

# THE SPECIAL RITES

## II.1. The "special" rites and the forms of differentiation of protection which emerge from the answers given by the states

Most legal systems provide for "differentiated" procedural rules. The matters and areas in which this differentiation operates coincide only in part. These choices either reflect the "domestic" peculiarities of the individual legal systems or show a partial "uniformity" of the European Union system.

The spheres and matters where, most commonly, the legal systems provide for "differentiated" procedural rules concern the protection of "sensitive" interests or of relevant "economic-social" impact, such as, for instance, immigration, planning, public contracts, environment, expropriation proceedings, taxation, elections and disputes with independent administrative authorities. There are also rites in which there is a common and generalised need for simplification and speeding-up of judicial protection, such as, for instance, in the case of access to documents, silence of the administration (in its different meanings in the various legal systems), in injunction proceedings and enforcement of administrative judgments and also in proceedings for damages.

In many cases the provision of special procedural rules is instrumental to providing greater protection with respect to particular areas that respond to national specificities: examples of this are the Hungarian and Polish systems that provide for a "simplified" protection for the issuance of certificates, or the Portuguese system in which a simplified procedure is regulated for litigation in the so called "mass procedures".

There is also a tendency for many legal systems to converge with regard to the provision of differentiated protection to ensure better safeguarding of fundamental rights (e.g. health or safety). In most jurisdictions, there are also "special" rules for the granting of interim measures. This point will be discussed in more detail below in Session III.

In some cases (e.g. in Bulgaria and Norway) the existence of "special" substantive rules (e.g. for the compensation of damage resulting from an unlawful administrative measure) does not correspond to a special procedural regime, the ordinary rules continue to apply.

In particular, in Germany and Norway, instead of providing for the recourse to differentiated procedural rules, the system anticipates the "specialness" of certain matters by applying a differentiated procedural regime to them (e.g. by providing for the speeding-up of the time-limits for requesting and inspecting administrative acts).

As for the source of the "special" discipline, in some countries, such as Italy, it is contained directly in the Code, in others it is in the legislative sources that generically regulate the administrative process (Austria, France, and the United Kingdom), in others still, it is contained in special laws (Belgium). Sometimes, as in Sweden, the legal provisions are accompanied by the possibility for individual courts to further "calibrate" the differentiation of protection in their internal procedures.

The states which answered in the affirmative with regard to the existence of "special" procedural rules also pointed out that the "differentiation" coincides, in most cases, with the provision of "*fast-tracked procedures*" for the lodging of an application at first instance, or for the conduct of the trial or for the adoption of the judicial decision or in the provision of exceptions to the ordinary procedural rules ("*simplified procedures*"). This emerges from the replies given by Austria, Croatia, the Czech Republic, France, Greece, Ireland, Malta, Poland, Romania, Serbia and Turkey.

In addition to these differentiating profiles, other countries add that in their legal systems there are some exceptions regarding "jurisdiction" of the administrative courts (Belgium, Finland, Latvia, Lithuania, Luxembourg, the Netherlands, Slovenia). With regard to this last profile, some countries specify that this exception consists in the preclusion, in certain disputes, of the possibility of appealing against decisions of first instance (in Latvia with regard to electoral disputes and in Luxembourg for immigration disputes and for those generated during the Covid-19 pandemic). In some cases, however, the specialness is determined by the possibility to appeal directly to the SAC (in Luxembourg and in Slovenia when dealing with electoral disputes).

Norway replied that, in general, there are no special rules in its legislation on time limits for lodging an appeal or for the course of the proceedings.

Some countries noted that the area of differentiation of procedural protection is much wider, involving also a greater extension of the powers of the judge, the widening of the adversarial process (Estonia), the type of rulings that can be made (Greece and Lithuania), the possibility for the judge to provide a more streamlined reasoning (Greece and Italy) or to take evidence more informally and more quickly. Greece also pointed out that interim measures *ante causam* can only be granted in regard to public contracts.

Further specificities reflecting "domestic" peculiarities also emerge from the replies.

According to the answer given by Cyprus, it emerges that the latter, within the area of "speciality", also includes cases in which the exertion of the hierarchical appeal is a condition for access to the administrative judgment (e.g. in matters of public contracts). Slovakia, on the other hand, indicated that each jurisdictional action has its own differentiated discipline and the greater speciality consists in the specific conditions – in addition to the "ordinary" ones – of the legitimacy to appeal.

It is also worth mentioning the reply from the Netherlands which pointed out that the administrative courts have the power to adopt an interim decision, allowing the administrative authority to correct, for example, a procedural defect or failure to state reasons. This procedure is called "*administrative loop*" ("*bestuurlijke lus*").

In their replies, most countries pointed out that "differentiated" procedural rules are established both "by subject matter" and by the jurisdictional actions which may be brought Austria, Belgium, Cyprus, Croatia, Finland,

Greece, Hungary, Italy, Latvia, the Netherlands, Portugal, Romania, Spain, Sweden Turkey and the United Kingdom). Other countries replied that the speciality concerned exclusively, or principally, "matters", but not actions (Czech Republic, France, Ireland, Lithuania, Luxembourg, Poland, Serbia, Slovenia).

In a very few cases, the differentiation of protection concerns only the actions which can be brought (Slovakia) and not specific matters.

### II.2. Judicial protection against "silences"

Almost all the countries replied that their legal systems provide for judicial action against the silence of the administration (Austria, Belgium, Bulgaria, Croatia, Cyprus, Czech Republic, Estonia, France, Germany, Greece, Hungary, Italy Latvia, Lithuania, Luxembourg, Malta, the Netherlands, Poland, Portugal, Romania, Serbia, Slovakia, Slovenia, Spain, Sweden, Turkey, the United Kingdom), but do not always clarify whether it refers to mere *inertia*, understood as failure to comply with the general obligation to provide, or to a silence with the value of consent or rejection.

Finland and Norway replied that no specific procedural action is provided for in their legislation for these purposes: in the Norwegian system, preference was given to procedural remedies, limiting judicial protection to actions for damages, while in the Finnish system only the Chancellor of Justice or the Ombudsman can react against silence in defence of "legality". On this point, Finland also specified that, even in the absence of any legal provision for an action by private individuals against the silence of the administration, a particularly protective line of case-law stated that the administrative judge, in order to prevent inertia resulting in an infringement of the individual's rights, may refer the matter to the competent administration by making express reference to its obligation to take a decision.

With regard to the source of regulation of the protection against silence, it was found that in only one legal system is it directly provided for by the Constitution (Cyprus), while in the others it is contained in general procedural provisions or special laws. In some countries (Lithuania and Spain) the discipline of judicial protection against silence is not properly qualified as "special", since it is considered as an "ordinary" remedy.

There is some convergence in substance and procedure.

In Belgium and Greece, for example, silence is equivalent, as a general rule, to rejection of the application. France's reply shows that although, in principle, silence takes on the value of consent, there are numerous provisions of the *Code des relations entre le public et l'administration* in which it takes on the value of implicit rejection ("*décision implicite de rejet*") and in these cases silence corresponds to a "*décision préalable*" that can be challenged directly before the administrative court.

The Czech Republic pointed out that a private individual who has exhausted his domestic remedies before an administrative authority without success may ask the court to compel it to give a decision on the substance of the matter. This procedure, the Czech Republic specifies, does not apply in cases where there are special laws that give silence the value of consent.

Turkey replied that, in addition to total inertia, the action to contest the adoption of a non-final measure by the Public Administration is also available instead of waiting for the final decision. In this case, the non-final decision is considered as a rejection of the application.

There are also differences with regard to the time limits for bringing an action against silence. In Luxembourg, the action can be brought three months after the administration should have issued its decision. In Poland it can be brought without any time limit. In Romania, the court, as well as setting a time limit, may impose a penalty on the administration for each additional day of delay.

### II.3. The enforcement of judgments of the administrative judge: rate of compliance and remedies against non-compliance

With reference to the data representing the rate of spontaneous compliance with the rulings of the administrative judge by the Administrations, this data tends to converge.

Most of the countries report that the Administration complies spontaneously, always or almost always, without indicating a reference percentage (Austria, Bulgaria, Cyprus, Estonia, Finland, Germany, Greece, Latvia, Lithuania, Portugal, Slovenia, Turkey, the United Kingdom), but underlining that this aspect is not particularly problematic.

Some countries report that the administration complies in more than 50% of cases (Belgium, Croatia, Czech Republic, France, Ireland, Italy, the

Netherlands, Romania, Slovakia, Spain, Sweden), others even more than 90% (Hungary, Luxembourg), recording a very low rate of appeals necessary to enforce judgments (Czech Republic, France).

Serbia does not indicate a percentage, as there is no remedy before the administrative court to challenge the non-enforcement of its judgments. Norway, also, does not indicate a number as there is no system of administrative jurisdiction. It is worth noting the peculiarity of Slovakia where, in those rare cases where the administration considers that the administrative judge has erred in his decision in law, it can challenge it in a new trial.

Many countries replied that in their own legal systems there are jurisdictional procedures, more or less articulated, to ensure the enforcement of administrative judgements (Austria, Belgium, Bulgaria, Croatia, France, Germany, Greece, Hungary, Ireland, Italy, Latvia, Romania, Spain). On this point, Cyprus pointed out that such a provision exists at constitutional level: Article 146.5A of the Constitution provides that both the Administrative Court and the Supreme Court have the power to assess whether their decisions which have become legally binding have been correctly and promptly executed and, if they have not, they may impose sanctions to the extent provided for by law. Cyprus further emphasised that guidelines for implementation have never been drawn up as there has been no need to do so, given the absolute rate of compliance by the administrations. For the enforcement of non-final decisions, suspension orders are adopted which, if disregarded by the administration, may constitute contempt of the Court. The Czech Republic also indicated that although a specific judicial procedure exists, it is never used.

Belgium, France and Germany replied that in their legal systems there are specific procedural actions for obtaining the full execution of the judgments of the courts of first instance and, in the event of non-compliance, a financial penalty may be imposed, quantified as a global amount, per unit of time (*astreinte*) or calibrated in relation to the individual infringement. On this point, Germany points out that an order by the administration to pay a sum of money to compensate for the non-execution of a decision is, however, not considered an effective remedy, as this sum is not paid in favour of the claimant, but to another authority, thus remaining within the public sector.

In Bulgaria, there are specific actions to enable both the administration and the individual citizen to obtain enforcement of judicial decisions (even if they are not final) or compensation for their non-execution or incorrect execution. Greece emphasised that "forced" enforcement actions can only be brought to "attack" the private property of the State.

Luxembourg pointed out that if the Administration, within three months of the judgment of annulment, does not adopt the consequent acts, the interested party may apply to the court which pronounced the judgment for the appointment of an extraordinary commissioner and that, in more than 95% of cases, the mere filing of such an application determines the immediate compliance with the judgment on the part of the Public Administration, with the resultant cessation of the matter in dispute. However, spontaneous compliance does not exclude the possibility of bringing an action for damages before the same court.

Some countries replied that there are no specific legal actions or procedures to ensure the full enforcement of the administrative judge's decisions (Malta, the Netherlands, Poland, Portugal, Serbia, Slovakia, Sweden, Turkey): nevertheless, it emerges from the answers given, that some legal systems provide for instruments for ("*enforcement*") that generally allow the "soliciting" or "order" of such enforcement.

Malta, for example, stated that its legislation contains *executive warrant procedures* which enable the interested party to request the enforcement of judgments. The Netherlands replied that the competence for the enforcement of judgments is, in general, vested in the ordinary judge, but the administrative judge may establish from the outset, in his decision, that failure to enforce it will entail the imposition of an *astreinte* (quantified by the judge himself). Estonia also noted out that its legislation provides for a mechanism of financial penalties (of 32,000 euros), which can be imposed by the administrative courts themselves in the event of non-compliance. Finland highlighted the observation that the administrative court does not, in principle, have the jurisdiction to enforce its decisions, but that the law provides for cases in which the interested party may challenge, in the courts, those administrative measures taken contrary to a previous court decision.

The replies of Portugal and Turkey showed that the non-enforcement of judicial decisions results in various liabilities on the part of the Administration. (in Portugal: disciplinary, civil and criminal). Austria also pointed out that the enforcement of judgments by *first instance administrative courts* is the specific responsibility of the *district administration authorities*, which are responsible for this.

In Sweden, on the contrary, in the rare cases where the Administration does not comply with judicial decisions, the interested party can only turn to supervisory bodies within the Administration. In Turkey, if the judgment is not complied with, an action for compensation for pecuniary and/or non-pecuniary damage may be brought before the competent administrative court.

The UK *enforcement* system, on the other hand, is quite peculiar. In this system, failure to comply with a *mandatory order* can be punished as "contempt of court" (see M v Home Office [1994] 1 AC 377) and result in a fine or imprisonment for up to two years. Conversely, the infringement of a "*declaration*" contained in a judgment does not give rise to such serious consequences, because of its non-coercive content, but the person concerned may take legal action to have it enforced. However, this is a remedy that is never resorted to, given the rate of immediate compliance with judicial decisions, by administrations.

## II.4. A regime of enforceability of judgments of first instance

As regards the enforceability of judgments at first instance, the replies given by the States reveal several different trends.

The first is that decisions of administrative courts of first instance are, in principle, immediately enforceable (Austria, Belgium, Czech Republic, France, Greece, Ireland, Italy Malta, the Netherlands, Norway, Romania, Spain, Turkey, the United Kingdom). The second is that decisions of the courts of first instance are enforceable only when they become "*final*" (*i.e.* no longer subject to appeal) (Bulgaria, Estonia, Hungary, Latvia, Poland, Portugal, Slovakia, Slovenia).

In Finland, as a rule, judgments are enforceable only when they become final, but they can also be enforced if (i) the law provides for it; (ii) their nature is such that they must be enforced immediately; (iii) enforcement cannot be deferred for reasons of public interest. Serbia pointed out that all decisions issued by the administrative courts have "mandatory" effects, but that only decisions that are no longer subject to appeal ("*final judgement*") are immediately enforceable, adding that, following judicial annulment, if the administration does not issue – immediately or within thirty days – a new measure, or does not execute the judicial decision, the interested party may, by means of a separate act, request the court to adopt the measure.

Some countries replied that only first instance decisions are not immediately enforceable (Croatia and Luxembourg). Others specified that first instance judgments take effect only if provided for by law or if declared provisionally enforceable by the court (Germany and Sweden). Lithuania replied on this point that first instance judgments are not immediately enforceable and that only SAC judgments are not appealable and therefore immediately enforceable.

There is also no agreement on the suspensive effect of the appeal.

In Cyprus, the enforceability of the judgment may be suspended not only at the request of the interested party but also subsequently, *ex proprio motu*, by the *Administrative Court*. There is, however, a specific procedure for opposition by the parties after the communication of the decision.

In some countries, the lodging of an appeal does not, as a rule, suspend the decision at first instance level (Finland, France). In France, however, the appeal against a judgment in electoral matters has a suspensive effect. In Romania, on the other hand, the lodging of an appeal has an automatic suspensive effect.

## II.5. The "exhaustion" of administrative discretion after judicial annulment

*The verification of the instruments available to the parties to contest any unlawfulness which may arise from a judgment annulling an administrative measure characterised by discretionary power, has led to difficulties for most countries in finding an immediate response within their own legal system because it is linked to the Italian system.*

In Italy, the judgment annulling an administrative measure characterised by discretionary power binds the Administration with regard to the illegitimacy recognised by the judgment (so-called "deduction"). The Council of State maintains that, in some cases, the discretionary power may be "reduced" either as a result of a self-imposed constraint by the public administration itself, or as a result of the outcome of the judgment (when, for example, the preliminary investigation has found that there were no other alternative practicable technical choices).

Not being in a position to give a precise answer, most countries stress, in general, that the administrative judge's review of discretionary decisions is rather limited and that there are no specific mechanisms for the progressive "reduction" of administrative discretion.

There is a general tendency to consider the annulment decisions of the court of first instance suitable for guiding the Administration, through its own motivation ("legal reasoning"), as to the correct re-exercise of administrative power. Some countries emphasise that judicial review is always limited to profiles of legitimacy and can never limit the discretion that characterises administrative action (Belgium, Bulgaria, Croatia, Hungary). Cyprus emphasised that the review is principally aimed at verifying the reasonableness of the decision. Estonia, Latvia and Portugal replied that the judge must verify that the administration has re-exercised its power according to the instructions indicated by the judge, but cannot directly replace it.

Some countries (France) replied by differentiating between the case in which the administration did not respond to a private party's request – by remaining silent, thus, not exercising its discretionary power – from that in which there was an express rejection. In the first instance, if the court finds that the administration has misrepresented ("méconnu") its discretionary power, denying the citizen the right to which he was entitled, the judicial decision leaves the administration with no alternative but to grant what was requested. The judgment in these cases contains an injunction ("injonction") to the administration to that effect. The second hypothesis leaves more room for manoeuvre for the administration: if it has wrongly rejected a private party's request, the judgment annulling the measure often contains an injunction ("injonction") not to grant the measure but to reconsider the matter. In such a case, the administration, although having originally given erroneous reasons for the first refusal, which was then annulled, may legitimately invoke another reason for the new refusal, by adopting a decision that will be independently contestable.

Some jurisdictions (the Czech Republic and Slovenia) pointed out in their replies that there is a general correspondence between the reduction of discretion and the acceptance of the grounds put forward by the claimant (at first instance or possibly on appeal). The Czech Republic stated that the reduction of administrative discretion is closely related to the principle of correspondence between "requested and pronounced", so that discretion is "reduced" according to the reasons for which the annulment of the measure was ordered.

Sweden observed that the "reduction" of discretion may be accentuated in the passage from the first instance to the appeal on account of the claimant's choice regarding which parts of the judgment are to be appealed: a choice which allows the claimant to obtain with priority ("precedence") a ruling by the SAC on the aspects of immediate interest with respect to the re-exercise of power.

Slovenia replied that the discretionary power may be reduced in exceptional cases in which, as there is an already established practice of the administration, the court is careful to avoid unequal or unfair treatment.

Romania replied that, as a rule, a judgment annulling an administrative act on the ground of excess of power obliges the administration to comply with the illegality established in the judgment; whereas, when the administrative judge suspends the execution of administrative acts, the discretionary power is "reduced" entirely by the effect of the judicial decision and the law. Thus, if a new administrative act is issued with the same content as the one suspended by the judge, it is automatically suspended.

The Netherlands reported that the system does not allow the administrative judge to annul further decisions similar to the one already annulled. However, there are mechanisms which allow the administrative judge to resolve disputes "once and for all". In this context, it is worth mentioning the rule that if the administration modifies the measure *sub iudice*, the appeal is automatically considered to be "extended" also to this new measure, unless the latter completely satisfies the applicant's claims. The reply emphasises that this mechanism fully guarantees the effectiveness of judicial protection, in that the interested party does not need to challenge the new measure. Another mechanism favouring the swift 'final' resolution of disputes is the previously mentioned ('administrative loop' – 'bestuurlijke lus') whereby the administrative courts may adopt an interim decision, allowing (or, if in the last resort, requiring) the administrative authority to remedy errors committed during the procedure (e.g. breaches of procedural rules or failure to state reasons). This instrument relieves the interested party of the burden of challenging new decisions taken by the administrative authority. Finally, Dutch law provides for the so-called "judicial loop" ("judiciële lus"), on the basis of which, in the event that the judgment of the SAC orders the administrative authority to take a new decision, the judgment may stipulate that the new measure can only be challenged before the same Court.

**SESSION III**
**INTERIM RELIEF**



# SESSION III
# INTERIM RELIEF

## III.1. The suspension of the measure as an "automatic" effect of the lodging of the grievance: systems that provide for it and limits to the rule

Most of the countries replied that the lodging of a judicial appeal does not automatically suspend the effectiveness of the measure, since the suspension must be the subject of an application by the interested party.

In reporting the data below of the only countries that answered the question in the affirmative or that, although answering in the negative, indicated some exceptional cases in which the suspension of the measure follows as an automatic effect upon the filing of the appeal, it should be noted that the automatic suspension, even if declared operational (Austria, Bulgaria, Croatia, Finland, Germany, Latvia, Malta, Portugal, Sweden), is not absolute but is subject to certain conditions, such as the timeliness and admissibility of the appeal (Austria) or its possible justification (Germany). In Austria, moreover, the authority may exclude the automatic suspensive effect if, following a balancing of opposing interests, it appears that urgent execution of the measure is necessary to avoid imminent danger.

In other countries, certain matters are exempted from the rule of automatic suspension by express legal provision. This exception may be reserved for specific matters (as in the case of asylum applications in Austria or municipal matters in Finland) or extended to the numerous expressly-listed cases of derogation (Latvia, Portugal, Sweden).

A different derogation mechanism operates in Germany, where, in certain matters, there is a presumption of non-suspensibility which hinders the application of the rule (such as taxation or police orders).

Finland referred to the automatic suspension of the judgment, pointing out that it follows from the procedural rule that court decisions cannot be enforced until they have become "*final*". It underlined, however, that this rule is derogated from in those cases where the appeal to the SAC is subject to a prior "*leave to appeal*": in these specific cases, the lodging of the appeal does not hinder the enforceability of the contested decision, with the consequent inoperability of the mechanism of automatic suspension.

Croatia too, referred to the suspension of the judgment, specifying that the rule of automatic suspension is also applicable in the event of an appeal.

Among the legal systems which, while answering the question in the negative, illustrated the exceptional cases in which the automatic suspension operates, a distinction should be made between those which provide for such a suspension at first instance only for specific matters (Czech Republic) or in exceptional cases expressly provided for by law (Slovenia), and those which illustrated the exceptional cases in which the appeal of the judgment before the higher court results in its immediate suspension (in social security matters in the Netherlands and in the case of appeals brought by the *Immigration and Asylum Chamber of the Upper Tribunal* in the United Kingdom).

Some countries replied that precautionary measures can be ordered *ex officio* by the judge (Cyprus, Estonia, Finland, Lithuania, Norway). On this point, Norway specified that the Court may decide, on its own initiative, to suspend the effectiveness of the contested measure, in certain cases only, such as in matters regarding social services.

## III.2. The types of precautionary measures and the generalised nature of the remedy

As for the types of interim measures, while some legal systems are atypical (Belgium, Czech Republic, Estonia, Finland, France, Germany, Greece, Hungary, Ireland, Italy, Latvia, Lithuania, Luxembourg, the Netherlands, Portugal, Slovenia, Spain, Sweden, the United Kingdom), others have only the suspension of the effectiveness of the measure (Bulgaria, Croatia, Cyprus, Norway Romania, Serbia, Slovakia, Turkey) or, more specifically, the suspension of the execution of the act or of the action of the Public Administration (Poland).

In some countries, the openness to forms of precautionary protection other than suspension operates exclusively in areas of EU relevance (Austria).

Some countries provided examples of atypical precautionary measures that can be granted: the admission of a candidate to a competition from which he had been excluded (Luxembourg), the granting of a provisional licence in the event of an appeal against the refusal (the Netherlands).

The absolute majority of the countries that replied to the questionnaire stated that interlocutory protection is a generalised remedy and, therefore, not limited to certain types of disputes.

In Hungary, interlocutory protection is excluded against administrative measures which (a) are taken in execution of a final court decision, (b) require the exercise of civil protection functions or the provision of services falling under national defence obligations; (c) concern defence and military areas and buildings.

Poland also clarified that the general application of interim protection is subject to exceptions provided by local laws which have come into force ("*provisions of local enactments which have come into force*") or in cases where the statute or the nature of the act (e.g. act of refusal) precludes it.

Romania specified that the suspension does not apply to acts adopted, in times of war, a state of siege or emergency, those relating to defence and national security or those adopted for the restoration of public order or to eliminate the consequences of natural disasters and epidemics.

Sweden, while affirming the general nature of the remedy, pointed out that there are particular matters, such as public contracts, where special rules apply as to the issues to be considered and the rules of evidence.

Ireland specified that interlocutory protection is by nature "equitable", this means that the Court may deny it even if the criteria set out in the *case law are met*.

## III.3. Conditions for the granting of precautionary measures and provision of security

With regard to the conditions for granting a request for interlocutory measures, it is generally necessary to demonstrate the existence of an urgent situation requiring immediate intervention, as well as a reasonable fear of damage or loss. In addition, some jurisdictions require profiles of the merits of the claim (Belgium, Estonia, France, Italy, Latvia, Lithuania, Luxembourg, the Netherlands, Norway, Portugal, Romania, Sweden, Turkey, the United Kingdom).

The relationship between the two requirements may vary from country to country: in Greece, for example, the manifest justification of the claim may be an alternative condition to injury.

Finland pointed out that the appearance of merits, although not a legal requirement, is in practice taken into account by the court in the interlocutory decision.

Some countries observed that when assessing the application for protective measures, the court generally balances any conflicting interests (e.g. Hungary, Slovenia, Spain).

The United Kingdom referred to a number of *case laws* according to which the claimant must show that he has a real prospect of a favourable outcome of the dispute and that the balancing of interests presupposes the adoption of the interim measure.

Some countries pointed out that non-contradiction to the public interest is considered a condition for granting suspensive measures (Czech Republic, Serbia, Slovakia). Cyprus pointed out that the manifest unlawfulness (self-evident and clearly deduced) of the contested decision reverses the rule that the public interest takes precedence over the claimant's interest when balancing it. In the Netherlands, too, the *prima facie* assessment of the illegality of the contested measure assumes autonomous relevance, so much so, that it alone can justify the granting of precautionary measures, even irrespective of the recurrence of the requirement of damage.

In Ireland, the Rules of Court and case law have established the conditions under which interim measures may be granted. The Court must verify, in the following order: (a) the seriousness of the claim brought before it; (b) the irreparability of the damage that the claimant would suffer as a result of the proceedings and (c) the reparability of the damage suffered by the administration. Finally, at the end of the process of verification of the existence of the above conditions, the Court balances the opposing interests in the light of the objective of maintaining the *status quo*.

Most countries replied that their legislations do not provide for the possibility of imposing bail (Austria, Belgium, Croatia, Czech Republic, Estonia, France, Germany, Greece, Latvia, Lithuania, Luxembourg, the Netherlands, Poland, Serbia, Slovakia, Sweden).

In addition to Italy, Bulgaria, Cyprus, Hungary, Malta, Portugal, Romania, Slovenia and Spain replied in the affirmative, specifying, however, that bail is only foreseen for specific cases (in case of suspension of tax measures and in other cases provided for by law).

In turn, Bulgaria specified that the court may order the payment of bail to allow the immediate enforcement of a measure subject to automatic suspensive effect if the administrative authority or the party against whom the measure has favourable effects so requests. In this case, the Court may set bail for them.

In Hungary and Norway, the bail is linked to the possibility that the protective measure may cause compensable damage. Hungary specifies that, when determining the bail, the court takes into account the degree of substantiation of the claim.

In Ireland, provision is made for the granting of bail only to guarantee the payment of court costs (*security of costs*). This form of security is also provided for in Norway, but applies only at the request of the administration involved and only to claimants who are not resident in an EEA State.

Latvia replied to the question by referring to the security deposit of €15 to be paid at the time of the application for interim measures, this deposit is fully refunded if the application is granted in whole or in part.

The Netherlands, after clarifying that there is no provision for the imposition of a security deposit for the application for protective measures, illustrated the rules applicable to the registration fees for the commencement of the interlocutory proceedings (the amount of which is similar to that applicable to proceedings on the merits) and the cases in which they may be reimbursed.

### III.4. Precautionary measures *ante causam*

As regards the possibility of introducing the precautionary request before the introduction of the case on the merits (*ante causam*), some countries replied that they were not aware of this remedy (Austria, Croatia, Cyprus,

Czech Republic, Finland, Latvia, Lithuania, Luxembourg, Poland, Slovakia, Slovenia, and Turkey. Poland, however, specifies that the administrative authority, having been preliminarily seized, may suspend the measure before the commencement of the proceedings).

Among the countries that provide for precautionary measures *ante causam*, Estonia, Germany, Norway, Serbia, Spain, and the United Kingdom, they do not expressly specify whether they lose their effectiveness if the appeal on the merits is not brought within the time limit, whereas this time-limit rule applies in Belgium, Bulgaria, Ireland, Italy, Malta, the Netherlands, Portugal and Romania.

In Italy the precautionary measure *ante causam* loses its effectiveness if, within fifteen days from its adoption, the appeal has not been notified. In any event, the measure granted loses effect sixty days after the date of its adoption, while only the provisional measures that have been confirmed in the course of the litigation in the collegiate court, remain effective.

Serbia replied that measures granted *ante causam* take effect irrespective of the commencement of proceedings on the merits. Norway and the United Kingdom emphasised that the determination of the duration of such measures is left to the Court to decide.

Sweden replied that although the possibility of applying for provisional measures *ante causam* was not expressly provided for, the particular flexibility of the procedure would allow the claimant to apply for them, specifying the merits at a later stage.

Particular mention should be made of those countries in which only certain provisional measures can be applied for on a stand-alone basis (e.g. *référé-liberté* in France, or the request to obtain evidence in advance in Hungary). In Greece, interlocutory measures *ante causam* are allowed only in the sphere of public contracts and remain effective irrespective of the introduction of proceedings on the merits.

## III.5. The interlocutory proceedings: terms, collegiate or monocratic nature of the ruling and the possibility of appeal

Some jurisdictions do not have specific rules on interlocutory proceedings (Austria, Croatia, Finland). They therefore follow the rules of the main proceedings, sometimes adapted only for minimal indications, such as the speeding-up of the procedure (Czech Republic).

Generally speaking, the interlocutory procedure is speeded up in comparison to ordinary procedures (Poland, Romania, Serbia, Slovenia, Spain, Sweden, Turkey) and may be characterised by a lighter adversarial process (Lithuania, the Netherlands), also in terms of it not requiring oral evidence (Germany, Hungary, Norway, Serbia, the United Kingdom) and a less complete preliminary investigation (Germany).

In some cases, the collegial or monocratic nature of the decision depends on the general rules of procedure of each country (Greece, Hungary, Latvia, Lithuania, Norway). In others, the protective decision is usually delivered by a single judge (Ireland, Luxembourg, Malta, the United Kingdom and, the Netherlands where the protective decision is delivered by a single judge at all stages of the procedure), except in the event of exceptional hypotheses, the subject-matter of which is particularly sensitive.

In Luxembourg, the judge who decides on the application for a protective measure may not be part of the panel that decides on the substance of the case, in compliance with the principle of impartiality set out in Article 6 ECHR.

In Portugal (as in Italy), collegiality is the rule, except in cases of extreme urgency. In Italy, if it is not possible to wait for the collegial hearing to be fixed, the president of the Regional Administrative Court or the president of a section of the Council of State or a judge delegated by them, rules on the application for a precautionary measure with a monocratic decree that loses its effects if it is not confirmed by a subsequent collegial decision.

The decision is always collegial in Serbia, Slovenia, and Spain.

In Portugal, the procedure to be followed differs depending on the type of protective measure requested (suspension, injunction, payment of provisional sums, preventive evidence, etc.).

In general, the precautionary order can be appealed before the SAC, irrespective of whether the appealed decision is issued by a single or collective court (Bulgaria, Croatia, Estonia, France, Latvia, Lithuania, Malta, Norway, Romania, Slovenia, Sweden, Turkey, and Spain, which, however, specifies that no appeal in cassation is possible against the precautionary decision).

In some countries, the possibility of appealing is excluded due to the temporary nature of the measure (Czech Republic, Finland). In others, it is only allowed for certain categories of defects (unconstitutionality in Germany or particularly important defects in Ireland) or after passing a "*test of eligibility*" of the appeal (Portugal, the United Kingdom).

In Luxembourg and the Netherlands, the single judgement taken on remand cannot be appealed.

The interim decision cannot be appealed in Serbia, even if it is always collegial. Hungary specified that interim measures rejecting the modification of previous decisions which reject the same application, cannot be appealed, in the absence of new legal or factual arguments.

In Greece provisional measures are not appealable, but may be revoked by the same court that issued them. Poland has made it clear that the protective order (always suspensive) can be reviewed at any time by the Court if circumstances change, irrespective of the party's request.

## III.6. Definition of the merits of the case in the interlocutory proceedings

In some countries, it is expressly provided for that, when examining the application for interim measures, the court may directly determine the merits of the case (Belgium, Greece, Italy, Luxembourg, the Netherlands, Portugal, Sweden). However, a number of conditions must be met: verification of the integrity of the adversarial process and of the preliminary investigation or the prior agreement of the parties in the Netherlands; the granting of a time-limit to the parties to defend themselves in writing with reference to the proposal for early settlement in Belgium where, in the event of opposition, the President may refer the matter to the ordinary procedure; the simplicity of the case and the urgency of its resolution in Portugal, where the parties must also be heard in advance on this point; the complete annexation of the parties' requests in Sweden.

The majority of the countries stated that there is no provision for determining the merits of the case in the interlocutory proceedings (Croatia, Czech Republic, Estonia, Finland, Hungary, Ireland, Latvia, Lithuania, Luxembourg, Malta, Norway, Poland, Romania, Serbia, Slovenia). Others replied that it is excluded by the autonomous nature of the interlocutory proceedings with respect to the main proceedings (France), by the lack of orality characterising the interlocutory proceedings (Germany) or by the interim nature of the interlocutory phase (Cyprus, the United Kingdom).

The United Kingdom, furthermore, pointed out that the interim nature of the interlocutory phase does not exclude the possibility that the granting of provisional measures may, in practice, settle the dispute definitively: in that case, a particularly rigorous assessment of the conditions for granting the requested measure is required. Luxembourg pointed out that the arguments used by the court to assess the merits of the application for provisional measures are indicative of the final resolution of the dispute.

## III.7. Suspension of the effects of the judgment as a protective measure on appeal

From the specific answers to the specific question, it emerged that the possibility for the SAC to suspend the enforceability of judicial decisions in case of appeal, is excluded only in a few countries (Bulgaria, Estonia, Germany, Greece, Latvia, Lithuania, Norway, Poland and Serbia, which means that the SAC can grant provisional measures only in the rare cases where it is the sole judge).

It is interesting to note that in Estonia, where this possibility is not permitted since the judgment is generally enforced only after it has become "*final*" (*i.e.* no longer subject to appeal), the possibility of a single instance appeal against any order for immediate enforcement of the judgment is nevertheless provided for.

In Romania, an appeal automatically suspends the enforcement of the contested judgment.

The Czech Republic and Finland replied that the suspension of the judgment on the substance of the case by the first court is allowed, although the possibility to appeal protective measures is not.

Luxembourg noted that such a measure can be granted, upon request, only by the same court whose decision is appealed and that this mechanism is considered as a compensation for the non-appealability of provisional measures. Cyprus stated that only the suspension of judgments of rejection is precluded.

In the United Kingdom, the suspension of the enforceability of a lower court judgment before the SAC is quite exceptional; it is the same court whose decision is challenged that decides, as a rule, on the application for suspension of its effects.

## III.8. Statistics on the average number of precautionary rulings

The lack of data prevented some countries from answering this question (Austria, Bulgaria, Cyprus, Finland, Malta and Spain).

Some countries only provided the absolute number of interim rulings made by the SAC:

- 3 in the UK in 2021 and 0 in 2020;
- less than 10 (Estonia):
- between 500 and 600 (Serbia);
- less than 1 000 (Belgium);
- around 2,100 as a first instance judge and around 5,600 as an appeal judge (Turkey);

In Ireland, due to the strict conditions in place for approaching the SAC, the likelihood of it being required to rule on the granting of an interim measure is almost non-existent.

Among the countries that were able to provide a percentage figure on the average number of interim relief decisions taken each year by the SAC as a proportion of total decisions, the results diverged considerably, although this overall percentage remained at less than 4%.

The percentage is below 1% in Croatia and Norway (where, moreover, most of the disputes concern relations between private individuals and do not involve the public administration).

In Portugal it is slightly above 1%. Around 3% in the Czech Republic, Lithuania, Poland (500 out of 15,000) and Sweden (183 out of 6,314). The percentage is between 3-4% in Germany, Latvia and France, where, however, there has been a significant increase in the number of rulings in connection with the health emergency in 2020 (in proportion, precautionary rulings have tripled compared to figures for the previous two years).

The average number of precautionary rulings is around 10% in Greece, 11% in Romania, 15% in Slovenia and 20% in the Netherlands. The Italian percentage of 39% is the second highest, surpassed only by Hungary, where 50% of appeals to the Supreme Court include interlocutory measures and where, in tax matters, the percentage is significantly higher as almost all appeals contain interlocutory measures.

# ACA-Europe Seminar
# “The application of general principles and clauses in the case law of contentious-administrative courts”

**Madrid, Spain**
**21 November 2022**
**General Report by the Supreme Court of Spain**

# Summary of the General Report of the Seminar "The application of general principles and clauses in the case law of contentious-administrative courts" held in Madrid, Spain, 21 November 2022

The topic covered in the seminar organized in Madrid, by the Spanish Supreme Administrative Court, focused on the principles and general clauses developed in the jurisprudence of the administrative courts of the countries participating in the questionnaire: the topic was examined from four different perspectives, through the administration – for each of them – of multiple-choice questions.

With five questions, an attempt was made to understand whether there are general principles and clauses in the legal system of the countries participating in the questionnaire that are capable of prevailing over rules of law, that can be used as the basis for jurisdictional decisions, and that, because of their cross-cutting relevance, can be considered applicable to all areas of public law. The answers given to these made it possible to ascertain the following.

In most countries, general principles of the legal system are considered applicable only where there are gaps in positive law. In some countries they may be applied even in the presence of written norms with respect to which they are in conflict: this results in the substantial disapplication of positive norms, which, moreover, in such a case is justified by the constitutional rank of the interests that the general principles protect and which has been accorded to them by the respective Constitutional Courts, or by the Supreme Administrative Courts.

In almost all countries, the most relevant general principles of the legal system have been, albeit to varying degrees, positivized: among the positivized principles are the principle of reasonableness of administrative acts; the principles of equality, transparency, impartiality, and non-discrimination; and the principles that impose procedural guarantees to protect the citizen. These are principles that, in the context of the decision, can assume diriment relevance or, simply, to reinforce an argument based, predominantly on positive norms. All countries reported that general principles are invoked and applied across the board, in all areas of public law.

The exception is Germany, where general principles have been transfused into statutory norms, which is why they do not serve as an independent yardstick for judgment.

In almost all countries (with the exception of Croatia), there are general principles specifically referable to public law, which coexist and are applicable together with other general principles: these are the principles of good administration, efficiency, effectiveness and transparency, legitimate expectations, official secrecy, subsidiarity, cooperation with the European Union, continuity of administrative action and public purpose of the Administration Only Italy appears to have specified that general principles referable specifically to administrative law have found recognition both at the level of the Constitution and ordinary law, assuming special and derogatory relevance.

One group of questions aimed to ascertain how general principles of European law are applied by national courts, proving decisive for the outcome of a judgment.

With reference to the question of whether the principles of European law have been expressly incorporated in the various domestic systems, rather varied positions emerged; however, it is possible to state that while in the Mediterranean countries the incorporation of the general principles of European law, in an explicit manner, has taken place, albeit with different nuances, in the northern and central European countries this has not been the case. In most of the questionnaire states, general principles of European law are invoked and taken into account in judicial practice even in matters for which there is not yet harmonized European Union legislation, or even to disapply, or interpret in a manner consistent with European principles, national rules that conflict with them.

With particular reference to the principle of reliance, most states have reported it to be a principle that has wide and transversal application, which has its basis in constitutional charters or because it is incorporated in certain legal texts and can lead to the annulment of the administrative act adopted in violation of it. Among the exceptions, it is worth mentioning: France, where the principle of reliance does not exist in national legislation, a reason why case law has played a fundamental role in the application of it, like the principle of legal certainty; and Norway, where the principle of reliance can only be invoked in liability suits against the public administration. In fact, therefore, the annulment of an administrative act for violation of the principle of reliance is more theoretical than practical eventuality.

With reference to the principle of good administration, to which Article 41 of the CDFUE alludes, it appears to be applied in most states across the board, although Art. 41 of the CDFUE does not have a counterpart in national legislation, also being able to lead, in the event of violation, to the annulment of the administrative act: this, for example, in the case of a lack of continuity of a service, legality, legal certainty, impartiality, the right of the interested party to be heard, the right of access to the acts relating to his or her legal sphere, the use of the addressee's native language in administrative acts. In some states, Article 41 of the CDFUE is considered to apply only with respect to the European institutions, or this principle is considered to essentially concern procedural legality, thus being able to lead to annulment only in cases of "serious violation". Among the exceptions worth mentioning are the United Kingdom and Sweden, which do not consider good administration to be an actionable situation in court.

The principles of necessity and proportionality are applied in all countries, with the exception of Norway and Malta. In some cases, although not explicitly positivized, the principle is implicit in the "proportionality test" that in some states is carried out in annulment processes. The scope of this principle is general, applying to both administrative acts and general provisions, serving as a mechanism for limiting the discretion of the public administration, which requires a balancing of the general and individual interest. The application of the principle of proportionality in judicial practice has expanded considerably, partly driven by precedents from the EU Court of Justice or the EDU Court.

The judicial practice of other states is taken into account for the purpose of applying principles derived from EU law, but mostly on an occasional basis: it is noted, in this regard, that the case law of the German Constitutional Court is the reference for various foreign jurisdictions, albeit on different matters (Austria as to the right to asylum, the

Czech Republic as to the principle of legitimate expectations, France as to the principle of proportionality; etc.). Some states have stated that precedents from the EDU Court and the EU Court of Justice are also occasionally considered.
Finally, it appears that in most states principles are identified that are considered common and, as such, considered to be a source of general principles of European law, as stated in Art. 6(3) TEU: the 'identification of such rights is carried out essentially, on the basis of the case law of the EU Court of Justice or the EDU Court, but sometimes also taking into consideration the case law of the ACA member states.
Some principles appear to be applied in judicial practice in a generalized and across-the-board manner.
This is the case with the principle of non-discrimination and gender equality, which is considered a fundamental right that renders unjustified privileges based on differences in personal characteristics, such as race, language, religion, and ideology; the principle of non-discrimination is considered implicit in that of equality. Some states have also pointed out the existence of specific norms in their legal systems to protect equality and non-discrimination: interestingly, these are particularly the states in the Balkan area (Czech Republic, Hungary, Slovakia, Bulgaria), which in the early 2000s passed laws aimed at promoting equal opportunities between men and women or having the purpose of setting criteria for verifying compliance with these values. In contrast, Sweden, the United Kingdom and Lithuania reported that the principle of equality is applied only in specific areas.
The principle of protection of minorities and fragile persons, appears to be applied, in most states, but with reference to specific areas With regard to the type of justification of administrative acts that infringe on fundamental or minority rights, it was found that in most countries it is required that such acts carry an enhanced justification, particularly in decisions on asylum (Austria, Bulgaria, Slovakia) and eviction of housing, where almost unanimously a justification that accounts for the balancing of conflicting interests is considered essential. However, as many as 13 countries (France, Germany, Hungary, Malta, Poland, Portugal, Slovenia, Sweden, Norway, the United Kingdom, Croatia, Estonia and Italy) stated that, on the one hand, in general no special justification is required for the administration to take measures detrimental to fragile groups, and on the other hand that in the absence of such a justification the act is not necessarily invalid.
States were asked whether in judicial practice administrative acts based on artificial intelligence or predictive mechanisms were challenged by invoking the principles of transparency, equality, and non-discrimination. In most cases the answer given was negative, albeit with some distinctions.
The questionnaire also sought to highlight the existence and application in judicial practice of general principles pertaining to specific subjects.
With regard to the area of administrative organization and administrative procedure, it was found that in most of the states surveyed the principles of decentralization and subsidiarity; the principle of publicity and transparency; the principle of proportionality; the principle of impartiality; and the principle of "self-correction" are applied; more divided were the responses given with regard to the principle of "non-formality," and the principle of gratuitousness.

In the area of administrative sanctions, the applicability of general principles concerning criminal sanctions was investigated. Many of the questionnaire states responded that the principles of criminal law are also applied to administrative sanctions, with different nuances: sometimes it is the legislature that regulate criminal and administrative proceedings in a similar manner, in other cases the homologation of the two proceedings concerns certain general principles, and has occurred by the jurisprudence of the Supreme Courts, and in the wake of the pronouncements of the European Court of Human Rights Many of the states have therefore reported to apply, to administrative sanctions: the principle of presumption of innocence and the right not to incriminate oneself; the principle of legality, whereby all elements defining the offense must be predetermined; the principle of non-retroactivity of the sanctioning rule; the principle of culpability; the principle of proportionality; the right to legal aid (although this right does not always also imply the state's obligation to pay the attorney's fees; in some cases it is limited to administrative sanctions of a punitive nature); the right to be heard; the principle that the act imposing a sanction must be reasoned; the principle that administrative offenses must be contested within a specified period of time; the principle of judicial protection; and the principle of double jeopardy. Regarding, however, the principle of separation of investigating and adjudicating authority, only a few countries have reported that they apply it.

In the area of subsidies and state aid, it has been found that in many states the principle of proportionality is applied in order to modulate or mitigate the consequences of not meeting the necessary requirements for accessing the benefit (Croatia, Cyprus, Czech Republic, Belgium, Estonia, Finland, Hungary, France, Luxembourg, Portugal, Slovakia, Slovenia and Norway).

In contrast, the area of public contracts tends to be subject to specific regulations or general principles. In the vast majority of countries there is a common legislative basis, but specific principles are applied at the stage of advertising the notice, selecting the contractor and awarding and concluding the contract: these principles are those of par condicio among candidates, non-discrimination, proportionality, transparency, free competition and economic efficiency, absence of conflict with the public interest, and best relationship between quality and supply. On the other hand, general principles, *i.e.*, those applicable to contracts between private parties, are applied to the next stage, execution. In France, the specificity of the principles applicable to public contracts is also evident in relation to the execution phase of the contract.

In the field of urban planning and the environment, they are applied. In almost all states, the precautionary principle, the polluter pays principle, the principles of sustainability, conservation of resources, efficient use of resources, prevention of waste in the use of resources, the principle of prevention, the right to a healthy environment.

In the area of taxation, one finds in the majority of states the application of the principle of legality, according to which tax penalties can be imposed only on the basis of formal rules; the principle of the economic capacity of the taxpayer (it is not applied in Latvia and Lithuania and the Czech Republic); the principle of equality and generality (the exception is the United Kingdom, where there is no such principle, which is the reason why tax legislation must rather comply with the principle of non-discrimination set out in the

CDFUE: different individuals can be taxed differently, without this being unlawful, as long as the principle of non-discrimination is not violated); principle of progressivity and its limit, according to which taxation cannot be excessively heavy: the application of this principle has also been reported by states, such as Sweden, whose level of taxation is known to be very high; Other principles mentioned by the questionnaire states are: the principle of non-retroactivity of rules imposing taxes, the principle of exclusive responsibility of the legislature and the principle of participation (Portugal): the principle of limited duration of tax regulations, the principle of allowing knowledge of facts, protection of personal data, good faith and feasibility (Serbia).

# General Report
# Madrid, 21 Novembre 2022

## I. General principles of law in the system of sources

**Question 1.**

**What place and function do general principles of law have in the system of sources of your country's legal system?**

- **They are applied where there are gaps in the law.**
- **They may be applied directly, even to the extent of displacing the initially applicable written law and prevailing over it.**

**Summary of answers**

- They are applied where there are gaps in the law (Austria, Belgium, Croatia, Czech Republic, Spain, Estonia, Finland, Germany, Italy, Lithuania, Portugal, Poland, Romania, Slovakia, Slovenia, Sweden, Norway)
- They may be applied directly, even to the extent of displacing the initially applicable written law and prevailing over it (Bulgaria, Cyprus, France, Greece, Hungary, Latvia, Luxembourg, Netherlands)

Most of the national reports (17 of the countries that answered the questionnaire, including Austria, Belgium, Croatia, Czech Republic, Spain, Estonia, Finland, Germany, Italy, Lithuania, Portugal, Poland, Romania, Slovakia, Slovenia, Sweden, Norway) indicate that general principles are applied where there are gaps in the law and are therefore subject to the written law.

Conversely, eight of the countries (Bulgaria, Cyprus, France, Greece, Hungary, Latvia, Luxembourg, Netherlands) confirm the feasibility of directly applying general principles, which may displace the initially applicable written law and prevail over the solution that would result from its application.

In this regard, Bulgaria indicates that although most general principles of law have been incorporated into positive law, based on the premise of Article 5 of the Civil Judicial Code that these are applied where there are gaps in the law, the case law of Bulgaria's Supreme Administrative Court has determined that these principles are directly applicable, and may pass over a normative provision that is in contradiction with the principle concerned.

Cyprus states that the general principles of law have been formed in a traditional manner by the judiciary through case law. However, in 1999 the developed general principles of administrative law were codified in a statute to safeguard administrative decision-making through the establishment of rules. Thus, the legal framework of administrative principles is governed by the General Principles of Administrative Law provided for in the 1999 Law (L. 158(I)/1999).

In France, general principles are generally subordinated to the written law. However, as the French Council of State has affirmed, there are some general principles that have constitutional value and are therefore binding on the law, such as the principle of equality and the principle of continuity in the provision of public service.

Greece states that according to case law, only those general principles with constitutional value can displace and prevail over the initially applicable written law.

Hungary states that the presence of the general principles of law can be observed at different levels of the entire body of sources of law in its legal system, being present not only in the binding framework of the Fundamental Law of Hungary of 1 January 2012, but also in the regulation of various fundamental rights, as constitutional requirements expressed in the decisions of the Constitutional Court and as principles in various general and sector-specific laws.

Latvia's report indicates that since the general principles of law arise from natural law, they constitute a criterion of legitimacy for written laws and for the legislator itself. Therefore, written laws must comply with the general principles of law, and it follows from this that these principles prevail over the written law.

Luxembourg states that traditionally, both the Council of State and the contentious-administrative courts had indicated the existence of general principles of law that have legislative value. However, the Constitutional Court has recently identified general principles of law that have supra-legislative value and are enshrined as general principles with constitutional value.

The Netherlands confirms that the general principles may also be applied directly, even to the extent that they prevail over the applicable written law, in what has been doctrinally referred to as "*contra legem* application of general principles". This *contra legem* application of general principles has been accepted by the Supreme Court of the Netherlands since the 1970s, although it makes it clear that there are limitations on their application (for example, the limitation provided for in Article 120 of the Constitution itself).

Serbia indicates that the general principles of law (including some derived from European Union law) are incorporated into the Constitution, laws and other written rules.

The United Kingdom, for its part, cannot offer an unambiguous answer to this question given the existence of two predominant sources of law in its legal system: written law and common law. Primary laws enacted by the UK Parliament take precedence over all other sources of law under the constitutional principle of parliamentary sovereignty. For legal matters and questions on which the Parliament has not enacted any legislation, or where a law requires interpretation, the law is given by common law. Common law is an evolving set of rules and principles developed by judges through case law over the centuries. Common law does not allow for any gaps: in principle, it will always provide a legal rule that must be applied in order to answer a legal problem. A number of fundamental constitutional principles and rights have been developed through common law, these being the closest things to "general principles of law" presented by the United Kingdom. Thus, although general principles cannot displace or prevail over primary laws passed by the Parliament, they can influence the way in which the courts interpret them.

Spain reports that Article 1.4 of the Spanish Civil Code states that "General legal principles shall apply in the absence of applicable written law or custom, without prejudice to the fact that they contribute to shaping the legal system". Based on this precept, case law indicates that general principles of law can be successfully cited in judicial practice only where there are no legal or customary rules. Thus, the Supreme Court of Spain's judgment 107/2005 of 3 March states that principles of law, "as subsidiary sources, after written law and custom, can be invoked only by justifying their strict necessity due to a deficiency in the written or customary legal system". However, the great majority of the most relevant principles in judicial practice have been incorporated into positive law through their recognition and inclusion in written laws, so that they tend to be invoked directly through citation of the laws in which they are enshrined.

**Question 2.**

**Can it be said that the most relevant general principles of law in your culture and legal tradition have been positivised, *i.e.* enshrined with legal status in your country's judicial system?**

- **Yes**
- **Yes, the most relevant ones (please indicate briefly the most notable of these)**
- **No**

**Summary of answers.**

- Yes (Bulgaria, Croatia, Cyprus, Czech Republic, Estonia, Finland, Germany, Greece, Hungary, Italy, Latvia, Lithuania, Poland, Portugal, Slovakia, Slovenia, Serbia, Spain, Sweden, Norway, United Kingdom)
- Yes, the most relevant ones (Austria, Belgium, France, Romania)
- No (Malta, Netherlands)

For the most part, the national reports gave an unambiguously positive response to this question, so we can say that the general principles of law have found explicit normative support in their various legal systems (see, in this regard, the reports of Bulgaria, Croatia, Cyprus, Czech Republic, Estonia, Finland, Germany, Greece, Hungary, Italy, Latvia, Lithuania, Poland, Portugal, Slovakia, Slovenia, Serbia, Spain, Sweden, Norway, United Kingdom).

Four countries said that the most relevant general principles have been enshrined in written rules.

In this regard, Austria indicates that the main principles of Public Law have been positivised in constitutional, procedural or administrative rules. These include the principles of *ex officio* investigation, the right to be heard, the principle of impartiality and reasoning, the right to a fair trial, the principle of *non bis in idem*, the principle of legality and definition of the constituent elements of the offence, and the principle of legitimate expectation.

Belgium indicates that among the most important principles to have found explicit normative recognition are the principles of equality and non-discrimination, the principle of reasoning (formal and material) for individual administrative acts, and the principle of proportionality (e.g. for authorisations of access to a service activity). In the field of public procurement, this is also true for the principles of equality, non-discrimination, transparency and proportionality.

France has a set of general principles of law identified by the Council of State that are unwritten and apply "even without a text", such as the principle of prohibition of dismissal of a pregnant woman on the grounds of circumstances related to her maternity within the framework of a contract under public law. However, certain principles have been expressly enshrined in positive law, such as the right to recourse for abuse of power, the principle of job reclassification, respect for privacy, and the protection of human dignity.

Luxembourg indicates the existence of a set of general principles that arise from case law but have been enshrined in legislation since the 1970s, and that seek to establish a set of procedural guarantees for citizens in their relations with the Public Administration. These include the principles of reasoning of administrative acts, good administration, rights of defence, the necessary participation of the citizen – to the extent possible – in the administrative decision, the principle of procedural collaboration by the Administration, the right of the citizen to be heard and to obtain the administrative record, and the Administration's obligation to provide the citizen with the necessary information.

Romania indicates, by way of example, that the body of general principles applicable to the Public Administration, as expressly set out in the Romanian Administrative Code, include the principle of legality, the principle of equality, the principle of transparency, the principle of proportionality, the principle of satisfaction of the public interest, the principle of impartiality, the principle of continuity and the principle of adaptability.

It should be noted that out of all the countries that replied to the questionnaire, only Malta and the Netherlands gave a negative answer to this question. In this regard, the Netherlands' report states that although there are a considerable number of principles that have been positivised in its legislation (duty of diligence, prohibition of misuse of power, the principle of proportionality and the duty of reasoning, among others), these are not the most relevant, pointing out that the principles of legal certainty and legitimate expectation have not been expressly reflected in the administrative rules.

**Question 3.**

**In the judicial practice of Public Law, are general principles of law frequently invoked and applied as a basis for decisions?**

- **They are frequently invoked and applied, and are relevant and decisive in the**

**settlement of disputes.**
- **They are frequently invoked and applied, although generally in a complementary manner, to reinforce challenging arguments based primarily on the interpretation and application of written rules.**
- **They are not frequently invoked and applied as a basis for decisions.**

**Summary of answers.**

- They are frequently invoked and applied, and are relevant and decisive in the settlement of disputes. (Austria, Bulgaria, Belgium, Cyprus, France, Hungary, Latvia, Luxembourg, Netherlands, United Kingdom)
- They are frequently invoked and applied, although generally in a complementary manner, to reinforce challenging arguments based primarily on the interpretation and application of written rules. (Spain, Croatia, Czech Republic, Estonia, Finland, Greece, Lithuania, Malta, Poland, Portugal, Romania, Slovakia, Slovenia, Norway, Sweden)
- They are not frequently invoked and applied as a basis for decisions. (Germany)

A notable majority of countries confirm that general principles of law are frequently applied in their legal systems (25 countries).

Thus, ten countries (Austria, Bulgaria, Belgium, Cyprus, France, Hungary, Latvia, Luxembourg, Netherlands, United Kingdom) state that these principles are not only frequently invoked and applied, but are also relevant and decisive for the resolution of disputes, thus acquiring considerable importance in those systems.

Meanwhile, fifteen countries report that in their legal systems, general principles are applied or invoked as a complement to the written rules, contributing to their proper interpretation.

Countries such as Austria, Greece, Spain, Slovenia and Serbia base this answer on the fact that the most relevant general principles of law have been incorporated, for the most part, into positive law, including in rules of a constitutional nature. This is why, if these principles are mentioned, it is often because the written rules that include and enshrine them are directly invoked.

Other countries such as Italy, Lithuania, Malta, Poland, Portugal, Romania and Norway say that although principles of law generally have a subsidiary role in the hierarchy of sources of law, they are often invoked in judicial practice. Thus, they serve not only to reinforce arguments based on the written rules, but also as tools for interpreting those rules when they are ambiguous or uncertain.

Slovakia, for its part, offers a mixed solution, stating that in its practical application, the bodies of the Public Administration make their decisions according to the letter of the written laws, but in disputed cases the general principles of law are taken directly as the basis of the decision (e.g. principles of public procurement).

The only country to say that the general principles of law are not frequently invoked and applied as a basis for decisions is Germany. In this regard, the German report justifies this answer from the perspective that most of the general principles have been transferred to the written laws and are therefore directly applicable.

**Question 4.**

**If you have answered yes to the previous question, can it be said that the invocation and application of general principles of law is done in a general and transverse way, in all areas or matters of Public Law?**

**Summary of answers.**

All the States surveyed gave a positive answer to this question, confirming that their courts apply general principles of law in a general and transverse way, in all areas or matters of Public Law.

**Question 5.**

**In your country's legal system, are there general principles specific to Administrative Law, independent of other general principles of law that are applied interchangeably in all sectors of the legal system, such as civil, criminal or labour matters?**

**Summary of answers.**

Almost all the States consulted confirm that they have potentially applicable principles specific to Administrative Law alongside other general principles.

The only exception is Croatia, where there are no general principles specific to Administrative Law.

As for Italy, although it has principles specific to Administrative Law, it adds that these exclude and displace the application of the other general principles, explaining that in its legal system, the general principles relating to Administrative Law are specific and included in both the Constitution and the written law, and may prevail over other general principles relating to different matters, as a result of the weighting exercised by the courts when deciding on a particular case.

As regards the taxonomy of these principles, it should be emphasised that many countries concur in including in their catalogues the principles of good administration (the Netherlands even differentiates between good procedural administration and good substantive administration), efficiency and effectiveness, legality and transparency.

Apart from this structural and common set of principles, it is rewarding to note the presence of other more endemic types, such as legitimate expectation (Germany); official secrecy (Austria); public service nature of the Administration (Czech Republic); substantial truth and amicable settlement (Slovakia); continuity of public service (Greece); one-stop shop and objective research (Lithuania); subsidiarity (Romania); officiality (Sweden); and electronic administration, open administration and cooperation with the European Union as set out in the Portuguese Code of Administrative Procedure.

Finally, the United Kingdom also has principles of Administrative Law that can be applied with other general principles, many of which have been developed by common law. Although certain principles of customary law will be relevant only to matters of public and administrative law, these types of dispute may require the application of general principles of a different nature.

## II. Common incorporation of general principles of law: European Union and horizontal dialogue

**Question 6.**

**Has your country's administrative legal system patently incorporated the general principles of European Union law?**

**Summary of answers.**

With regard to the incorporation of the general principles of European Union law into national legal systems, the survey is heterogeneous in this respect.

Thus, in attempting to establish some kind of systematic model, it can be seen that the major Mediterranean States say they have not experienced major difficulties in incorporating the general principles of European Union law into their existing bodies of law. This is the case with France, which has accepted the binding nature of the general principles of European Union law for national acts since the Council of State clearly affirmed in 2001 the applicability to domestic law of the general principles of Union law through the Assembly's Freymuth and FNSEA rulings.

Italy too embraces these types of principles, irrespective of the fact that the general principles of impartiality and good administration are enshrined in Article 97 of the Italian constitution, since this does not preclude the incorporation of the general principles of European Union law.

Portugal, meanwhile, emphasises the role of the national legislator in the transposition of Directives. Finally, Spain once again answers in the affirmative on this point, although it admits that there has been some complexity when institutions outside its legal tradition have been incorporated into Spanish law, such as the transposition of the Directive on services in the internal market, which entailed limitation of the traditional administrative "authorisation regime", with other mechanisms such as self-responsibility or citizen self-control gaining ground.

Cyprus, for its part, confirms that most of the general principles of EU law applied by the Court of Justice of the European Union in determining the legality of administrative measures, such as legal certainty, equal treatment, proportionality, good administration and respect for fundamental rights, are principles enshrined in national legislation, stressing that they are also safeguarded by the judiciary in established judicial precedents.

Of the Baltic states, only Latvia does not incorporate the general principles of Union law. Estonia and Lithuania frequently recognise and apply them in their legal systems, with many of them coinciding with legal principles derived from their own constitutional charters.

Conversely, it should be noted that in Nordic countries such as Finland and Sweden, no special or specific incorporation of these supranational principles has been necessary, since they were already recognised and enshrined in the country's legislation and procedural practice. In the same situation are Central European States such as Germany, Slovakia (Article 7 of its Constitution provides that "The legally binding acts of the European Communities and the European Union shall prevail over the laws of the Slovak Republic"), the Netherlands and Poland, in contrast to neighbouring States that do fit them into their systems such as Austria, Croatia, Serbia, Hungary, Romania and the Czech Republic, with the latter also acknowledging problems of fit with regard, for example, to the principle of public participation in procedures relating to environmental protection, where the Czech legislator's decision to restrict the access of environmental NGOs to the procedures under the Construction Law caused controversy.

Norway is a singular case, since despite not being a member of the European Union, it applies the relevant principles in the context of the European Economic Area (EEA) Agreement of 2016, incorporating them through an adaptation of "EEA law" which provides that the Agreement applies as Norwegian law and that in the event of a conflict between a legislative act designed to ensure compliance with EEA law and other provisions of Norwegian law, the rule of compliance with EEA law will prevail.

Finally, the United Kingdom does not consider this incorporation of the general principles of European Union law into its domestic system to be necessary, although many of these principles find expression in customary law. Thus, Section 6 of the European Union (Withdrawal) Act of 2018 establishes that the validity, meaning or effect of any retained EU law is to be decided in accordance with the general principles of EU law as they stood on 31 [sic] November 2020.

**Question 7.**

**Is it common in your country's judicial practice for the specific general principles of European Union law to be invoked and taken into account in areas where there is no regulatory harmonisation?**

- **Yes, for certain matters**
- **No, not generally**

**Summary of answers.**

Most of the States that responded to this question answered in the affirmative, citing circumstances in which the general principles of European Union law are frequently invoked and taken into account in areas where there is no harmonisation of legislation. This was mentioned, for example, by the Czech Republic, Greece, Slovenia and Spain with reference to the area of non-harmonised tax law. Poland also highlighted, in particular, the applicability of the right to good administration in those areas that are not harmonised. Italy indicates that the general principles of EU law are invoked and taken into account on a par with the general principles of its domestic law. Bulgaria, for its part, highlighted the principle of proportionality.

Some States answered "no" to this question: Austria states that these principles are invoked and taken into account only if they can be drawn from its domestic legislation, as is also the case with Finland. France, Malta and Germany stress that they are invoked only in the area of European Union law. Slovakia's answer is also negative, as are those of Norway and the United Kingdom, even though these are States that do not belong or have ceased to belong to the European Union. In particular, we see in the case of the UK that, irrespective of the above, almost all of the principles find expression in its own "common law".

**Question 8.**

**When applying the general principles set out in European Union law, and when it is found that the general European principle applicable to the dispute in question conflicts in some way with national law, has the dispute been resolved through a solution involving the displacement and non-application of the national rule in order to give way to the general European principle?**

- **Yes**
- **This solution has been chosen in some cases, while in others different solutions or answers have been used**

**Summary of answers.**

The great majority of States that responded to this question answered in the affirmative.

In particular, France notes that in the decision on the case of the National Union for the Pharmaceutical Industry (SNIP) of 3 December 2001, the French Administrative Court gave a clear and definitive opinion on the delicate question of the ranking of national law and the general principles of the Union's legal system in the hierarchy of rules. The Council of State reviewed the law in the light of two general principles of EU law, namely legal certainty and legitimate expectation, thus accepting that these principles have a supra-legislative value. In the wake of the Council of State's SNIP ruling, other decisions refer to the general principles of the EU legal system, stressing that they have "the same value as the Treaties".

Malta underlined and highlighted the principle of consistent interpretation in its answer to this question. And Romania says that since the general principles of European Union law are, together with primary sources and secondary law, one of the sources of European law, in the event of a conflict between the national rules and a general principle of the European Union, the domestic judge must apply the principle of supremacy of the Union, while stressing the importance of the pre-judicial mechanism before the European Court of Justice.

The answer to this question from Norway and the United Kingdom is negative.

**Question 9.**

**Is it common in judicial practice for the principle of legitimate expectation to be invoked and taken into account?**

- **Yes, as a transversal principle**
- **Yes, but only in certain sector-specific matters and areas harmonised by Union law (please indicate what these are)**
- **No.**

**Summary of answers.**

The majority of States responded to this question by indicating that it is common for the principle of legitimate expectation to invoke and take into account as a transversal principle.

Some of these States said that this principle arises directly from their constitutional texts in the sense interpreted by their constitutional courts. These include Austria, Czech Republic, Estonia, Luxembourg, Portugal and Slovenia. It is a principle that has been incorporated into domestic legal texts in States such as Finland, Lithuania and Poland.

Some States responded by pointing out the connection between the principle of legitimate expectation and other principles. In this regard, Cyprus linked it to good faith and *stare decisis*, Austria to the principle of equality, and the United Kingdom to the doctrine of *estoppel*.

The Netherlands, for its part, makes it clear that the scope of application of this principle is broader in its own case than in other States, since it can also operate *contra legem*.

The answer was negative in the case of Norway and also in the case of France. However, in the latter case, it is clear that this principle is applicable in the field of European Union law and that it has given rise to intense doctrinal and jurisprudential debate.

In the cases of Hungary, Romania, Sweden and the United Kingdom, the answer was that the invocation and consideration of this principle is limited to certain sector-specific areas harmonised by Union law.

**Question 10.**

**Can taking the principle of legitimate expectation into account even result in the annulment of administrative decisions that are contrary to or violate those principles?**

- **Yes**
- **No, these principles are applied only in order to provide for compensation or reparation when they are violated in some way by the decisions of the Administration.**

**Summary of answers.**

Yes, in some specific cases.

All the countries except Norway chose this option, although in most cases it is stated either that it does not happen frequently, that it is subject to strict conditions or that it is taken into consideration to modulate the analysis of the contested measure's compliance with the law.

Spain states that the scope of this principle has, for the most part, concerned the analysis of the Administration's liability, and the United Kingdom that, if it is possible for the Administration to act fairly without satisfying the principle of legitimate expectation, the court may then grant a different remedy or benefit, or order the Administration to consider its decision taking legitimate expectation into account as a relevant factor.

The Netherlands, while stating that violation of this principle, as set out in domestic law, can result in the annulment of administrative decisions, adds that it is more difficult for the application of the European principle of legitimate expectation to lead to such a result, since that principle sets higher requirements than its Dutch equivalent. Sweden states that this principle has not had a major impact on case law in cases that do not concern EU law.

Luxembourg states that a *contra legem* application of the principle of legitimate expectation would not in principle be possible, but that, since the enshrinement of this principle by its Constitutional Court, this solution should be called upon to evolve, although the administrative court has not yet had the occasion to give its opinion.

France states that the principle of legitimate expectation does not exist in its domestic law, and that the role of the judge has been decisive in the evolution of the principles of protection of legitimate expectation and legal certainty.

Norway is the only country to have answered in the negative, as it considers that these principles play a role only in order to provide for reparation or compensation when they are violated in some way by the decisions of the Administration. It adds that the expectations of an individual will not normally be compensated, although this will depend on the basis of the expectations and on the circumstances that led to the decision against them.

**Question 11.**

**Has the "principle of good administration" referred to in Article 41 of the Charter of Fundamental Rights of the European Union been adopted and applied in your country's judicial practice?**

- **Yes, as a transversal principle**
- **Only in certain sector-specific matters and areas harmonised by Union law (please indicate what these are)**
- **Not commonly applied**

**Summary of answers.**

Most of the countries apply this principle in their judicial practice, even where it is not reflected as such in the respective constitutions or national laws, since it is implicit in other principles that do form part of their domestic systems.

Some of the principles cited by the above-mentioned countries in which the principle of good administration is considered to be implicit are those of objectivity, effectiveness, impartiality, the right to be heard, access to personal records, and the right to obtain a reasoned decision without undue delay.

Romania answers that it is applied only in certain matters or areas, citing the exercise of public functions and the supervision of financial activity.

Austria, France, Malta, Norway, the Netherlands, the United Kingdom and Sweden answered in the negative, although Malta states that despite not being specifically provided for in its domestic law, it is commonly applied in judicial practice.

Austria, France and the Netherlands state that Article 41 of the Charter of Fundamental Rights of the European Union concerns the institutions of the European Union and does not refer directly to the Member States or their institutions. The Netherlands says that the principle of good administration reflects general legal principles of EU law, and is applied by the Dutch courts when a case falls within the scope of application of Union law.

The United Kingdom states that the Charter of Fundamental Rights of the European Union was not identified in the European Union (Withdrawal) Act 2018 as European Union law to be retained, and therefore no longer has any application in the United Kingdom.

Sweden states that although it has been introduced into national law, it is not regarded as an enforceable individual right.

And Norway, while stating that much of the content of the principle of good administration is applied in Norwegian law, is not established as a specific principle or right of the individual to have his/her affairs handled fairly and within a reasonable time.

**Question 12.**

**Can taking the principle of good administration into account even result in the annulment of administrative decisions that are contrary to or violate that principle?**

- **Yes, in some specific cases.**
- **This would never be possible because, among other reasons, this principle applies solely as a guideline for conduct within the Administration and cannot be invoked by the citizen.**

**Summary of answers.**

The majority of countries answer in the affirmative, with some of them linking the annulment of administrative decisions to the violation of proximate principles or to the violation of one or more of the components of that principle.

Some of the principles or rights identified by the different countries that can be invoked and whose violation can lead to the annulment of the administrative act are continuity of public services, legality, legal certainty, effectiveness, impartiality, the right to be heard, to have access to one's own personal file, to obtain a reasoned decision without undue delay, and to use one's mother tongue.

Germany states that this principle primarily concerns the formal legality of an administrative act, and procedural defects will result in annulment of the decision only in the event of very serious violations. Austria states that the principle of good administration, as laid down in Article 41 of the Charter of Fundamental Rights of the European Union, concerns the institutions of the EU, not national institutions, but that the principle of good administration is also enshrined in its law on administrative procedure. The Czech Republic, for its part, states that although this is a principle that serves mainly as a guide for the conduct of the Administration, it can nevertheless be invoked and its violation can result in the annulment of the administrative decision. Slovakia notes that in the field of university self-government, on which the general provisions of the administrative procedures do not apply, the Supreme Court has repeatedly annulled decisions of public bodies with reference to the European regulation on the principles of good administration.

Portugal, the United Kingdom and Sweden answer in the negative. Portugal states that control of the courts is in line with strict legality, so it can hardly, in itself, be a cause of nullity. The United Kingdom justifies its answer that the principle is not applicable in its country, although various customary rules of public law can be explained as aspects of good administration. Sweden states that it is not regarded as an enforceable individual right.

**Question 13.**

**Is it common in judicial practice for the principle of necessity and proportionality of administrative measures that limit or restrict access to or the exercise of an economic activity to be invoked and taken into account?**

**Summary of answers.**

The majority of the participating States concur in assigning a positivist or basic character to this principle, violation of which results in the nullity of the administrative act or general provision. There are only two exceptions: Malta and Norway, where this principle is not applied.

But this principle is not only administrative in nature: in some States it is either enshrined in the constitution itself or elevated to the status of a constitutional principle. Countries that have it enshrined in their constitution include Greece (Articles 5 and 25 of the Greek Constitution guarantee the right to economic freedom and the principle of proportionality), Italy (under

Article 41 of the Italian Constitution, the right to economic initiative can only be limited for social reasons), Latvia (Article 1 of the Constitution) and Slovenia (the Constitution uses it as a criterion for assessing interference in an individual human right – private property, free economic initiative, etc.).

As a constitutional principle, it results from a declaration to that effect made by the respective Constitutional Court: this is the case in Romania, whose Constitutional Court has declared that the principle of proportionality must be recognised as a constitutional principle (Decision 157/1998 and Judgment 161/1998), and also in Luxembourg, where the Constitutional Court, based on the application of this principle as a general principle, has formally declared it to be a principle with constitutional value since the judgment of 19 March 2021.

These categories of necessity and proportionality can also be used as a principle implicit in the constitutional order as part of what is known as the "proportionality test": this is the case in the Czech Republic (in proceedings for annulment of legal provisions) or the Netherlands (whose Council of State declares that this proportionality test encompasses the three elements of appropriateness, necessity and proportionality *stricto sensu*). For its part, Estonia regards a restriction of the right to take action as a cause of unconstitutionality.

From an administrative perspective, it is stated that the principle of necessity and proportionality operates in a general way as a parameter of legality of the actions of the public authorities, both in the adoption of administrative acts and in the adoption of general provisions, and is applied in all decision-making areas (Cyprus) or in all legal relations between the Administration and citizens (Latvia).

It also has a characteristic projection that manifests itself as a mechanism for limiting administrative discretion, weighing the general interest against the individual interest. Countries that answered along these lines included Portugal (restrictive measures must observe "fair proportion" in respect of the cost/benefit weighting), Cyprus (proportionality consists of the correlation between the administrative decision and the legitimate purpose for which it is designed), Latvia (the restriction of individual rights is justified only insofar as it represents a significant benefit to society), Serbia (the imposition of obligations must be effected through the adoption of measures that are less restrictive or more beneficial for the party concerned, as long as they achieve the aim of the regulation) and the Netherlands (the adverse consequences of an order directed at the person concerned cannot be disproportionate to the ends pursued by that order).

The application of this principle in the judicial practice of the participating States is becoming more and more widespread, with emphasis on its application in specific areas such as: the revision of restrictive measures during the COVID-19 pandemic (Czech Republic and Finland); the exercise of certain professions, notably the business of photography (Austria); public procurement, taxation and access to and use of European funds (Romania, Court of Cassation judgments of 22 February and 10 June 2021); taxation (Slovakia, judgment of the Constitutional Court of 29 June 2010); taxes and regulation of public advertising fees (Slovenia); restriction of use of beach property and prohibition of reforestation (Sweden); disputes concerning the Administration's refusal to grant a licence or permit necessary for the exercise of an economic activity (Bulgaria); and in matters of public order and administrative policy, freedom of assembly, freedom of trade and industry, and as a criterion for reviewing administrative sanctions or certain regulatory decisions on economic activity, such as concentration authorisations (France, Benjamin judgment of 19 May 1933, Council of State judgments of 22 June 1951, 13 March 1968 and 21 December 2012).

This application is carried out not only within the framework of the principles of the legal system concerned, but also in the light of the case law of the Court of Justice of the European Union (France) or of the European Convention on Human Rights (United Kingdom).

**Question 14.**

**With regard to any of the above principles (legitimate expectation, necessity, proportionality or good administration) or other principles, has your country's Supreme Court taken into consideration the interpretation and manner of application of these principles by other European national high jurisdictions?**

**Summary of answers.**

The answers given by the participating States range from those that do not take the decisions of other jurisdictions into consideration (Croatia, Hungary, Lithuania, Poland, Sweden, Norway and the United Kingdom) to those where the case law of other States is occasionally taken into account, either on the basis of the proximity or affinity of the legal systems or in the prosecution of certain matters. In the first of these two cases – proximity or affinity – we find

Cyprus (in relation to the Greek Council of State, given that its public law applies the Greek administrative system), Greece (whose legal system is inspired by French and German law); Malta (in respect of the jurisdictions of Italy and the United Kingdom); Slovenia (in respect of the jurisdictions of Germany, France, Ireland and Luxembourg); and Slovakia (in respect of the Czech Republic, particularly in matters governed by European Union law).

In the second case, where the case law of other States is occasionally taken into account in respect of certain matters, we find: Austria (which follows the case law of the German Federal Constitutional Court on asylum matters), the Czech Republic (which draws on the case law of the German Federal Constitutional Court with regard to the principle of legitimate trust), France (which relies on the case law of the German Federal Constitutional Court and the CJEU with regard to the principle of proportionality), Italy (with regard to pronouncements concerning COVID-19), Portugal (which is inspired by German constitutional case law with regard to the application of the "metadata law"), and the Netherlands (which is inspired by German case law with regard to the proportionality test).

Some countries single out the taking into consideration of the case law of the CJEU and/or the ECtHR: Latvia, the Netherlands, Luxembourg and Serbia.

Finally, other countries state that they only occasionally take such decisions into consideration, but without giving any further details in this regard: Germany and Romania.

**Question 15.**

**According to Article 6, paragraph 3 of the Treaty on European Union, fundamental rights that result from the constitutional traditions common to the Member States shall constitute general principles of the Union's law. Has your country's Supreme Court identified any of these common constitutional traditions?**

**Summary of answers.**

Most of the participating States answer this question in the affirmative, in the sense that such identification is made especially on the basis of the case law of the Court of Justice of the European Union or of the European Court of Human Rights.

However, we can find some cases in which the answer is nuanced. For example, Germany states that such identification can be found in the case law of the Federal Constitutional Court and, to a lesser extent, in that of the Supreme Administrative Court.

Luxembourg states that its Constitutional Court, particularly in Judgment 146 of 19 March 2021, enshrines the notion of a common basis in the recognition of certain fundamental rights provided for in parallel by the Luxembourg Constitution, the European Convention on Human Rights and the Charter of Fundamental Rights of the European Union.

Spain says that the Spanish Supreme Court has taken into consideration decisions of the French Court of Cassation concerning the application of principles associated with the freedom to provide services and with proportionality in matters of town planning that affect the exercise of economic activities (e.g. properties for tourist use), as well as decisions of the German Constitutional Court in relation to the limits of the principle of economic capacity. Recently, in the judicial response to the COVID-19 pandemic, the Spanish Supreme Court has applied general principles of law similar to those considered by other Supreme Courts within the scope of the ACA (such as the French Council of State or thc Italian Council of State), arriving at common solutions to ensure the upholding of constitutional values or the defence of public order.

Estonia states that, while it is not known that the Administrative Law Chamber of the Supreme Court has made explicit reference to the case law of other European national high jurisdictions, the case law of other countries is investigated as a source of inspiration when difficult and novel disputes are encountered.

France states that the domestic courts interpret and apply the provisions relating to fundamental rights in a variable manner, making it difficult to identify common bases between the Member States. However, it says that rights such as privacy and a fair trial or the principles of legality and proportionality in relation to criminal offences and penalties derive from constitutional traditions common to the Member States and identified as such by the Council of State. In this regard, it notes that the right to education guaranteed by Article 14 of the Charter of Fundamental Rights of the European Union and the principle of legality and proportionality of criminal offences and penalties enshrined in Article 49 of the Charter derive from rules that were already common to many Member States.

Conversely, the Netherlands and Norway say that no such identification is made, with Norway pointing out that such a link with the CJEU has not been considered because it is not a member of the European Union.

## III. General principles and fundamental rights

**Question 16.**

**What status and importance does the principle of non-discrimination and gender equality have in your country's judicial practice?**

- **It is a principle commonly and generally taken into consideration, in a transversal manner.**
- **It is a principle that is taken into consideration and applied in certain legal relations and sector-specific areas.**

**Summary of answers.**

The principle of equality is considered to be a fundamental right by almost all the surveyed countries, and is seen as inspiring judicial practice in a transversal manner. For France, this is the principle that governs the operation of public services, as outlined in 1951 by the Council of State.

It is a generalised criterion that the principle of equality includes gender equality, so that privileges arising from personal characteristics are excluded, and therefore the principle of non-discrimination is implicit.

Finland, for its part, notes that gender equality is the most prolific issue in judicial decisions on the application of the principle since the entry into force of the Law on Equality between Men and Women in 1986. With regard to disability, it refers to a court ruling that found negligence on the part of an airline that did not take reasonable measures to accommodate a disabled person.

In Austria, the Constitutional Court declared it to be objectively unjustified, in the civil realm, for a married woman to be given the option of adding her maiden name when no such provision was made for men. In the area of employment, among others, the age difference between men and women for retirement purposes, or in respect of the right to severance pay for civil servants, was deemed unconstitutional.

France, for its part, highlights the principle of equality before the law, especially with regard to equality of access to public functions, with relevant case law going back as far as 1954 (the Barel case), which defended the need for impartiality and neutrality as a corollary of equality between candidates. Moreover, since the Law of 10 July 1975, most civil service posts must be offered to men and women, except those reserved for "service reasons". Finally, this inclusive interpretation of the principle of equality has been reinforced by European law, extending the application of the principle to foreign nationals of Member States of the European Union.

Some States highlight the existence of specific rules on equality and discrimination. For example, the Czech Republic cites the Anti-Discrimination Law transposing some European directives in this area; Hungary the 2003 Equality of Treatment and Promotion of Equal Opportunities Law; Slovakia the Anti-Discrimination Law of 2004, which establishes the legal basis for compliance with the principle of equality of treatment in the country's legal system, transposing European anti-discrimination legislation. In Slovakia there is the Law on Equal Opportunities for Men and Women, and in Norway the Equality and Anti-Discrimination Law, which applies to all sectors of society. Bulgaria mentions the Anti-Discrimination Law, and in Spain there is Organic Law 3/2007 of 22 March on the effective equality of women and men.

Portugal adds that among the case law recognising the principle of equality, with regard to its non-discrimination and gender equality aspects, the following decisions of its Constitutional Court stand out: Decision 186/90 enshrining the binding nature of the principle for the public sectors in the legislative, judicial and governmental realms, and Decision 412/02, where the principle of non-discrimination prohibits any difference in treatment on the basis of subjective criteria, such as race, language, religion or ideology, among others.

Both Romania and Cyprus state that, within the scope of the principle of equality, there are cases in which measures are taken to enable certain groups to be placed at a level equivalent to others.

The Supreme Court of Romania mentions measures taken by public authorities, or by the private sector, for the benefit of a person or group of persons in order to ensure the natural development and effective achievement of equality of opportunity with respect to other persons. Meanwhile, Cyprus's constitution incorporates the principle of relative equality, whereby not every difference of treatment will give rise to discrimination because sometimes the difference will be justified by the objectively identifiable circumstances, with the aim of mitigating the causes that give rise to such discrimination, as provided for in Law no. 146 (I)/2009 regulating employment for people with disabilities, which was applied in the Tsikkasa case on 3 September 2015 when the judgment recognised the right of physical education teachers with disabilities to have equal career opportunities. Bulgaria cites the Supreme Court's referral for a preliminary ruling in relation to the prohibition of discrimination against people with disabilities (C-824/19).

Finally, Sweden, the United Kingdom and Lithuania consider the principle of equality to be applicable, but for certain legal relations and specific sectors.

Sweden states that it applies to public procurement subject to the European legal framework, and adds that Chapter 1 of Section 9 of the Government Instrument states that the Courts, the Administration and any public body must act on the basis of objectivity and impartiality. It also states that the Supreme Court does not hear cases relating to discrimination, but that this is a matter for the lower courts.

In the United Kingdom, the Equality Act 2010 protects against discrimination for reasons of gender in employment, housing or public services. It points out that in any case, unjustified discrimination may form the subject of a claim for violation of public law, but for violation of the "common law" requirement of rationality.

Finally, in Lithuania the principle of equality breaks the principle of gender equality in practice.

**Question 17.**

**In the judicial practice of your country, is the principle of protection of particularly vulnerable groups (e.g. minors, women, people with disabilities) invoked and applied?**

- **Yes, in a general, open and transversal manner.**
- **Yes, for certain groups that are predetermined and identified in the different sector-specific rules (give a significant example)**
- **No**

**Summary of answers.**

In general, most of the countries extensively apply the principle of protection of vulnerable groups, although these groups are not specified in a particular list.

Austria highlights the application of the principle in asylum proceedings requested by unaccompanied minors, in which both the legal adviser and the minor's legal representative must be present at every interview and hearing that takes place in the proceedings. The Czech Republic adds, among other things, the right to access to justice for economically excluded people and the right people with illnesses to have their cases handled preferentially, depending on the type of illness that they have.

Estonia states that the practice of this principle of protection is linked to the principle of predicable investigation, in both judicial and administrative contexts, in order to ensure that the absence of legal training of the affected person does not curtail any of his or her due rights.

This being an obligation enshrined in international law, Finland states that the principle is invoked and applied pursuant to international instruments such as the Convention on the Rights of the Child and the Convention on the Rights of Persons with Disabilities.

France highlights its Law of 10 July 1987 imposing a minimum quota of posts reserved for people with disabilities (6%), and since 2005 a contribution must be made to funds for the inclusion of people with disabilities in the civil service. In 2020, the Council of State enshrined the liability of the State in the event of any failure to comply with this obligation.

Hungary mentions that its Law on Proceedings before the General Public Administration 2016 includes measures to ensure the protection and confidentiality of the personal data of minors and adults with disabilities in hearings or witness statements.

Latvia, for its part, applies this principle to groups of socially vulnerable people, in relation to the country's socio-economic situation: single-parent families, homeless people, victims of people trafficking, children, victims of violence, people with disabilities, ex-convicts, large families and the elderly, among others.

Germany states that the principle of protection of vulnerable groups is provided for in its domestic law, and the specific situation of the group concerned will be taken into account when considering its fundamental rights.

Italy, meanwhile, cites the Decree annulled in 2010 whereby emergency measures, such as surveillance and profiling, were adopted in relation to members of Roma communities settled on the outskirts of the most important Italian cities. The Council of State considered that the grounds of emergency did not legitimise discriminatory treatment based on the fact of settlement per se.

In Slovenia, the Italian and Hungarian communities, as well as Roma communities, are given special protection by the Constitution (Art. 65).

In Luxembourg, the protection of vulnerable groups is extended to the health field, especially in the light of the severity of the COVID-19 pandemic, with two rulings delivered by the Constitutional Court on laws that adopted restrictive measures to combat the pandemic and interfered with fundamental freedoms.

Portugal cites the 2017 "Inclusive Courts" project examining the courts' relations with minorities, with a view to conducting a critical examination of the multicultural case law of the Portuguese courts in relation to international human rights standards, and comparing the experiences of US and European courts.

Countries that do not recognise the principle of special protection of vulnerable persons as a principle generally applied in their judicial system include Lithuania, the Netherlands and the United Kingdom.

Lithuania points out that this does not mean there has been any non-compliance with, for example, the Council of Europe's Recommendation 1740 (2010) and the case law of the European Court of Human Rights with regard to the adoption of measures to protect vulnerable persons when they are removed from buildings.

The Netherlands states that although this principle has not been recognised as such in judicial practice, it is considered to be a manifestation of the principle of proportionality, which is expressly provided for in its legal system. Thus, in cases of eviction, the presence of minors must be an aspect taken into account, as indicated by the Administrative Jurisdiction Division of the Council of State. In addition, there is specific legislation protecting certain groups, such as adolescents and people with disabilities or chronic illness.

Finally, in the United Kingdom the principle is applied in linkage with the provision contained in the rules that protect, where applicable, persons with particular characteristics. The characteristics eligible for protection are itemised in the Equality Act 2010: age, disability, gender reassignment, marriage and civil partnership, pregnancy and maternity, race and religion, and the authorities are obliged to avoid situations of discrimination or harassment.

**Question 18.**

**Do the judicial bodies demand enhanced reasoning in cases where the contested administrative measure or decision (e.g. eviction from housing, granting of nationality) affects these vulnerable groups (e.g. minors, women, people with disabilities) or has an impact on other constitutional values such as protection of the family?**

- **No special reasoning is required in these cases.**
- **Yes, and its absence results in the nullity of the decision.**

**Summary of answers.**

In most of the countries that responded to the survey, enhanced reasoning of administrative measures affecting vulnerable groups, or affecting other constitutional values such as the family, is an essential element guaranteed by their administrative legal system.

Many national systems require such reasoning in cases relating to asylum, especially – as Austria indicates – when taking decisions to return unaccompanied minors to their country of origin. Bulgaria also mentions that the Supreme Court has issued a series of rulings on the assessment of asylum applications submitted by minors, which must be reasoned by the Administration in terms of what they call the "quality of the candidate". If this reasoning is not provided, the annulment of the administrative decision may be granted.

One country in which case law has addressed the importance of the reasoning of administrative decisions in respect of vulnerable groups is Slovakia, as happened in the examination of a case of refusal of asylum for the applicant and his sick youngest child with heart disease. The court's decision emphasised the necessity for administrative bodies to test for signs of vulnerability (judgment of 13 December 2017).

This approach is also followed by Spain, as enshrined in STS 151/2021 of 17 December, which lays down the requirement for the administrative decision to be taken in the light of the personal circumstances of the applicant.

With regard to evictions, there is a unanimous stance of weighting the conflicting interests when a minor or vulnerable person is involved, and

Spain, moreover, reiterates this with respect to the judges competent to authorise entry into the home (STS 1197/2021 of 4 October).

The Italian courts have required the Administration to assess the possible absence of guarantees of protection for an immigrant in his/her country of origin, when he/she belongs to a vulnerable group. The Czech Republic adds, with regard to foreigners involved in administrative proceedings, the need to take into account their ability to get by in the country's language.

In Luxembourg, the requirement for enhanced reasoning is considered to be a logical consequence of the application of the constitutional principle of proportionality, in order to ascertain the reasons for interfering in the natural rights of the individual as provided for in the country's constitution, such as life or health.

Lithuania stresses that although the principle of protection of vulnerable groups is not provided for in its legal system, this does not mean that such circumstances are not taken into account, not only in the judicial decision, but also in the administrative process, to determine whether the measure to be adopted is appropriate.

In addition, thirteen countries (France, Germany, Hungary, Malta, Poland, Portugal, Slovenia, Sweden, Norway, United Kingdom, Croatia, Estonia and Italy) state, on the one hand, that in general no special reasoning is required of the Administration in order to adopt measures affecting vulnerable groups; and, on the other hand, that the absence of such reasoning does not result in the nullity of the decision.

In this regard, Sweden states that the principles of freedom to litigate and freedom of proof are enshrined in its legal system, and therefore in most cases the burden of proof does not apply as an obligation for either party.

Italy, Portugal, Croatia and Estonia point out that the absence of a general obligation of enhanced reasoning in these cases is not an obstacle to this being done, if provided for in the specific legislation, given that discretionary power is exercised by the administrative body, or when – as Sweden points out – it is necessary to provide reasoning of the State intervention that the measure entails.

Finally, the case law of the United Kingdom determined in 2019 that there is no obligation under common law to provide reasoning of an administrative decision, although there have been differing opinions, focusing on the need to allow the person concerned to know the reasons in order to appeal, considering this criterion to be superior to the nature of the decision taken or the characteristics of the person concerned ((Help Refugees Ltd) v. Secretary of State for the Home Department [2018]).

**Question 19.**

**In your judicial practice, have disputes been raised regarding the issue of the principles of transparency, equality and non-discrimination in relation to decisions based on artificial intelligence or predictive data management systems?**

- **Yes**
- **These principles are not frequently invoked, but some examples exist.**
- **No.**

**Summary of answers.**

The majority of the answers are in the negative, with some nuances.

France states that the Council of State has not received any appeal against administrative decisions taken by or with the help of an artificial intelligence (AI) system on the grounds of the opaque or discriminatory nature of that system. However, appeals have been made in three cases where the legality of such systems was questioned.

One of these concerned the transparency of the algorithmic processing used to allocate places at higher education institutions to students who have passed the baccalaureate ("*Parcoursup*" system). The institutions are authorised to use algorithmic processing to achieve the best possible match between supply and demand for courses, with decisions not fully automated but with the participation of a committee and the institution's director. In essence, it was ruled that the secrecy of the deliberations of the educational teams responsible for examining applications precluded communication of the source codes of the programs used by the centres, but that firstly, applicants who had received a rejection decision could obtain information about the criteria used by the centre and their weighting, including, where applicable, the criteria used by the algorithmic processing, and secondly, upon completion of the procedure, each institution must publish the criteria according to which the applications were examined, specifying the extent to which algorithmic processing was used to carry out that examination.

In the other two cases, the processing of the personal data necessary for the design and implementation of AI decision-making support systems was criticised on the basis of the GDPR. The question of transparency and respect for the principles of equality and non-discrimination was not discussed in the first case (decision of 30 December 2021, *Sté Gerbi avocat victimes & préjudices* and others, no. 440376 et al., relating to the "DataJust" project, the purpose of which was to identify the determining factors for the amount of compensation due in the event of personal injury and to develop an indicative frame of reference for compensation). The second case, relating to the automated data collection system ("web scraping") of the tax and customs authority, is still pending.

Hungary, for its part, states that its judicial bodies are familiar with the new data management technologies and services. The efforts made to use these tools in decision-making processes are visible, but no significant proceedings have taken place. Artificial intelligence and data management systems are not used in judicial adjudication, so there have not been any disputes relating to such systems.

Belgium reports that to date, the judgments of the Council of State do not yet mention any grounds based on violation of the principle of non-discrimination, transparency and (adequate) reasoning of the contested act in relation to the use of AI by the authority in making a decision. However, it is assumed that these procedures are already (more or less) frequently used, for example in the context of detecting tax fraud or social security fraud, or when allocating a place (enrolment of a student in a school knowing that such enrolment is not necessarily at the school "of his/her choice"), etc. It is expected that this will not be long in coming, for example as a result of an appeal against an administrative decision denying access (violation of the principle of transparency) to the algorithms.

Other countries report that these principles are not frequently invoked from this particular perspective, but that some examples exist.

For example, Cyprus states that some of the artificial intelligence systems used in that country have been analysed by its Supreme Court. However, when the Court reviews the legality of a contested decision that was made by automated systems, its competence does not extend to questions of a technical nature. The Court will only intervene if, after taking all the facts of the case into account, it finds that the conclusions of the public body cannot be upheld, result from an error of fact or law, exceed its discretionary powers, are contrary to administrative principles or encroach upon constitutional rights.

Italy states that the use of electronic means in the judicial process is not widespread in that country. It is used mainly for decisions that do not involve any discretion, because in these cases it is more difficult to prepare the algorithm that includes the elements to be taken into account. Only in these cases can the correct preparation of the algorithm with respect to the principles in question be relevant for the judgment.

The response from the Netherlands states that the issue of transparency has been raised in relation to decisions based on the "AERIUS Calculator" software. This application is used to calculate nitrogen levels. The calculation requires a large amount of data. In this connection, the problem has arisen as to the extent to which that data must be available to the parties to the process. The Council of State does not explicitly mention the principles of transparency and non-discrimination, but does not mention the risk of unequal treatment of the parties to the process. In such cases of unequal treatment, ministers and secretaries of state are obliged to disclose the choices made and the data involved, so that they are accessible to third parties.

The United Kingdom says that although decision-making based on artificial intelligence is not widespread, there has been increasing controversy about discrimination in this context. It cites the problem of the use of facial recognition, concluding that this can produce results that involve indirect discrimination based on sex and race.

Finally, Poland states that the administrative courts apply the principles of transparency, equality and non-discrimination, but that there is little connection with decisions based on artificial intelligence systems, since there have not been many cases of decisions taken by such systems.

## IV. General principles in certain sector-specific areas of public law

### IV.1. Organisation and administrative procedure

**Question 20.**

**In the administrative organisation, do the principles of decentralisation and subsidiarity apply?**

- **Yes.**
- **No.**

- **Not generally, but in certain areas or sectors (in this case, explain your answer briefly)**

**Summary of answers.**

Most of the answers are in the affirmative.

Luxembourg states that it relies primarily on the case law of the Constitutional Court, which has recognised in various judgments that the provisions of the European Charter of Local Self-Government of 15 May 1985, ratified by the Grand Duchy of Luxembourg in a Law dated 18 March 1987, overlap with the provisions of Article 107(1) of the Constitution enshrining the principle of local self-government. This means that, in a spirit of subsidiarity, the Constitutional Court analyses the conformity of certain laws concerning local matters not only in relation to Article 107, but also in relation to the corresponding – and often more precise – articles of the Charter of Local Self-Government. Whenever the Constitutional Court has had to make a ruling, the preliminary referral has come from the Administrative Court. In some cases, the Administrative Court has had to rule in the final instance and apply, through transposition, the principles adopted by the Constitutional Court, in particular on the basis of the principle of subsidiarity and the Charter of Local Self-Government, together with the principle of local self-government enshrined in Article 107 of the Constitution.

Only Sweden and the United Kingdom answer in the negative.

Finally, some countries answer that these principles do not apply generally, but in certain areas or sectors.

For example, Belgium states that decentralisation is organised, as a rule, by or under the law. Decentralisation implies the granting of legal personality to an autonomous entity (in principle, under the control of a supervisory authority). The granting of legal personality requires the intervention of the legislator. The decentralisation of local and provincial authorities, on the other hand, is enshrined in the Constitution (Art. 162). Once decentralisation is organised by law, the principle of subsidiarity for the decentralised entity is recognised and protected. However, this principle is applied rather through the principle of proportionality.

Germany says it is organised as a federal State. This means that a degree of decentralisation is part of its DNA. Therefore, decentralisation and subsidiarity cannot be described as general principles, but both categories exist in political and administrative culture.

Malta reports that due to geographical considerations, most administrative functions are effectively centralised, but that some decentralised aspects of administration are entrusted to local or regional bodies.

**Question 21.**

**Are the general principles set out below applicable to the procedure for formulating administrative acts and provisions?**

**Principle of publicity and transparency**

- **Yes**
- **No**

**Principle of proportionality**

- **Yes**
- **No**

**Principle of impartiality**

- **Yes**
- **No**

**Principle of anti-formalism**

- **Yes**
- **No**

**Principle of gratuitousness.**

- **Yes**
- **No**

**Principle of self-correction (enforceable decision, without the need for judicial assistance)**

- **Yes**
- **No**

**(If you consider it appropriate, please indicate any other general principles of administrative procedure different from the above.)**

**Summary of answers.**

A) Principle of publicity and transparency

The large majority of the answers are in the affirmative.
Belgium states that this principle is applicable in relation to public procurement, concessions and administrative law on property.
Austria, Germany and the Netherlands answer in the negative.

B) Principle of proportionality
Again, a clear majority of the countries answer in the affirmative. Austria, Norway and the United Kingdom answer in the negative.

C) Principle of impartiality
All answers are in the affirmative.

D) Principle of anti-formalism
On this point, here is more division. Croatia, Cyprus, the Czech Republic, Estonia, France, Hungary, Italy, Latvia, Luxembourg, Malta, Portugal, Slovakia and Norway answer in the affirmative.
Austria, Finland, Germany, Greece, Lithuania, the Netherlands, Romania, Slovenia and the United Kingdom answer in the negative.
Belgium says it should be borne in mind that Article 14, § 1, paragraph 2 of the Consolidated Acts on the Council of State provides that, with regard to appeals for annulment due to substantial formal defects, or those required under penalty of nullity, excess or misuse of powers, brought against the acts and regulations of the various administrative authorities (Art. 14, § 1, paragraph 1): "the irregularities referred to in the first paragraph shall give rise to annulment only if they have influenced the direction of the decision taken, deprived the interested parties of a guarantee or had the effect of affecting the competence of the author of the act" (interest of the stated grounds).

E) Principle of gratuitousness
Croatia, Cyprus, Estonia, Hungary, Latvia, Luxembourg, Malta, Portugal, Romania, Slovakia, Slovenia and Norway answer in the affirmative.
Austria, the Czech Republic, Finland, France, Greece, Italy, Lithuania, the Netherlands and the United Kingdom answer in the negative.
Belgium states that the principle of "gratuitousness" is not recognised as such, since the public service is provided/financed either (i) by taxes or (ii) by tax revenue (and therefore, in the latter case, "gratuitously", *i.e.* with no direct economic compensation). However, it is understood that,

on equal terms, the interested party must have access to the service of general (economic) interest, *i.e.* "universal", if necessary at a reasonable price (remuneration).
It should be noted that both Germany and Sweden report difficulties in giving an answer on this point because it is not sufficiently clear what this principle means.

F) Principle of self-correction
The large majority of countries answer in the affirmative.
Belgium points out that the enforcement of an administrative decision requires the intervention of the judge, except where there is express legal authorisation (warrant/"*dwangbevel*") or urgent need.
Austria, Lithuania and the Netherlands answer in the negative.
Again, Germany states that it is not sufficiently clear what this principle means.

G) Other general principles
Cyprus mentions the right to be heard, the principle of good faith, the principle of adequate investigation and the principle of good record-keeping.
The Czech Republic states that some basic principles worth mentioning include the principle of non-abuse of administrative discretion, the principle of accordance with the public interest, the principle of substantive truth, the principle of administration as a public service, the principle of courtesy and assistance, the principle of providing information about rights and remedies, the principle of enabling interested parties to assert their legitimate rights and interests, the principle of amicable resolution of disputes, the principle of effectiveness and efficiency, and the principle of cooperation and collaboration between the administrative authorities.
This country stresses the principle of publicity and transparency, noting that although one of the principles of the administrative process is that of non-publicity, there are certain instruments that ensure the publicity and transparency of administrative activities carried out by the authorities.
France refers to the principle of non-retroactivity of administrative acts, the principle of the right of defence and the right to appeal against any administrative act for abuse of power.
Latvia indicates the following principles that it considers must also be applied: 1) Principle of respect for the rights of private persons. Taking

into account the scope of the law, institutions and courts must facilitate the protection of the rights and interests of private persons. 2) Principle of the rule of law. The decisions of institutions and courts must comply with the law. Courts and institutions must act in accordance with the powers conferred upon them by law. 3) Principle of reasonable application of legal provisions: basic interpretation methods must be used when carrying out the relevant legal provisions. 4) Principle of priority of laws. Administrative acts favourable to a private person that regulate legal relations with regard to an aspect vital to a democracy must be carried out on the basis of the principles established by the constitution or laws. 5) Principle of procedural fairness. Courts and institutions must respect objectivity.

Slovakia considers it important to highlight the principle of substantive truth (investigative principle). This principle allows the authority to establish objective facts.

## IV.2. Administrative sanctions

**Question 22.**

**Are the general principles of criminal law applied or projected in the area of administrative sanctions law? (Indicate the answer that you consider best reflects your legislation and practice.)**

- **Yes.**
- **Yes, although with nuances arising from the different natures of criminal and administrative offences**
- **Not in relation to minor, lesser or trivial infractions.**
- **Only in relation to infractions that can be characterised as "criminal" in accordance with the doctrine of the ECtHR**

**Summary of answers.**

The Spanish Supreme Court has recognised that the substantive principles underlying the criminal law system are applicable, with certain nuances, to administrative sanctions law, since they are both manifestations of the State's punitive system, and has projected on to measures aimed at exercising the Administration's sanctioning powers the principles of legality, definition of the constituent elements of the offence and culpability, as well as procedural guarantees of the following rights: the right to defence, with proscription of any lack of defence representation; the right to legal assistance, which can be transferred under certain conditions; the right to be informed of the accusation, with the unavoidable consequence of the unalterability of the allegations; the right to the presumption of innocence, which means that the burden of proof of the constitutive facts of the offence lies with the Administration, with prohibition of the use of evidence obtained in violation of fundamental rights; the right not to incriminate oneself; and the right to use appropriate means of proof for the defence.

Most of the surveyed countries also consider, with nuances, that the principles of criminal law are also applicable to administrative sanctions law, so that in Austria, for example, there are no significant differences in administrative criminal law proceedings other than the following: principle of investigation: in general, the criminal administrative authorities are both "prosecutors" and "judges", with some exceptions; representation by a lawyer in cases of appeal before the administrative courts of first instance is not mandatory; the principles of publicity, orality and immediacy apply only to proceedings before the administrative courts of first instance, and not those before the administrative authorities.

In the case of Belgium, in general, any punitive decision may be taken only by taking into account the right of defence and the principle of *non bis in idem*. This is the case, for example, with disciplinary sanctions. In addition, where the sanction is likely to constitute a criminal charge (*i.e.* "punitive" administrative sanctions), certain general principles of criminal law must be applied (e.g. guarantees of the right of access to a judge), but with nuances deriving from the different natures of criminal sanctions and administrative sanctions. The general principles of criminal law (respect for the rights of defence, assistance of a lawyer, access to files, accusatory principle, principle of *non bis in idem*, principle of (strict) legality, no offence or punishment without law, etc.) apply with respect to administrative infractions (and sanctions) that can be characterised as "criminal" in accordance with the doctrine of the ECtHR. That being said, the general principles of law (in general) apply in the context of "pure" administrative sanctions that are not considered to be "criminal" sanctions within the meaning of Art. 6 ECHR (*audi alteram partem*, principle of diligence, reasonableness, proportionality, reasoning, etc). The principle of *non bis in idem* does not apply if an act is punished criminally and also by disciplinary means, since these are sanctions "of a different order".

In Cyprus, an administrative sanction is distinguished from a criminal sanction because a criminal prosecution can be carried out only in accordance with the provisions of the Constitution, and therefore a criminal sanction requires a constitutionally acceptable finding of guilt without which that penalty could not have been imposed. In the case "República contra Demand Shipping Co. Ltd (1994) 3 C.L.R. 460", the Supreme Court declared, by a majority judgment, that the imposition of a pecuniary administrative sanction was not a criminal indictment under Article 12 of the Constitution, but an administrative sanction imposed by a public body for administrative infractions of the relevant legal provisions. In this regard, it is established case law that an administrative sanction is one imposed by a competent administrative authority and that it is distinguished from criminal sanctions imposed by criminal courts. In making the distinction, the Engel criteria serve as a starting point and a guide for the Cypriot courts. While the ECtHR's independent interpretation of the concept of "criminal prosecution" laid the basis for a "progressive extension of the application of the criminal guarantees of Article 6", Cyprus's case law takes a fairly dominant and consistent view that the less "harsh" categories of criminal law must be maintained within the sphere of administrative law, so that the criminal guarantees are not necessarily applied with their full rigour.

Moreover, the principle of legality – *nullum crimen nulla poena* – applies in a similar way to administrative offences that incur administrative sanctions. Therefore, a competent public body cannot impose any administrative sanction without legal authorisation and subsequent non-compliance or non-compliance by a regulated company/institution/person. Therefore, a violation is identified by a competent public body mandated by law to regulate a group of persons for the public interest. In this way, the public body supervises, enforces the law and imposes administrative sanctions on offenders. In short, administrative procedures are safeguarded by principles similar but not identical to those of criminal law. Likewise, administrative sanctions do not infringe Article 6 of the ECHR since they may be subject to a judicial control that satisfies Article 6.1 of the ECHR.

With regard to the Czech Republic, although the Supreme Administrative Court has repeatedly held that the principles of criminal law are applicable, in particular, with regard to liability for infractions in the area of administrative sanctions law, the new Law on Liability for Administrative Infractions and Proceedings (which is based on those findings) nevertheless holds that there is scope for judicial practice to apply or project other principles of criminal law in the area of administrative sanctions. The differences between criminal law and administrative sanctions law deriving from the different natures of criminal offences and administrative offences are found mainly at procedural level (for example, criminal proceedings are governed by the principle of publicity, the principle of defence and legal assistance, there are more procedural safeguards to protect the rights of the accused, etc.).

In the case of France, if the power to impose sanctions remains highly disputed, this is even more true with regard to the procedural guarantees of the affected persons, particularly in relation to the right of defence. The Constitutional Council has specified a number of conditions that must be satisfied in order for the attribution of a sanctioning power to independent administrative authorities to be constitutionally admissible: - a law must establish the power to impose sanctions; - the rights of defence must be respected; - the parties must be offered the possibility of appealing the authority's decision before a court, as well as the possibility of the court suspending an immediately enforceable decision; - in addition, the sanctions imposed must be proportionate, and their combination with strictly criminal sanctions must not exceed the maximum penalty of the most serious sanction.

The Greek Council of State has also recognised the application, with some nuances, of the substantive principles of criminal law to administrative sanctions law and disciplinary law, both manifestations of the State's punitive system. It has transposed the principles of legality, definition of the constituent elements of the offence and culpability, as well as procedural guarantees of the following rights: the right to defence, prohibiting any loss or limitation of the means of defence; the right to be assisted by a lawyer; the right to be informed of the accusation, with the unavoidable consequence of the unalterability of the allegations; the right to the presumption of innocence, with prohibition of the use of evidence obtained in violation of fundamental rights; the right not to incriminate oneself; the right to use appropriate means of proof for the defence; the principle of non-retroactivity of sanctioning provisions; the principle of *ne bis in idem*, and finally the publicity of the process.

As far as Hungary is concerned, there are separate laws regulating statutory offences (Law no. II of 2012) and sanctions imposed for infractions of administrative law, such as warnings, administrative fines, prohibition of conducting an activity, and confiscation (Law no. CXXV of 2017). Similarly, certain general principles of criminal law apply in the case of statutory offences (Law no. II of 2012), for example the principle of presumption of innocence. Meanwhile, in the case of infractions of administrative law (Law no. CXXV of 2017), we can also find a number of principles such as proportionality. These principles are invoked in the above-mentioned laws.

Similarly, in Italy, the general principles relating to administrative sanctions are laid down in Law no. 689 of 24 November 1981. They are based on the criminal law model, but with significant differences, for example with regard to the effects of the law on the time and subjective element of the offence.

Mention should also be made of the case of Lithuania, where the Constitutional Court has stated that constitutional principles must be respected when the legislator establishes administrative liability for infractions of the law. The entire legal system is based on the rule of law, which, among other things, presupposes the proportionality of the sanction. According to the doctrine of the Constitutional Court, the measures taken must not only be proportional, but must also reflect lawful objectives of general importance, and the rights of the individual must not be restricted any more than is necessary to achieve those objectives. There must also be the possibility of individualising a sanction. It is important to note that the Constitutional Court has placed emphasis on situations in which the nature of the sanction applied (for example, rigour) coincides with the criminal punishment; in such cases, the procedural rights conferred on the person must be the same as those provided for in the Constitution (*i.e.* those constitutional rights are not reserved only to defendants in a criminal trial). This applies even if the sanction is designated "economic" in the law that establishes it.

In Luxembourg, in general the Administrative Court recognises by transposition the general principles applicable in criminal matters, including in the area of administrative sanctions, particularly insofar as they fall within the autonomous concept of criminal law defined by the European Court of

Human Rights. In the field of European Union law, the Administrative Court has placed special emphasis on the application of the fundamental principle of proportionality, particularly in relation to greenhouse-gas emission quotas in the context of the transposition of the Kyoto Protocol by European Union legislation, as has also been applied in the Grand Duchy of Luxembourg. (Administrative Court, 7 February 2019, register no. 40990C, and Administrative Court, 7 July 2020, register no. 40990CA).

In the case of Poland, the Polish Code of Administrative Procedure distinguishes the principles of criminal law in the field of administrative sanctions. However, its content is partly similar to that of the criminal law.

In Portugal, the concept of an administrative sanction can be defined as a punitive measure applied in administrative relations when an administrative infraction is committed. Thus, the sanction takes the form of a sanctioning administrative act, combining the pursuit of the public interest and the punitive aspect. Meanwhile, the criminal sanction, as a basic expression of public punishment, protects "primary interests", *i.e.* the legal values and assets essential to community life, such as personal integrity, life, freedom, and tangible and intangible heritage. The transposition of the principles of criminal law into administrative sanctions law does not happen automatically, but to the extent necessary to preserve the essential values that underlie the constitutional norm and are compatible with the nature of the sanctioning administrative procedure.

In the case of Romania, in the area of administrative liability, administrative sanctions are applied after a summary procedure by members of the public administration, and in the great majority of cases the sanctions are applied by administrative bodies. The administrative law procedure does not offer the same guarantees as those enjoyed by a person accused of a criminal offence.

In the case of Norway, the applicable general principles of criminal law include a number of fundamental substantive and procedural guarantees, but the scope of their application varies to some extent depending on the seriousness of the case and the nature of the administrative proceeding. Infractions that can be characterised as "criminal" in accordance with the doctrine of the ECtHR entail the application of general principles of criminal law close to or fully on a par with criminal proceedings. For less serious offences and proceedings, some of the general principles are not applies to the same extent.

Other countries state that there is no specific legislation or case law establishing that the general principles of criminal law apply in cases of administrative sanctions.

This is the case with Finland, although it says that most of the principles listed in the next question are also central principles of administrative law and therefore apply in matters relating to administrative sanctions.

In the case of Germany, administrative sanctions are not known to German administrative law. Administrative law can be applied by declaring its infraction by the individual as a crime or a misdemeanour.

As regards Sweden, unlike the Spanish Supreme Court, the Swedish Supreme Court has not ruled on the question of whether the substantive principles on which the criminal system is based are applicable to the law on administrative sanctions. Similarly, administrative sanctions are not codified in the Swedish criminal system, but are handled by the administrative courts. However, the principle of legality and the burden of proof are applicable in the administrative procedure rules relating to administrative sanctions.

The situation is different in Slovakia, where the scope of administrative sanctions is codified not in a single legal norm, but in a number of specific laws. Any gaps in the legislation are filled through appropriate application of the principles of criminal law, while proportionality depends on the individual circumstances of the case, so there is no automatic annulment of these principles. The principles of criminal law are those explicitly enshrined in the Code of Criminal Procedure (principles of criminal procedure), as with the principles for the imposition of penalties (e.g. principle of absorption).

The legal system of the Republic of Serbia provides the opportunity to issue and determine administrative measures of a criminal nature, provided for by laws regulating specific administrative matters. The administrative measures are those determined by the Commission for Protection of Competition requiring a market participant to pay a certain amount of money, not exceeding 10% of the total annual revenue earned in the territory of the Republic of Serbia, if, for example, it abuses its dominant position. In addition, the Law on Protection of Competition provides for a procedural sanction of EUR 500 to EUR 5,000 per day of action in breach of the decision issued by the Commission for Protection of Competition during the proceedings, which does not act in accordance with that order in certain circumstances. Procedural sanctions may not amount to more than 10% of the total annual revenue calculated in accordance with Article 7 of Law on Protection of Competition.

The measures aimed at the protection of competition, as well as the procedural sanctions, are of a punitive nature, but their application is in line with Union law due to the approval of the Law on Protection of Competition. In addition, in accordance with the Law on Protection of Competition, there are also measures aimed at eliminating damage to competition that are implemented by issuing orders for the execution of certain actions or for the prohibition of certain behaviours ("behavioural" measures). The administrative measures are determined by separate laws regulating specific administrative fields, regardless of whether there are any offences prescribed for those specific administrative fields. Finally, disciplinary proceedings against prosecutors are carried out in accordance with the Law on the Public Prosecutor's Office and the Rules on Disciplinary Procedure and Disciplinary Liability of Prosecutors and Deputy Prosecutors. Matters not covered by the regulations of Article 1 of that Law are governed by the provisions of the Criminal Code.

Finally, with regard to infractions that can be characterised as "criminal" in accordance with the doctrine of the ECtHR, in the United Kingdom, government departments may, in certain areas, impose administrative sanctions as alternatives to the initiation of criminal proceedings. For example, with regard to benefit fraud, the Department of Work and Pensions can offer an administrative sanction to a person when the case is not considered to be so serious as to consider the possibility of initiating court proceedings at first instance. A person can choose to accept this penalty without any admission of guilt and without many of the same processes and principles of criminal law being applied. In general, however, the strengthened protections associated with criminal law apply only when infractions of administrative measures can be characterised as criminal in line with the ECtHR.

In Estonia, the scope of application of sanctioning administrative law is currently quite limited, since there is no established system of administrative offences, and even less serious offences (misdemeanours) are subject to the general part of criminal law and the jurisdiction of the criminal courts. However, punitive administrative sanctions do exist (for example, disciplinary sanctions against prisoners or officials). In these cases, Estonia's Supreme Court has applied the general principles of criminal law that derive from the Constitution and the case law of the ECtHR.

In the case of Latvia, according to the judicial practice of the Supreme Court, the principles of criminal law can be applied to tax fines. Because of the punitive nature and the amount of such fines, they can be considered to be criminal fines within the meaning of Articles 6 and 7 of the European Convention on Human Rights. There are no other cases before the Administrative Court in which the principles of criminal law can be applied.

In Malta, the predominant interpretation seems to be that the general principles of criminal law apply only in cases where the administrative sanction imposed reaches a certain threshold and can therefore be considered to be a criminal sanction. In previous years, there have been some notable cases in which administrative sanctions have been challenged on the basis that they provide for criminal sanctions without the additional guarantees available in the context of criminal proceedings.

In the Netherlands, general principles of law that are specific to criminal law (such as the presumption of innocence) apply only to infractions that can be described as "criminal" in accordance with the doctrine of the ECtHR. General principles of law that are not specific to criminal law (such as the principle of proportionality and the principle of reasoning of the sanctioning decision) apply to all administrative sanctions.

In the case of Slovenia, the country's legal system traditionally considers that all infractions of the law that must be sanctioned fall within the scope of criminal law and not administrative law and jurisdiction. Consequently, "criminal sanctions" and "sanctions for minor offences" are regulated as sanctions for different criminal acts. The system of criminal sanctions is regulated by the Penal Code and covers "sanctions", "warnings" and "security measures". Sanctions for minor offences, *i.e.* less serious criminal acts, are numerous, for example, "fine", "warning", "deportation of non-nationals", "seizure of items", etc., and all are systematically regulated by the Minor Offences Law.

"Administrative sanctions" is a relatively new legal (statutory) term in Slovenian legislation. However, this does not mean that they do not exist. Systematic regulation (the Minor Offences Law) refers here to the possible regulation of the imposition of sanctions on legal persons for administrative infractions. Therefore, administrative sanctions will be regulated by different statutes (*lex specialis*) outside the Minor Offences Law, but these have not yet been passed. The administrative sanctions and the applicable principles are not (yet) defined as such in the country's legislation, administrative practice and case law. Consequently, the only legal basis for the application of the principles of criminal law in administrative matters is currently the ECtHR.

Since administrative sanctions are not yet a general feature in the Slovenian legal system, and since acts that in future will presumably be punished by administrative sanctions are currently treated as minor offences, the Slovenian legal system for minor offences could be regarded as a kind of hybrid system. The administrative authorities are competent to supervise the correct application of the regulations (law) and the proper performance of inspection procedures, and also function as minor offences authorities (at first instance). There is no prohibition for an official of an administrative authority acting as a minor offences authority who finds a breach of the law to initiate or even terminate the minor infraction procedure. However, it should be noted that the judicial review of the sanctions imposed is carried out by the criminal rather than the administrative courts.

<u>Question 23.</u>

**If you answered yes to the previous question, could you specify whether or not the following general principles on administrative sanctions are applied or to what extent?**

**Principle of presumption of innocence and right not to incriminate oneself or plead guilty:**

- **Yes**
- **No**
- **With nuances**

**Principles of legality and definition of the constituent elements of the offence:**

- **Yes**
- **No**
- **With nuances**

**Principle of non-retroactivity of sanctioning provisions:**

- **Yes**
- **No**
- **With nuances**

**Principle of culpability:**

- **Yes**
- **No**
- **With nuances**

**Principle of proportionality**

- **Yes**
- **No**
- **With nuances**

**Principle of defence and legal assistance:**

- **Yes**
- **No**
- **With nuances**

**(If you consider it appropriate, please indicate any other general principles of administrative sanctions law different from the above)**

<u>Summary of answers.</u>

A) Principle of presumption of innocence and right not to incriminate oneself or plead guilty. Most of the countries surveyed apply these principles.

In the case of Belgium, however, due to a cooperation requirement specific to the administrative procedure, it is not impossible for the inertia or silence of a person charged with an administrative offence to harm that person's defence. That being said, in disciplinary matters (a "quasi-judicial" issue), (recent) case law seems to align with the criminal case law accepting that the accused is free to choose the defence of his/her choice, including the right to remain silent.

In Finland, the burden of proof in cases of administrative sanctions generally falls on the Administration. The right not to incriminate oneself can be applied in some situations of administrative sanctions.

In the case of France, the decision of the Constitutional Council of 10 June 2009 censuring the "HADOPI" law revises the constitutional case law on administrative sanctions. The Constitutional Council adds itself to the list of "guarantees" that must govern the imposition of administrative sanctions. It enshrines the applicability of the principle of presump-

tion of innocence in censuring the law on the basis of Article 9 of the Declaration of the Rights of Man and of the Citizen.
In the case of the Netherlands, this principle is generally applied only to punitive administrative sanctions.
This principle is not applied in Sweden.

B) Principles of legality and definition of the constituent elements of the offence. All surveyed countries that answered this question apply these principles.
In the case of Belgium, however, in disciplinary matters, for example where the alleged conduct remains vague ("acts endangering the proper functioning of the service or the dignity of the public function"), the criminal law principle of *nullem crimen sine lege* is not applied. There is no exhaustive list of ethical rules that can be violated. The administrative authority judges at its discretion (under the supervision of the judge) what it considers to be misconduct.
In Cyprus, the principle of legality is held to be the most substantive and essential principle for a democratic State that respects the rule of law and acts primarily in the public interest.
In the case of France, like the Council of State, the Constitutional Council ensures that the infraction is "defined in sufficiently clear and precise terms to exclude arbitrariness". However, the Constitutional Council observes a certain flexibility in stating that "applied outside the criminal law, the requirement for a definition of the sanctioned infractions is satisfied, in administrative matters, with reference to the obligations to which the holder of an administrative authorisation is subject pursuant to laws and regulations". In the Assembly decision of 7 July 2004, the Council of State endorsed this case law, stating that "infringements could be defined in terms of the obligations to which a person is subject by virtue of the activity that he/she carries on, the profession to which he/she belongs or the institution to which he/she belongs". Reversing the previous case law, the Council of State thus ruled that the principle of legality of infractions also applies to disciplinary sanctions imposed on members of the regulated professions. It should be noted, however, that it does not apply to the disciplinary sanctions that the administrative authority has the power to impose on public officials placed under its authority. Thus, although the principle of legality applies to "any sanction

that has the nature of a penalty", there is flexibility in cases where there is a "prior relationship" (of special subjection) between the administration and the sanctioned person.

C) Principle of non-retroactivity of sanctioning provisions:
All surveyed countries that answered this question apply this principle. In the case of France, the principle of non-retroactivity of criminal law applies only if its provisions are more stringent. However, in the area of sanctions, particularly criminal sanctions, the principle of application of the newer, more lenient law (the principle of retroactivity *in mitius*) states that if a new law is more lenient than the old one, it is applied retroactively to acts committed before their entry into force (Art. 112-1 of the Penal Code). It has been enshrined as a constitutional principle by the Constitutional Council. The Council of State applies it in the area of administrative sanctions when it acts as a court of full jurisdiction.

D) Principle of culpability:
Most of the countries surveyed apply this principle.
In the case of Belgium, this principle means that if the burden of proof falls on the administrative authority, the answer is in the affirmative. If by "principle of culpability" we mean the need for a moral element (intent), the answer is in the negative.
In the Czech Republic, the principle of culpability in administrative sanctions law applies to persons who are not employers. However, in the case of employers and legal entities, strict liability applies for offences based on the imputability of the conduct of the persons concerned (employees, etc.). Conversely, in criminal law there is no distinction between the criminal liability of employers and non-employers (liability in both cases is based on the principle of culpability). And although the criminal liability of legal entities is also based on the imputability of the conduct of the persons concerned on behalf of, in the interest of or in the course of the activities of the legal entities, their criminal liability, unlike liability for crimes, is not strict. Legal entities can be held criminally liable only if the persons whose conduct can be imputed to them are culpable, hence the principle of culpability applies. Another significant nuance between criminal and administrative sanctions law is the degree of culpability required for the person to be held liable. While criminal

law requires intent (unless the written law expressly states otherwise), negligence is sufficient in administrative sanctions law (again, unless the written law expressly states otherwise).
This principle does not apply in Finland.
France states that the dominant trend in that country is for a simple "material fault" to be sufficient. It may not be an exaggeration to see signs of an opposite trend in tax law in which the administration is obliged to prove the offender's bad faith or fraud.
This principle does not apply in Romania either.
In the case of the Netherlands, this principle is generally applied only to punitive administrative sanctions.

E) Principle of proportionality:
Most of the countries surveyed apply this principle.
In the case of Italy, the principle of proportionality is not included among the general principles of administrative sanctions laid down in Law no. 689 of 1981. Although it is widely applied in judicial practice to determine whether the level of the sanction exceeds the seriousness of the sanctioned conduct, the law gives the public authority the power to graduate the sanction.
In Norway, to the extent that the infraction can be characterised as "criminal" in accordance with the doctrine of the ECtHR, the response must be determined on the basis of criteria that promote proportionality, such as the scope and effects of the infraction, the degree of culpability of the private individual or entity, etc. For administrative procedures relating to the withdrawal or restriction of a public licence, there is also a stricter principle of proportionality.
The United Kingdom answers in the negative.

F) Principle of defence and legal assistance:
Most of the countries surveyed apply this principle.
Spain states that in sanction proceedings, the sanctioned person has the right to be assisted by a lawyer, but if they do not appoint a lawyer and pay the related fees out of their own pocket, the Spanish State will not provide them with a duty lawyer. The duty lawyer system is a service provided by lawyers who, on a rotating basis, defend citizens who, due to lack of funds or in certain situations of special protection (minors, de-

tainees, foreigners "without papers", victims of gender-based violence, etc.) require "free justice." Conversely, in criminal proceedings under Spanish law, if the accused does not appoint a lawyer to defend them, the Spanish State must provide the arrested person with a lawyer through the *Colegio de Abogados* [Spanish Bar Association].)

In Austria, representation by a lawyer is not mandatory (either before the administrative authority or before the administrative court of first instance). However, if required, in the interest of delivering justice, and particularly in the interest of an adequate defence, a defendant may be assigned a duty lawyer for judicial proceedings at his/her request if he/she cannot bear the costs of his/her defence without this making it difficult to cover the basic necessities of life. In assessing whether the assignment of a duty lawyer is necessary, in the interest of delivering justice, the difficulty of the situation in fact and in law, the particular personal circumstances of the defendant and the particular consequences of the case for the accused must be taken into account.

As regards Belgium, this principle applies when the matter concerns a "punitive" administrative sanction or the right of defence within the meaning of Article 6 of the ECHR, and also in the case of a disciplinary sanction or a "pure" administrative sanction (e.g. in socio-economic matters, the withdrawal of an approval, authorisation or licence), with the authority making its position known in writing. Legal assistance may be granted free of charge for proceedings before administrative courts.

In the case of Cyprus, the principle of natural justice is based on "two pillars" of procedural fairness known as "the rule against bias" and "the right to be heard". The right to be heard is enjoyed by any person who is affected by the disciplinary or sanctioning act or measure or who is prejudiced in any way, and can be exercised as a litigant in person or with a lawyer, either orally or in writing. With regard to free legal assistance, the legal framework is governed by the Legal Assistance Law of 2002. Under its provisions, free legal assistance is available to eligible applicants under certain conditions and for certain proceedings, but these do not include proceedings relating to administrative sanctions.

In the Czech Republic, in administrative sanctions proceedings, offenders have the right to be assisted by a lawyer, but the State does not provide them with a duty lawyer if they do not appoint one or cannot afford to pay for one. However, although the Law on Liability for Administrative Infractions and Proceedings does not enshrine the right to free legal assistance for citizens who, due to lack of funds, cannot afford a lawyer, the Law on Defence provides the option (not only for offenders in sanction proceedings, but in general) to file a request – accompanied by documents declaring income, assets, etc. – with the Bar Association of the Czech Republic. If certain conditions are met, the Bar Association appoints a duty lawyer who then provides free legal consultation or the legal services for which the request was filed. The costs of sanctioning administrative procedures are borne by the State. In addition, the law regulating proceedings before administrative courts enshrines the right of persons entitled to exemption from legal fees, if necessary to protect their rights, to request the appointment of a legal representative by the court (again, the costs are again borne by the State). Conversely, in criminal proceedings under Czech law, the State automatically provides the accused with a lawyer if he/she does not appoint one him/herself. However, this applies only to certain situations (e.g. if the accused is in custody, persons with limited legal capacity, etc.) expressly listed in the Code of Criminal Procedure.

In Finland, legal assistance is generally available in administrative judicial matters for persons with low income who cannot afford a lawyer on their own.

In the case of Luxembourg, appeals before the Administrative Court can be brought only by a lawyer with full court training, including the final examination for judicial training, which corresponds to the former office of prosecutor. Legal assistance is not regulated by the Administrative Court, but jointly by the bar associations and the Ministry of Justice.

In the Netherlands, in cases of general criminal law and in cases of detention (including temporary custody in immigration cases), the accused or the applicant is entitled to legal assistance. In administrative and civil law cases in general, all parties have the right to defend themselves and to be represented by a lawyer, but only parties with incomes below a certain threshold are entitled to free legal assistance.

In Portugal, in accordance with the General Regime for Administrative Offences (GRAO), the accused has the right to be accompanied by a lawyer chosen at any stage of the proceedings. In addition, the administrative authority will appoint a defence lawyer for the accused, either on its own initiative or at his/her request, in accordance with the legal assistance legislation, provided that the circumstances of the case show the need or desirability for the accused to be assisted.

In Slovakia, in general, the right to defence can be exercised by the accused him/herself or through a defence lawyer. The law does not demand mandatory representation by a lawyer in sanction proceedings before a public administration body, but the accused has the right to choose to be represented by a defence lawyer. In criminal proceedings, there is a mandatory requirement, in certain circumstances, for the accused to be represented by a lawyer (for example, if he/she is being detained, is devoid of legal capacity, if the case involves a particularly serious offence, if the case is against a minor, etc.). In administrative judicial proceedings, with some exceptions, the law provides for mandatory legal representation by a lawyer as a procedural requirement. At both stages, in administrative proceedings and in judicial administrative proceedings, the accused has the right to request legal assistance if the preconditions are met.

In Norway, although a private individual or entity is always granted the right to be represented by a lawyer, as well as the right to a defence that includes the use of appropriate means (evidence) to contradict or challenge the authorities' factual or legal assessments, the costs of hiring such a lawyer are not automatically paid or reimbursed by the authorities in proceedings for less serious cases.

The United Kingdom, Italy and Latvia do not apply this principle.

G) Principle of hearing.

Most of the countries surveyed apply this principle.

In the case of Belgium, this principle applies in cases involving a "punitive" administrative sanction, a disciplinary sanction or, in the case of a "pure" administrative sanction (*audi alteram partem*), with the authority making its position known in writing (often in the context of a withdrawal of an authorisation, licence, etc. in socio-economic matters).

In Slovakia, infractions are always dealt with before an administrative authority in accordance with the Law on Infractions. In other cases, the general rules on administrative procedures (Administrative Procedure Law) impose an obligation on the administrative authorities to order an oral hearing only if this is required due to the nature of the case, in particular if it helps to clarify the case, or if it is provided for by a special law.

In Norway, although the principle of hearing both parties is always applied, there is no general principle of oral hearing that applies to all administrative sanctions procedures.

Latvia answers in the negative.

H) Principle of separation between investigating authority and decision-making authority This principle is applied in some countries.

In the case of Austria, as a general rule, the criminal administrative authorities are both "prosecutors" and "judges". There are exceptions in respect of disciplinary procedures, where a disciplinary lawyer initiates a judicial process.

In the case of Belgium, this principle applies with the nuance that the principle of impartiality in administrative matters knows these limits and is therefore less absolute than for the courts, particularly when the law provides otherwise or when this principle conflicts with the structure of the organisation in such a way that the application of this principle will make a decision impossible. In any event, there remains access to an (administrative) court of "full jurisdiction" within the meaning of Article 6 of the ECHR.

In Cyprus, the case law of the European Court of Human Rights on this question is consistent with the fact that an administrative body combining the functions of investigation, prosecution, judgment and imposition of penalties cannot be "independent and impartial" within the meaning of Article 6 of the ECHR. However, the case law establishes that this defect can be remedied when the parties have the right to appeal the decisions of such bodies/authorities before judicial bodies with full competence or power to exercise sufficient control, including the power to nullify questions of fact and law and overturn the contested decision, and capable of ensuring that the procedure as a whole is compatible with Article 6 of the ECHR.

The example is given of the case Sigma Radio Television Ltd v. Cyprus, no. 32181/04 and 35122/05 of 21 July 2011, where the ECtHR considered that the combination of different functions of the Cyprus Radio Television Authority (CRTA) gave rise, in the Court's opinion, to legitimate concerns that the CRTA lacked the necessary structural impartiality to comply with the requirements of Article 6 of the Convention. Nonetheless, the ECtHR reiterated that even where an adjudicatory body, including an administrative one as in the present case, which determines disputes over “civil rights and obligations” does not comply with Article 6 § 1 in some respect, no violation of the Convention can be found if the proceedings before that body are “subject to subsequent control” by a judicial body that has “full” jurisdiction and does provide the guarantees of Article 6 § 1. In this regard, the ECtHR considered that the judicial remedy provided for in Article 146 of the Constitution was sufficient to comply with Article 6 of the Convention.

In the case of Estonia, administrative sanctions are decided by the administrative authorities, which also investigate the cases. However, these decisions are subject to review in the administrative judicial system, which has full jurisdiction to examine all relevant questions of fact and law.

In the case of France, although the impartiality of the sanction procedure of certain administrative authorities could be affirmed, this could not be said for all authorities. For example, the implementation of the sanctioning power of ARCEP [*Autorité de Régulation des Communications Électroniques, des Postes et de la Distribution de la Presse* – Electronic Communications, Postal and Print Media Distribution Regulatory Authority] was recently challenged by Orange as part of a QPC in 2019, due to a question of impartiality. The law provides that ARCEP’s College may participate in training on dispute resolution, prosecution and investigation. There is therefore no separation between the teams responsible for prosecuting, investigating and sanctioning, unlike other authorities with sanctioning power such as the *Autorité des Marchés Financiers* (AMF). Orange believes that in the absence of any such clearly dissociated organisation, there are real doubts about the constitutionality of ARCEP’s sanctioning power. However, Orange chose to withdraw this QPC on 26 September 2019 and doubts about ARCEP’s impartiality remain unanswered, which could prove problematic in view of the potential litigation arising from the development of the 5G network in France.

On the other hand, the Council of State has been able to affirm that since the decision of an independent administrative authority may form the subject of an appeal before a court of full jurisdiction, “the fact that the

proceedings before [that authority] do not comply in all respects with the requirements of [Article 6 of the European Convention on Human Rights] cannot lead in all cases to a violation of the right to a fair trial".
In Italy, the principle in question is not included among the general principles of administrative sanctions laid down in Law no. 689 of 1981, but it is applied in judicial practice. For example, the internal organisational measures of the prosecuting public authority are sometimes considered to be illegitimate if they do not comply with that principle, especially if the administrative body that decides on the sanction has an economic interest that can be traced back directly to the prosecuting authority.
In Poland, the administrative procedure and the final decision are issued by the same administrative authority. If a decision is final, it may be subject to a judicial control.
In Romania, in the case of administrative liability of public officials (other than the most senior public officials), the disciplinary committees responsible for investigating disciplinary matters are made up of officials of the same authority that takes the disciplinary decision.
This principle is not applied by countries such as the United Kingdom, the Czech Republic, Finland, Latvia, Lithuania, the Netherlands, Slovakia, Sweden and Norway.

I) Principle of reasoning of the sanctioning decision
All surveyed countries that answered this question apply this principle.
In Austria, in general, administrative criminal decisions must include a reasoning. However, in some cases the administrative authorities (instead of issuing an administrative criminal decision) may issue a sanction notice without any prior investigation in expedited proceedings. No reasoning of the sanction notice is required. If the accused subsequently files an admissible appeal against this sanction notice, the ordinary procedure will be initiated and the administrative authority may, where applicable, issue a sanctioning administrative decision (with due reasoning).
In the case of Belgium, this principle is applied in the same way as any administrative decision, under the Law of 29 July 1991 on the formal reasoning of administrative acts.
In the case of the United Kingdom, for certain administrative sanctions, the body that imposes them must provide the reasons for them. For ex-

ample, when the Competition and Markets Authority imposes sanctions for various breaches of research requirements, it is obliged to provide the reasons for those sanctions. In other circumstances – for example in cases involving benefit fraud – it is not necessary to provide the reasons, although the person concerned must be informed that there are grounds for criminal prosecution.

In France, before the entry into force of Law no. 79-587 of 11 July 1979, the rule was that the administration did not have to give reasons for its decisions, unless the law provided otherwise. According to the Council of State, the legislator sought to impose on an authority imposing a sanction "the obligation to specify in its decision the accusations that it intends to make against the person concerned, so that the person concerned can know, solely from reading the decision notified to him/her, the reasons for the sanction imposed on him/her". The contentious-administrative judge adopts a circumspect position with regard to the content of the reasoning. It is therefore not necessary for the administrative authority to respond to all allegations put before it, nor to attach a specific reasoning to the sanction, other than the main grounds, that would constitute an additional sanction, such as the decision to make the main sanction public.

As regards the reasoning of imposed sanctions before the court, for example by the disciplinary sections of the professional bodies which, as has been said, are a specialised administrative court, it is up to the judicial body to determine the facts with sufficient precision so that the Council of State can exercise its control, making reference to the specific cases examined for its review.

The Law of 11 July 1979 now enshrines the principle of reasoning of unfavourable individual decisions and of individual decisions that provide exceptions to the general rules established by the law or by regulations. However, there are two important exceptions to the reasoning requirement in respect of these two categories of acts. The first concerns cases of extreme urgency. However, if the person concerned so requests, within the time limit for the disputed appeal, the authority that took the decision must inform him/her of the reasons within one month. The second exception concerns cases where disclosure of the reasons for the decision would jeopardise medical confidentiality or other secrets, such as governmental and national defence deliberations.

J) Principle of time-barring of administrative infractions and sanctions
Most of the countries surveyed apply this principle.
In the case of Belgium, this principle is applied by virtue of the legal provisions and, where appropriate (in the absence of an explicit rule) through the principle of "reasonable time".
Countries that do not apply this principle include the United Kingdom, Finland and Latvia.

K) Principle of judicial protection
All surveyed countries that answered this question apply this principle.
In the case of **Belgium**, this principle is applied through an appeal for annulment before the Council of State or another judicial body expressly designated by law.

L) Principle of double instance
Most of the countries surveyed apply this principle.
Spain states that the Plenary of the Contentious-Administrative Division of the Supreme Court recently delivered two judgments on 25 November 2021 (RRCA/8156/2020 and 8158/2020) establishing as doctrine that the requirement for review by a higher tribunal of a judgment confirming an administrative decision imposing a criminal sanction, as referred to in Article 2 of Protocol 7 to the European Convention on Human Rights, in the interpretation given by the ECtHR judgment of 30 June 2020 in Saquetti v. Spain, can be satisfied by the filing of an appeal for cassation, the admission of which shall be subject to assessment of whether the criminal nature of the sanctioned offence is justified in the notice of appeal in the terms established by the ECtHR, as well as the basis of the offences imputed in the appealed judgment confirming the administrative sanctioning decision.
In the United Kingdom, in certain contexts, such as cases brought before the above-mentioned Competition and Markets Authority, there is the possibility of appealing to an independent court. In other cases, there is the possibility of seeking judicial review in a common law court of a decision imposing a sanction. In both cases, there is the possibility of filing other appeals.

In the Czech Republic, in criminal proceedings before the courts, the principle of double instance is applied (the accused always has the right to appeal), with the possibility of filing an extraordinary appeal before the Supreme Court. In the area of administrative sanctions law, the answer to the question differs. With regard to liability for offences, the proceedings are initially carried out by the administrative authorities, and the principle of double instance applies (in most cases, the accused has the right to appeal to a higher administrative authority). Moreover, since the offences typified in Czech legislation generally meet the so-called Engel criteria, the accused can also challenge the final decisions of the administrative authorities in the courts and subsequently file a cassation complaint with the Supreme Administrative Court. Therefore, the principle of double instance applies. However, with regard for example to the disciplinary liability of judges, disciplinary proceedings (which, as the Constitutional Court has held, do not meet the Engel criteria) are conducted in a single instance by the Supreme Administrative Court.

In Finland, the decisions of administrative courts can be appealed before the Supreme Administrative Court, provided authorisation to appeal is granted.

In the case of Latvia, according to the judicial practice of the Supreme Administrative Court, the following principles of criminal law are also applicable to fines under tax law: -Principle of term of validity of the law This principle provides that a law that recognises an offence as non-punishable, reduces the penalty or is beneficial for a person, unless otherwise provided by the applicable law, has retroactive effect, *i.e.* it applies to offences committed before the entry into force of the applicable law; -Inadmissibility of double jeopardy (*ne bis in idem*). This principle establishes the right not to be sanctioned repeatedly for the same unlawful act.

There are other countries where this principle is not applied, such as Belgium and Greece.

M) Other principles

In the case of Portugal, the principles of administrative sanctions law include, in addition to those mentioned above, (i) the principle of investigation; (ii) the principle of reservation of law; (iii) the principle of due process; and (iv) the principle of prohibition of analogy.

## IV.3. Subsidies and public aid

### Question 24.

**Is the principle of proportionality applied in order to modulate the consequences of non-compliance by a beneficiary of public subsidies, aid or resources, or in the area of regulated sectors?**

- **Yes (in this case, explain briefly in what areas and with what consequences or effects)**
- **No.**

### Summary of answers.

In most of the countries surveyed, the principle of proportionality is applied to modulate the consequences of non-compliance with the requirements of public subsidies, aid or resources, mitigating the negative effects on the basis of considerations such as the degree of partial compliance identified. This is the case for Croatia, Cyprus, the Czech Republic, Belgium, Estonia, Finland, Hungary, France, Luxembourg, Portugal, Slovakia, Slovenia and Norway.

Spain states that the principle of proportionality is used in these cases to modulate the consequences of an undisputed non-compliance, tempering the negative effects according to either the degree of partial compliance identified or the inexcusable third-party intervention as a determining cause of the non-compliance. Thus, for example, the principle of proportionality, of jurisprudential origin, has been expressly enshrined in the *Ley General de Subvenciones* [General Law on Subsidies], Article 37.2 of which (in relation to Art. 17.3.n) provides that when compliance with the obligations and conditions of the subsidy closely approximates total compliance and the actions of the parties concerned are unequivocally geared towards fulfilment of their commitments, the amount to be repaid will be determined by the application of certain criteria, and the principle of proportionality must be satisfied (see, in particular, STS 186/2020 of 12 February). To give another example, in the regulated energy sector, case law has held that the right to be paid the premium tariff should not be lost when delay in the fulfilment of formal obligations (registration) or material obligations (feed-in of energy into the network) is due to the actions of a third party (either the Administration or the energy distributor), without finding any lack of diligence on the part of the facility's owner.

This modulation or tempering of the consequences of non-compliance is conceived as a concrete expression of the principle of proportionality (see, in particular, STS 1261/2017 of 26 October and STS 1517/2017 of 5 October).

In the case of Belgium, provided that the administrative authority has discretionary powers in this context, judicial control will be carried out as in other areas (among others) according to the principle of proportionality. More broadly, however, it should be noted that the texts often provide for an obligation of restitution, and that the related disputes are generally regarded as disputes relating to subjective rights and therefore do not fall within the competence of the Council of State.

In Cyprus, the principles of due investigation and proportionality apply to all administrative decisions in all areas of the civil service, regardless of whether the decision concerns a beneficiary or simply a person or body subject to the authority's administration. The administration is bound by these principles, and if a contested decision does not comply with them, it will be annulled by the court.

In the Czech Republic, although the principle of proportionality is a transverse principle applied to all external activities of the public administration, in the field of public subsidies and other types of public aid, the contentious-administrative courts have ruled that the principle of proportionality must be applied in order to determine the amount of the fine to be imposed on a beneficiary who has infringed budgetary discipline or, if the subsidy has not yet been paid to the beneficiary, to determine the amount of the subsidy that will not be released.

In the case of France, when a public authority withdraws a subsidy due to misconduct, a judicial appeal before the administrative judge is possible. The judge will assess the fault alleged by the public authority, as well as its proportionality with the sanction of withdrawing the subsidy. The judge assesses the legality of the withdrawal, and does not only consider the manifest errors of assessment committed by the public authority.

In Hungary, this principle applies in various areas, such as agricultural aid or job creation subsidies. The Hungarian Curia case of 22 January 2019, which concerned a subsidy granted for the provision of village care services, is mentioned. The beneficiary (in this case, a local government body) failed to comply with its administrative obligations, and the administrative authority hearing the complaint issued an order for the entire subsidy to be recovered. The Curia considered that the administrative decision, which did not impose a proportionate reimbursement obligation consistent with the facts of the case, violated the relevant legislation (the Public Finance Law). In 2019, almost 50 cases of this type were pending before the Hungarian Curia.

In Portugal, the principle of proportionality applicable to public subsidies if there is a breach of obligation within the regulated market, specifically in the electricity sector, the Regulation on Commercial Relations in the Electricity and Gas Sectors provides that failure to comply with the clause concerning the loyalty period constitutes an obligation for the party in breach to compensate the other party, in accordance with the stipulated terms. In this context, "the compensation due shall be provided and shall not exceed the direct economic loss for the supplier or market participant involved in the aggregation from the time of termination of the contract, including the costs of investments or pooled services already provided under the contract" (Article 19, nos. 6 and 7).

Slovenia states that the Supreme Court has taken various decisions in which it has confirmed that the general principle of proportionality must also apply in these cases, and has also referred to the principles of the subsidy system established by European Union law (e.g. in agriculture).

In the case of Serbia, Article 52 of the Law on the Control of State Legal Aid sets out the administrative measures adopted by the Commission. In the subsequent monitoring procedure, the Commission can decide to impose behavioural measures requiring the repayment of State aid or other administrative measures in accordance with this Law. The Commission can impose the measure aimed at eliminating inconsistencies, *i.e.* prevention of the granting of State aid, which specifically involves the temporary or permanent suspension of the provision of State aid (behavioural measure). If it determines any such inconsistency, the Commission issues an order for the providers of State aid to take appropriate measures without delay to reimburse the relevant amount of the State aid, plus statutory default interest, from the day of use of that aid until the day of reimbursement of the amount used, and also to immediately suspend the provision of the unused amount of the State aid (return measure). Exceptionally, the Commission may waive the reimbursement of default interest, contrary to the provisions of paragraph 3 of this Article, provided that the lender shows that such action would result in the user's bankruptcy or cessation of business activity. The Commission informs the competent authority for State audit activities, *i.e.* budgetary inspection, of the measures adopted in paragraph 1 of this Article.

On the other hand, there are a number of countries where, in the obtaining of public aid or resources, the relationship between public and private parties after the funding is considered to be a private relationship governed by the principles of civil law relating to breach of legal obligations in this area, including proportionality between the infraction and the resulting sanction. However, if the subsidies or aid have an EU origin, the resources received unduly must in any case be recovered in full in accordance with the relevant EU legislation.

This is the case for both Italy and Austria, where the civil courts are competent to rule on such cases. For example, a regulation of the Minister of Finance establishes general guidelines for the granting of subsidies from federal funds, although there is no Supreme Court case law relating to this question. Other general principles applicable to subsidies include effectiveness, transparency, economy, efficiency and desirability.

Finally, in a number of countries, the principle of proportionality is not applied in order to modulate the consequences of non-compliance by a beneficiary of public subsidies, aid or resources. These include the United Kingdom, Germany (no answer given), Greece, Latvia, Lithuania, Malta, Romania, the Netherlands, Poland and Sweden.

In the case of Latvia, it is stated that the principle of proportionality in the context of State aid is interpreted as meaning that the State aid measure (amount and intensity) should be limited to the minimum necessary to induce the companies concerned to undertake additional investments or activities on their own, *i.e.* the same result could not be achieved if the amount of aid were lower. If the aid exceeds the minimum necessary, its recipient will obtain excessive benefits that could unnecessarily distort competition and therefore cannot be said to be compatible with the EU's single market. According to judicial practice, the principle of financial precaution must also be taken into account in this area. This principle is intended to ensure that public finances are not invested in projects whose success there are objective reasons to doubt, since otherwise the country runs an excessive risk of wasting public money.

For its part, the Netherlands says that when an administrative authority has a discretionary power to reclaim subsidies, the application of the principle of proportionality can lead to a reduction in the amount that must be repaid by the beneficiary. However, when an administrative authority has the obligation to reclaim subsidies, the principle of proportionality does not apply. This is the case, for example, when the obligation to reclaim subsidies is based on EU law.

## IV.4. Contracting by public bodies

**Question 25.**

**Is contracting by public bodies governed by different principles from contracting between private individuals and entities?**

- **Yes. Although based on a common foundation, administrative procurement contracts are governed by different principles from civil or private contracts.**
- **There are specific principles applicable to contracting by public bodies as regards the procedure for advertising and selecting contractors and the award of the contract, but the performance, execution and effects of the contract are governed by principles substantially the same as those applicable to private contracting.**
- **No, public and private contracting are essentially governed by the same rules and principles**

**(If you consider it appropriate, please indicate any other general principles of contracting by public bodies different from the above)**

**Summary of answers.**

In Austria there are specific principles applicable to contracting by public bodies as regards the procedure for advertising and selecting contractors and the award of the contract, but the performance, execution and effects of the contract are governed by principles substantially the same as those applicable to private contracting. In particular, in Austria the general principles of public procurement procedures include the principles of equal treatment of all candidates and tenderers, non-discrimination, proportionality, transparency, free and fair competition and economic efficiency, as well as the principle of awarding contracts to authorised, capable and reliable contractors at reasonable prices (see sec. 20 para. 1, Federal Procurement Act 2018-Bundesvergabegesetz 2018, BVergG 2018, *https://www.ris.bka.gv.at/Geltende-Fassung.wxe?Abfrage=Bundesnormen&Gesetzesnummer= 20010295*).

In Belgium, public contracting is governed, in principle, by rules different from those applicable to private contracting. The former is governed by the Law of 17 June 2016 on public contracting, and the latter by the relevant provisions of the Civil Code (Articles 1787-1799 of the "old" Civil Code). It should be noted that the "authorities" subject to the Law of 17 June 2016 may be public authorities in the organic sense of the term, or legal persons under private law that provide a service of general interest. The system of judicial control of the decisions taken by the contracting parties (public or private) depends on the nature of the contracting authority: for the decisions of public parties, the Council of State is competent; for the decisions of private parties, the ordinary courts (in principle, the commercial courts) are competent. The Constitutional Court has ruled that the two types of judicial procedures offer equivalent protection and that there is therefore no discrimination between two categories of complainants (Judgment no. 157/2020 of 26 November 2020). This does not prevent the rules on competence from being confusing for economic operators.

In Croatia, Malta and Serbia, contracting by public bodies, although based on a common foundation, is governed by principles different from those applicable to civil or private contracting.

In particular, in Serbia, the provisions of Articles 22 to 26 constitute the administrative contract instrument. The administrative contract is a mutually binding written document which, when required by a separate law, is signed by the authority and the other party, and which creates, modifies or eliminates the legal relationship in administrative matters. The content of the administrative contract must not be contrary to the public interest or the legal interest of third parties. If, due to circumstances subsequent to the conclusion of an administrative contract that could not have been anticipated at the time of the conclusion of that contract, the fulfilment of the obligations of one of the contracting parties becomes significantly more difficult, they may request the other contracting party to amend the contract and adapt it to the new circumstances. The administrative authority dismisses the party's request by issuing a decision in the event that the conditions for amendment of the contract are not met, or if such amendment of the contract would cause a harm to the public interest that would be greater than the harm suffered by the party. The public authority can terminate the contract by issuing a decision with a precise reference and a clear explanation of the reasons for the termination. If the administrative authority fails to fulfil its contractual obligation, the contractor does not have the option of terminating the administrative contract, but can raise objections. Application of this law and laws governing contracts and extracontractual liability (laws torts [sic]).

In Cyprus, Hungary, Lithuania, Luxembourg, the Netherlands, Poland, Portugal, Romania, Slovakia, Slovenia, Spain, Sweden, Norway and the United Kingdom, there are specific principles applicable to contracting by public bodies as regards the procedure for advertising and selecting contractors and the award of the contract, but the performance, execution and effects of the contract are governed by principles substantially the same as those applicable to private contracting.

In Portugal, in accordance with the Public Procurement Code (approved by Decree-Law no. 18/2008 of 29 January, with Amendment no. 25/2021 of 21 July), in the preparation and execution of public contracts, the general principles of the Constitution of the Portuguese Republic and the Code of Administrative Procedure must be complied with, as well as the principles of competition, publicity, comparability and intangibility of tenders (Articles 1-A; 4, no. 1; 72, 56 and 70).

In the Slovak Republic, the effectiveness of contracts in the field of public procurement is linked to their publication in the Central Register of Contracts.

In the Czech Republic, there are specific principles applicable to contracting by public bodies as regards the procedure for advertising and selecting contractors and the award of the contract, but the performance, execution and effects of the contract are governed by principles substantially the same as those applicable to private contracting.

In Estonia, although contracting by public bodies has a common basis with contracting between individuals, administrative contracting is governed by principles different from those applicable to civil or private contracting. In particular, the general principles applicable to public procurement include transparency, verifiability, proportionality, equality of treatment and non-discrimination, effective use of competition and public funds, non-distortion of competition, absence of conflicts of interest, economic and purposeful application of funds, best price-quality ratio, and absence of prejudice to public interests and the rights of the persons in respect of whom the duty must be fulfilled (see § 3 of the Public Procurement Act, available in English: *https://www.riigiteataja.ee/en/eli/513072020002/consolide*, and § 5 of the Administrative Co-operation Act, available at *https://www.riigiteataja.ee/en/eli/522112021003/consolide*).

Similarly, in Finland, although contracting by public bodies has a common basis with contracting between individuals, administrative contracting is governed by principles different from those applicable to civil or private contracting.

In France, although contracting by public bodies has a common basis with contracting between individuals, administrative contracting is governed by principles different from those applicable to civil or private contracting. It is in the execution stage of the contract that the difference between public and private contracting is really seen. Under a public contract, the contractor has prerogatives conferred on it by virtue of the administrative nature of the contract. The following are reserved for administrative contracts: 1.- The power to unilaterally modify the contract. This power, created by case law, has been codified in Article L. 2194-2 of the Public Order Code: "*When the buyer unilaterally submits to this book a modification to an administrative contract, the contracting party shall have the right to maintain the financial value of the contract, in accordance with the provisions of Article L.*6". According to the Council of State, this implies that the additional costs incurred by the unilateral modification must be fully compensated by the public person (EC Sect. (CE Sect. 27 October 1978, City of Saint-Malo, Rec. 401). Moreover, in the absence of any explicit indication of this modification option in the contract, private contracts are in principle intangible. 2.- Termination of the contract for simple reasons of public interest. The public person always has the right to unilaterally terminate the contract for reasons of general interest, even in the absence of a contractual clause to that effect. The price paid for exercising this right is the full compensation of the contractor who, by definition, has not committed any fault. However, this right to compensation can have its limits in practice, since certain contracts, particularly "purchase orders", do not specify an amount committed by the Administration, thus depriving the contractor of the possibility of seeking compensation. This option of termination is a matter of public policy, and a contractual clause that deprives the public person of that option will be considered null and void.

Conversely, this option cannot be accepted in the context of a private market, because it is fundamentally unbalanced. Moreover, where public contracts protect the interests of the public contracting authority, private contracts offer their contractors some protection in the event of a breach by the contracting party of its contractual obligations. This protection is enshrined, in particular, in the principle of *exceptio non adimpleti contractus*, which allows a party to a contract to withhold its own performance until the other party has duly performed its own obligations towards that first party. Moreover, unlike public contracts, private contracts can include deferred payment clauses and can be freely concluded at provisional prices.

In Germany, Greece, Italy and Latvia, contracting by public bodies, although based on a common foundation, is governed by principles different from those applicable to civil or private contracting.

## IV.5. Town planning and environment

**Question 26.**

**Could you say whether the following principles of environmental law are invoked and applied in your judicial practice?**

**Precautionary principle**

- **Yes**
- **No**
- **Occasionally, or on a limited basis (in this case, explain your answer briefly)**

**"Polluter pays" principle**

- **Yes**
- **No**
- **Occasionally, or on a limited basis (in this case, explain your answer briefly)**

**(If you consider it appropriate, please indicate any other general town planning or environmental principles different from the above)**

**Summary of answers.**

A) Precautionary principle
In Austria, Belgium, Croatia, Cyprus, Czech Republic, Estonia, Finland, France, Germany, Greece, Hungary, Italy, Latvia, Luxembourg, Malta,

the Netherlands, Poland, Portugal, Romania, Slovakia, Slovenia, Spain, Serbia and Norway, the environmental precautionary principle is invoked and applied.

In Lithuania, the environmental precautionary principle has been applied occasionally or on a limited basis, as there have been only a few cases in which this principle has been invoked (particularly in relation to the management of hazardous waste).

In Sweden, the Supreme Contentious-Administrative Court does not deal with cases or matters relating to town planning or the environment. These cases are the responsibility of the Land and Environment Courts, where the Land and Environment Court of Appeal is the highest instance. Therefore, Sweden's Supreme Contentious-Administrative Court states that it cannot contribute answers to the questions in Section 5.

In the **United Kingdom** too, the environmental precautionary principle has been applied occasionally. The courts will not challenge the government's failure to apply the precautionary principle as a matter of routine (*R (Duddridge) v. Secretary of State for Trade and Industry* [1995] Env L.R. 151). However, the courts have accepted that where the government has sought to apply the precautionary principle using a specific or identifiable mechanism or methodology, a challenge can be filed on the basis that the government did not follow those mechanisms [R (*Amvac Chemical UK Ltd) contra Secretary of State for Environment, Food and Rural Affairs* [2001] EWHC 1011).

The precautionary principle has been incorporated into UK domestic law in a limited sense by Article 17 of the Environment Act 2021. This requires the Secretary of State to prepare a policy statement setting out how certain environmental principles must be interpreted and applied proportionately by government ministers when formulating policies. The precautionary principle with regard to the environment is one of these principles.

B) "Polluter pays" principle

In Austria, Belgium, Croatia, Cyprus, the Czech Republic, Estonia, Finland, France, Germany, Greece, Hungary, Italy, Latvia, Lithuania, Luxembourg, Malta, Poland, Portugal, Romania, Slovakia, Slovenia, Spain, Serbia and Norway, the "polluter pays" principle is also invoked and applied.

C) Other principles

Other examples of environmental principles in Austrian legislation are the principles of sustainability, conservation of resources, efficiency of resources, and waste prevention and separation (sec. 1 Waste Management Act-Abfallwirtschaftsgesetz 2002, AWG 2002, *https://www.ris.bka.gv.at/GeltendeFassung.wxe?Abfrage=Bundesnormen&Gesetzesnummer= 20002086*).

In Estonia, there is also application of the principle of high-level protection of the environment, the principle of integration (considerations that ensure a high level of protection of the environment must be taken into account as guidelines for the development of all areas of life in order to ensure sustainable development), the principle of prevention, and the principle of economic use of natural resources.

The Fundamental Law of Hungary recognises and endorses the right to a healthy environment, enshrines the "polluter pays" principle and prohibits the import of polluting waste [Article XXI of the Fundamental Law]. According to Article XXI of the Fundamental Law: "*(1) Hungary shall recognise and endorse the right of everyone to a healthy environment. (2) Anyone who causes damage to the environment shall be obliged to restore it or to bear the costs of restoration, as provided for by an Act. (3) The transport of polluting waste into the territory of Hungary for the purpose of disposal shall be prohibited*".

Decision no. 4/2019 (III.7.) of the Constitutional Court of Hungary summarised the practical application, in particular with regard to the principle of non-derogation, of Article XXI of the Fundamental Law and the obligation to protect natural resources referred to in Article P) of the Fundamental Law. As regards the right to a healthy environment, the Constitutional Court emphasised that in regulating the strengthened system of values concerning the environment, the legislator must demonstrate that the new regulation does not constitute a retrograde step from the level of environmental protection achieved and therefore does not cause irreversible damage. However, a backward or retrograde step must be examined using the fundamental law test: it must be decided whether the regulation falls within the scope of application of the right to a healthy environment and whether a backward or retrograde step in the level of protection can be detected; if so, can the restriction involved in the backward step be justified by the criteria of necessity and proportionality?

In Latvia, in accordance with the Environmental Protection Law, the State's environmental policy will be developed and decisions will be taken that may affect the environment or human health, respecting the following principles of environmental protection: the principle of prevention, whereby a person must prevent as far as possible the occurrence of pollution and other adverse effects harmful to the environment or human health, or, if this is not possible, must prevent its spread and its negative consequences; the principle of assessment, whereby the effect of any activity or measure that could substantively affect the environment or human health must be assessed prior to the authorisation or initiation of that activity or measure. An activity or measure that could have adverse effects on the environment or human health, even if all environmental protection requirements are met, will be permitted in such a case only if the expected positive result for the public as a whole is greater than the damage caused by the activity or measure in question to the environment and the public.

In the field of construction, the following principles apply: the principle of architectonic quality, whereby structures are designed by balancing the functional, aesthetic, social, cultural, historical, technological and economic aspects of the construction and also the interests of the initiator of the construction and the public, emphasising the individual identity of the natural or urban landscape and integrating this organically into the cultural environment, thus enriching it and creating a living space of good quality; the principle of technical engineering quality, whereby the technical engineering solution of the structure is safe for use, as well as economically and technologically efficient; the principle of openness, whereby the construction process is open and the public is informed about the planned construction and the decisions taken in this regard; the principle of public participation, whereby, in the cases specified in this Law, public discussion of the intended construction is guaranteed; the principle of sustainable construction, whereby a quality living environment is created for present and future generations during the construction process, increasing the efficient use of renewable energy resources and promoting the efficient use of other natural resources to that end; the principle of environmental accessibility, whereby that environment is created during the construction process, in which any person can move around comfortably and use the structure according to its intended use.

In the Netherlands, the "polluter pays" principle is invoked and applied in the country's judicial practice only occasionally or on a limited basis. The "polluter pays" principle is not considered to be a general principle that can be invoked and applied in the judicial practice of the Administrative Jurisdiction Division of the Council of State (AJD). However, it is common practice for the legislator and the administrative authorities to refer to this "principle" when formulating legislation and policy.

In Portugal, in accordance with Law no. 19/2014 of 14 April, the Framework Law on the Environment, in addition to the principles already mentioned, others can be invoked, namely: the principle of sustainable development; the principle of intra- and inter-generational responsibility; and the principle of environmental education (Article 3(a) and (d) and Article 4(d)).

In its practicc, the Supreme Court of Slovenia has also highlighted the precautionary and preventive principles, which are defined as fundamental environmental principles by Article 191, para. 2, of the Treaty on the Functioning of the European Union and Articles 8 and 7 of the Environmental Protection Act.

In the United Kingdom, the "polluter pays" principle is invoked and applied in the country's judicial practice only occasionally or on a limited basis. Although the "polluter pays" principle is given some expression in the legislation (see, for example, Part IIA of the Environmental Protection Act 1990 concerning Waste on Land), the courts have hesitated to adopt the principle as a more general basis for liability. For example, the House of Lords held in R (*National Grid Gas plc/Environment Agency* [2007] UKHL 30) that the "polluter pays" principle was not a basis for extending liability under the Part IIA regime to the successors-in-title of past polluters. However, the "polluter pays" principle has been incorporated into UK domestic law in a limited sense by Article 17 of the Environment Act 2021. This requires the Secretary of State to prepare a policy statement setting out how certain environmental principles must be interpreted and applied proportionately by government ministers when formulating policies. These include the "polluter pays" principle.

## IV.6. Taxation

**Question 27.**

**In tax matters, are the following principles applied in your legislation and judicial practice? Principle of legality: Tax liability can be established only by rules with legal status.**

- **Yes**
- **No**
- **With nuances (in this case, explain your answer briefly)**

**Principle of economic or contributory capacity**

- **Yes**
- **No**
- **With nuances (in this case, explain your answer briefly)**

**Principles of equality and generality**

- **Yes**
- **No**
- **With nuances (in this case, explain your answer briefly)**

**Principle of progressiveness and its limit: non-confiscatory taxation**

- **Yes**
- **No**
- **With nuances (in this case, explain your answer briefly)**

**(If you consider it appropriate, please indicate any other general principles of tax law different from the above)**

**Summary of answers.**

A) Principle of legality: Tax liability can be established only by rules with legal status.
In Austria, Belgium, Croatia, Cyprus, Czech Republic, Estonia, Finland, France, Germany, Greece, Hungary, Italy, Latvia, Luxembourg, Malta, the Netherlands, Poland, Portugal, Romania, Slovakia, Slovenia, Spain, Serbia, Norway and the United Kingdom, the principle of legality is invoked and applied in tax matters.

B) Principle of economic or contributory capacity

In Austrian legislation and practice, the "principle of economic or contributory capacity" is applied with nuances, because although the principle of economic or contributory capacity is one of the most fundamental principles of the Income Tax Act, there are other areas of tax law where this principle is not applied, such as the Value Added Tax Act.
In the legislation and practice of the Slovak Republic, the "principle of economic or contributory capacity" is also applied with nuances. The "with nuances" answer applies whenever the principle of "contributory capacity" means the principle of capacity to pay, whereby taxes take account of a taxpayer's capacity to pay. Exceptions to the principle of taxation on the basis of a taxpayer's capacity to pay include the tax on sales of real estate assets.
In the legislation and practice of Belgium, Croatia, Cyprus, Estonia, Finland, France, Germany, Greece, Hungary, Italy, Luxembourg, Malta, Poland, Portugal, Romania, Slovenia, Spain, Sweden, Serbia, Norway and the United Kingdom, the "principle of economic or contributory capacity" is applied.
For example, by Decision no. X Ips 367/2015 of 30 August 2017, the Slovenian Supreme Court ruled that income tax should be based on an objective net principle that ensures tax fairness. This means that the costs incurred in obtaining an income must be deducted, since only the (positive) difference is what actually represents an increase in the taxpayer's assets (economic power).
In the legislation and practice of the Czech Republic, the "principle of economic or contributory capacity" is applied with nuances. The principle of economic or contributory capacity is not a guiding principle. However, the Tax Code provides several instruments that allow the current economic or contributory capacity of a taxpayer to be taken into account. These include exemption from taxes, which is an exceptional option provided for only in certain specific statutes (for example, in the Law on Budgetary Rules, which authorizes the tax authorities to waive the fine imposed for breach of budgetary discipline). There is also the possibility of a massive waiver by the Minister of Finance in the event of emergencies, particularly natural disasters. In addition, if a tax that led to a penalty has been paid, the tax authorities can exempt up to 75% of that penalty. Similarly, the Tax Code allows the waiver of penalties

for late filing or default interest, while expressly establishing that in assessing the extent to which the penalty (or interest) will be exempt, the tax authorities will take into account whether the taxpayer's economic or social circumstances justify the severity of the penalty incurred (or of the interest charged). In addition to exemptions, there are also other mitigating instruments related to the payment of taxes, such as deferral of payment or allowing the taxpayer to pay the tax in instalments. Most of the conditions set out in the Tax Code for this procedure relate to economic or contributory capacity (e.g. whether immediate payment would cause serious harm to the taxpayer, or whether the subsistence of the taxpayer or his/her dependants would be threatened, etc.).

In Latvia and Lithuania, the principle of economic or contributory capacity is not applied.

C) Principles of equality and generality

In the legislation and practice of Austria, Belgium, Croatia, Cyprus, the Czech Republic, Estonia, Finland, Germany, Greece, Hungary, Italy, Latvia, Lithuania, Luxembourg, Malta, the Netherlands, Poland, Portugal, Romania, Slovakia, Slovenia, Sweden, Serbia and Norway, the principles of equality and generality are applied.

In French legislation and practice, the principles of equality and generality are applied with nuances. The principle of equality under French tax law does not preclude the legislator from pronouncing differently on different situations or making exceptions to equality on grounds of general interest, provided that, in both cases, the resulting difference in treatment is directly related to the purpose of the establishing law.

In the United Kingdom, there is no general principle of equality and generality in tax legislation. However, Article 14 of the European Convention on Human Rights protects against the imposition of tax obligations in a discriminatory manner. Nevertheless, provided that it is not discriminatory, different persons can be taxed at different rates without this being unlawful (see, for example, *Inland Revenue Commissioners/ The National Federation of Self-Employed & Small Businesses Limited* [1982] AC 617).

D) Principle of progressiveness and its limit: non-confiscatory taxation

In Austria, the principle of progressiveness and its limit: non-confiscatory taxation is applied with nuances, since not all tax rates are established progressively in Austrian tax law. Examples of such progressive tax rates are income tax, where the rate is established progressively on the basis of annual income, and the licence tax provided for by the Gambling Act. Rules that stipulate confiscatory taxes (which result in an excessive burden on taxpayers) are unconstitutional (see, inter alia, the Judgment of the Constitutional Court of the Republic of Austria VfGH 11.3.1977, B274/74, *https://www.ris.bka.gv.at/Dokumente/Vfgh/JFR_19770311_74B00274_01/JFR_19770311_74B00274_01.pdf*). Other important principles of Austrian income tax law include individual taxation, periodic taxation, taxation of net income, and universality or territoriality.

In Belgium, the principle of progressiveness and its limit: non-confiscatory taxation is applied. The Belgian Constitutional Court has ruled, for example, that "B.15.6 In the present case, the legislator has disproportionately undermined both the testator's right to dispose of his property and the legatee's legitimate expectation of receiving it, by fixing a rate that is inconsistent with the taxes imposed for other forms of transmission of property and those affecting other categories of heirs". This case concerned an inheritance tax at a rate of 95%. The Court went on to state that: "While it is the political choice of the tax legislator to apply different rates to different taxes and to tax different categories of heirs, it is manifestly disproportionate to apply, with regard to inheritance tax, such a high rate unjustified by any specific objective of the category of taxpayers in question and taking into account only the budgetary objective pursued. B.15.7. Insofar as the rate applicable to the amount exceeding EUR 175,000 is greater than 80%, Article 1 of the contested Decree is not compatible with Articles 10, 11 and 172 of the Constitution and must be annulled to that extent".

In Croatia, Cyprus, Estonia, Finland, France, Germany, Greece, Hungary, Italy, Luxembourg, Malta, the Netherlands, Poland, Portugal, Slovakia, Slovenia, Spain, Sweden, Serbia and Norway, the principle of progressiveness and its limit: non-confiscatory taxation is applied.

In Hungary, as in all administrative procedures, the provisions of the Fundamental Law must also be respected and applied in tax-related administrative procedures. Law no. CL of 2017 on tax rules expressly sets out specific sectoral principles such as (Part I, Chapter I): the requirement for the correct (intentional) exercise of rights (prohibition of abuse of rights), the requirement to assess a contract on the basis of its content (authenticity clause), the requirement to assess a transaction on the basis of the economic results, the requirement to assess contracts between related companies, the taxation in Hungary of income covered by an international contract, and the possibility of applying an estimate in the event of any improper exercise of rights.

In the Slovak Republic, the rate of personal income tax depends on the amount of taxable income. Up to a certain level of taxable income, a lower tax rate (19%) will be applied, with a higher rate (25%) being applied when that limit is exceeded. This limit is based annually on the amount of the minimum applicable taxable income level. The dual rate for income tax (15% and 21%) also applies to corporation tax. Article 11 of the Income Tax Act also defines the establishment of the tax-free income allowance, which means that below a certain limit, income is not subject to tax.

By Resolution no. U-I-113/17 of 30 September 2020 (RS Official Gazette no. 145/20), the Slovenian Constitutional Court ruled on an application by the Administrative Court to review the constitutionality of Article 68.A of the Tax Procedure Act, which determined that a tax rate of 70% would be applied to undeclared income. The regulation on the taxation of undeclared income that was in force before the contested regulation made the rate applicable to these taxes dependent on the rates derived from the Income Tax Act (which sets a maximum rate of 50% for the highest income bracket.) The Constitutional Court therefore proceeded from the assessment that in determining a tax rate of 70%, the legislator substantially promulgated – in addition to the tax calculated according to the income tax rate in force – an increase, *i.e.* a surcharge on the normal income tax rate. The surcharge serves to deter taxpayers from violating tax law obligations and to encourage them to fulfil those obligations. The Constitutional Court considered that in promulgating a surcharge, the legislator did not pursue the objective of financing public expenditure nor any of the socio-political objectives (within the framework of social or economic policy) which, in accordance with the constitutional determination of taxes and the case law of the Constitutional Court, are acceptable objectives of taxes. It therefore concluded that in constitutional terms, the surcharge is not a tax, but a measure intended to: 1) repair the damage suffered by the public finances and revenues due to violations of the obligation to declare income; 2) annul the benefits obtained by taxpayers as a result of such violations (*i.e.* a restorative measure); or 3) sanction taxpayers for such violations (*i.e.* a punitive measure). The Constitutional Court repealed this provision on the grounds that the tax rate of 70% determined therein exceeded the tax rate prescribed by the regulation previously in force on the taxation of undeclared income.

In the Czech Republic, Latvia, Lithuania and Romania, the principle of progressiveness and its limit: non-confiscatory taxation is not applied.

However, Latvia has adopted a principle of progressiveness for personal income tax, which means that people with lower incomes pay less tax and those with higher incomes pay more. The Latvian tax administration operates in accordance with the "adviser first" principle, which establishes that the main objective is not to penalise, but to achieve cooperation between companies and supervisory authorities in order to ensure that companies know and understand their obligations and fulfil them in good faith. The tax legislation also applies the principles of proportionality, legality, equality and other principles of administrative law.

The principle of progressiveness in tax matters is implicitly established in Luxembourg's system with regard to the direct taxes that fall under the jurisdiction of the administrative courts, and it operates in such a way that there is a prohibition of taxation of the substance in the sense that no tax should in principle exceed 50%.

In Portugal, in accordance with the Constitution of the Portuguese Republic and the General Tax Law (approved by Decree-Law no. 398/98 of 17 December, last amended by Law no. 7/2021 of 26 September), in addition to the principles mentioned above, other principles may be invoked, namely: the principle of prohibition of tax retroactivity (Article 103 of the Constitution); the principle of exclusive responsibility to legislate (Article 165, 1, subparagraph i) of the Constitution); and the principle of participation (Article 60 of the General Tax Law).

According to the Law on Tax Procedure and Tax Administration of the Republic of Serbia, the following principles of tax procedure are prescribed: principle of legality, principle of time limit of tax regulations, principle of enabling insight in facts, principle of protection of secret data in the tax procedure, principle of acting in good faith, principle of facticity.

In the United Kingdom, taxation is generally applied progressively, but there is no general principle that it should be so applied or that there are limits based on the principle of non-confiscatory taxation. The form and amount of taxes fall within the competence of the Parliament. The Human Rights Act 1998, which gives some force to the Convention rights by virtue of the European Court of Human Rights, can affect the interpretation of tax statutes in order to provide a limited degree of protection against confiscatory taxes.

Taxes are established by Acts of Parliament. This is interpreted with the aim of ensuring that the Parliament's basic intention to impose a tax is restricted and the scope for unlawful tax evasion is minimised.

# ACA-Europe Seminar
# "The judge and inert administration. Administrative discretionary power"

**Riga, Latvia**
**27 April 2023**
**General Report by the Supreme Court of the Republic of Latvia**

# Summary of the General Report of the Seminar "The judge and inert administration. Administrative discretionary power" held in Riga, Latvia, 27 Avril 2023

The seminar and the preparatory questionnaire addressed two substantive issues which characterise administrative action:
a) the inertia of the public administration in dealing with the requests of private parties. Starting from the provisions on the obligation to provide and the time limits for concluding procedures, the aim was to ascertain whether there were or not procedural remedies to protect individuals and the role of the administrative judge;
b) the exercise of discretionary power by the administration and judicial review of such acts.
The report summarises the main indications emerging from the responses of ACA-EUROPE members, observers and guests.
The report is divided into three sections:
1) the first provides an overview of the legislation and application of procedural time limits;
2) the second focuses on national rules concerning the administrative silence, the role and jurisdiction of the courts in the proceedings against fictitious acts resulting from administrative silence, and other procedural remedies provided by different national jurisdictions;
3) the third examines issues relating to the exercise of discretionary power by the administration, its definition, the distinction from margin of appreciation in the interpretation of undefined legal concepts, the criteria and methods for determining when there is an exercise of discretionary power, and the limits of judicial review.
According to the answers to the questionnaire, it is common in a large number of Member States to have time limits for the conclusion of administrative procedures, which are mainly set by general provisions on the activities of public administration or by procedural law, but sometimes also contained in sectoral laws.
On average, the general time limits vary from 20 days in Latvia, to 30 days in Italy, Romania and Croatia, to 60 days in France and Malta. There are also some jurisdictions, such as Slovakia, where the Code of Administrative Procedure provides that the administrative authority must decide simple matters immediately, and within 30 days from the opening date of procedures, in other cases.
Many countries have stated that in the absence of fixed time limits, or even in the presence of them, the principle of 'reasonable time' (Belgium, Bulgaria, Croatia, Greece, Latvia), as a corollary of the principles of good administration and legal certainty, can be applied to all administrative decisions and that the reasonableness of the duration of the procedure must be assessed in relation to the concrete case and also in relation to the intermediate stages of the procedure.
The concepts of 'reasonable time' and 'without undue/unnecessary delay', recurring in many national legal systems, tend to be vague and their reasonableness/congruity must be assessed in relation to the concrete case.

In almost all Member States, the legal systems allow the authorities to extend administrative time limits, in a reasoned manner, with the exception of a limited number of countries in which, their extension is not permitted or is irrelevant in the absence of a general provision on time limits for the conclusion of the procedure.

A further differentiation between the different legal systems is related to the possibility of contesting and challenging the decision by which the administration extends the time limits, a possibility admitted in most Member States, but with different procedural remedies that in some cases have the administrative decision as their object, in others the possible harmful consequences of the administrative decision within the entire procedure.

In almost all Member States, it is provided that the administration may adopt a decision unfavourable to the applicant or potential addressee even after the expiry of the time limit, although this possibility is related to specific provisions in each Member State.

Some countries provide for the possibility of claiming compensation or actual damages if the authority's failure to meet a time limit has caused financial loss or even non-financial damage.

Failure to comply with established administrative time limits is reported as a recurring problem by eight Member States, which identify the reasons as a lack of organisational capacity of the institutions, a shortage of human and/or financial resources, inadequate timing in relation to the complexity of the procedures, and a lack of planning capacity in relation to the quantity of applications in some specific areas.

It is worth noting, however, that even those Member States that did not characterise the failure to comply with time limits for the conclusion of procedures as a frequent problem, referred in their replies to the organisational capacity of the institutions as the main reason for the delays.

Finally, most jurisdictions provide for penalties or liability for administrative authorities and/or their officials as a result of failure to comply with procedural time limits, and a significant number of countries, with the exception of the United Kingdom, reported that failure to comply with time limits may result in disciplinary or administrative liability of officials. Some of the Member States also provide for criminal liability in the most serious cases, while others require the competent authority to pay a penalty for each day's delay or to reimburse all or part of the fees that the applicant has paid for submitting the unprocessed application.

With regard to the administrative silence, an examination of the replies to the questionnaire reveals that only a few national legal systems contain a general definition of the administrative silence, whereas in most countries it is an institution that is essentially of a judicial nature for the protection of private individuals.

Most national legal systems provide for both models of tacit consent – where inaction is equivalent to granting the application (the positive model of administrative silence) – and tacit refusal – where inaction is equivalent to rejection of the application (the negative model of administrative silence) – or at least one of the two. In some countries, models of silence constitute a general principle of the legal system, whereas in others they exist only if specifically provided for by law.

When specifically asked which regulatory model of administrative silence is most typical for the national legal system, 11 countries indicated the negative model, while 7 countries the model of positive model. The other countries reported that none of these models could be considered typical because, in most areas of law, administrative silence means neither denial nor assent and the relevant models are applied as exceptions.

In a number of member states, the positive model has been introduced by transposing into national legislation the model of the tacit consent referred to in Article 13(4) of Directive 2006/123/EC of the European Parliament and of the Council of 12 December 2006 on services in the internal market, with the main purpose of simplifying administrative procedures or protecting the rights of citizens and businesses in the event of failure to comply with administrative time limits, or with both purposes.

As regards the types of administrative procedures to which the negative model can be applied, all countries indicate procedures initiated on the basis of an application or claim by a citizen, while only a few admit it in relation to procedures initiated *ex officio*.

Concerning proceedings rules, all national legal systems do not provide for a special action to appeal against a tacit refusal, but there are in the various judicial systems a few procedural specificities with regard to the need to file a hierarchical administrative appeal or to the provision of procedural time limits distinct from the ordinary ones.

With regard to the type of review exercised on the silence-denial, some countries affirm that the court may annul the 'implicit refusal' and order the administrative authority to issue a decision, but it is not competent to decide on the issue itself, judicial review being limited to the legitimacy of the act and not extending to the merits of administrative decisions. Other countries state that the court may also decide the issue on the merits, pointing out that this is normally possible in cases where the administration has no discretion or where discretion has been exhausted.

On the question of whether the national legal system provides for any prohibitions or restrictions on the application of the positive model, most respondents answered in the negative, since this model mainly applies only to specific cases provided for by law without prejudice, even in systems that provide for it as a general rule, to the limitations that may derive from general legal principles, in particular the principle of legal certainty and the protection of the rights of third parties, or from international and European obligations, national security, public order, and the nature of the interests involved (environment, taxation, etc.).

Finally, where neither of the two models of silence apply, most countries allow for the possibility of an appeal against silence or inaction, which can be lodged with an administrative authority or an administrative court.

All countries indicate that national laws do not provide specific remedies for interested third parties against an "implied decision" to accept an application. However, in most countries, if such an 'implied decision' of acceptance affects the rights or interests of a third party, the latter has the right to challenge it through a complaint to the competent administrative authority that 'tacitly approved' the application, to special administrative review bodies or before the administrative court.

In all Member States, authorities are obliged to correctly and timely execute a court ruling in an administrative case. Most countries provide for appropriate legal remedies in the event of failure by an authority to comply with this obligation, such as fines or administrative or, in serious cases, even criminal liability of the public official, as well as remedies for judicial enforcement of decisions.

All countries report that discretion is present in national legal systems, although a few contain an explicit definition of it, as it is a concept mainly developed by case law and doctrine. The definitions provided indicate a similar conception in the various national legal systems: the administrative authority has discretionary power if, in order to make a decision, it has the freedom to assess the facts according to which it can choose between several decisions, all equally lawful.

A large number of countries stated that there is no distinction between administrative discretion and margin of appreciation in the interpretation of undefined legal concepts in the legal system.

Most of the counties indicated that discretion is related to the part of the legal consequences of the legal provision, meanwhile, the margin of appreciation is related to the part of the legal provision's hypothesis (legal conditions) in cases where it contains an undefined legal concept and the administrative authority must assess its content and conclude – on the basis of an overall assessment – whether or not a given state of affairs falls within the scope of that concept.

According to most answers, discretionary power is generally indicated by the use of expressions such as 'may', 'is authorised to', 'has the possibility of', and gives the administrative authority freedom of content.

With regard to the judicial review of the use of discretionary power by the administrative authority, all the countries reported that it tends to be limited to verifying the exercise of discretionary power in accordance with the law, since it is not possible for judges to modify or annul administrative decisions if they deem them merely inappropriate. A separate discussion deserves the review of discretionary acts that have entailed a violation or limitation of fundamental rights, with respect to which most countries have reported a strengthened and more incisive judicial review that can go as far as replacing the administrative decision taken by the administration. Lastly, it should be noted that there is a general tendency in the control of discretionary power where it is based on technical rules not to limit it to manifest error or manifest unreasonableness, but to verify its reliability according to the laws of science and technology.

# Table of Contents

**3. Administrative discretionary power**

3.1. Definition of discretionary power

3.2. The distinction between discretion and margin of appreciation in the interpretation of undefined legal concepts

3.3. Characteristics, criteria, or methods for determining the administrative discretionary power in a particular case

3.4. Judicial review of the use of discretionary power by the authority

3.5. Judicial review of the use of discretionary power by the authority that has resulted in a restriction of human rights

# General Report
# Riga, 27 April 2023

## Introduction

The ACA-Europe seminar organised in Riga on 27 April 2023, and the questionnaire in preparation for the seminar addresses the issue of inert administration and the role and competence of the courts in this regard, as well as issues of administrative discretionary power.

The questionnaire was answered by 32 ACA members, observers and guests: Austria, Albania, Belgium, Bulgaria, Croatia, Cyprus, the Czech Republic, Estonia, Finland, France, Germany, Greece, Hungary, Ireland, Italy, Latvia, Lithuania, Luxembourg, Malta, the Netherlands, Norway, Poland, Portugal, Romania, Serbia, Slovakia, Slovenia, Spain, Switzerland, Sweden, Türkiye and the United Kingdom.

This General Report presents a summary of the information provided by all the national responses to a questionnaire in order to gather information on the issues to be addressed at the seminar. It is not possible to give a detailed account of all the information provided by the reporters. However, the aim of this report is to provide a comprehensive overview of the main subjects and areas of discussion, which will be addressed during the seminar, as well as to highlight similarities and differences in the information provided by reporters.

The report is divided into three main sections. The first section provides an overview of the provide insights into the regulation and application of procedural time limits. The second section focuses on the current national regulations of the administrative silence, the role and competence of the courts in the process of appeal against fictitious acts resulting from administrative silence, as well as other legal remedies available in this regard. The final third section examines issues of administrative discretionary power, in particular, definition of discretionary power and its distinction from margin of appreciation in the interpretation of undefined legal concepts, criteria and methods for determining the administrative discretionary power and a judicial control limits in this regard.

# 1. Administrative time limits

## *1.1. General principles for setting time limits*

The majority of ACA members have indicated in their national reports that their legal system sets specific administrative time limits within which authorities must take administrative decisions or complete administrative actions. While nine members (*Belgium, Estonia, Finland, Germany, Ireland, Luxemburg, Sweden, Switzerland and United Kingdom*) have specified that such time limits are set only in certain areas of law.

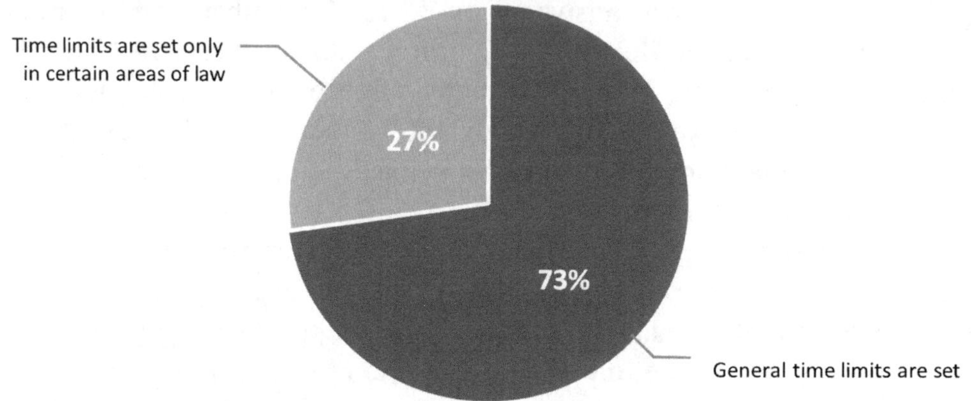


*Figure 1. Determination of time limits*

As regards where the relevant administrative time limits have been set, most ACA members indicated that they are set both in the national general code of administrative law or administrative procedure law and special laws (*Austria, Bulgaria, Croatia, Czech Republic, Germany, Greece, Hungary, Latvia, Lithuania, Portugal, Romania, Serbia, Slovakia, Spain, Switzerland, Türkiye and Norway*).

In such a case, national general code of administrative law or administrative procedure law usually sets general administrative time limits, while special law specify derogations from these time limits.

For example, *Austria* indicated that the general provisions of the administrative time limits are stipulated in the General Administrative Procedure Act. However, these provisions are applied only if administrative regulations do not provide otherwise.

*Lithuania* stated, that general administrative time limits are set out in the Law on Public Administration, providing that the subject of public administration must make an administrative decision on a person's request or complaint within 20 working days from the date of receipt of such a request or complaint. The special laws may also specify other time limits that can be shorter or longer than the general time limit of 20 working days.

Along with the national general code of administrative law or administrative procedure law and special laws, some members noted that administrative time limits are also set elsewhere (*Albania, Cyprus*, *France, Italy and Netherlands*).

*The Netherlands* has specified that the time limit for deciding upon an objection follows from the case law. *Italy* indicated that if terms exceeding ninety days are necessary for the conclusion of the proceedings, due to the administrative organization, nature of public interests, and the complexity of the proceeding, the state administrations and national public bodies adopt decrees to establish them on the proposal of the Ministers for public function and simplification of the legislation.

*Cyprus* stated that alongside other provisions, Article 29 of the Constitution safeguards, as a fundamental right of the individual, speedy administration imposing a duty upon State authorities to address petitions (written requests) and complaints of individuals in a manner befitting a society ordered by law. It expressly stipulates that an administrative authority must respond to a petition or complaint within 30 days.

*Albania* stated that sub-legal acts are issued based on and in accordance with ad hoc law.

Some members indicated that administrative time limits are set only in the general code of administrative law or administrative procedure law (*Poland and Slovenia*) or only in special laws (*Belgium, Estonia, Finland, Ireland, Luxemburg, Sweden and United Kingdom*).

For example, *Finland* stated that there is no general administrative time limit within which authorities must make administrative decisions or complete administrative action. However, the requirement of timeliness can be derived from Section 21 of the Constitution of Finland. Administrative Procedure Act also states that an administrative matter must be considered without undue delay. In addition, there are several statutory time limits laid out in specific acts.

*Malta* specified that administrative time limits in their legal system are set in the code of civil procedure.

According to the national reports, the procedures and time limits within which authorities have to take decisions or actions vary considerably among countries. However, in identifying common points, it needs to be noted that a large number of member states provide certain general time limits for the authorities. Members have mainly indicated that these time limits are set by the national general code of administrative law or administrative procedure law. However, in some cases, they may also be set by specific laws (*Albania, Bulgaria, Croatia, France, Hungary, Italy, Latvia, Lithuania, Malta, Netherlands, Portugal, Romania, Serbia, Slovakia, Slovenia, Spain and Türkiye*).

For example, in *Lithuania* the general administrative time limit in which administrative decisions are made is 20 working days from the date of receipt of request or complaint, in *Latvia* – one month, in *Italy* and *Romania* – 30 days, in *France* and *Malta* – two months.

*Croatia* stated that general administrative time limits are set in the General administrative procedure act, providing that the authority shall issue a decision within 30 days from the day of receipt of the submission. In cases when the investigatory procedure is performed, the authority is obliged to issue a decision and deliver it to the party within 60 days from the day of receipt of the submission. The special laws may also specify other time limits.

In *Slovakia,* according to the Administrative Procedure Code, the administrative authority shall decide immediately (without delay) in simple matters. In other cases, the administrative authority shall decide the matter within 30 days from the opening date of the proceedings.

*Spain* indicated that the procedural time limits established in the different regulations vary depending on the nature of the procedure and the complexity of the issues to be examined. If no specific time limits are set in the corresponding sectoral regulation, the general time limit established in the Law on the Common Administrative Procedure applies.

*Hungary* has stated that in relation to the three types of procedures specified in the Administrative Authority Procedures Act, three general time limits are set for the competent authorities: (1) twenty-four hours in case of automatic decision-making, (2) eight days for summary proceedings and (3) sixty days for full proceedings (see the reply to point 1 above).

A significant number of countries also indicated that the concept of "reasonable time" for setting administrative time limits is applied in their legal system or case law. In general, as most national reports indicate, the concept is a guiding principle according to which authorities should ensure good administration in its activities. Several countries also indicated that the concept applies in cases where the law does not clearly set a time limit for action. In such cases, the authorities are obliged to act within a reasonable time (*Belgium, Bulgaria, Croatia, Greece, Latvia, Lithuania and Netherlands*).

In this regard, *Belgium* noted that the principle of "reasonable time", which derives from the general principle of good administration and legal certainty, can be applied to all administrative decisions. Furthermore, the reasonableness of the duration of the procedure must be assessed not only in relation to the overall duration of the procedure but also with the procedural steps in between.

*Hungary* reported that the Fundamental Law of Hungary states that everyone shall have the right to have his or her affairs handled impartially, fairly and within a reasonable time by the authorities. The same right can be found, as an element of the principle of legality, among the fundamental principles of the Administrative Authority Procedures Act.

*Slovenia* indicated that it is deemed that the specified time limits set out in the law are reflecting the "reasonable time" needed to decide on the subject matter. There is a general principle recognized in the Constitution as well as in subsequent the General administrative procedure act interpretation to support the necessity to decide in a reasonable time in general.

*Slovakia's* report notes that the concept of "reasonable time" is a legally indefinite term, the content of which is defined by administrative authorities in their decision-making practice. Reasonableness is to be assessed on a case-by-case basis, concerning the nature of the matter and the administrative authority´s workload.

According to the *Türkiye* report, the principles of "decision making in a reasonable time" and "notifying the decision without delay" are included in Article 6 "Principles of Good Administration" of the Regulation on the Procedures and Principles Regarding the Implementation of the Law on the Ombudsman Institution. Thus, the principle of "reasonable time" is one of the criteria used in Ombudsman audits.

At the same time, several member states (*Austria, Czech Republic, Estonia, Finland, Germany, Luxemburg, Norway, Poland, Sweden and United Kingdom*) have indicated a different type of approach to setting time limits: their legal systems do not provide for general time limits for decisions or actions by the administrative authorities, but the general rule states that administrative authorities are obliged to act without undue delay or without unnecessary delay. However, specific time limits may be provided by some specific legal acts.

*The Czech Republic* states that generally according to the Code of Administrative Procedure the administrative authority shall deal with matters without undue delay. The Supreme Administrative Court has concluded that the assessment of failure to act within reasonable time limit is a relative issue. (Un)reasonableness of the length of the proceedings has to be examined and conclusions must be made with regard to factors that directly affect the proceedings, such as complexity of the subject-matter, requirements for taking of evidence, the conduct and procedural activities of parties etc. Conversely, conditions of operation of the administrative authority (such as human resources, internal organisation or workload) cannot be taken into account.

In *Estonia,* according to the Administrative Procedure Act, administrative procedure shall be purposeful, efficient and straightforward and conducted without undue delay. Specific legal acts sometimes contain certain time limits for administrative procedure, but if that is not the case, the limitation is "no undue delay". Finland has also indicated a similar principle.

Also, in *Norway,* it follows from the Public Administration Act that cases shall be prepared and decided "without undue delay". Moreover, it follows that if it is expected that it will take a disproportionately long time before an application can be answered, the administrative agency that received the application shall as soon as possible provide a provisional reply. In the provisional reply the reason why the application cannot be dealt with earlier shall be explained, and it shall, as far as possible, be stated when a reply can be expected. In cases concerning individual decisions, a provisional reply shall be if an application cannot be answered within one month of its being received.

*Sweden* indicated that the Parliamentary Ombudsman and other supervisory authorities make reports and decisions on what reasonable time for a particular issue might be and these serve as guidance for the administration in general.

## *1.2. Extension of time limits*

The absolute majority of national reports indicate that the legal system allows authorities to extend administrative time limits. Only a few countries indicated that such a possibility is not provided (*Austria, Croatia, Finland, Malta, Norway and Türkiye*).

Clearly, as explained by *Austria, Finland* and *Norway*, such an extension of administrative time limits is not relevant and common for those countries whose legal system does not provide specific administrative time limits. Consequently, also the question of the right of persons to complain about the authority's decision to extend the time limit is not relevant.

Some countries pointed out that such an extension of time limits is rather exceptional and only provided in specific cases (*Estonia, Hungary, Luxemburg, Slovenia and Sweden*).

*Estonia* pointed out that the possibility of extending the time limit depends on the special law which sets the time limit. For example, the General Part of the Environmental Code Act allows the extension of the time limit for issuing an environmental permit simply "if there appear circumstances which do not allow deciding on the issue of the permit within this time limit." The person may have a right of action depending on the circumstances.

In *Luxemburg*, the extension of administrative time limits is only possible in cases where the law exceptionally sets a time limit for the authority to take a decision. Normally, in such cases, the law allows the competent authority to extend the time limit once for a certain period if the case is complex. The decision to extend the time limit must be properly motivated.

*Slovenia* indicated that, generally, it is not possible to extend administrative time limits. However, there are some specific regulations in this regard, e.g. based on the Freedom of information act, administrative authority must decide on the party's application within 20 days, but in complex cases this time limit can be extended for additional 30 days, if the decision of the decision-making body decides that it is necessary in a specific case.

*Hungary* stated that the Administrative Authority Procedures Act does not allow the authorities to extend the time limit set for the administration of a case, nor does it provide for such an extension. However, a separate Act of Parliament may allow such an extension.

All other member states indicated that their legal system at least partially allows the administrative authorities to extend the administrative time limit.

For example, in *Portugal*, time limits can be exceeded when there is a particularly complex procedure or difficulties in obtaining evidence. In these situations, the burden of proof regarding the need to extend the deadline for a better decision lies within the Administration.

*Albania* indicated that the public authority shall meet some criteria/requirements to extend the time limit for the conclusion of the administrative procedure:

1) The extension must not explicitly be forbidden by law;
2) The extension may be done in justified and objective cases;
3) The time limit may be extended for complex cases (such as a combination of administrative procedures, a large number of subjects, unification of administrative procedures, special investigation for the purposes of decision-making, a large volume of evidences, etc.);
4) The time limit may be extended only once, for the maximum and no more than the initial time limit;
5) The time limit may be extended to the extent it is necessary for the conclusion of the procedure;
6) The time limit may be extended by an interim decision in accordance with the principle of proportionality;
7) The extension of the time limit shall be notified to the party before the expiration of the initial time limit.

All the above requirements do not allow for the extension to be arbitrary or unjustified but are in favor of the fair and objective resolution of administrative case.

In the case of *Bulgaria*, the time limit may be extended if it is necessary to give other individuals or organisations the opportunity to object or is necessary to obtain the consent or opinion of another authority.

*Ireland* stated that some legislation specifically permits the extension of time for certain bodies within a specific service, whilst other bodies allow for the extension of time-based on discretion.

National reports indicate differences in regulations and case law regarding the rights of a person to complain about the authority's decision to extend the time limit.

Six member states reported that in their legal system there is no such right to complain about an extension decision (*Hungary, Netherlands, Norway, Poland, Serbia and Slovenia*).

The Council of State of The Netherlands indicated that although the extension of the decision period can have unpleasant consequences for the applicant (it will take longer before construction or the intended use can start, for example), it is in principle not possible to object against this decision.

In *Poland*, the decision to extend the time limit is made in the form of an order of an authority and this order cannot be appealed.

Ten member states reported that such rights exist in their legal system (*Czech Republic, Greece, Ireland, Italy, Latvia, Portugal, Romania, Slovakia, Switzerland and United Kingdom*).

*The Czech Republic* indicated that participants generally have the right to appeal the decision to extend the time limit. However, some special laws provide exceptions. For example, due to the fact that the time limit for dealing with a request to provide information is not extended by issuing a formal decision, but only by informing the person who submitted the request, the extension cannot be appealed. In contrast, according to the Act on Free Movement of Services, the administrative authority has to issue a formal decision on the extension of the time limit under this provision which, on the other hand, also explicitly excludes the possibility of appealing against such a decision.

*Ireland* also indicated that it is generally possible to appeal a negative decision in an application to extend the time limit of a particular service. However, there are no specified legal remedies available for a right to complain about an authority's decision to extend the time limit.

*Italian* case law has admitted the appeal against the acts by which the authority requests unnecessary formalities or issues decisions that circumvent the content of the request or otherwise suspend the procedure without a deadline.

*Latvia* reported that according to the Administrative Procedure Law the decision on the extension of the time limit may be contested to a higher authority in accordance with the procedures regarding subordination. If there is no such higher authority, as well as the decision on the extension of the time limit of the higher authority, it may be appealed directly to the court. The court shall examine the complaint in a written procedure at one instance, with no right of appeal.

Some countries pointed out that the question about the right of persons to appeal against the authority's decision to extend the time limit could not be answered unequivocally (*Albania, Estonia, France, Germany, Lithuania and Luxemburg*).

*France* pointed out that, in general, persons do not have the appeal against the authority's decision to extend the time limit. However, such an appeal cannot be excluded if the particular decision is unfounded and affects the interests of the person concerned.

In *Germany*, the law does not regulate this issue. Nevertheless, the decision about the extension must be considered a procedural decision that cannot be subject to separate litigation. The legality of extending the time limit could, therefore, only be the object of judicial scrutiny in litigation of material compensation for a supposedly delayed permission.

Also, in *Lithuania*, the law does not provide a person's right to complain about the authority's decision to extend the time limit. The Supreme Administrative Court of Lithuania has stated that the decision to extend the administrative procedure is only an intermediate procedural document that does not cause independent legal consequences and, according to consistent court practice, cannot be the independent subject of an administrative dispute. Nevertheless, the reasons for the extension may be assessed when (if) the final administrative decision is challenged before the courts.

*Albania* reported that whereas the legislator does offer explicit provision in this regard, there are two approaches to challenging the interim decisions on the extension of time limits for the administrative procedure. On the one hand, their appeal is considered along with the final decision, on the other hand, their appeal is submitted immediately following their notification.

*Luxemburg* stated that in rare cases where the authority is obliged to reply within a certain time limit and extends that time limit, the applicant could theoretically complain about the authority's decision. However, in such a case, there would be a question of the admissibility and classification of such a complaint.

National reports indicate that almost all ACA member states (28 members in total) provide that an administrative decision unfavourable to the submitter or the potential addressee of the decision can still be made after the expiry of the time limit. However, several countries have highlighted some specificities in this regard.

For example, in *Cyprus*, no administrative decision can be reached if an excessive period of time has passed, which essentially influences the legal and real conditions. In fact, a challenged favourable decision to an interested party may be annulled by the court if the decision was taken in breach of the 'reasonable time' rule and by the time the decision was taken, the legal or real conditions have changed.

*France*, in this regard, noted that, unless the law provides otherwise, if the authority fails to take a decision within the time limit set by law, the claim is deemed to have been granted. The case law of the French Conseil d'Etat states that the authority may annul or revoke such a fictitious decision conferring rights on its own initiative or at the request of a third party only if it is unlawful and if the annulment or revocation takes place within four months of the decision.

*Finland* indicated that there are instances where unfavourable decisions cannot be made after the expiry of a given time limit (typically in matters initiated by authorities.

*Greece* also pointed out that in cases with a strict time limit and not an indicative one, the administrative decision cannot be made after the expiry of such time limit, whether or not the decision is unfavourable to the submitter. In these cases, if the authority makes a decision after the expiry of the strict time limit, this decision is not enforceable because the authority that issued this decision had no jurisdiction to issue such a decision.

*Malta* noted that such a decision is possible unless the addressee has already taken legal action.

*Portugal* indicated that pursuant to the Code for the Administrative Procedure the unofficial initiative procedures that may lead to issuing a decision containing unfavourable effects to the interested parties expires in the absence of a decision within 120 days' time.

*Albania* stated that, as a rule, the legislation requires compliance with the time limits for the conclusion of legal administrative actions. Albeit, in practice, it occurs that an administrative action may be completed out of the time limit set out by law. Code of Administrative Procedure offers a permitting approach in this regard states that failure to comply with the time-limits should be justified by the competent authority to the superior body, or by the competent official to his/her own superior within 10 (ten) days from the expiry of the time-limit or the end of state of emergency.

*The Czech Republic* indicated that no decision (whether favourable or unfavourable) can be made after the time limit has expired if the law provides a fictitious decision upon the expiry of the time limit. Norway also indicated that in cases where the claim is deemed to be granted as the time limit expires, the authority is generally prohibited from making a decision that is unfavourable to the potential addressee after the expiry of the time limit.

Some countries also noted that if such a failure by the authority to meet a time limit has caused a financial loss or non-financial damage to a person, a persona is entitled to claim appropriate compensation (*Estonia, Greece, Italy and Latvia*).

### *1.3. Non-compliance with time limits*

Failing to comply with established administrative time limits is reported as a common problem by eight member states (*France, Italy, Netherlands, Poland, Portugal, Serbia Slovakia and Slovenia*). A lack of institutional capacity is mainly cited as the main reasons for non-compliance with administrative time limits. However, some of the specificities identified by countries are also worth mentioning.

*Italy* reported that situations where an authority does not take administrative decisions or perform administrative actions within the time limit set by law are usually related to lack of resources within the authority (e.g. lack of staff), the improper organisation of administrative activities and inappropriate time limit provided for a complex proceeding (for example, if many advices need to be obtained).

In *Slovakia* the causes of the inactivity by public administration bodies are varied. Indeed, individual and, in a few cases, systemic failures by authorities and legal as well as non-legal causes can be identified. The legal causes of the inactivity lie in the deficient or missing regulation. Non-legal causes include a lack of financial resources that has impacts in terms of personnel and material.

*France*, *Poland* and *Slovenia* have indicated that, besides the lack of institutional capacity, a large number of applications on certain administrative matters to administrative bodies that have limited capacity is also a problem. *France* identified such administrative matters as asylum, urban planning and social assistance, while *Slovenia* highlighted cases related to work visas and permits.

Also, in *the Netherlands*, the problem is especially challenging in the context of asylum law, where the Immigration and Naturalisation Service has to deal with many applications, and in the cases of large compensation projects. Since the right to compensation depends mainly on the facts of the case, the Tax Service (Belastingdienst) has significant problems deciding timely the thousands of applications it is confronted with.

Although the other member states did not identify failing to comply with established administrative time limits as a common problem, lack of institutional capacity was also cited as a primary reason for time delays.

*Germany* indicated that time limits are difficult to abide by partly because of lack of staff, and partly because of the complexity of the law, which demands very complex administrative decisions (*i.e.* in urban planning etc.).

*Albania* noted that it used to be a common problem. However, since 2016, following the introduction of the amended Code of Administrative Procedure, a greater awareness of state administration for completing the administrative actions in due time is evident. This occurs due to the digitalization of services that are getting electronic (online). The authorities' failure to meet the time limit, aside from a lack of institutional capacity, is also sometimes caused by a lack of organizational skills of the institution to make a decision in due time and in any case the approaches of officials to obtain an unlawful benefit in corruptive means (criminal offence).

It is also worth mentioning the cases observed by Supreme Administrative Court of *the Czech Republic* in which administrative authorities were inactive due to their opposition to the case law (in particular, the tax authorities were refusing to pay interests related to verification of VAT deduction claims).

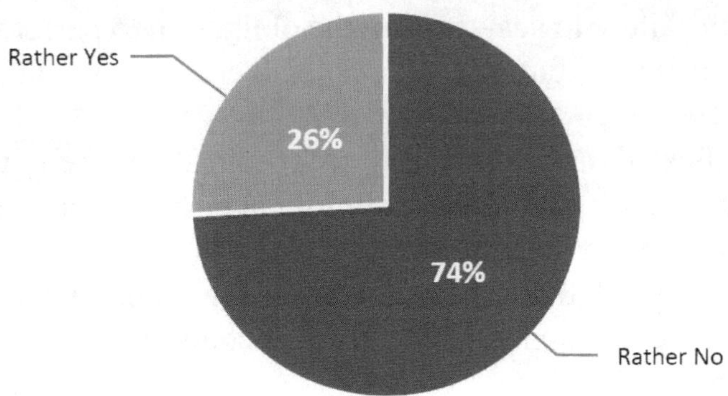


*Figure 2. Is a non-compliance with the time limits a common issue?*

On the question of whether there are any penalties or liability for the authorities or their staff for not complying with the time limits, only three member states indicated that their legal system does not provide such remedies (*France, Malta and Romania*).

In a significant number of countries, not complying with time limits in certain circumstances might result in staff being held liable to disciplinary or administrative action (*Albania, Austria, Belgium, Bulgaria, Cyprus, Czech Republic, Estonia, Finland, Greece, Italy, Latvia, Lithuania, Poland, Portugal, Slovakia, Slovenia, Spain, Sweden and Norway*).

In *Spain*, the Law on Common Administrative Procedure states that the staff in the service of the Public Administrations who are responsible for the handling of cases, as well as the heads of the administrative bodies competent to investigate and resolve them, are directly responsible, within the scope of their competences, for compliance with the legal obligation to issue a written decision within the deadline. Failure to comply with this obligation shall give rise to disciplinary liability without prejudice to any other liability that may arise in accordance with the applicable regulations. *Italy* also stated that according to the Administrative Procedure Law, failure or delay to issue the final decision is an element of individual performance assessment and disciplinary and administrative-accounting responsibility of the defaulting official.

The Supreme Administrative Court of *Lithuania* has stated that when applying disciplinary liability to civil servants for the failure to act, manifested by failure to perform procedural actions established by legal acts within the established terms, there must be assessed not only the objective basis of responsibility for failure to act – having the obligation to perform the actions established by legal acts, but also the subjective basis – the ability to act as required by law.

*Slovenia* indicated that disciplinary proceedings may be initiated against an individual civil servant if there are additional circumstances, e.g. showing a lack of due attention to the case.

*Ireland*, however, stated that there may be only internal disciplinary procedures where the competence of the staff to comply with procedural time limits is in question.

*Finland* indicated that questions of dealing with cases of undue delay are, in practice, perhaps most typically handled by the Parliamentary Ombudsman and the Chancellor of Justice, who supervise the activities of authorities and can investigate complaints concerning the undue delay in administrative decision-making. They can e.g. issue a reprimand to an authority or official concerned.

In addition, some of the countries (*Albania, Austria, Italy, Norway and Sweden*) also provide criminal liability in certain grave cases.

For example, in *Italy*, in accordance with the Criminal Code the public official or the person responsible for a public service who, within 30 days of the request, does not perform the act of his office and does not answer to explain the reasons for the delay, is punished with imprisonment up to a year or with a fine up to 1032 euros.

Some countries have also identified other measures.

In *Hungary* the Administrative Authority Procedures Act sanctions the exceeding of the time limit set for the administration of cases by imposing on the authority the obligation to pay fees and charges, and by exempting the client from paying the procedural costs.

*The Netherlands*, in 2009, adopted the Act on Penalty Payments in Case of Late Decisions. The essence of this Act is that an administrative body that does not decide in time on an application will have to pay a penalty payment for each day that the body is in default. This penalty has its boundaries. The maximum number of days that a periodic penalty payment can be forfeited is set at 42 days.

*Norway* indicated that in certain areas, such as spatial planning, failing to comply with the time limits could entail that the relevant authority would have to reimburse, either partly or in full, fees that the applicant has paid in order to have the authority decide the application.

In *United Kingdom* any remedy would be directed at the public authority and would not extend to staff.

## 2. Administrative silence

### *2.1. Administrative silence as a legal concept*

Only a few national legislations contain a general definition of administrative silence (*Czech Republic, Greece, Italy, Romania, Serbia and Slovenia*).

For example, in the *Czech Republic*, the administrative silence is defined as a failure to act within a specific or reasonable time limit.

In *Italy*, according to the Administrative Procedure Law, the silence of the public administration is a misbehaviour of the administration who is obliged to conclude the proceeding by adopting a final decision within the time limit.

In *Slovenia*, if the administrative decision was not issued within the statutory set time limit, it is considered that the administrative silence (silence of administration) has occurred.

The *Greece's* Administrative Procedural Code contains a slightly broader definition: administrative silence occurs in cases where an authority is obliged to take an administrative decision but fails to do so within a specific time limit set by a special law, after the day of the submission of the petition. If a specific time limit is not set by law, administrative silence occurs when an authority is obliged to take an administrative decision but fails to take this decision within three months after the day of the submission of the petition.

*Romania* indicated that according to Administrative Litigation Law, not replying to the applicant within 30 days of registration of the application (unless otherwise provided by law) is defined by the concept of "failure to settle a petition within the legal time limit" and is considered an assimilated (atypical) administrative act.

Other national reports indicated that the "administrative silence" is not clearly defined as a general legal concept in their national legislation. However, it is present and is used in one form or another in certain administrative regulations and jurisprudence almost in all countries.

For example, *Spain* indicated that the concept of administrative silence has been included in the Spanish legal system for many years, and it is currently referred to the Common Administrative Procedure that address the lack of a written decision within the established time limit, and regulates the effects of the Administration's silence.

*Portugal* stated that in the doctrine silence can be "understood as the absence of a decision by the Administration concerning a petition addressed to it by an individual".

In *Slovakia*, the legal theory uses the term "fiction of decision/fictitious decision", which is the consequence of inaction by an administrative authority.

## *2.2. Legal models of administrative silence*

Administrative silence by the administrative authorities can have different effects. The authorities' silence, or failure to take a decision within the set time limit, may be deemed to be a refusal to take such a decision (negative model of administrative silence) or, in the opposite case, a claim not refused in due time is deemed granted (positive model of administrative silence). At the same time, administrative silence also may not have any specific effects and mean neither refusal nor granting of the application. However, a person may, for example, take action against the administrative authority's inaction.

National reports indicated that most legal systems provide both positive and negative models of administrative silence, or at least one of them. Moreover, in some countries, the relevant models are provided as a general principle in the case of administrative silence, while in others, they exist only in cases specifically provided for by law.

The negative model of administrative silence as a general principle in the case of administrative silence is established in *Belgium, Greece, Latvia, Luxemburg, Malta, Romania, Slovenia, Türkiye*. It means that administrative silence shall be recognised as a deemed refusal of a claim unless the law provides otherwise.

In certain areas of law, the negative model of administrative silence is provided in Albania, Bulgaria, Cyprus, Czech Republic, France, Greece, Ireland, Italy, Norway, Serbia Slovakia, Spain and United Kingdom.

For example, only one example of this model can be found in the *Czech* legal system: deemed refusal of a request to provide environmental information according to the Act on the Right to Environmental Information.

*Italia* indicated that their legal system provides a negative model but the law should explicitly provide that administrative silence is to be considered as a rejection of the claim.

*Estonia* stated that where not otherwise provided by law, administrative silence has a similar effect as refusal. However, nowhere in law it is explicitly stated that administrative silence equals refusal to grant the application.

In some countries where a negative model of administrative silence used to exist, indicated that it is no longer present in their legal system. In *the Netherlands*, before 2009, the case law of the Administrative High Court left it up to the parties whether the administrative silence should be considered as a fictitious refusal. If the administrative body wanted its silence to be considered a refusal, it only had to motivate this in its statement of defence. However, this model does not exist anymore. Also, in *Portugal* the current Code for the Administrative Procedure of 2015 does not provide, any longer, the negative effects of silence as a tacit act of refusal, enshrined in its previous that is now repealed.

Also, *Albania, Austria, Finland, Germany, Hungary, Lithuania, Poland and Switzerland* indicated that the negative model of administrative silence is not provided in their legal system.

Five countries have indicated the positive model of administrative silence as a general principle in the case of administrative silence in their legal systems (*France, Italy, Netherlands and Spain*).

In *Italy*, the Administrative Procedure Law states that the silence of public administration shall be deemed to constitute assent for all proceedings initiated by a request for an administrative act.

Similarly, in *Spain*, in procedures initiated at the request of the interested party, the law has sought to establish a general positive model of administrative silence, although with relevant exceptions.

The positive model of administrative silence also applies in other countries in certain areas provided for by law or as an exception (*Austria, Belgium, Bulgaria, Cyprus, Czech Republic, Estonia, Finland, Germany, Greece, Hungary, Ireland, Latvia, Lithuania, Luxemburg, Norway, Poland, Portugal, Romania, Slovakia, Slovenia, Sweden, Türkiye and United Kingdom*). In several countries, this model was mainly implemented by transposing the positive silence model provided for in Article 13(4) of Directive 2006/123/EC of the European Parliament and of the Council of 12 December 2006 on services in the internal market into national legislation.

On the question of which regulatory model of administrative silence is more typical for national legal system 11 countries (*Belgium, Bulgaria, Greece, Latvia, Luxemburg, Malta, Romania, Slovenia, Sweden, Türkiye and United Kingdom*) indicated the negative model of administrative silence, while 7 countries indicated the positive model of administrative silence (*Austria, France, Hungary, Italy, Netherlands, Poland and Spain*). Meanwhile, the rest of the countries indicated that none of these models could be considered typical because, in most areas of law, administrative silence means neither refusal nor granting of the application, and the models are rather applied as exceptions.

## *2.3. The negative model of administrative silence*

This section of General Report summarises the responses of those ACA member states with a negative model of administrative silence in their legal system.

### *Types of administrative procedures the negative model can be applied to*

All of the countries on the question of the types of administrative procedures that the negative model can be applied to, stated that the model is applicable to procedures that are initiated on the basis of an application or claim by a person (*Belgium, Bulgaria, Croatia, Cyprus, Czech Republic, Estonia, France, Ireland, Italy, Latvia, Luxemburg, Malta, Norway, Romania, Slovakia, Türkiye and United Kingdom*).

Only a few countries indicated that the negative model of administrative silence could also be applied to *ex officio* or other procedures (*Greece, Slovenia, Spain and Serbia*).

As *Slovenia* has stated, in any proceedings brought against the party (on an application or *ex officio*), the administrative silence presupposes a negative decision for the party (its application denied or imposition of new obligations on the party.

*Spain* indicated that for procedures initiated on the basis of applications, the negative silence model applies: (1) in those cases in which a rule with the status of law or a rule of European Union or international law applicable in Spain establishes otherwise; (2) in procedures relating to the exercise of the right to petition; (3) in those cases whose upholding would result in the transfer to the applicant or third parties of powers relating to the public domain or the public service, in proceedings which involve the exercise of activities that may damage the environment and in procedures demanding the liability of the Public Administrations, as well as (4) in proceedings challenging acts and provisions of the public administration.

But for *ex officio* procedures: (1) in the case of procedures which may result in the recognition or, where appropriate, the establishment of rights or other favourable legal situations, the interested parties who have appeared in the proceedings shall understand their claims dismissed due to administrative silence; (2) in procedures in which the administration exercises powers to impose penalties or, in general, powers to intervene which may have unfavourable or burdensome effects, the proceedings shall lapse due to administrative silence.

### ***The process for appealing against a "fictitious refusal"***

The majority of countries reported that the negative or rejection effects of the expiration of the time limit without a written decision having been issued are produced immediately or automatically due to the expiry of the time limit, and national regulation does not provide any extra actions in order for the person to be able to appeal the refusal (*Bulgaria, Cyprus, Czech Republic, Greece, Ireland, Italy, Latvia, Norway, Serbia, Slovakia, Slovenia, Türkiye and United Kingdom*).

Some of these countries, however, pointed out that if the party wishes to challenge or appeal a rejection due to administrative silence, the party may have to justify that this silence has occurred, for example, by providing a copy, receipt or certification of the initial application, which initiated the administrative procedure that has not been resolved within the time limit (*Cyprus, France, Greece, Latvia, Luxemburg, Spain, Türkiye and United Kingdom*).

*Belgium* reported that in the case of the classic negative model, three preconditions must be identified:

1) a statement addressed to the competent administrative authority, made by the interested party;
2) the administrative authority must be obliged to take a decision;
3) the administrative authority must remain silent for four months.

Once these preconditions have been met, the "fictitious refusal" is subject to appeal.

*Poland* indicated that the general rules of administrative silence regulated in the Code of administrative procedure offer a possibility for a petitioner to receive proof of the authority accepting his application being silent for a prescribed time period.

*Malta* stated that the applicant has to provide proof of silence. However, the report does not provide any details.

*Luxemburg* indicated that all cases are different. Thus, the administrative judge must analyse on a case-by-case basis whether, in a particular case, the law provides that administrative silence is deemed to be a refusal.

Based on the national replies, it can be concluded that in almost all countries, the "fictitious refusal" resulting from administrative silence can be appealed before a higher authority (if any) and/or a court, with the majority of rapporteurs indicating no differences in the appeals process for "fictitious refusals" resulting from administrative silence from the general appeals process.

Only *Czech Republic* indicated that administrative courts do not review "fictitious refusals" but subsequent decisions on the merits of appellate administrative authorities (if the refusal is appealed). The administrative proceedings, thus, should always end with a standard decision on merits with reasoning, and the court can either annul the decision and refer the case back to the administrative authority or dismiss an action against the decision as unfounded. However, it should be noted that such a process is based on a single provision – the Act on the Right to Environmental Information – which is the only law that provides for the negative model of administrative silence in the Czech Republic.

A few countries highlighted some specificities of the process.

For example, *Cyprus* indicated that some statutes include provisions for hierarchical recourses or complaints to be made to higher authorities before lodging a recourse to the Administrative Court. For example, the Right of Access to Information of the Public Domain Law provides for the filing of a complaint to the Commissioner of Information if the administrative authority has failed to respond to a request or has violated the time frames.

*Serbia* indicated that in the appeal procedure due to the silence of the first instance administrative body the same authority acts in relation to the general appeal procedure. Its procedure differs from the general appeal procedure. In the appeal procedure, the second-instance authority requests that the first-instance authority shall inform the second-instance authority why it failed to issue a decision in a timely manner. If the second instance authority finds that the first-instance authority did not issue a decision within the time limit specified by law for a justified reason, it extends the deadline for issuing a decision for a period as long as the justified reason lasted, and 30 days at the latest. If the second-instance body finds that there is no justified reason for failing to issue the decision within the deadline specified by law, it decides on the administrative matter by itself or orders the first-instance body to issue a decision within a period no longer than 15 days. If the first-instance authority does not issue a decision again within the deadline set by the second-instance authority, it decides on the administrative matter by itself.

*Slovenia* noted that the only difference is that the appellate authority will ask first instance administrative authority for the reasons for the delay.

*Italy* specified that in the case of "fictitious refusal" the applicant will not be able to complain about the unlawfulness of the fictitious refusal for lack of reasoning.

In *Luxembourg*, there is a difference concerning time limits. The general time limit for action against a decision of the administrative authority is three months. It must be observed. Otherwise, the appeal will be declared inadmissible. As regards fictitious refusal, the individual is not obliged to act. He/she may prefer to wait until the administrative authority actually decides. The mechanism of fictitious refusal has traditionally been understood as a way of making the silent administration react. This is why the Luxembourg legal system has never provided that, in case of a fictitious refusal a person would be obliged to act within three months.

*France* indicated that in cases where the silence of the administrative authority is considered as a negative decision, and unless otherwise provided by law, the interested party has two months to lodge an appeal from the date of the fictitious negative decision. The applicant must prove by any available means the date on which the application was submitted to the administrative authority.

*Türkiye* also has a specific procedural provision – if the request is not replied to within thirty days, it shall be deemed to be dismissed. The persons concerned may brought an action to the Council of State, administrative and tax courts, depending on the subject of the case, within the time limits running from the end of thirty-day period. If the response given by the authorities within the thirty-day period is not final, the person concerned may either regard this response as dismissal or bring an action regarding this response as dismissal or wait for the final response. In this case, the time limit for the action shall not run. However, the waiting period cannot exceed four months from the date of application. In the case of not filing an action or dismissal of action due to the time limit, if a response is given by the authorities after the end of the thirty-day period, an action might be brought within sixty days from the notification of the response.

***Competence of the court in relation to the "fictitious refusal"***

According to national reports, there are some differences in the competence of national courts in cases where the "fictitious refusal" is found to be unjustified.

Eight countries indicated that the court's competence extends only to the annulment of such a "fictitious refusal" and ordering the administrative authority to issue a decision, but the court has no competence to decide upon the matter itself (*Bulgaria, Cyprus, France, Luxemburg, Malta, Norway, Sweden and United Kingdom*).

*Cyprus* specified that the reason the court cannot decide the matter itself is that the role of the administrative court in a recourse for judicial review is limited to testing the legality and not the correctness of administrative decisions. Two exceptions exist by virtue of the Administrative Court's Law of 2015. In asylum and tax recourses, the administrative court has jurisdiction to review both the legality and the correctness of the decision and to substitute the administration's decision with its own. However, in tax recourses where the applicant challenges the omission generated from inaction where the action is due in law, the administrative court has no jurisdiction to review the correctness of the omission. The matter must first be decided by the administrative authority in order to execute its legal obligation by issuing a decision.

In *Norway*, generally the courts competence is limited to ruling on the validity of the decision. As a consequence, the court's judgments in these matters will only rule that the decision – be it a regular one or a "fictitious refusal" constituted by the relevant rules on the negative mode – is invalid. It would then be for the relevant public body to examine or re-examine the matter, taking into account the ruling and findings of the courts. The courts would, at least generally, not set a specific time limit, but as always, the decision would have to be made "without undue delay" and in accordance with any other fixed time limits that might apply.

*Luxemburg* indicated that the administrative judge, following the classic procedure of the action for annulment, has the competence to annul the "fictitious refusal" and refer the case back to the administrative authority to decide upon the matter. However, if the competent administrative authority does not comply within three months of the referral, the party who received the annulment judgment may submit a request to the court that pronounced the annulment in question for the appointment of a special commissioner. In practice, in 98% of the cases, the request for the appointment of a special commissioner causes the administration to react and it takes a decision.

Once an administrative decision is taken, the request for the institution of a special commissioner becomes irrelevant.

Meanwhile, eleven countries stated that the court can also decide upon the matter itself (*Belgium, Croatia, Germany, Greece, Italy, Latvia, Romania, Serbia, Slovenia, Spain* and *Türkiye*).

In *Greece*, according to the Administrative Procedural Code, if a court finds a deemed refusal of a claim resulting from an administrative silence to be unjustified, it shall assign the authority to examine the petition and issue a relevant decision. In cases where the Tax Authorities have failed to issue a decision within a specific time limit, the court shall abrogate the administrative silence and decide upon the existence and the content of a right or an obligation.

*Romania* stated that, as a rule, the court may order the administrative authority to issue a decision within a certain time limit and may determine the application of certain penalties for each day of delay. If the court does not set a time limit, the administrative authority must comply with the obligation within 30 days from the date the court decision becomes final.

If the court has all the evidence necessary to verify that the conditions laid down by law for a favourable outcome of the plaintiff's application have been met, without further reassessment by the public authority, it may itself decide on the matter in dispute or oblige the public authority to issue an administrative decision with a certain content.

*Slovenia* similarly mentioned that if the court finds that the lawsuit is well-founded, it will mostly order the administrative body to issue a decision with a certain content in a certain time limit or if additional conditions are met (all of the facts are already determined or were determined by the court), the court can also decide on the case (dispute of full jurisdiction). The judgment will replace the decision of the authority.

*Serbia* indicated that if the court has the necessary facts and the nature of the subject matter allows/permits it, it can directly resolve the administrative matter with its judgment.

*Spain* reported that once the appeal has been lodged against the presumed rejection, the court has the same capacity to study, hear and resolve the case as if it were dealing with the challenge of an explicit act. It is a different matter that, precisely because it is a rejection due to administrative silence, in the absence of a written administrative decision, the court may lack essential data to decide on its own. In such a scenario, it would be possible to give a judgment ordering the administration to issue a written decision in accordance with the rules and details established by the court.

Meanwhile, all the countries where the court is competent to decide upon the matter itself instead of the "silent" authority indicated that this is only possible in cases in which the authority has no discretionary power or it is limited to zero (where a provision of applicable law requires that a specific content decision be issued and the authority is no longer required to carry out considerations of usefulness).

***Legal remedies if the authority does not comply with the court's decision***

From national reports, it is generally clear that all countries apply the principle that authorities are obliged to properly and in good time enforce a judgment or another decision directed against it, rendered or taken by a court in an administrative case. Most countries also provide various legal remedies in the case of an authority's noncompliance with this obligation.

Several countries indicated that if a court order to issue a decision is not complied with, the administrative authority may face financial penalties (*Albania, Bulgaria, Estonia, Germany, Greece, Latvia and Spain*).

For example, in *Bulgaria*, in accordance with the Code of Administrative Procedure, the responsible official who does not implement a court decision in force may be fined. The minimum financial penalty is about 100 EUR, and the maximum is about 1000 EUR.

*Latvia* also indicated that according to the Administrative Procedure Law, a court may impose a pecuniary penalty on the responsible official. The minimum pecuniary penalty shall be 50 EUR, the maximum – 5000 EUR. A person may ask a court to re-impose the pecuniary penalty until the head of an authority or another official enforces or terminates the activity specified in a court ruling. A repeated pecuniary penalty may be imposed not earlier than after seven days.

Some countries, as a possible legal remedy, also indicated administrative or, in grave cases, even criminal liability of a public official who does not implement the judicial decision (*Albania, Spain, Sweden and Türkiye*).

Similarly, the *United Kingdom* indicated that failure to comply with a court order could, in theory, generate proceedings for contempt of court. Sanctions for contempt of court include imprisonment, fines and seizure of assets.

*Croatia* stated that if the authority does not enforce the judgment within a certain period, the party can demand enforcement of the judgment from the court of the first instance. *Romania* reported that if the authority does not willingly execute the judgment, it is enforced by compulsory execution, following a special procedure provided by the Administrative Litigation Act.

The *Italian* legal system provides a wide range of legal remedies. The claimant may submit a complaint concerning the non-compliant execution of the judgment, and it shall be examined by the court, which issued the judgment, or by the Council of State if the judgment has been amended on appeal. In deciding the execution, a court may:

1) Order compliance, giving prescriptions, including by determining the content of the administrative act or by issuing it instead of the administration;
2) Annul the decision taken in breach of the res judicata;
3) In the event of compliance with judgments, which have not been res judicata or other measures (e.g., interim measures), determine the modalities of enforcement, considering the acts issued in violation of the decision to be ineffective;
4) Appoint an ad acta commissioner;
5) Impose a pecuniary penalty due for any subsequent infringement or non-compliance, or for any delay in the execution of the res judicata.

As in *Italy*, some other countries also pointed out that in certain or exceptional cases, the court has the competence to decide on the matter itself and replace the decision of the authority (*Poland, Serbia and Slovenia*).

Some countries indicated that their national legal system does not provide any specific legal remedies if an authority has failed to comply properly with a court order to issue a decision.

*Norway* stated that as the issue of authorities failing to comply properly with court orders is not a common issue, the legal remedies against said failure have not been thoroughly explored in practice. It has, however, been argued that should the authority's failure become flagrant enough, the courts could set specific time limits for when the decision must be made, and in extreme instances, possibly even decide on the matter itself.

Also, *Swedish* legislation is based on the assumption that public authorities will always follow a court's decision, if they do not, criminal responsibility may follow. If an authority does not comply with a courts ordering, a case concerning damages can be directed against the authority and a complaint to the Parliamentary ombudsman may also be done, resulting in an investigation and possible critique or prosecution.

The *Czech* Code on Administrative Justice also does not contain provisions for the enforcement of decisions of administrative courts. Therefore, if the administrative authority does not voluntarily comply with the order imposed by an enforceable judgment, it is necessary to seek compliance by applying for judicial enforcement, which is entrusted to civil courts or via enforcement officers.

*Cyprus* indicated that generally, administrative authorities observe and comply with the court's judgments, and until now, no statute has been enacted in this regard. However, three bills to regulate the obligation of administrative authorities to active compliance with judgments are currently pending before the Parliament.

## *2.4. The positive model of administrative silence*

This section of General Report summarises the responses of those ACA member states with a positive model of administrative silence in their legal system.

### *The purpose of the positive model*

14 countries noted that the main purpose of the positive model in their legal system is to simplify certain administrative procedures (*Austria, Cyprus, Estonia, Finland, Germany, Greece, Ireland, Italy, Latvia, Lithuania, Netherlands, Poland, Romania and Türkiye*). 6 countries identified the protection

of individuals' rights in the case of non-compliance with administrative time limits as the main purpose of the model (*Bulgaria, Croatia, Slovakia, Slovenia, Spain and Norway*). 7 countries identified both (*Albania, Czech Republic, France, Hungary, Luxemburg, Portugal and United Kingdom*).

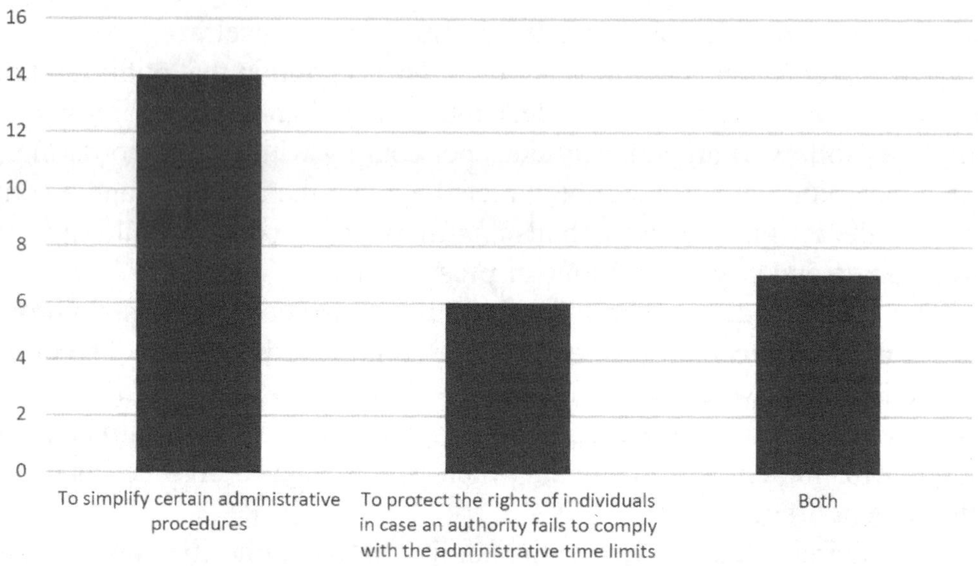


*Figure 3. The purpose of the positive model*

The prevalence of the purpose of simplifying and speeding up administrative processes is probably related to the fact that, as it was already mentioned in the section "Administrative silence", in several countries, the positive model of administrative silence was mainly implemented by transposing the positive silence model provided for in Article 13(4) of Directive 2006/123/EC of the European Parliament and of the Council of 12 December 2006 on services in the internal market into national legislation. The relevant provision states that failing a response within the time period set or extended, authorisation shall be deemed to have been granted. The purpose of such regulation is mainly related to reducing the administrative burden for the establishment and development of services, as well as simplifying and modernising public administration. This is also the explanation provided by the reports of several countries: *Cyprus, Finland, Germany, Greece, Ireland, Latvia, Lithuania, Poland and Romania*.

In the *Austrian* legal system, it is apparent from the preparatory works of the few provisions establishing a positive model of administrative silence that this model is only to be applied to cases where further examinations are not considered necessary.

*Italy* indicated that the positive model of administrative silence is a tool to simplify administrative procedures and to ensure legal certainty, which is fundamental in procedures involving economic interests linked to investments. Article 20 of the Administrative Procedure Law provides that the silence of public administration be deemed to constitute assent for all proceedings initiated by a request for an administrative act.

With regard to the protection of individuals' rights as the main purpose of the model, the national reports indicate the following.

The *Spanish* legal system imposes on the administration the legal obligation to issue a written decision in all cases. From this perspective, the positive effect of administrative silence constitutes a guarantee for citizens, who can have their applications upheld even when the deadline for doing so has expired and the administration has not issued a written decision as it should have done.

*Bulgaria* mentioned that on the grounds for the bill amending and supplementing the Code of Administrative Procedure, the institute of "tacit consent" is presented as an effective measure for the protection of citizens against the administrative authorities in cases where an authority fails to comply with administrative time limits. This institute reduces the administrative burden and increases the discipline to meet time limits.

*The Czech Republic* indicated that the positive model of administrative silence generally serves both of these purposes. The main purpose depends on the type of decision and regulatory context.

*Portugal* similarly pointed out that in the national legal order, the tacit approval ensures, on the one hand, the procedural speed and, on the other hand, guarantees the protection of rights, which exercise depends on an administrative control.

*France* explained that the 2013 reform of the regulation, which set the positive model of administrative silence as a general principle, was aimed at simplifying the relationship between the administrative authorities and citizens and modernising public action by reducing administrative procedures.

Also, the risk of illegal tacit decisions was expected to act as an incentive for the administration to take decisions within a shorter timeframe.

***Restrictions on the application of the positive model***

On the question of whether the national legal system contained any prohibitions or restrictions on the application of the positive model in certain areas of law, most respondents answered in the negative, indicating that as the positive model mainly applies only to specific cases provided for by law no such prohibitions or restrictions are needed. (*Albania, Austria, Bulgaria, Estonia, Germany, Greece, Latvia, Norway, Poland, Romania, Slovenia and Türkiye*).

For example, *Austria* stated that the positive model of administrative silence is not a general legal principle in the Austrian legal system but an exception that is only to be applied when explicitly stated.

*Poland* specified that the fundamental limitation of the use of tacit settlement of a case results from the fact that this solution can be used only when a specific act so provides. In other words, it is the legislator who arbitrarily indicates in which areas a case can be settled tacitly.

*Albania* also pointed out that the law establishing the positive model of administrative silence provides that it should be regulated by a special law, without limiting the nature and types of special laws depending on the areas of law.

*Finland, Ireland* and *Slovakia* also indicated without further specifying that no such prohibitions or restrictions exist in their legal systems.

*Cyprus, Lithuania, Luxemburg and the United Kingdom* also reported that there are no prohibitions or restrictions on the application of the positive model in their legal system. However, as a possible restriction highlighted by the above-mentioned Directive 2006/123/EC, that imposes certain restrictions by defining services and areas where its provisions (including Article 13(4) in relation to the positive model of administrative silence) cannot be applied. It is clear that the relevant provisions should be taken into account by the countries where the Directive has been implemented.

*The Czech Republic* stated that the legal system does not contain any specific prohibitions or restrictions on the application of the positive model. However, prohibitions or restrictions may arise from general legal principles – namely, the principle of legal certainty and protection of the rights of third parties. According to the explanatory memorandum to the Code on Administrative Procedure, there were attempts to introduce the positive model as the general regulatory model of administrative silence during the discussions on the length of the time limit for issuing a decision. The memorandum states that this model was not introduced as general because it "cannot be accepted generally in administrative proceedings, in particular, because of the protection of the rights of third parties".

*Hungary* indicated that prohibitions on the use of the positive model could be found in individual sectoral rules. One example is the restriction in the Government Decree on Weapons and Ammunition, according to which no lawful silence is possible in the licensing process provided for in the Act on Firearms and Ammunition.

In the *Italian* legal system, some exceptions to the positive model of silence consent are provided for the legislator to safeguard interests for which a formal procedure is required. These are cases relating to procedures aimed at the protection of cultural heritage of the environment or decisions issued by the national defence, public security, immigration, health and public safety administrations.

In addition, the cases in which European legislation requires the issue of a formal administrative decision and those in which the law qualifies the silence of the administration as a refusal of the claim are excluded from the positive model of silence.

*Portugal* stated that the new Code for the Administrative Procedure announces as exceptional rule of tacit approval, eliminating the list of situations applied in the previous regime.

In the *French* legal system, the positive model of administrative silence is the general rule. However, the law sets a number of restrictions. The positive model does not apply where: the action does not concern an individual decision; the action is of a financial nature; the granting of an indirect action is incompatible with France's international and European obligations; the action relating the protection of national security, constitutional freedoms and principles and public order and, finally, in relations between the administration and its officials.

*Spain* as exceptions to the positive model indicated cases where administrative silence has a negative effect: (i) in those cases in which a rule with the status of law or a rule of European Union or international law applicable in Spain establishes otherwise; (ii) in procedures relating to the exercise of the right to petition; (iii) in those proceedings whose outcome would result in the transfer to the applicant or third parties of powers relating to the public domain or the public service; in proceedings which involve the exercise of activities that may damage the environment, and in proceedings concerning the liability of the Public Administrations, as well as (iv) in proceedings challenging acts and provisions and in *ex officio* review proceedings initiated at the request of the interested parties.

*The Netherlands* indicated that such a fictitious positive decision, for example, an environmental permit for the construction of a structure or the felling of a tree, may be at the expense of the public interest, which requires careful consideration of whether the criteria for granting a permit have been met and that, if not, the license will be denied. In addition, the public interest sometimes requires that certain conditions be attached to a licence. A fictitious positive decision could therefore be at the expense of the interests of third parties who cannot know that a positive decision has been taken and who may miss objection or appeal periods as a result. Therefore, some mitigating provisions have been made.

***Tacit approval of the claim***

National reports indicate that in the majority of countries, a moment when a person's claim is deemed to have been granted is the moment when the time limit set for handling a request expires (*Albania, Austria, Bulgaria, Croatia, Cyprus, Czech Republic, Finland, France, Greece, Hungary, Ireland, Italy, Latvia, Lithuania, Norway, Poland, Romania, Slovakia, Slovenia, Spain and Türkiye*). In other words, a person's claim is deemed to have been granted immediately after the expiry of the time limit.

Some countries indicated more specific rules.

*Estonia* stated that a moment when the person's claim is deemed to have been granted depends on the specific provisions. Sometimes the application is deemed to have been granted once a certain amount of time has passed (for example, 10 days in case of a building notice or use and occupancy notice; 30 days in case of an activity licence), but there are also instances where the reaction time for the authority is not directly limited, but the application or declaration is deemed to have been granted immediately upon registration (for example notice of economic activities).

In *the Netherlands*, the applicable time limits are laid down in specific laws or follow the General Administrative Law Act. The legal consequences associated with a positive fictitious decision take effect three days after the decision period has expired without being used.

*Portugal* specified that in accordance with the Code for the Administrative Procedure, the time limit considered for the tacit approval is the notification period. It means the law considers "that there is tacit approval if the act's notification is not sent until the first working day following the decision's deadline".

*The United Kingdom* reported that the specific moment an application is deemed to have been granted would depend on the provision in question. For example, the licence for a sex establishment is deemed to remain in force from the moment it expires until the withdrawal or determination of the application, and the notification is deemed approved after the expiry of 28 days from the date the application was received by the planning authority.

On the question of whether the person has to get any kind of confirmation or proof that the claim has been granted, 11 countries stated that no such confirmation or proof is required (*Austria, Croatia, Cyprus, Greece, Italy, Latvia, Norway, Portugal, Slovenia, Spain, Türkiye and United Kingdom*).

*Greece*, however, pointed out that when a petition to grant an authorisation is submitted, the authority shall issue a confirmation of receipt of a such petition that states the time limit within which the authority shall examine the petition, the legal remedies that are provided in case of rejection of the petition and a declaration that if the competent authority does not examine the petition within the statutory time limit, the authorisation is deemed to have been granted.

Meanwhile, 10 countries indicated that a person has a legal right to receive confirmation or proof that the claim has been granted (*Albania, Czech Republic, Finland, France, Germany, Hungary, Ireland, Lithuania, Luxemburg, Poland and Romania*).

*Finland* specified that in situations where authorisation is deemed to have been granted, a document indicating the same shall be issued to the applicant for the authorisation.

*Luxemburg* indicated that, in general, the person does not need to obtain confirmation or proof that the application has been granted. However, the law sometimes expressly provides that, on the initiative of the applicant who has obtained tacit authorisation, the competent authority must issue the documents relating to the authorisation without delay.

*Albania* reported that after exceeding the time limit, the party may request the issuance of a written confirmation as approved in silence. The confirmation shall contain the text of the request, the date of its submission and the fact that the public body has failed to notify its decision within the time limit.

If the authority does not issue a confirmation within seven days from the date of the party's request or at the same time does not issue the requested administrative act, the party may bring a lawsuit before the competent court for administrative matters in order to clarify the rights and obligations between the plaintiff and the public body.

The party also may request written confirmation through a judicial proceeding if the public body has failed to issue it upon the party's request.

In *the Netherlands,* the administrative authority is obliged to notify the fictitious order within two weeks after it has been granted, stating that the order has been granted *ex officio*. If the administrative authority fails to publish the order, the applicant may declare the administrative authority to be in default. If the administrative authority does not make the notification within two weeks, it will forfeit a penalty for each day that it is in default.

*Estonia* pointed out that if an activity licence is required to be entered in the register, also in the case of a "silent" activity licence, the authority enters the data of the activity licence in the register on the working day following the expiry of the time limit. Similarly, the *Czech Republic* noted that the administrative authority shall, without undue delay, make an entry in the file that the authorisation to provide some service has been granted and enter the holder of the authorisation in the relevant register. Upon request, it shall issue a certificate to the holder.

### *Legal remedies available to third parties affected by the "fictitious decision" of granting a claim*

All rapporteurs indicated that their national regulation does not provide any specific or special legal remedies available to third parties affected by the "fictitious decision" of granting a claim. However, in most countries if such "fictitious decision" of granting a claim affects the rights or legal interests of a third party, that party has the right to complain against the decision.

*Cyprus* explained that a third party may complain to the competent administrative authority which has "fictitiously approved" the claim or to the Commissioner for Administration and the Protection of Human Rights (Ombudsman).

Also, if the third party's existing and direct legitimate interest is affected by the "fictitious approval" he or she may lodge a recourse to the Administrative Court under Article 146 of the Constitution.

*The Czech Republic* indicated that generally according to the special laws, only the participants of a proceeding have the right to appeal against such a "fictitious decision".

However, third parties may try to initiate administrative review proceedings, which shall be commenced if the administrative authorities discover (on the basis of their own official activity or the initiative of a participant or third party) facts that give rise to reasonable doubts that a decision is in accordance with the law.

Third parties may also try to seek judicial protection. The right to bring an action against an administrative decision does not derive from previous participation in the administrative proceedings. This action may be brought by whoever claims to have been deprived of his rights by an administrative act that concerns his/her rights and/or obligations. This option, however, is just theoretical.

*Germany* specified that a third party may recruit to all remedies which are available against a "real" decision. The calculation of the time limit for the third party remedy starts with the existence of the fictitious permission, thus three months after the application.

*Bulgaria* and *Hungary* stated that the "fictitious decision" of granting a claim generally should not affect any third parties.

Bulgaria explained that according to the Code of Administrative Procedure, tacit approval may not impose obligations and affect the legal rights and interests of individuals and institutions other than the applicant. In case of violation of this prohibition, the third parties concerned have the right to submit a claim.

*Hungary* also specified that the positive model shall not apply where the case involves an opposing party.

### *Annulment of the "fictitious decision" of granting a claim*

According to national reports, no country has any special or certain procedure that allows annulling a "fictitious decision" of granting a claim. However, most countries indicated that such an annulment, where there are grounds, is possible according to the general procedure.

For example, *Cyprus* indicated that an applicant may request the cancellation of "fictitious decision" by writing to the issuing administrative authority. Also, an interested, prejudiced party, whose direct legitimate interest has been affected by the "fictitious decision", can contest in court the decision requesting its annulment. There is no special procedure. The only observation that can be made here relates to the strict constitutional time limit within which acts, decisions and omissions of the administration can be challenged by way of judicial review. In the case of a "fictitious decision", where there is no communication of the act/decision, the 75-day strict constitutional time limit is activated once the prejudiced party gains knowledge of the decision.

Other countries also referred to specific rules on setting time limits for appeals in cases where the decision has not been notified to the person.

*Croatia* indicated that according to the Act of Administrative disputes, if an individual decision has not been delivered to the party in accordance with the delivery rules, an appeal may be submitted within 90 days from the day when the party has become aware or could have become aware of the decision, and no later than within five years after the deadline.

In *Latvia*, according to the Administrative Procedure Law, if a decision restricts the rights or legal interests of a private person, but the private person has not been notified thereof, an application may be submitted within one month from the day when the private person has become aware thereof but not later than within one year from the day this decision comes into effect.

Some countries also indicated that, in certain cases, the authority has the right to annul the decision itself.

*Italy* explained that it is always possible, in the presence of a set of conditions and in the balancing of all the interests involved, for the public administration to annul *ex officio* its expressed or tacit decisions for defects of legitimacy or for opportunity reasons.

*The Netherlands* stated that the administrative authority may impose conditions on the decision or can even withdraw the decision "insofar as this is necessary to prevent serious damage to the public interest". The administrative body can only do this within six weeks of the fictitious decision and, in doing so, must compensate for any damage, for example, if a person who has been granted the permit has already started the activities that are licensed with it. This procedure also serves the interests of third parties. Application of these "corrective measures" is only allowed in exceptional cases.

In *Spain,* decisions obtained due to the positive effect of administrative silence can be challenged through ordinary channels, just like explicit acts. Furthermore, Article 47 of the Law on Common Administrative Procedure establishes that "explicit or presumed acts contrary to the legal system by which powers or rights are acquired" will be null and void "when the essential requirements for their acquisition are lacking". When faced with these acts that are null and void or legally void, the administration may also promote their *ex officio* review and declare them null and void, always after hearing the interested party and in accordance with a specific procedure.

### *Implementation of the positive silence model provided for in Directive 2006/123/EC*

All countries where the Directive was to be implemented indicated that it had been implemented in national law on services and various specific pieces of legislation regulating the particular area of law.

Several national reports also clarified that any potential implementation of the positive model of administrative silence in accordance with Article 13(4) of the Directive was made in the light of the Directive's provision that different arrangements may be put in place, where justified by overriding reasons relating to the public interest, including a legitimate interest of third parties. In this regard, some countries (*Greece, Latvia, Poland and Portugal*) indicated that a special working group was set up within the responsible ministries in order to undertake and monitor the various stages of the Directive's implementation and to assess in which areas and which services the positive model could be applied, in particular whether the application is not contrary to the public interest.

By way of example, in *Greece* and *Latvia* it was recognised that in the sector of education services, such a model may be in contradiction with the public interest and is not applicable in this area. *Cyprus* indicated that positive silence is contrary to the public interest with regard to aliens and immigration as well as citizenship. The *Finnish* report also lists a number of areas where the principle does not apply, such as financial and insurance services, transport services, the services of temporary work agencies, health care and pharmacy e.g.

In addition to these restrictions, *Estonia* also pointed out that the positive silence model is also not applied if an activity licence must be granted with secondary conditions.

The national reports also contained an extensive list of services and areas where the principle of positive silence has been implemented. *Spain* indicated that the relevant provisions of the Directive are taken on board and generalised in numerous sectors of administrative practice, such as, for example, the industrial, energy, construction, services, transport and communications sectors. *Germany* identified the following specific areas of law: rail infrastructure, urban planning (partly), chemical labs, energy market regulation, trade with agricultural property, public transport and import of infectious material. *Lithuania* specified that legal areas where the positive silence model is implemented are very different: natural gas sector, electricity sector, issuance of permits to purchase, keep or carry weapons, issuance of licenses for the wholesale and retail sale of alcohol products etc.

In addition, in the context of the implementation of the Directive, *Italy* pointed to the introduction of a single point contact, through which service providers can carry out, by electronic means, all the formalities necessary for access to and operation of an economic activity and obtain information and assistance.

No country has reported any difficulties in implementing the Directive in the national legal system.

However, the *Czech Republic* considered it worth noting that the explanatory memorandum to the act, which amended 23 special laws to transpose the positive model, does not indicate on what basis the model was implemented in these special laws and not in others (which would come into consideration), or why these laws provide for fictitious decisions only for certain authorisation procedures and not for others. It is thus unclear whether the implementation was done after careful consideration for which authorisation procedures this model could be introduced and for which it could be not due to "overriding reasons relating to the public interest, including a legitimate interest of third parties".

*Belgium* pointed out that although general rules have been adopted, the implementation of the positive silence model provided for in the Directive has still not been implemented in a unified and coherent manner. Rather, its implementation is dealt with on a case-by-case basis.

### *2.5. Other legal remedies*

#### *Legal remedies in situations of administrative silence where the law does not regulate it neither in accordance with the positive, nor the negative model*

Several countries, in relation to other existing legal remedies, indicated that one or both of the silence models provided in the national legal system generally cover all situations and there is, in principle, no need for other solutions. The national reports of *Albania, Belgium, Greece, Latvia, Luxemburg, Slovenia and Türkiye* indicated this.

For example, in Slovenia, the general negative model is applicable in all situations. The *Latvian* and *Türkiyeish* administrative legal system also provides the negative model as a general principle in the case of administrative silence unless a specific provision states otherwise. *Albania*, meanwhile, emphasised that the situation of administrative silence is regulated in accordance with the positive model of administrative silence, and there are no other institutes related to the administrative silence.

*Spain* and *Norway* also pointed out that, in general, the regulation of the positive model and the negative model covers any possible administrative file. However, they clarified a few more options.

In *Spain*, Articles 29 and 30 of the Law on Administrative Jurisdiction 29/1998 provide for cases of jurisdictional challenges that can be brought in the absence of a written decision by the Administration, but to which the general concept of administrative silence cannot be applied. Article 29 regulates the so-called appeal against the inactivity of the Administration, in reference to the possibility of appealing to the court in the event of failure to comply with a specific material benefit that has already been recognised in favour of the interested party. In turn, Article 30 regulates the appeal against a so-called “de facto act”, in reference to the possible challenge against an action carried out by the Administration without competence or completely disregarding any legal procedure.

*Norway* explained that the most prominent additional legal remedy would be a complaint to the national Ombudsman. Ombudsman would then have the competence to examine to the case at hand and to issue a reasoned decision. In such a decision, Ombudsman could examine whether and why the relevant public authority has not acted in accordance with the relevant time limits. Should Ombudsman reach such a conclusion, Ombudsman could also recommend that the relevant authority re-examine the case.

Similar to Norway, also *Cyprus, Finland* and *Sweden* mentioned the possibility of submitting a complaint to the Ombudsman, Chancellor of Justice (in *Finland*) and Commissioner for Administration (in *Cyprus*).

Most countries, as a possible legal remedy in case of the administrative silence if it is not addressed by any of the models, indicated an appeal against the silence or inaction, which can be lodged with an authority or an administrative court (*Austria, Bulgaria, Croatia, Cyprus, Czech Republic, Estonia, France, Germany, Hungary, Ireland, Italy, Lithuania, Poland, Portugal, Switzerland and United Kingdom*).

In particular, the *Czech* regulatory model of administrative silence is based on measures against inaction. It means that if an administrative authority is inactive, its superior authority shall (ex officio or on request of a participant of the proceedings): 1) order the inactive administrative authority to take necessary measures to remedy the situation or issue a decision within the time limit; 2) take over the case; 3) delegate the case to another administrative authority in its administrative district; 4) reasonably extend the time limit if it can be reasonably expected that the inactive administrative authority will issue the decision within the extended time limit and if such a measure is more advantageous to the participants. If the superior administrative authority is also inactive, it is possible to seek judicial protection.

*France* stated that the refusal of an authority to take an action or make a decision can be appealed to an administrative court. This can lead to the decision being annulled and the administration being ordered to act in a certain direction within a time limit set by a judge, imposing a penalty if necessary. Such refusal or failure to act may also give rise to administrative liability on the part of the relevant administrative authorities.

In *Hungary*, Act on the Administrative Court Procedure provides a separate type of action: a lawsuit that can be brought against an administrative body for failure to fulfil its statutory obligation to perform an administrative act. The function of the so-called “action for failure to act” is to provide the party with legal protection against infringements of the law caused by the passive action of the public administration.

Moreover, the Court stated that in such a case, there is no supervisory (remedy) procedure in the proceedings of the administrative authority, and no conditions can be imposed on a person which it cannot fulfil within the legal framework.

*Italy* explained that according to the Administrative Procedure Code, the applicant may appeal against the silence, which does not mean a fictitious positive or negative decision. The object of the special rite is the inaction of the administration, which is required to issue a decision at the request of the party.

The Court orders the administration to provide within the time limit not exceeding thirty days and has the power to appoint a commissioner ad acta to replace the administration that does not comply with the order to issue the final decision. The court may rule on the merits of the claim only when it is a mandatory decision or when the authority is no longer required to carry out considerations of usefulness, or there is no need to carry out investigations.

*Estonia* stated that if a person wants to dispute an administrative omission or delay, the person must file a mandatory action (for the court to order the authority to act), for which the time limit is quite lenient: one year from the date when the authority should have issued the administrative act, or in case no deadline is provided by law, two years from the application. In case of a mandatory action, the court has two options: either to order the authority to make a specific decision or simply to order the authority to decide on the application.

*The United Kingdom* also pointed out that in the context of administrative silence, the most important public law remedy is the mandatory order. Mandatory orders are available when a public authority is in dereliction of a public duty. They have the effect of compelling the authority to act in light of its obligations.

In addition, *Slovakia* also pointed to the possibility of a motion addressed to a public prosecutor.

The *Netherlands*, for its part, offers a different solution. As stated in the report, besides the fictitious decision, the forfeit of a penalty is an important way to “hurry up” the administrative authority. In this case, the administrative body will have to be given a notice of default. After receiving this notice and two weeks after the decision period has expired, the administrative authority will forfeit a penalty.

In the absence of an order after sending a notice of default, the applicant can also immediately appeal to the court. The judge then has the following possibilities:

1) In case the appeal is well-founded, he can determine the height of the penalty that the administrative body has to pay.
2) In case the appeal is well-founded and the administrative body has still not notified a decision, the judge might oblige the administrative body to give a notification within two weeks after the judge's decision has been sent to the administrative body. The judge might also oblige the body to pay an additional judicial penalty payment.

***Compensation for financial loss or non-financial damage that has been caused as a result of the administrative silence***

A notable majority of countries confirmed that, generally, a person is entitled to claim a compensation for financial loss or non-financial damage which has been caused as a result of the administrative silence of the authority.

Only *Ireland* and *the United Kingdom* replied differently.

*Ireland* indicated that a person is not entitled to claim such compensation. However, a person may be entitled to an award of damages or costs as a result of a judicial court order.

*The United Kingdom* explained that damages are not generally available as a public law remedy. However, claimants may be able to establish that a public law illegality is also actionable in private law, for instance, for negligence, breach of statutory duty or misfeasance in public office.

Several countries (*Bulgaria, Greece, France, Lithuania, Luxemburg and Netherlands*) emphasised that, in order to claim compensation, the loss or damage must be the result of the illegal administrative silence of the authority, and the causal link between the administrative silence of the authority and the damage must be proven.

*Croatia* and *Latvia* specified that compensation cannot be claimed for any procedural violation, but only for a violation if it has caused a significant infringement of rights or legal interests of a person.

In *Italy*, the Administrative Procedure Law provides compensation for unjust damage resulting from the unlawful exercise or lack of activity if the authority issues a positive decision requested by the party after the time limit set by law, or if the delay or failure to issue a negative decision causes damage.

In *Portugal,* the natural reconstitution rule prevails, that is, the pecuniary compensation will only be considered when natural reconstitution is not possible.

*The Czech Republic* indicated that if the non-financial (non-material) damage has been caused by maladministration in the form of a failure to comply with time limits, specific circumstances shall be taken into account in determining the amount of appropriate compensation. In particular, the overall length and complexity of the proceedings, the conduct of the public authority during the proceedings, the conduct of the injured party which contributed to delays and whether he/she used available remedies against inaction, and the importance of the subject-matter of the proceedings to the injured party.

In *Switzerland*, the Federal Court held that the fault of the person claiming compensation may be the reason for breaking the direct causal link between an unlawful action of the institution and the loss caused. If there is a risk that the party concerned could be harmed by the excessive length of the proceedings, it is obliged to inform the institution so that it can speed up the procedure. If the institution does not react, the party must submit a complaint to the competent authority. The party may claim compensation only if these measures have remained unanswered by the institution. If the above measures are not taken, the victim himself may be considered to be complicit in the proceedings relating to compensation for damages.

*Hungary* additionally pointed out that the legal person exercising public authority shall be liable for damage caused by the exercise of public authority. If the person exercising public authority is not a legal person, liability for the damage shall be borne by the administrative body having legal personality under which the administrative body has acted in the case is operating.

Furthermore, according to the established jurisdiction, errors in the application or interpretation of the law in the exercise of public authority in individual cases shall only give rise to liability for damages if they are manifestly serious.

## *2.6. Case law and regulation in non-harmonised sectors of law*

### *National case law where regulation on administrative silence has been found unfounded or inapplicable*

A majority of respondents indicated that the issue of national regulation on administrative silence had not been dealt with in their case law. *Bulgaria, the Czech Republic, Germany, the Netherlands, Romania* and *Spain* are the only countries mentioning such case law.

*The Czech Republic* indicated, by way of example, a case of shared broadcasting licenses, where the Supreme Administrative Court found that the fiction of positive decision cannot be applied.

In *Germany*, the Federal Administrative Court has found that the violation of the general obligation of speedy conduct of administrative procedure does not trigger a fictitious permit as foreseen in the Code of Administrative Procedure; this is only the case if this consequence is expressly provided for in a specific rule.

*Spain* explained that there are frequent administrative disputes in which the question of whether or not there has been a positive or negative effect of administrative silence is raised, which is why there are numerous rulings on this issue, depending on the different nature of the case in question. However, no individual case has been specified.

*The Netherlands* described a case concerning administrative penalty. As stated before, in *the Netherlands*, if an administrative body has still not decided on an application during the appeal process, the administrative court might impose a so-called judicial penalty. In addition to the judicial penalty, Dutch law provides an administrative penalty. The latter is a penalty the government automatically owes if it does not decide within the statutory period. The Temporary Penalty Suspension Act excludes both judicial and administrative penalty payments in asylum cases when the Immigration and Nationalisation Service does not make a decision on an asylum application in time.

This is contrary to the principle of effective legal protection. It is important for legal certainty and confidence in the government that the State Secretary decides on asylum applications in good time. Without a judicial penalty, a foreign national has no effective means of persuading the State Secretary to make a decision in time.

However, the Administrative Jurisdiction Division did rule that abolishing the administrative penalty in asylum cases is not contrary to the European principle of effective legal protection. Unlike a judicial penalty, the government automatically owes an administrative penalty. This penalty is, therefore, not a means for a citizen to persuade the government to make a timely decision.

***Case law on the application or interpretation of the positive model provided for in Article 13(4) of Directive 2006/123/EC***

Only seven respondents reported the following case law on applying or interpreting the positive model provided for in the Directive (*Belgium, Germany, Lithuania, Netherlands, Poland, Spain and United Kingdom*).

*Germany* indicated that outside of the competence of the Federal Administrative Court, the Federal Social Court has found that in the public health insurance system, a treatment is considered granted if the health insurance does not decide on a corresponding petition within the given time limit.

The Supreme Administrative Court of *Lithuania* has invoked the fiction of positive silence on multiple occasions whilst examining cases on issuing authorisations and licences. In a string of cases dealing with renewable solar energy and the issuance of licences to this effect, the Court emphasised that a decision on the issuance of licences should be taken without prejudice to the set time limits by public bodies. The positive model of administrative silence was enshrined in Article 17(2) of the Law on Electricity, which stated that if a properly submitted application for a permit is not answered within the specified time, it is considered that a positive decision on the permit issuance has been made. The Court stated that by relying on this provision, a person gained the right to carry out licensed activities in accordance with the requirements provided by legal acts and did not have to reapply for the issuance of the licence. According to the Court, under such regulation, the legislator, on the one hand, promoted good administration by public entities while, on the other hand, establishing an additional, exclusive pathway for the protection of the rights and legitimate interests of individuals. The Court repeated these statements in later cases.

In *the Netherlands*, the Rotterdam district court examined a case concerning granting a permit (*ex officio*) to exploit a restaurant. Art. 3 para 2 of the Liquor and Catering Law and the general local regulation state that the regulation on positive decisions in the event of late decisions of section 4.1.3.3 of the General Administrative Law Act does not apply.

The plaintiff argued that the aforementioned provisions of the general local regulation were non-binding because these articles had not been reported to the European Commission. The District Court stated that this does not follow the Services Directive.

The explanation provided with the particular general local regulation states that introducing a positive silence model may pose a risk to public health, as a permit may be issued without sufficient assessment. Because the local government determines which license applications are assessed in co-administration, it is impossible to regulate in the formal law which licenses are subject to a positive administrative silence and which licenses are not.

In *Poland*, in cases before the Supreme Administrative Court, operators applied for television broadcasting licences. Citing the general provision – article 11 (9) of the Freedom of Economic Activity Act, they considered that the concession had been granted to them by tacit consent.

The Supreme Administrative Court ruled in these cases that it, therefore, follows from the wording of the Directive 2006/123/EC and the justification of the draft Act on the provision of services in the territory of the Republic of Poland that, in view of the intended systemic objectives of the national legislator, the material scope of Article 11(9) of the Act on freedom of economic activity should be defined taking into account the exclusions and limitations contained in Directive. The Court, therefore, held that the provision of Article 11(9) of the cited Act was not applicable in the case for granting a concession for the distribution of television programs in the part concerning the concession fee.

In *the United Kingdom*, the Upper Tribunal considered a local housing authority's appeal against a decision of the First-tier Tribunal upholding the respondents' applications for licences under the Housing Act 2004. The respondents cross-appealed, arguing that the licences were deemed to have been granted to them after a reasonable time pursuant to Regulations 19 and 20 of the Provision of Services Regulations 2009, which gives effect in English law to Article 13 of Directive 2006/123/EC. According to Regulation 19, authorisation procedures and formalities had to be processed "within a reasonable period" which was fixed and made public in advance. Regulation 20 provided that applications had to be acknowledged "as quickly as possible". The respondents argued that, on the basis that the licences were deemed granted before they were refused, they could not have been refused at a later date.

The Upper Tribunal held that there was no material difference between the wording of Regulations 19 and 20 and the wording of Article 13 of Directive 2006/123/EC, the purpose of which was to clarify the exact time at which authorisation was deemed to be granted if not previously refused or expressly granted. The Upper Tribunal held that the purpose of Article 13 and Regulation 19 would be defeated if the latter were to be interpreted as meaning that, in any case where an authority did not publicise in advance and notify the fixed period within which an application would be determined, there would be a deemed grant after the expiry of a reasonable period of time, as that would enable authorities which did not specify such a period to fall back on an uncertain period of time and leave applicants vulnerable to delay. In the instant case, the First-tier Tribunal had correctly concluded that the authority had published a decision not to specify a fixed period of time on the basis that it was justified in not doing so by an overriding public interest in safety within Regulation 19(6). The respondents' cross-appeal was therefore dismissed.

The *Belgian* and *Spanish* case law addressed the relevant provision of the Directive indirectly.

### *A question to the Court of Justice of the European Union in order for it to make a preliminary ruling in a case concerning national regulation on administrative silence*

No country has indicated such a question to the Court of Justice of the European Union.

However, it is worth mentioning *Portugal's* observation, given that European Union law has "zero tolerance" for tacit acts in environmental matters and providing Portuguese legislation with such cases of tacit approval regarding environmental permits, it should not be despised that such a request should be made.

### *National regulation on administrative silence in non-harmonised sectors of law*

#### Construction, spatial development planning, and environmental protection

The national responses of *Croatia, Finland, Romania, Sweden* and *the United Kingdom* indicate that there are no special rules on administrative silence in their national legislation concerning this area of law.

According to the reports of other ACA members, national regulation on administrative silence in this area of law varies; moreover, in several countries, it is highly fragmented. Some relevant examples are provided below.

*Poland* indicated that only the positive model of administrative silence applies in these areas of law. Regarding construction law, the tacit consent of the authority refers to the notification of construction works.

The Polish legislator has also provided the construction of "tacit cooperation" of the authorities when issuing decisions in the framework of opinions and agreements on the establishment of spatial development conditions in law related to the natural environment.

In the *Italian* legal system, the positive model of silence is the general rule. Some exceptions are provided in cases relating to procedures aimed at the protection of cultural heritage or the environment.

*Spain* indicated that the different urban planning regulations typically provide a positive effect of administrative silence in relation to applications for urban planning licences (licences for buildings).

*Cyprus* stated that an example of positive silence is stipulated in section 18(3) of the Town Planning Law. This section provides that failure to respond within three months on an application for an extension on the validity of a planning permit deems the application approved, and the permit's validity is extended for another year.

In other cases, unless the positive silence model is adopted in the applicable statute, there is a right to recourse under Article 29.2 of the Constitution for the administration to respond, a right to a recourse which arises out of 3-month administrative silence which is deemed as a refusal to satisfy a claim under section 36 of the General Principles of Administrative Law or under Article 146 of the Constitution for recourse for judicial review if there has been a failure to act (omission) on the part of the public authority when action is legally prescribed.

In *Norway*, the positive model following from Article 13(4) of the Directive applies to the construction area in so far as the relevant service falls within the scope of The Services Act.

For questions on spatial development planning, the positive model generally applies by virtue of special laws.

For questions of environmental protection, a variation of the negative model applies in instances where the relevant authority does not order someone to clean up; this decision can be appealed against by others with a legal interest in doing so.

In *the Czech Republic*, the Building Act no longer provides fictitious decisions. However, the Building Act still provides fictitious binding opinions. A binding opinion is a written opinion elaborated by the "concerned" administrative authority on the basis of law; it is not a decision, but its content is binding for the operative part of the decision of the competent administrative authority. If the binding opinion is not issued within the time limit, it is deemed positive without any conditions. Generally, this fiction applies to all binding opinions under the Building Act processes. However, Art. 4(12) precludes this fiction's application to certain binding opinions, essentially – important environmental opinions.

*Estonia* stated that construction is one of the areas of law where the legislator has decided to implement a positive silence model, albeit for only cases of minor importance.

In *Germany*, the General Railroad Act provides that permission to start the operation of a railroad is considered granted if the competent authority does not decide in deviation of the petition within six weeks. Also, the Federal Building Code provides in several regulations that the permission of certain planning decisions is to be considered granted if the competent authority does not decide in deviation of the petition within a certain time limit.

*Slovakia* indicated that the Construction Act regulation related to the procedure for issuing a building permit contains provisions on the fiction of the positive opinion issued by the competent authority (e.g., if a nature protection authority fails to notify its opinion with regard to the construction that is subject to the building permit procedure within the prescribed time-limit, its consent, in terms of its interests pursued, shall be deemed to be given).

In the national law of *Albania*, silent approval is provided by specific law that deals with object construction or territorial development planning, specifically law "On territorial planning and development". This law provides that tacit approval shall mean the act of obtaining the right to develop, carry out works or use buildings without the approval of the planning authority if the approval or refusal of the request has not been issued within the terms provided by the relevant provisions herein.

Also, in *Lithuania*, there are some provisions implementing the positive model of administrative silence, mostly in the regulation of the territory planning process. The Law on Environmental Impact Assessment of Planned Economic Activities provides the positive administrative silence model approach in approval of the environmental impact assessment program and report.

*Ireland, Portugal* and *Türkiye* also pointed out that a positive model of silence can be found in some legal provisions in this area of law.

In *Switzerland*, generally, neither the Confederation nor the cantons provide for any model of silence in these areas of law.

However, there are exceptions. An example is the law on the protection of nature, monuments, and territories in the canton of Vaud. This law states that the owner of a site listed on the cantonal register must inform the Department of Safety and Environment of any works he intends to carry out. An investigation must be started within three months of the owner's notification of the planned works. Otherwise, permission to carry out the works shall be deemed to have been granted.

In *Greece*, the general principle of the negative model is mainly applied in this area of law. However, some provisions regulate the positive model. For instance, in case of sitting of a tourist port within an existing port, the Tourist Port Committee is obliged, before expressing its opinion, to forward the relevant file to the competent authority of the Ministry of Maritime Affairs and Insular Policy in order to express its opinion within the time limit of two months whether the tourist port will obstruct the operation of the existing port. If the Ministry of Maritime Affairs and Insular Policy does not express an opinion within the mentioned time limit, it shall be regarded that the above Ministry has expressed a positive opinion.

Also, in *Latvia*, the general principle of the negative model is mainly applied in this area of law. As an exception in accordance with Article 13(4) of Directive 2006/123/EC positive model is implemented in the Construction Act, providing for administrative authorities to issue a permit, note, and coordination by default.

In *Luxemburg*, for building permits, the general rules on a negative model of administrative silence apply in all cases where an individual administrative decision is taken.

In the area of environmental protection, the general rules on the negative administrative silence model also apply to applications for permission to build or carry out certain activities in a green area.

Also, in *Bulgaria*, *Serbia* and *Slovenia*, a general negative model of administrative silence is applied in a particular area of law.

*Hungary*, for its part, points out that the positive model applies according to the general rules in this area of law.

The *Netherlands* emphasised that a new environmental law will be applicable in the near future: the Environment and Planning Act. The positive model of administrative silence will no longer apply, whereas it currently does. Most permits granted under the construction of the positive model relate to a service. Many of these services consist of activities that place a burden on the environment and may also be in conflict with European law. Moreover, the assessment of a permit requires customization in which various interests must be weighed up. There is insufficient space for this when a permit is granted *ex officio*.

**Social security**

Fourteen respondents replied that there are no special rules on the administrative silence in their national legislation concerning this area of law (*Albania, Croatia, Czech Republic, Estonia, Finland, Ireland, Lithuania, Luxemburg, Norway, Poland, Romania, Sweden, Switzerland and United Kingdom*).

According to the reports of other respondents, national regulation on administrative silence in this area of law varies; moreover, in several countries, it is highly fragmented. Some relevant examples are provided below.

In the *Italian* legal system, social security is a matter for ordinary courts, not administrative ones. However, there are exceptional cases of silence assent (e.g., automatic registration of public employees to the retirement funds). The general rule is the negative model (e.g., any administrative request to the National Social Security Institute).

In *Greece*, the general principle of the negative model is mainly applied in this area of law.

In *Latvia*, the general principle of the negative model is mainly applied in this area of law.

As an exception in accordance with the Article 13(4) of Directive regulations provide for social service providers to be registered in the register by default (if within one month after receipt of the application from the service provider the Ministry does not request additional information and documents, does not take and notify the decision to refuse to register the service provider, it shall be regarded that the service provider has been registered in the register).

Also, in *Bulgaria*, *Serbia*, *Slovenia* and *Türkiye*, a general negative model of administrative silence is applied in the area of social security.

*Portugal* noted that in the Law of Access to Law and Courts, the absence of a final decision by the Social Security services on the request for legal aid leads, within thirty days, to the approval of a tacit act.

*Spanish* Royal Legislative Decree, which approves the revised text of the General Social Security Act, establishes in Article 129 that "In procedures initiated at the request of the interested parties, once the maximum period for issuing and notifying a decision established by the regulation governing the procedure in question has elapsed without a written decision having been issued, the request shall be understood to have been rejected due to administrative silence. Exceptions to the provisions of the previous paragraph are those procedures relating to the registration of companies and to the affiliation, registration, deregistration and variations in the details of workers initiated at the request of the interested parties, as well as those relating to special agreements, in which the lack of a written decision within the established period shall have the effect of granting the respective request due to administrative silence".

*Hungary* indicated that the positive model applies according to the general rules in this area of law.

In *Austria*, the Federal Act on Hospitals and Sanatoria stipulates that a contract between insurance institutions and hospitals whose legal entity is not a region is considered to be approved by the regional government if it does not refuse the approval in writing within a given time limit.

*Slovakia* indicated that the positive model of administrative silence in this field is enshrined in the Act on Social Work and the Conditions for the Performance of Certain Professional Activities in the Field of Social Affairs and the Family regarding registration with the Slovak Chamber of Social Workers and Social Work Assistants.

*Germany* explained that in the public health insurance system, a treatment is considered granted if the health insurance does not decide on a corresponding petition within the given time limit.

**Freedom of information**

The national responses of thirteen respondents indicate that there are no special rules on administrative silence in their national legislation concerning this area of law (*Albania, Austria, Croatia, Estonia, Finland, Lithuania, Netherlands, Poland, Portugal, Romania, Spain, Switzerland and United Kingdom*).

According to the reports of other respondents, it can be concluded that the negative silence model prevails in this area. Some relevant examples are provided below.

In *Bulgaria, Greece, Latvia, Norway, Serbia, Slovakia, Slovenia* and *Türkiye*, a negative model of administrative silence is applied in the areas of freedom of information.

In the *Czech Republic*, the negative model of administrative silence is provided for in Environmental Information Act.

This model was also provided for in the Act on Free Access to Information. However, this model did not prove to be functional because the administrative courts could not review such fictitious decisions for lack of reasons and could only annul these decisions. Since then, there are no "fictitious refusals".

In *France*, contrary to the general positive model of administrative silence, if an authority does not reply to requests for information and documents within one month, it is deemed to have refused to provide them.

*Germany* noted that the Freedom in Information Act provides for a time limit of one month to answer a request. However, the violation of this time limit does not automatically result in a fictitious positive decision.

*Italy* indicated that the Administrative Procedure Law provides that a request for access to administrative documents is deemed refused after 30 days. The applicant may submit a request for a review to the responsible authority for corruption and transparency. The applicant may challenge the refusal before the Administrative Court or, in the case of regional administrations or local authorities, bring the matter before the local Ombudsman. In the latter case, access is deemed to be granted if the Ombudsman does not confirm the refusal or postponement within 30 days of receiving the Ombudsman's communication.

*Ireland* explained that both the positive and negative silence models can be found in the Freedom of Information Act.

In *Hungary*, the positive model applies in this area of law according to the general rules.

## 3. Administrative discretionary power

### *3.1. Definition of discretionary power*

All countries indicated that discretion is generally understood and commonly used in their legal system. Only in a few countries is it explicitly defined in a statute; most respondents indicated that the definition and interpretation of discretion has been established in case law or doctrine.

The definitions provided by the countries indicate a similar conception of discretion in national legal systems.

For example, *Bulgaria* stated that discretion allows the administrative authority to assess whether, when, and how to act to take the most appropriate administrative decision in each case.

In *the Czech Republic*, administrative discretionary power is generally recognized in situations when a legal norm does not entail a single legal consequence if its hypothesis is fulfilled. Therefore, the legal norm provides administrative authorities with possibility to choose from two or more solutions after considering all the specific circumstances of the case.

*Estonia* indicated that according to the Administrative Procedure Act, the right of discretion is an authorisation granted to an administrative authority by law to consider making a resolution or choose between different resolutions. The right of discretion shall be exercised in accordance with the limits of authorisation, the purpose of discretion and the general principles of justice, taking into account relevant facts and considering legitimate interests.

*France* explained that the administrative authority has discretion if, to make a decision, it has the freedom to assess the facts according to which it can choose between several decisions, all of which would be equally lawful.

*Hungary* stated that a discretionary administrative decision is a decision in which the authority bases its decision on a piece of legislation that only defines the framework of the decision. A discretionary decision is also a decision where the legal provision defining the options for a decision does not specify the conditions and criteria for the decision. An administrative decision is not a discretionary decision if the authority decides on the basis of an assessment of the evidence necessary to reach a decision by applying a legal rule which does not provide for discretionary powers.

*Latvia* noted that in the case of discretion, once the preconditions for applying a legal provision have been established, the authority may choose from several alternative legal consequences provided for in the legal provision rather than applying one specific consequence.

*Lithuania* indicated that According to the Supreme Administrative Court, the right of discretion of the administrative authority is understood as the power that gives the subject of administration a certain freedom of action in making decisions, enabling it to choose from several legally possible options of behaviour the one that it considers to be the most suitable.

In *Slovakia*, the Recommendation of the Committee of Ministers concerning the exercise of discretionary powers by administrative authorities defines discretionary power as a power that leaves an administrative authority some degree of latitude as regards the decision to be taken, enabling it to choose from among several legally admissible decisions the one which it finds to be the most appropriate.

In *Spain*, case law defines discretionary acts as those that result from freedom of choice between equally fair alternatives or options with the same legal effect, brought to the subjective judgement of the administration.

*Serbia* explained that a discretionary administrative act is an act the contents of which are not formerly determined, but the authority issuing such act has the option to select one of two or more legally equal possibilities.

*The United Kingdom* indicated that to say that there is a discretion presupposes that there is no unique legal answer to the problem.

### *3.2. The distinction between discretion and margin of appreciation in the interpretation of undefined legal concepts*

Eleven respondents indicated no distinction between discretion and margin of appreciation (scope of appraisal) in the interpretation of undefined legal concepts in their legal system (*Belgium, Croatia, Cyprus, Ireland, Hungary, Lithuania, Romania, Serbia, Slovakia, Slovenia and Türkiye*) and *Bulgaria* has not provided an answer to this question. Other countries indicated that such a distinction is in place.

Most of the counties indicated that discretion is related to the part of the legal consequences of the legal provision. Meanwhile, the margin of appreciation is related to the part of the legal provision's hypothesis (legal conditions) in cases where it contains an undefined legal concept that needs to be specified.

At the same time, most national reports explained that, unlike discretion, which, as mentioned in question 1, means that the administrative authority has the freedom to choose among several alternative and legally permissible actions with the same legal effect, when authorities have to specify undefined legal concepts, the law generally allows only one – objective, fair and truthful – decision.

In particular, *Austria* explained that discretion, in a narrow sense, refers to margins that are intentionally granted to the administration by the legislator. In contrast, the legislator does not intend to grant discretion to the administrative authority when using undefined legal concepts. Undefined legal concepts are the result of the use of imprecise legal terms. Their contents and meanings have to be determined through interpretation. If, even after applying all methods of interpretation, no specific content emerges, the provision is not precise enough and infringes Art. 18 of the Federal Constitutional Law. However, if a provision allows for several interpretations, preference shall be given to the interpretation enabling the provision to be in conformity with the Constitution.

*The Czech Republic* explained that if the hypothesis of the legal norm contains an undefined legal concept, the administrative authority must assess its content and conclude – based on an all-round assessment – whether or not a particular state of facts falls within the scope of such a concept. According to the case law, firstly, the administrative authority must generally define what falls or may fall within the scope of the undefined legal concept and apply this abstract definition to the case at hand. If the hypothesis of a legal norm containing an undefined legal concept is fulfilled, the administrative authority has no choice but to proceed as envisaged by relevant rules for such a situation (to apply the legal consequences).

In the *Greek* legal system, the margin of appreciation is recognized in cases where the authorities specify undefined legal concepts on the basis of common experience.

*Italy* indicated that the margin of appreciation is the margin of discretion when the legislator grants the authority the freedom to decide whether an element of a legal rule containing an indefinite legal concept is satisfied. The authority has no discretion to decide but only to fill the concept of content.

*Spain* stated that discretionality implies the recognition of a freedom of choice for the holder of the right, so that within the margin conferred by the enabling rule, any of the different options that could be exercised are legally permitted, and any of them can be chosen, given that such options have the same legal effect. On the other hand, when the right is exercised applying indeterminate legal concepts, there is no such freedom of choice between options with the same legal effect, but rather, when the legal concept applied presents some degree of indeterminacy or imprecision in its wording, such a concept can and must be individualised in its practical application in such a way as to identify the specific solution that is fair and appropriate to the circumstances of the case under consideration.

A different approach is described by *Latvia*, that, for its part, pointed out that it is generally considered possible to determine only one correct content of an undefined legal concept. However, in such a case, the authority has no margin of appreciation.

The margin of appreciation could be recognized in exceptional cases, where it may not be possible to identify a single legally correct content of the undefined legal concept in the specific factual circumstances of the case. In such cases, an assessment is required, which can only be carried out objectively by the authority concerned. In such a case, the authority has a margin of appreciation, *i.e.*, the freedom to fill with content the undefined legal concept according to the factual circumstances of the case.

Similarly, *Norway* also pointed out that generally, the authorities are not offered any margin of appreciation in the interpretation of undefined legal concepts. In certain cases, it could, nevertheless, follow from an interpretation of the relevant provisions that the authorities are offered some degree of appreciation with regard to the assessment of whether the facts of the case at hand, are covered by the undefined legal concept (e.g., whether a planned construction project will, in the view of the municipality, have “good visual qualities” when assessed in conjunction with its’ natural surroundings and placement).

Noteworthy are also some other national responses in this regard.

*Albanian* legal system makes a distinction between discretion and margin of appreciation by the public administration body. The appreciation of the public body exists in any case, even in the situation of discretion as the body is obliged to investigate and to complete administrative actions on this basis.

In the framework of the appreciation, the public body considers the evidences, investigates thoroughly and comprehensively, evaluating the circumstances of the case in relation to the applicable law, to reach an administrative decision. Almost in any case, the decision is taken in compliance with the due process.

Also, in *the United Kingdom,* the distinction is recognized. As explained in the report, it sometimes being said that the interpretation (or application) of an undefined legal concept calls for an evaluative judgment rather than an exercise of discretion. Generally, the interpretation of legal concepts is assigned to the judgment of the court rather than an administrative body, whereas administrative discretion is conferred on public authorities. However, it may be found as a matter of interpretation of the legal concept that the evaluative judgment to be made in applying it is primarily reserved to the public authority, in which case the lawful limits of its function are in practice the same as for the exercise of discretion (in particular, it must make a decision which it not irrational).

### *3.3. Characteristics, criteria, or methods for determining the administrative discretionary power in a particular case*

Most national reports indicated that the determination of whether an administrative authority has discretion is mainly based on the assessment of the structure and wording of a legal norm. This method of identifying discretion was pointed out by most of the respondents: *Austria, Bulgaria, Croatia, Cyprus, Czech Republic, Estonia, Finland, France, Germany, Greece, Hungary, Italy, Latvia, Netherlands, Norway, Poland, Portugal, Serbia, Slovakia, Slovenia, Sweden, Türkiye and Switzerland.*

In this regard, firstly, most countries indicated that in the case when administrative authority has a freedom to decide whether to issue or not to issue a decision, discretion is usually indicated by the use of the words “may”, “allowed”, “can”, “should”, “it is permissible”, “have the right” in the particular legal provision.

Slovenia, as an example, mentioned the following provision: the administrative authority can grant citizenship to a foreigner, bypassing the general rules, if he is a descendant of a Slovenian citizen and has lived in Slovenia for at least one year prior the date of the application for citizenship and also meets additional conditions regarding economic security, not being part of any criminal proceedings, [...].

However, Austria highlighted that the mere use of the expression "may" does not constitute discretionary power if the law does not provide for criteria according to which the discretion is to be exercised. The law must determine a standard according to which the discretion is to be exercised; otherwise, it is unconstitutional.

Norway indicated that in some instances, the discretion might not follow directly from the provision itself. In such a case, the preparatory works could show that the legislator has intended for the authority to be offered discretion, even if terms like "may" have not been included in the provision itself. This could be the case if the assessment requires specific knowledge or, for example, if it presupposes broader assessments on a societal scale.

Estonia also highlighted that occasionally, if the wording is not clear, interpretation in conformity with the Constitution or EU law is also used.

Secondly, discretion may also be recognised where administrative authority has a freedom of content which means that an applicable legal provision prescribes that a decision is to be issued but does not determine specific content thereof. An authority shall issue such a decision by taking into account of the frameworks laid down in the applicable legal provision.

In this regard, for example, Latvia indicated that a legal provision may contain a precise list (catalogue) of possible legal consequences or define a range (field) of possible legal consequences, allowing to choose any legal consequences within the range (e.g., the provision provides that the authority shall impose a fine of between EUR 100 and EUR 5000).

Similarly, Slovakia noted that an administrative authority applies discretion by choosing the type of sanction when imposing penalties for administrative offenses provided that the law allows for alternatives, or when deciding on the amount of the fine within the range set by the law.

A similar approach was described by Albania, indicating that discretion is provided by law when it provides for the minimum and maximum opportunities of the public body and the body takes a decision within these limits.

Most countries also indicated that administrative discretionary power (or margin of appreciation if distinguished) could be recognised if the particular provision contains undefined legal concepts.

Slovakia stated that discretion is also when the administrative body gives the content of undefined terms such as "principles of morality", "good faith", or "reasonable time limit" in the process of applying the law.

Türkiye also explained that administration has discretion power in cases where legal provisions use not-so-clear terms such as "public safety, general health, public order requirements". The administration has discretion to fill in these ambiguous concepts. However, it should also be noted that if vague concepts have an objective value, administration has no discretion power. For example, the concept of "immorality and decency" has an objective value in law.

The Czech Republic explained that undefined legal concepts are mostly abstract nouns or nouns with adjectives (such as "public interest" or "substantial change"). Therefore, it is usually not a problem to recognize them in the legal system and thus determine if administrative authorities have margin of appreciation.

In this regard, it is important to mention that Latvia, for its part, offers a different explanation concerning determining the margin of appreciation. As Latvia pointed out, two elements must be established:

1) the description of the preconditions for the application of the legal norm in the part of the legal circumstances of the provision contains an undefined legal concept;
2) there are objective reasons for the margin of appreciation, *i.e.*, it is not possible to identify a single legally correct content of the undefined legal concept and an assessment is required which can only be carried out objectively by the authority concerned.

*Latvia* also highlighted that the following situations are recognised as objective reasons for recognising the margin of appreciation:

1) an assessment has to be made for a unique non-reproducible situation (e.g., an assessment for an oral examination that is not recorded or otherwise fixed);
2) an assessment is based on personal experience (e.g., in the case of assessment of civil servants);
3) an assessment is mainly based on political considerations or concerns the right of the administration to decide on its own organisation;

4) an assessment is complex, based on non-legal standards or political values, and adopted by a collegial body composed, for example, of experts in different fields or representatives of different social groups.

In addition to all the above, it also follows from some national reports that discretion may in some cases arise from the nature of the matter itself.

*Greece* and *Hungary* indicated that in cases where the administrative authority issues regulatory administrative acts it is recognized that the authority has discretionary power. In this case, the authority may adopt provisions that serve the public interest in a better way.

*Türkiye* noted that the administrative authority has discretion in the subject matter of the administrative action. For example, according to the regulation regulating aid to students in need, if the faculty administration has the right to choose one of the options of giving books, providing clothing, food aid, or providing shelter, there exists discretion here.

### *3.4. Judicial review of the use of discretionary power by the authority*

Regarding the judicial review of the use of discretion by the administrative authority, all reporting parties indicated that, in general, judicial control of such decisions is limited to the question of where the administrative authority has exercised its discretion in accordance with the law. Furthermore, the courts cannot generally amend or annul administrative decisions because they consider another exercise of discretion more appropriate.

In particular, *Cyprus* noted that when reviewing the legality of a decision, the court examines the decision in order to ascertain whether:

1) there is a clear statutory legitimacy of discretion and its extent;
2) the public organ has exercised its discretionary powers;
3) there has been sufficient enquiry of all relevant facts for the discretion to have been exercised correctly, reasonably and under no misconception and
4) there was due reasoning for the decision.

In *the Czech Republic*, the Supreme Administrative Court ruled that the court may only review whether the administrative authority has not departed from considerations set in law, whether the reasoning of the contested decision is in accordance with the rules of logical thinking, and whether the premises of such reasoning have been established by due process of law.

*Estonia* indicated that when assessing the lawfulness of an administrative act issued as a result of the exercise of discretionary power, the court does not conduct a separate assessment of the expediency of a discretionary decision. When verifying the lawfulness of an administrative act or measure, the court does not exercise discretionary power instead of administrative authority. What this means in practice is that if one of the important reasons that formed the basis of the authority's discretionary decision is deemed unlawful or irrelevant by the court, the court cannot assess whether the authority would/should have taken the same decision even without that part of the reasoning – thus, the decision must be annulled.

*Greece* also explained that if the court establishes an incorrect use of discretion, this is a ground for annulment of the decision. If a petition to issue a decision was submitted before an authority and the competent authority did not issue such decision, the court cannot itself specify the content of the decision, because the content of the decision must be determined by the authority in the exercise of its discretion.

In *Hungary*, the Administrative Court Procedure Act sets out the limits of the discretionary power of the administrative court by stating that, in addition to the general aspects of review, "[i]n the context of the legality of an administrative act carried out within discretionary powers, the court shall also examine whether the administrative body exercised its powers within the limits of its discretionary powers, whether the criteria for discretion and their reasonableness can be ascertained from the document containing the administrative act".

Administrative Court of *Lithuania* adheres to its consistent practice that in the event where public authorities are given relatively wide discretion, in the implementation of certain legal norms or policy in a certain area, the courts examine only whether the subject of public administration, exercising its discretion, did not make a clear error (in the assessment of circumstances and application of law), did not abuse authority (power), did not manifestly exceed the limits of discretion.

*Spain* stated that case law resorts to methods for the control of discretionary powers such as the control of the facts determining them as well as the regulated aspects, the observance of the procedure, the application of the general principles of prohibition of arbitrariness or misuse of power, or the implementation of general principles of law such as the principle of proportionality, among others.

In this regard, it should also be noted that some countries indicated an expansion of judicial control.

In particular, *Poland* indicated that the court is limited in its ability to review discretionary decisions, but at the same time seeks to expand it due to ensure the subjective right to a court to the fullest extent possible, as well as to protect the citizen from unilateral actions by administrative authorities.

It is pointed out in the legal scholarship that the concept of the directives of choice of legal consequences and the concept of the legality of purpose (goal), on the one hand, limit the freedom of the authority to decide on the shape of the decision and, at the same time, extend the scope of judicial review exercised by administrative courts over discretionary decisions. Especially, the concept of the legality of the purpose allows for a very wide control of the discretionary decision by the administrative court, and in fact allows for full control of decisions issued within discretionary power of the administration.

The administrative courts sometimes turn also to the criterion of reasonableness as a premise for reviewing discretionary decisions. It is also argued in the legal scholarship that, in administrative discretion cases, it is becoming increasingly common for administrative courts to reach for the principle of proportionality as a criterion for the control of discretionary power.

*Italy* pointed to the transition from a formal check on the existence of reasoning to the correctness and logic of the decision, which is a step towards a stronger review of administrative discretion.

A fundamental step in the evolution of the control of discretionary power is related to technical discretion, in which the administration's choice is grounded on technical rules. Initially, the judge exercised a weak review being able to annul acts based on evidently unreliable technical assessments. For now, the administrative judge's review is full and exclusive, although it can never substitute the choice of administration.

*Luxembourg* pointed out that the court's assessment of the discretion of the authorities was previously limited to the assessment of manifest error. However, this approach has given rise to controversy and confusion, in particular as to the meaning of the term "manifest".

In its 2010 judgment, the Administrative Court clarified its position, stating that a judge may annul an administrative authority's decision only for an error of discretion. Such an error may take the form of a disproportionate application of a rule of law to factual elements. The judge's review of legality is thus carried out as a proportionality review.

*France* also pointed out that the administrative court has extended the scope of its judicial review. There are generally three types of discretionary control a judge can exercise:

1) Limited control: the judge has no control over the administrative assessment of the facts and is limited to superficial control, which is limited to identifying a manifest error of assessment. Recognising the discretion of the administration, it is considered that the court has the competence only to correct grave and manifest errors.
2) Ordinary legal control of the facts: the judge checks whether the nature of the facts of the case corresponds to the factual conditions laid down in the documents.
3) The control of ultimate legality or so-called proportionality: it is used when the administrative decisions reviewed by the judge infringe fundamental rights or fundamental freedoms.

In addition, some countries also indicated certain exceptions.

*Latvia* and *Portugal* emphasised that judicial control could be different where administrative discretion is limited to zero (despite the textual formulation of a legal provision indicating discretion, only one particular legal consequence can be legally correct). In such a case, the court can fully examine whether the authority has applied the only correct legal consequence. If the authority has not done so, the court may annul the unfavourable decision or order the authority to issue a decision of a specific content.

*Slovakia* stated that the only exception to the principle that courts should not substitute their discretion for the discretion of the administrative authority constitutes an exercise of mitigating power by a judge in cases where an administrative authority has imposed a penalty manifestly disproportionate to the nature of the act and its consequences.

*Romania* indicated that judicial review of the use of discretionary power might not be carried out in the case of administrative acts of public authorities concerning their relations with Parliament, acts of command of a military nature, administrative acts for the amendment or abolition of which another judicial procedure is provided for by organic law.

In contrast to the limited judicial review in case of discretion, most countries indicated that there is a complete judicial review over the interpretation of undefined legal concepts.

For example, *the Czech Republic* explained that the interpretation of an undefined legal concept and its application to a particular situation may be the subject of full (unlimited) judicial review as it falls within the review of (un)lawfulness of contested administrative decisions. Therefore, administrative authorities are bound by courts' interpretation of an undefined legal concept and their assessment of whether or not a particular state of facts fulfils the concept.

*Greece* indicated that in such a case, the court, having taken into account the common experience, shall examine whether or not the authority has correctly assessed the specification of an undefined legal concept. If the assessment is found to be incorrect, then the court shall make its own assessment.

*Spain* also explained that when it comes to the interpretation and application of undefined legal concepts, the courts are fully empowered to carry out a full judicial review of the administrative decision, being able not only to annul it but even to replace it with a more appropriate one, when the conclusion is reached that, based on the particular circumstances of the matter examined and the evidence provided, the fairest solution is different from the one reached by the administration.

Meanwhile, some countries highlighted the limited control of the courts in cases where the authorities are found to have a margin of appreciation in interpreting undefined legal concepts.

*Latvia* emphasised that, if the authority has a margin of appreciation (exceptional cases where it is not possible to determine the single legally correct content of an undefined legal concept and an assessment is required which can only be objectively carried out by the authority concerned), the court can only examine whether there has been a manifest error of assessment or an essential procedural violation.

*Estonia* stated that when resolving disputes related to a margin of appreciation, the court is not forbidden from exercising an extensive control, including replacing the authority's assessment with that of the court. However, the court may be more restrained, especially when the assessment requires specific non-legal knowledge or experience and the interference with subjective rights is not serious.

The Supreme Court has explained that the court's control over the margin of appreciation may range from full control to a test of rationality to even a test of obvious errors, depending on the thoroughness of the regulation, the necessity of non-legal knowledge needed for the assessment and the seriousness of the restriction of subjective rights.

*Norway* pointed out that, in the context of discretion, certain provisions may lead to the conclusion that judicial review should be less intense to a certain extent and the assessment of the authorities must be taken into account. In such a case, the courts would still assess whether the facts of the case at hand are covered by the relevant legal provision, but they would offer some level of appreciation to the authority's assessment of the question. Should the courts, taking this margin into account, find that the facts of the case are not covered by the relevant legal provisions, the decision would generally be considered invalid.

*Portugal* stated that the "margin of free assessment" only admits a single decision that is wanted by the law. Therefore – even when the administration has a "margin of free assessment" namely to fulfil undetermined concepts using technical judgements, rules of experience or reasonability – its decisions may be challenged, although this jurisdictional appreciation is limited to cases of error or breach of the fundamental legal principles that govern the administrative activity.

### *3.5. Judicial review of the use of discretionary power by the authority that has resulted in a restriction of human rights*

Most national reports indicate that judicial review of the use of discretionary power by the authority that has resulted in a restriction of human rights is more intense. This approach has been clearly pointed out by *Bulgaria, Croatia, Cyprus, Estonia, Finland, France, Greece, Ireland, Italy, Latvia, Lithuania, the Netherlands, Norway, Poland, Slovakia, Slovenia, Sweden and the United Kingdom*.

Most countries indicate that in such cases, the courts are more rigorous in assessing the principle of proportionality or even the intensity of the proportionality test is generally the same as in cases with no administrative discretion.

In particular, *Estonia* stated that the intensity of judicial review must be more thorough in case of a serious restriction of human rights. However, the court may still not exercise discretion instead of the authority.

*Finland* explained that restrictions of fundamental rights and liberties and human rights must comply with certain criteria such as proportionality and necessity. Thus, an authority's use of discretionary power resulting in the restriction of a human right would most likely receive heightened scrutiny during judicial review.

*Greece* indicated that judicial review is affected by the fact that discretionary power used by the authority has resulted in a restriction of human rights. In such cases, the courts are usually more rigorous in assessing the principle of proportionality. If the restriction is found to be not proportionate, the court annuls the unfavourable decision that restricts the human rights according to the Constitution, the European Convention on Human Rights and the Charter of Fundamental Rights of the European Union where applicable. In taking this approach, the courts seek to assess proportionality with the same scrutiny as the European Court of Human Rights and the Court of Justice of the European Union.

*Ireland* stated that whilst the judicial review is not in itself a remedy to review the discretionary powers of a public authority but rather of the decision-making process emanating from the use of that power, such powers are reviewable in circumstances where the Human Rights of an aggrieved person are concerned.

Judicial review is concerned with the Courts exercising their constitutional duty to ensure that powers, governmental and administrative, are exercised within the law and the Constitution and in a manner consistent with the rights of individuals affected by them: "Where fundamental human rights are at stake, the courts may and will subject administrative decisions to particularly careful and thorough review".

*Italy* stated that if the discretionary power used by the authority has resulted in a restriction of human rights, the court is more rigorous in its assessment of the principle of proportionality, even if it is never possible to substitute its assessment for the assessment of the authority.

*Lithuania* explained that in such cases, the court very carefully analyses the situation through the prism of the principle of proportionality. In this respect, if the restriction is found to be disproportionate, administrative acts may be annulled.

Referring to the recent judgment of the Grand Chamber of the Administrative Jurisdiction Division of the Council of State, *the Netherlands* indicated that the intensity of the test of the principle of proportionality is determined by the degree of policy space the government has to make a decision and purpose that the decision serves and what its weight is. It is also important to determine whether and to what extent the interests of the citizens and businesses involved are affected. Here, human rights play an essential role. The more heavily these interests weigh, the more serious the adverse consequences of the decision or the decision violates human rights, and the more intensive the assessment will be by the administrative court.

The Constitution of the *Slovak Republic* provides that the review of any decisions concerning fundamental rights and freedoms should not be excluded from the court's jurisdiction. Thus, if a discretionary power used by the administrative authority had resulted in a restriction of human rights, a judicial review by the administrative court would be possible even though otherwise inadmissible.

*Norway* indicated that should the decision entail such a restriction, the courts would have to assess whether that restriction is justifiable, *i.e.*, whether it is prescribed by, pursues a legitimate aim, law, and is proportionate. In assessing the proportionality of the restriction, the courts would generally conduct a full and unlimited assessment. Furthermore, the intensity of the review of the proportionality of the restriction would, in these instances, generally be the same as in cases of no administrative discretion. Regardless of whether there is an element of administrative discretion or not, the courts will, should they find that said restriction on human rights is not proportionate, and thus not justified, order that the decision is invalid.

Also, the *United Kingdom* explained that where alleged violations of fundamental rights are relevant to a rationality review of an exercise of administrative discretion, the courts will apply a more demanding approach to scrutiny than they otherwise would. Since the Human Rights Act came into force, the courts have adopted proportionality as the appropriate standard of review in claims in which the exercise of administrative discretion is alleged to have engaged rights protected under that Act, subject to considerations of deference which will be considered within the proportionality analysis.

Moreover, some countries highlighted that in taking this approach, the courts seek to assess proportionality with the same rigour and scrutiny as the European Court of Human Rights (*Greece, Latvia, Norway*).

At the same time, most national reports indicated that even if the court finds that the authority's discretion has resulted in a violation of human rights, it can only annul the particular decision. Only *Latvia* highlighted that the courts in such a case might also substitute their own assessment for the assessment of the authority.

In this regard, it is also worth mentioning the explanation given by Germany and Slovenia.

*Slovenia* stated that, in principle, there is no room for the use of the discretionary power of the administrative authority in the enforcement of human rights and also other legal rights of the parties. The right of a party must be recognized in full if the statutory conditions are met. Any interference or restriction of human rights must always pass a strict test of proportionality.

Similarly, *Germany* noted that in such situations, the principle of proportionality would only render legal the decision that has the least impact on human rights. All other decisions will thus be illegal. In such a situation, it is often found that discretion is reduced to zero.

The other countries mainly emphasise the obligation of the authorities to exercise discretion in accordance with human rights and also highlight the obligation of the authorities to provide reasons with particular rigour and intensity when the decision affects the essential core of fundamental rights. Furthermore, it is generally noted that the courts are competent to review such a decision by the authorities, but it is not specified whether and how the judicial review is affected in such a case.

# ACA-Europe Colloquium
# “Services to citizens and social rights”

**Naples, Italy**
**26 June 2023**
**General Report by the Italian Council of State**

# Summary of the General Report of the Colloquium "Services to citizens and social rights" held in Naples, Italy, 26 June 2023

The topic of services to citizens and social rights was chosen because it relates to areas, such as health protection, employment, education and the right to housing, which traditionally do not fall within the direct competence of the European Union.
This means that the laws of the Member States are not harmonised and it is possible that the protection of legal positions in these areas may vary considerably from one country to another.
The purpose of this study was to enrich the comparative experience resulting from mutual knowledge of the different legal systems and to verify the possibility of achieving a common standard of legal protection of individuals, particularly the most vulnerable, by the Supreme Administrative Courts.
The report summarises the main indications emerging from the answers given by the respondents to the questionnaire and it is divided into three parts:
1) the first, which is of a substantive nature, is devoted to the identification of social rights in the different legal systems, the guarantees offered and their implementation even in times of crisis;
2) the second focuses on judicial protection, on the identification of the court competent to hear disputes relating to social rights, on trade unions, on the rites and actions provided for by each procedural system;
3) the third aims to illustrate the most emblematic rulings in relation to the different types of social rights and to allow a comparison of cases actually decided.
The replies to the questionnaire show that in almost all ACA Member States the source of legislation governing the main social rights (work, education, health, social security, legal, economic and social protection of families) is the Constitution or the ordinary law. Common law is responsible for the implementation of constitutionally protected social rights and related services (maternity benefits, right to a minimum wage, invalidity and/ or sickness pension), while regulatory acts are responsible for the detailed rules.
In some countries, international treaties – the European Convention for the Protection of Human Rights and Fundamental Freedoms, the International Covenant on Economic, Social and Cultural Rights – also provide the legal basis for the recognition of social rights, as they are binding once ratified.
Moreover, the fundamental role of the Supreme Administrative Courts is evident not only in terms of the effectiveness of the protection of social rights, but also in terms of the establishment of new rights, such as access to the internet, the right to water (Slovenia), the right to sustainable development in environmental matters (Italy, France, Lithuania), subsequently positively regulated by the legislator, as well as in terms of the extension of the recipients of benefits related to this type of legal situation (Germany).
This last interpretative activity is particularly important in view of the social groups of recipients of benefits and services, consisting of so-called weak subjects, and the high

impact that recent emergency periods, connected to the pandemic and the energy crisis following armed conflicts, have had on them.

In all legal systems, with the exception of Spain, there is a non – tangible core of social rights which cannot be sacrificed because of limited financial resources and, in the event of the need to curb public expenditure, in almost all Member States there is no indiscriminate reduction in the resources allocated to the implementation of the various rights. In many countries the balancing of the conflicting needs is the responsibility of the constitutional court, in the Netherlands it is the responsibility of the legislator, in Germany the responsibility is shared between the government and parliament, while in Ireland it is the responsibility of the Minister for Finance.

If the limitations result from individual acts, the ordinary or administrative court has jurisdiction depending on the type of act, except in France, Greece, Estonia and Austria where the administrative court always has jurisdiction.

In most countries, social benefits are provided by public entities, private entities included in the public system and private entities on a voluntary basis.

In particular, in a number of countries (Italy, Ireland, Croatia, Luxembourg) private entities must be authorized on the basis of an accreditation mechanism and specific service contracts in order to be integrated into the public system in a structured way.

Associations and private bodies have an important role to play in the provision of the benefits necessary to guarantee social rights, without prejudice to the central role of public intervention.

In almost all Member States, non-state territorial levels of government have administrative and regulatory powers in the area of social rights (with the exception of Cyprus, Ireland and Turkey), being able to admit, exclude or condition access to social benefits in some areas (with the exception of Germany, Switzerland, Portugal and Hungary where they can do so in any area).

In most countries, EU and non-EU citizens have access to social rights benefits in certain areas.

In almost all Member States, non-EU citizens generally have access to health care, including emergency care, regardless of residence and administrative situation (Italy, Greece, France, Finland, Croatia, Belgium, Czech Republic).

Common to all Member States of the ACA is the introduction in recent years of special social benefits to cope with short and medium-term emergencies – pandemic, energy crisis, banking and financial crisis -, consisting of aid to companies, tax exemptions, special funds for workers in companies in crisis, subsidies for groups in difficulty, employment measures, subsidies and aid for families, price freezes on basic foodstuffs, bonuses for household utilities, maximum resale prices for electricity, natural gas and oil.

An equally shared trend is the lack of special rules on judicial protection for the special support measures introduced during the emergencies of the last few years, since the rules on the division of competences between judges remained unchanged, as did the remedies provided by individual legal systems.

On the other hand, the situation of the various legal systems in relation to the judicial protection of social rights is much more varied and diverse.

In most countries, jurisdiction over disputes relating to social rights is assigned for specific matters to the ordinary court or to a different special court and only on a residual basis to the administrative court. In Montenegro, the Czech Republic, Serbia, Sweden and Hungary, jurisdiction over disputes relating to social rights belongs exclusively to the administrative court, whereas in Belgium and Ireland it belongs to the ordinary court. In countries where social rights disputes are not exclusively within the jurisdiction of ordinary or administrative courts, the division of jurisdiction is highly articulated.

In many Member States, administrative jurisdiction includes disputes relating to social security, education, health, social assistance, maternity protection, employment protection and vocational training, but there are some important exceptions or clarifications to be made since the allocation may depend on several factors, such as a choice made by the legislator, the existence of a public-sector employment relationship underlying the social right at issue, the subjective legal position invoked in the case, and the nature of the subjects involved.

The administrative court has jurisdiction over the legality of administrative acts adopted by the public administration or other public entities to organise and regulate the provision of social services in all the countries examined (with the exception of Slovakia and Switzerland).

In all countries, the division of jurisdiction is also reflected in the power of administrative courts to deal with administrative acts and/or proceedings for the award or recognition of subsidies, aids, benefits and other services relating to social rights.

Common to all procedural systems are the remedies for the protection of social rights, which consist in the annulment of measures both of a general organisational nature and of recognition of benefits to individuals and an order that the administration pay compensation for damages in a specific form, *i.e.* the payment to an individual of subsidies/aids/benefits unlawfully denied, or in equivalent.

In some countries there are fast-track or simplified procedures, or in some special cases, in relation to the protection of social rights (Greece, Luxembourg, Spain). Alternative dispute resolution (ADR) exists in almost all the countries surveyed (with the exception of Albania, Belgium, Bulgaria, Croatia, Finland, Ireland, Slovenia and Turkey), often on a general basis. Mediation may be optional or compulsory before going to court in those jurisdictions that provide for it.

An overall analysis of the replies shows that, even in the absence of ad hoc legislation, the decisions of the competent judges have, from time to time, been the source of the extension of this type of rights and related benefits to non-beneficiaries, first and foremost non-EU nationals, irrespective of their status in the Member State concerned.

Finally, common problems in ensuring effective protection of social rights have been identified, such as:

a) the lack of financial resources, which requires a careful balancing of the various interests involved;

b) the lack of awareness among individuals of their social rights and the benefits they confer, often also due to the complexity of the administrative procedures required to obtain them;

c) the inadequacy of the legal framework, which is subject to frequent changes and which also affects the proper use of discretionary powers by administrations, which are often reluctant to extend the range of beneficiaries.
The role of the Supreme Administrative Courts has also proved to be important in relation to the above critical points, not only in deciding individual cases, but also for the principles that have been affirmed and for the conforming function of future administrative action.

# General Report
# Naples, 26 June 2023

In view of the seminar organised by the Italian Council of State in collaboration with ACA-Europe on[1] 26 June 2023 in Naples, a questionnaire was sent to all member Courts of the Association containing questions concerning the regulation and protection that each country offers to so-called "social rights". The seminar aims to examine in depth the approach of the Supreme Administrative Courts to "social rights".

This report has been prepared on the basis of the replies received from the following countries: Albania, Austria, Belgium, Bulgaria, Croatia, Cyprus, Czech Republic, Estonia, Finland, France, Germany, Greece, Ireland, Italy, Latvia, Lithuania, Luxembourg, Malta, Montenegro, Netherlands, Poland, Portugal, Serbia, Slovakia, Slovenia, Spain, Sweden, Switzerland, Türkiye and Hungary.

The report summarises and collates the main indications from the data provided.

The report was prepared by a working group coordinated by Prof. Marcello Clarich and composed of the lawyers Gianlorenzo Ioannides, Francesca Romani, Claudia Serra.

## FIRST PART
## SOCIAL RIGHTS: THE GUARANTEES OFFERED BY NATIONAL SYSTEMS AND THEIR IMPLEMENTATION IN TIMES OF "CRISIS"

### 1.1.

Before examining the approach of the Supreme Administrative Courts to "social rights" it is necessary to clarify what source of law governs the main

[1] ACA-Europe is a European association composed of the Councils of State and/or the Supreme Administrative Courts of the 34 Member States: the 27 countries of the European Union; Albania, Montenegro, Serbia and Türkiye, as observers; Norway, Switzerland and Great Britain, as host states. The Court of Justice of the European Union also participates in the meetings.

social rights such as the right to work, education, health, social security, economic and social legal protection of families.

First, all countries regulate the main social rights in the Constitution.

The Constitutions contain a non-exhaustive catalogue of social rights recognised within each country. For example, in Switzerland, in addition to the rights expressly mentioned in the Constitution, which are directly invoked before the courts, article 41 of the Constitution, which guarantees social objectives, should be taken into particular account. These objectives are primarily addressed to the legislative authority that is under a duty to implement them. They are not directly invoked before the courts, but serve to guide the judge in interpreting the law.

On the other hand, the ordinary law regulates social rights concerning more specific services, such as maternity benefits, the right to a guaranteed minimum wage, the pension system for invalidity and/or illness.

The ordinary law regulates in detail the various social rights mentioned in the Constitution and the services related to them. It is then up to the regulatory acts to regulate the rules implementing the ordinary law.

Additionally, in some countries international treaties (such as the European Convention for the Protection of Human Rights and Fundamental Freedoms or the International Covenant on Economic, Social and Cultural Rights), being binding on the countries where they have been ratified, can constitute the legal basis for the recognition of social rights.

## 1.2.

Having outlined the legal sources governing social rights, it is necessary to identify the social benefits provided by public administrations in the implementation of the various rights.

All countries provide subsidies and aid to people living in poverty; aid and support in job search (with the exception of Montenegro); a solidarity-based health system that provides equitable access to services regardless of the extent to which citizens contribute to funding the system; social housing; assistance to disabled people; economic aid and benefits to families, especially allowances for expenses incurred in the early years of life of children and for their education.

However, in the federal states (Austria, Switzerland) the amount of the various benefits granted at central level may differ from the federal level because of the amount of resources that provincial laws allocate to the various welfare programmes.

## 1.3.

In most countries (except Albania, Estonia, Germany, Latvia, Luxembourg, the Netherlands, Czech Republic, Slovakia, Sweden, Türkiye), in addition to the social rights traditionally recognised by the various Constitutions and laws in force, new rights have emerged, such as the right to access the Internet, the right to water and other "common goods".

This was achieved in various ways through the application of general principles and clauses (Italy, Bulgaria, France, Greece), the interpretation of the case-law (Italy, Belgium, France, Greece, Ireland, Montenegro, Spain, Switzerland), following regulatory intervention (Austria, Belgium, Bulgaria, Cyprus, Finland, France, Greece, Ireland, Lithuania, Poland, Portugal, Serbia, Slovenia, Spain, Hungary), or through negotiations carried out by trade unions and private associations (Croatia, France, Montenegro, Slovenia).

To cite one example, Article 70a of the Slovenian Constitution, which was introduced as a result of the 2016 reform, provides that every Slovenian citizen has the right to drinking water, which is considered to be a public good managed exclusively by the State.

In Germany, there has been no creation of new rights, but every citizen has equal access to any new benefit provided by a public institution. No new social rights have emerged in Luxembourg, but the ordinary law and its implementing measures provide in ever more detail how existing social rights are to be exercised in order to make them more effective.

Some countries mention the introduction of the right to the environment and the protection of sustainable development (France, Lithuania).

## 1.4.

However, in all countries, budgetary constraints and measures to curb public spending can limit the effectiveness of social rights.

The Member States of the European Union refer, in particular, to the measures introduced in each state following the implementation of the Treaty of 2 March 2012 on Stability, Coordination and Governance in the Economic and Monetary Union.

For example, in Italy, with the introduction of the balanced budget principle, preference has been given to selective interventions to protect certain social rights considered to be more worthy rather than to operate a system of indiscriminate cuts. Almost all countries have tried to briefly explain how the non-indiscriminate cuts of rights in periods of containment of public spending are carried out.

In Cyprus, measures taken to deal with periods of economic crisis must not violate any provisions of the Constitution (in particular articles governing fundamental and social rights) and international conventions ratified by the Republic. However, public interference must pursue the public interest and must not jeopardize the dignified life of citizens (a fundamental right provided for in the Constitution).

In Albania, on the other hand, emphasis is given to the economic crisis caused by the COVID-19 pandemic, which has also had an impact on the system of guaranteeing social rights.

## 1.5.

The comparison of the responses revealed that in almost all countries (with the exception of Malta, the Netherlands, Slovakia and Spain) there is an intangible core of social rights, even in specific areas, which cannot be sacrificed due to the limited financial resources.

In this regard in Switzerland, although Article 36(4) of the Constitution provides that 'the essence of fundamental rights is inviolable', full compliance with that article may become impossible if the cantons face material crises.

In Spain, it is not the prerogative of the State to guarantee an essential nucleus of social rights. However, in some cases, such as the right to study or the public social security system, the basis of protection is provided for in the Constitution, but the various benefits and their extension is remitted to ordinary law. However, there is no minimum constitutional guarantee.

**1.6.**

In countries that responded positively to the previous question, the core of social rights that cannot be sacrificed is identified either by the Constitution (Italy, Austria, Belgium, Bulgaria, Cyprus, Czech Republic, Estonia, Finland, France, Germany, Hungary, Ireland, Latvia, Lithuania, Luxembourg, Poland, Portugal, Montenegro, Serbia), or by ordinary laws (Albania, Belgium, Finland, France, Greece, Slovenia, Sweden, Türkiye), or by case law (Italy, Albania, Austria, Belgium, Cyprus, Estonia, France, Greece, Ireland, Latvia, Lithuania, Luxembourg, Poland, Portugal, Czech Republic, Serbia, Sweden, Switzerland, Türkiye) or by the regulatory provisions (Belgium).

In Hungary and implicitly in other countries, the proportionality-necessity test is the tool to assess the necessity and measure of the restriction of the fundamental right whose essential content cannot be limited under any circumstances. In the Czech Republic, the rationality test is the means of revising the rules governing social rights if the revision involves a limitation of these rights.

The limitation of social rights cannot affect the fundamental principle, present in every country, of protection and guarantee of human dignity and must take place in compliance with the principle of equal treatment and non-discrimination.

**1.7.**

As to how the scarcity of available financial resources may impact the effectiveness of social rights, in some countries social rights must be guaranteed regardless of budgetary constraints (Montenegro and Slovakia). This is the case even though the economic situation and income of the population may be reflected in the amount of certain social benefits, regulated by legislation (Slovakia).

In no country, however, do budgetary needs always prevail over social rights.

In most countries a balance must be achieved between the conflicting needs (Italy, Albania, Cyprus, Serbia, Sweden, Spain, Slovenia, Portugal, Poland, the Netherlands, Lithuania, Latvia, Malta, Ireland, Hungary, Greece,

Germany, France, Finland, Estonia, Czech Republic, Croatia, Bulgaria, Belgium, Austria, Switzerland, Luxembourg, Türkiye).

Where legal provisions restrict or otherwise affect social rights, the task of balancing the opposite needs lies with the Constitutional Court, when it is called upon to assess the constitutionality of the provisions in question (Italy, Albania, Belgium, Bulgaria, Croatia, Estonia, Lithuania, Poland, Portugal, Czech Republic, Serbia, Austria, Luxembourg, Spain).

If, on the other hand, the limitations arise from specific acts or measures, it will be the competent court (ordinary or administrative, depending on the sector involved or the type of act) to decide on the individual case (Italy, Albania, Bulgaria, Croatia, Finland, Greece, Luxembourg, Lithuania, Poland, Slovenia, Spain) or, in some cases only the Administrative Court (Austria, Estonia, France, Greece, Serbia and Sweden).

In the Netherlands, the search for balance lies mainly with the legislator, not the courts.

In Ireland, the Minister for Public Expenditure is responsible for balancing financial resources.

In Germany, it is the responsibility of the government and parliament to negotiate and determine the budget for all expenses, including social expenditure.

## 1.8.

To cope with the short and medium-term emergencies of recent years (pandemic, energy crisis, banking and financial crisis) special social benefits have been introduced in all countries.

The main measures were: aid to enterprises, tax exemptions, special fund for workers of companies in crisis (Italy, Albania, Austria, Bulgaria, Cyprus, Croatia, Estonia, Finland, France, Germany, Greece, Ireland, Lithuania, Latvia, Luxembourg, Malta, Montenegro, the Netherlands, Poland, Portugal, Serbia, Slovakia, Slovenia, Spain, Switzerland, Sweden, Hungary), special fund for pensioners and other categories in difficulty (Albania), employment measures (Belgium).

Some countries have also planned other actions to support social welfare with regard to food, housing, health, transport and childcare (Ireland, Spain and Türkiye) as well as subsidies and aid for families who have suffered a decrease in income due to the pandemic (Latvia and France). In Hungary, among other measures which proved to be very useful for the most deprived, there was a freeze in the prices of certain food products and the introduction of a subsidy for household users.

In Slovenia, as a result of energy crisis the following measures have been introduced: determination of the maximum resale price of electricity, natural gas and oil, aid for the business sector, energy solidarity subsidies for socially vulnerable groups of citizens due to the impact of rising energy prices, one-off subsidies for beneficiaries of family allowances. In Poland, special gas tariffs have also been introduced for poor families, as well as for hospitals, schools, nurseries and cultural institutions.

Some countries have taken measures to compensate households for rising energy and fuel prices (Austria, the Netherlands, Latvia, Greece and Hungary). Subsidies for electricity to run certain medical devices used by some consumers (Hungary) as well as assistance to pensioners to cope with rising energy prices (Croatia) were also introduced.

Many countries have provided subsidies for businesses and households to help counter the negative effects of rising energy costs (Belgium, Estonia, Finland, Czech Republic and Sweden).

In France, due to the war in Ukraine and the consequent increase in energy prices, a special energy voucher for 2022 was introduced for the benefit of 12 million households, as well as a subsidy for large energy-consuming companies for the payment of gas and electricity bills. A fuel allowance was also provided for workers who use a vehicle for work purposes.

**1.9.**

In no country has the special support measures introduced to deal with the emergencies of recent years been accompanied by special rules that have altered the ordinary division of competences between administrative judges and other judges in the areas concerned.

In the case of the Czech Republic, the measures introduced did not provide for derogations from the ordinary division of responsibilities between administrative and civil courts, but provided for derogations from powers within the administrative justice system. In fact, the special jurisdiction of the Supreme Administrative Court has been provided for to decide on applications for annulment of pandemic measures issued by the Ministry of Health. In other cases, regional courts have retained such responsibility.

## 1.10.

In most countries social benefits are provided by public entities, private entities included in the public system and private entities on a voluntary basis (Italy, Albania, Austria, Belgium, Bulgaria, Croatia, Estonia, Finland, France, Germany, Ireland, Lithuania, Luxembourg, Malta, the Netherlands, Poland, Portugal, Serbia, Slovakia, Slovenia, Spain, Sweden, Switzerland, Türkiye, Hungary).

In some countries social benefits are provided only by public entities and private entities included in the public system (Montenegro), while in other countries by public and private entities on a voluntary basis (Latvia and Greece).

In particular, in a number of countries private entities are authorised, on the basis of an accreditation and authorisation mechanism and special service contracts, to carry out public health functions (Italy, Albania, Croatia, Cyprus, Ireland, Luxembourg, Poland, Czech Republic, Slovakia and Sweden) in order to be included in a structured manner in the public system.

The role of associations and private bodies in securing benefits related to social rights is often recognised, without prejudice to the centrality of public intervention (Italy, Albania, Slovakia).

In Finland, social benefits can be provided both by public entities and, on a contractual basis, by private individuals, but functions involving the exercise of administrative powers (such as placing a child in care and non-voluntary psychiatric treatment) can only be performed by public entities.

In Switzerland, in the field of social and emergency assistance, in addition to State aid, people in need can receive assistance from private institutions; in the field of health, the state (in this case the cantons) grants reductions in premiums to insured persons of modest means. Health insurance companies reimburse the insured for the costs of care, assistive products and transport under compulsory health insurance.

The Czech Republic's health insurance system is based on the principle of compulsory redistributive payment based on income, the principle of insurance obligation and the principle of the free choice of the health insurance company. These companies are independent and separate entities from the state that manage health insurance funds.

## 1.11.

In most countries, non-state territorial government levels have administrative and regulatory powers in the field of social rights (Albania, Austria, Belgium, Bulgaria, Croatia, Estonia, Finland, France, Germany, Greece, Italy, Latvia, Lithuania, Luxembourg, Montenegro, Netherlands, Poland, Portugal, Czech Republic, Serbia, Slovakia, Slovenia, Spain, Sweden, Switzerland, Hungary).

In some countries, non-state territorial government levels do not have administrative and regulatory powers in this area (Cyprus, Ireland Malta, and Türkiye).

## 1.12.

In most countries where these territorial levels of government have administrative and regulatory powers in the field of social rights, they can admit, exclude or condition access to social benefits, but only in certain sectors (Italy, Albania, Austria, Belgium, Bulgaria, Croatia, Estonia, Finland, France, Greece, Latvia, Lithuania, Luxembourg, Montenegro, Netherlands, Czech Republic, Serbia, Slovakia, Slovenia, Spain, Sweden).

In other countries (Germany, Switzerland, Portugal, Hungary) territorial levels of government have the power to admit, exclude or condition access to social benefits in any sector, without limitation.

In the case of Poland, however, territorial levels of non-state government do not have the power to admit, exclude or condition access to social benefits.

Administrative functions – including those relating to the recognition of specific benefits – in Italy and Albania are assigned in accordance with the principle of vertical subsidiarity. In Sweden too, many administrative functions are carried out by local governments which have a constitutionally recognised right to self-government.

In general, local and regional authorities have legislative and administrative competences in the field of social rights based on the distribution of competences and cannot intervene in matters reserved for the central state.

For example, in Italy, with the exception of certain matters reserved to the State (immigration, social security), most of the matters relating to social rights are attributed by the Constitution to the laws of the State and Regions. The regions therefore have broad regulatory power, in accordance with the general principles laid down by state law.

In the case of Spain, the Autonomous Communities have multiple competences in the field of social rights, both at legislative and administrative level, depending on the distribution of competences.

In Albania most matters relating to social rights are attributed by the Constitution to the State, which can further delegate such matters to local governments in accordance with the general principles established by state law.

In Serbia, local territorial entities have the right to recognise or exclude or condition social benefits in areas that are governed by their general acts and financed from their budget.

In Latvia, local governments can adopt regulations and guidelines to regulate the provision of social benefits within their territories, in accordance with the general framework established by national legislation. This includes defining eligibility criteria for social benefits, determining the level and duration of assistance, and monitoring compliance with relevant laws and regulations.

In Greece, the State has the power to adopt legislation on social rights, while local authorities are charged with the implementation of social policies.

In France, the State does not have a monopoly on social assistance: the *departments* occupy an important place in the allocation of certain social benefits while the territorial authorities are competent, within their areas of competence defined by the legislator, to grant or refuse social aid under the conditions and criteria laid down in laws and regulations.

## 1.13.

In most countries, non-EU citizens can access social rights benefits in some domains (Italy, Albania, Austria, Belgium, Cyprus, Croatia, Estonia, Greece, Ireland, Latvia, Lithuania, Luxembourg, Montenegro, Poland, Portugal, Czech Republic, Serbia, Slovenia, Sweden, Hungary).

In some countries, non-EU citizens can benefit in all areas of social rights (France, Finland, Germany, the Netherlands, Slovakia, Spain, Switzerland).

In many countries, everyone, including illegally resident non-EU citizens, is guaranteed the right to emergency healthcare (Albania, Belgium, Croatia, Estonia, Finland, France, Greece, Italy, Luxembourg, Czech Republic, Slovenia and Sweden).

Moreover, in many countries, legally resident non-EU citizens have access to health care and other social benefits (Albania, Cyprus, Estonia, Finland, France, Greece, Ireland, Italy, Lithuania, Malta, the Netherlands, Poland, Serbia, Slovenia, Spain and Sweden).

In Switzerland, the criterion is residence and/or work, rather than nationality: people domiciled and/or employed in Switzerland are obliged to take out insurance and are therefore entitled to social insurance benefits.

In Spain, foreigners can access essential social services and benefits regardless of their administrative status.

In Luxembourg, legally resident non-EU citizens have full access to healthcare as well as Luxembourg citizens and, in general, all social rights.

In Hungary, non-EU citizens working in the country become insured and are entitled to all benefits provided for by the social security system.

In Germany, in principle, the rules of German social law do not distinguish between Germans, EU citizens and non-EU nationals: social benefits are slightly reduced for foreigners who apply for refugee status during the application procedure.

Healthcare in Austria is based on a model of compulsory social insurance based on employment, not residence or nationality. Other social benefits, such as family allowance or childcare allowance, may instead require residence status in Austria. The right to certain social benefits for third-country nationals, such as social assistance, may also be linked to the existence of agreements under international law.

## SECOND PART

## JUDICIAL PROTECTION OF SOCIAL RIGHTS

### 2.1.

Jurisdiction over disputes relating to social rights belongs exclusively to the Administrative Court in Montenegro, Czech Republic, Serbia, Sweden, Hungary.

In some countries, on the other hand, jurisdiction is assigned to the ordinary court (Albania, Bulgaria, Cyprus, Croatia, Estonia, Finland, France, Italy, Luxembourg, the Netherlands, Slovakia, Spain, Türkiye) and/or to a different special court (Cyprus, Finland, Germany, Greece, Luxembourg, Slovenia, Switzerland, Spain, Portugal), while remaining general to the administrative court. In Greece, for example, disputes over pensions for civil servants are decided by the Court of Auditors. In Germany, the matter falls primarily within the jurisdiction of the Federal Social Court. Also in Slovenia there are "Social Courts", in relation to whose decisions, however the judge of last instance is the Supreme Court. In Switzerland, similarly, there are cantonal insurance courts against whose decisions it is possible to appeal to the Federal Court.

In Austria and Latvia, the general jurisdiction of the administrative court is accompanied by that of the Constitutional Court, when the questions concern the constitutional legitimacy of legislative acts, including social rights provided for in the Constitution.

In Lithuania and Poland, the distinction between ordinary and administrative jurisdiction depends on the subject-matter of the dispute: matters relating to the merits of decisions of public administrations fall within the ordinary jurisdiction, while matters relating to legality fall within the administrative jurisdiction. Finally, in Belgium, Ireland and Malta, such disputes are decided by the ordinary court, since there is no general special administrative jurisdiction. In Belgium there may be cases, explicitly provided for by law, in which certain disputes are attributed to administrative courts.

## 2.2.

The division of jurisdiction of disputes concerning social rights is highly structured.

In almost all countries, administrative jurisdiction includes disputes relating to social security, education, health, social assistance, maternity protection, labour protection and vocational training, but there are some important exceptions or clarifications to be made.

In Albania, Austria, Estonia, France, Italy, Lithuania, Poland, the jurisdiction over some of the matters mentioned does not belong exclusively to the administrative court, as in some cases the same matters also fall within the ordinary jurisdiction. The combining of competences may depend on several factors, such as the legislator's choice, the existence of a public employment relationship underlying the social law at issue in the proceedings, the subjective legal position raised in the court, the nature of the persons involved.

In many cases disputes relating to labour protection and vocational training, and social security matters, belong to the jurisdiction of the employment judge, who may be part of the ordinary jurisdiction, or a special judge. In particular, such disputes, as well as those relating to the protection of maternity rights, fall within the ordinary jurisdiction of employment in Belgium and the Netherlands, as well as in Portugal, where, however, they belong to administrative jurisdiction in the case of public employment; also in Bulgaria and Croatia labour law disputes belong to the ordinary jurisdiction, except in the case of civil servants, where the jurisdiction is administrative. In Italy, similarly, social security disputes fall under the ordinary jurisdiction of employment. In Finland and Spain, on the other hand, social security disputes are attributed to a special court, the Insurance Court. In Cyprus, the labour court is also a special court and decides disputes on the protection of motherhood and paternity. In Germany and Luxembourg all disputes in the matters referred to above belong to a special jurisdiction with competence over social matters. In Slovenia, the jurisdiction is divided between special judges in social matters, administrative judges and ordinary judges.

In Slovakia, disputes relating to certain work activities, mainly related to security and defense, are covered by administrative jurisdiction, while all other labour protection disputes belong to ordinary jurisdiction. In Belgium and Malta, on the other hand, the absence of a general administrative jurisdiction determines that the division of jurisdiction between the ordinary judge and the special judges depends on specific regulatory provisions.

## 2.3.

The administrative judge has jurisdiction over the legality of administrative acts adopted by the public administration or other public entities in order to organise and regulate the provision of social services in all the countries examined, except in Slovakia and Switzerland, where organisational measures cannot be appealed, save those which take concrete decisions against the administrators.

Moreover, in Cyprus, Estonia, the Netherlands and Sweden, the administrative judge may decide on the legality of regulatory and organisational measures only indirectly and in the context of litigation having as its main object a measure relating to an individual decision.

In Ireland and Malta, the ordinary judge has the same power in the absence of administrative jurisdiction.

## 2.4.

In all countries, the distribution of jurisdiction described above is reflected in the power of administrative courts to also deal with administrative acts and/or procedures for the award or recognition of subsidies, aids, benefits and other services related to social rights.

Thus, for example, in Belgium all social matters fall generally within the jurisdiction of the ordinary judge, whereas the Council of State can only hear disputes expressly attributed to its jurisdiction. Social security matters in Spain fall within the special jurisdiction of the Social Courts; in Italy, on the other hand, within the ordinary jurisdiction of employment.

In Ireland, as mentioned above, the ordinary court deals with such matters in the absence of administrative jurisdiction.

## 2.5.

The administrative court in some legal systems can only verify the regularity of the procedures and, if necessary, annul them, but cannot take decisions replacing those annulled (Cyprus, Luxembourg, Czech Republic). Similarly, in Ireland, the judge having jurisdiction to examine the legality of administrative proceedings and measures can only verify their legality, and not the merits. In the Czech Republic, the administrative judge may require the administration to adopt a new measure, including principles which deprive the latter of any discretion. In Luxembourg, on the other hand, the administrative judge may decide on the substance in certain specific cases provided for by law, such as in the case of social security. In other jurisdictions, on the other hand, the administrative judge may also verify whether the individual is entitled to receive the benefit which has been wrongly denied, by adopting a decision replacing that of the contested administration which he or she deemed unlawful (Austria, France, Latvia, Lithuania, Montenegro, Portugal, Slovakia, Spain, Sweden, Türkiye). This is also possible in Bulgaria, except in cases where the measure which unlawfully denied the benefit has been annulled on the grounds of incompetence, in which case the relevant administration will be ordered to provide the benefit, or if there are other reasons why the Court is unable to decide, it will order the Administration to take a decision, including by providing binding instructions.

In many cases, the administrative judge can decide on the substance only if the annulled act is not the result of a discretionary choice of the Administration (Albania, Croatia, Estonia, Finland, Germany, Italy, the Netherlands, Poland, Serbia, Slovenia); if the Administration can exercise discretion, even after the contested measure has been annulled, the judge can only order that a new measure be adopted.

In Belgium, thc cxtcnt of the court's powers depends on the subject-matter of the proceedings, if it is a subjective right, it can decide on the merits; if, on the other hand, it is a question of the administration exceeding its power, the court can only annul the act.

In Switzerland, the administrative judge may enter into the merits of the questions covered by the measures submitted to him for examination, even if the limits of its power are established at cantonal and non-federal level, so there are differences in their scope.

Finally, in Hungary, the extent of the administrative judge's powers in matters of social rights depends on sectoral disciplines.

**2.6.**

The types of remedies that the administrative court can order for the protection of social rights include the annulment of administrative measures and a judgment against the administration.

The measures that can be annulled include both organisational measures and the concrete recognition of benefits. The court may order the administration to pay compensation in a specific form, that is to say, the disbursement to an individual of the unlawfully denied benefits, or its equivalent.

Different countries have adopted different solutions compared to the powers that each of them specifically grants to the administrative judge.

In Belgium and Poland, the administrative judge has all the powers mentioned above, except for an order for compensation in a specific form. In Cyprus, the Czech Republic and Slovakia the administrative court has the power to annul decisions of the public administration deemed unlawful, while compensation for any damage resulting from them can only be claimed from the ordinary judge. In Sweden, where the administrative judge may also enter into the merits of decisions of the public administration and itself exercise discretionary choices and order the disbursement of an unlawfully denied benefit, the same court cannot, however, order the public administration to pay compensation in the form of damages, which can only be claimed from the civil courts.

In Bulgaria, the administrative judge may annul measures and order the administration to pay compensation for damage caused by an act found to be unlawful. Similarly, a judge having jurisdiction in Ireland may only annul the unlawful administrative decision and, where appropriate, order the public administration to pay compensation for equivalent. The administrative court has similar powers in Austria, Croatia, Estonia, Finland and Italy, where it can also order the Administration to adopt specific measures. Condemnation in a specific form, in countries where this is possible, is permitted within the limits – set out above – of the powers conferred on the administrative court with respect to the exercise of the discretionary activity of the public administration. Thus in some countries this is always allowed (Austria, Croatia, Estonia, Greece, Lithuania, Portugal, Slovenia, Spain, Sweden, Türkiye) while in other systems it is possible only if there is no margin of discretion (Albania, Finland, Italy, Latvia, the Netherlands, Serbia) or in cases where it is expressly provided for by law (Luxembourg, Hungary).

In France, the administrative judge sitting in disputes relating to social rights has every necessary power, including, in addition to all those mentioned above, also the power to order the Administration to pay penalties.

In Italy, there is also a form of *class action* for the efficiency of the public administration, by which the breach of the period within which the proceedings must be concluded, the failure to adopt mandatory measures and the lack of adequate levels of benefits, including in the field of social rights, can be challenged.

**2.7.**

In some countries there are accelerated or simplified procedures in relation to the protection of social rights (Austria, Bulgaria, Greece, France, Lithuania, Luxembourg, Spain, Portugal, Türkiye). For example, in Greece in the field of pensions, the citizen can first turn to a dedicated committee set up in the administration, and only later to the administrative judge; the private individual may also act in this matter without the assistance of a lawyer. In Luxembourg, the procedure at first instance is subject to shortened time limits. In Spain, all disputes falling within the jurisdiction of the Social Courts are subject to an accelerated and simplified rite, and there is also a simplified procedure before the administrative court for certain matters. In Poland, there are no simplified or accelerated procedures in general terms, but can be provided for in sector-based regulations.

In Albania, Croatia, Italy except for social security matters, which fall under ordinary jurisdiction and are subject to the labour proceedings, which are simplified and accelerated, there are no accelerated or simplified procedures. Similarly, in Slovenia, matters falling within the jurisdiction of the Social Courts are subject to a simplified and accelerated procedure, while there is no simplified social procedure for the proceedings before the administrative court. In Cyprus, only disputes relating to labour law falling under the special jurisdiction of the Industrial Disputes Tribunal are subject to expedited proceedings.

However, there are no specific accelerated or simplified procedures for the protection of social rights in Belgium, Estonia, Germany, Ireland, Latvia, Montenegro, the Netherlands, the Czech Republic, Slovakia, Serbia, and Sweden. There are no accelerated or simplified procedures in Finland, but it is mandatory to request a review of the decision before it can be brought before the court.

Specific protective measures relating to social rights are provided for in Hungary.

There are no simplified procedures in Switzerland either at cantonal or federal level. However, it is expected, in general terms, that the proceedings before the cantonal insurance courts should take place quickly and easily.

In Malta when the violation of a social right is alleged to be also a violation of a fundamental human right (recognised by the Constitution or by the substantive provisions of the European Convention on Human Rights or one of its protocols, or recognised by both), the applicant needs to file an application before the First Hall Civil Court and then has a right to appeal before the Constitutional Court.

## 2.8.

In almost all the countries considered, arrangements for ADR (*alternative dispute resolution*) are often generally available and are not specific to the social rights sector.

There are no alternative dispute resolution procedures in the field of social rights in Albania, Belgium, Bulgaria, Croatia, Finland, Ireland, Slovenia, Sweden and Türkiye.

Mediation may be a possibility (Estonia, Germany, Latvia, Luxembourg, Poland, Serbia, Spain, and Hungary) or a mandatory passage before it can be brought before the competent court. Compulsory mediation can always be provided (Cyprus) or only with reference to certain subjects (France, Italy, Lithuania, Malta).

In some countries, mediation is only possible when the disputed issue falls under ordinary jurisdiction (Cyprus, Estonia, Greece, Italy, and Czech Republic).

In France there is generally a mediation procedure which may be initiated spontaneously by the parties or by order of the court; preventive mediation is then mandatory in some areas, including some disputes concerning social rights.

In Italy, alternative dispute resolution procedures are in place in some areas, and are mandatory only within the ordinary jurisdiction; none of them are directly related to social rights.

In the Netherlands, optional mediation, including in relations between private individuals and the public administration, has been introduced into practice, in the absence of a legislative provision. In Switzerland, alternative dispute resolution procedures under public law are neither prohibited nor expressly authorised in general terms, but there are certain areas in which disputes may be referred to a cantonal arbitration tribunal.

## 2.9.

With few exceptions (Austria, Belgium, Estonia, France, the Netherlands, Portugal) all the systems covered by the analysis identify the scarcity of economic resources as one of the main problems the administrative judge encounters in ensuring effective protection of social rights, and which imposes a delicate balancing activity, and sometimes limits the scope of action allowed to the judge. The scarcity of resources, which leads to a lower quality and limited distribution of benefits, is sometimes accompanied by a lack of awareness among individuals of their social rights (Albania, Croatia, Greece, Slovakia, Türkiye), which is also due to the complexity of administrative procedures sometimes required to obtain benefits (Czech Republic).

Other frequently encountered problems are related to the work of the public administration necessary to guarantee social rights. Thus, in some cases there is a misuse of discretionary powers, which results in the adoption of unlawful decisions and requires the intervention of the judge who may review decision (Bulgaria, Ireland, Slovakia, and Slovenia). Another problem encountered is the resistance to enforcement of the decisions of the judge (Albania, Croatia, Italy, Montenegro, Poland, Slovakia, Serbia, Sweden and Türkiye).

A further problem is the inadequacy of both the regulatory framework, which is subject to frequent changes, and the criteria for the recognition of social benefits (Estonia, the Netherlands, Slovakia, Hungary and Sweden).

# THIRD PART

# PRACTICAL CASES

## 3.1.

In the first question of the third part, respondents were asked to explain a case which occurred in their own system, in which the administrative judge had held that an act or measure adversely affecting social rights was unlawful because it infringed the 'essential core' of those social rights which cannot be restricted for any reason.

For example, in Austria, a provision of the *Familienlastenausgleichgesetz* (FAG) which did not grant a family allowance if a child was already married was considered to be in breach of the principle of equality enshrined in Article 7 of the Constitution[1].

In Belgium, the ordinary judge with jurisdiction over these disputes found that it infringed the principle of human dignity by the complete interruption of the supply of water to a citizen who was very late in paying the bills.

In Bulgaria, an ordinary judge found that the administrative authority had infringed the prohibition against discrimination in refusing to grant a woman, a single mother, the family allowance provided for families in which only one parent is living, as she had not demonstrated that she was not married and had not shown that her children had been recognised by their father or that he had died.

In Switzerland, a federal court held that it was contrary to the fundamental right to aid in situations of need (Article 12 of the Constitution) to cut the welfare benefits for a person who had refused to participate in an unpaid employment programme[2].

The Supreme Court of Cyprus has held that any form of difference in direct or indirect treatment between men and women in matters of wages, professional status, violates the constitutionally protected right to equality (Article 28 of the Constitution). The Court states that the prohibition of direct or indirect pay differentiations on the basis of gender is protected by the Constitution in absolute terms[3].

In a recent judgment, the Constitutional Review Chamber of the Supreme Court of Estonia ruled that the right to receive state assistance in case of need cannot be considered to have been violated as long as the state offers minimal means of living. In the case referred to above, there was no breach of law since the applicant's need for assistance had been adequately satisfied by the social security system[4].

The Supreme Administrative Court of the Czech Republic held that the decision of the Ministry of Health, during the COVID-19 pandemic, to close

---

[1] Judge of 18 March 1980, G 35/79, only available in German: *https://www.ris.bka.gv.at/Dokumente/Vfgh/JFT_10199682_79G00035_00/JFT_10199682_79G00035_00.pdf*).

[2] Arrêt du Tribunal fédéral publié aux ATF 142 I 1 consid. 7.

[3] *Melpo Gregoriou v. Municipality of Nicosia (no.1) (1991) 4 C.L.R, 3005.*

[4] Judgment of the Constitutional Review Chamber of the Supreme Court of Estonia, 5.5.2020, no. 5-20-1/15.

home schools (an alternative to standard education) during the Covid-19 pandemic undermined the essential core of the right to education[5].

The Finnish Supreme Administrative Court held that the right to education also included the free home-school transport service and that service was also to be offered to a disabled child, who, following a decision by the school Headmaster, had to be taken home half way through the school day[6].

In a number of judgments, the Greek Council of State considered the insufficiently justified reduction to pensions made by the legislature to be unconstitutional, stating that it was an attack on the very core of the right to pensions[7].

In Hungary, the Supreme Court annulled the decision of the administrative authority to reject the application for a widow's pension made by a widow divorced from her husband but who had continued to live with him as a civil partner, only on the ground that in the last year of life their cohabitation had been interrupted. In fact, the condition of the man's health had made it impossible for the woman to take care of him who had been assisted by the couple's son[8].

In Latvia, the Supreme Administrative Court has appealed to the Constitutional Court in order to ascertain whether the minimum amount of the State pension complies with Article 109 of the Constitution, which provides that everyone is entitled to social assistance in old age. It was noted that this amount could not even satisfy the basic needs of the person; therefore, it was declared that the relevant legislation was unconstitutional in that it undermined the right of human dignity. A reported case in Türkiye also concerns social security.

The Supreme Administrative Court of Romania held that the impossibility of challenging the decision of a Medical Committee on the determination of the ability to work in order to obtain recognition of an invalidity pension infringed the rights of the person[9].

Also in pension matters, the Supreme Administrative Court of Portugal held that an order for the repayment of debts arising from failure to pay

---

[5] Judge of the Supreme Administrative Court of 18 August 2021, No. 1 Ao 3/2021-52.

[6] Case KHO 2019:7 (ECLI:FI:KHO:2019:7).

[7] Ass. 2287-2290/2015.

[8] Kfv.VII.37.764/2019.

[9] Administrative Chamber of the Supreme Court (ACSC), decision no. 113, dated 22.7.2021.

social security contributions with the full value of the claimant's pension infringed the fundamental right to social security.

The Irish Supreme Court held that a provision in the Refugee Act (1996) restricting the right to work for asylum seekers was contrary to the Constitution when applied to the period prior to the final determination of the asylum application[10]. The Court held that the right to work entails a freedom to seek employment which cannot be limited without substantial justification.

The Lithuanian Court held that the non-recognition of benefits against a pregnant voluntary female soldier was in breach of the maternity protection provisions on account of the fact that she had not acquired 12 months of sickness and maternity insurance due to her voluntary military service in Afghanistan[11].

The Luxembourg Court has authorised certain building works in a protected zone. The alterations are necessary to adapt the property to the needs of the handicapped owner. The Court, recalling Article 11 of the Constitution, concluded that rights relating to the fundamental principle of the protection of human dignity include in particular the rooting of the human being in his territory and in his family context. In particular, they include the right for a person who has lived for a long time in his home, to be able to transform it in such a way as to make it compatible with his or her disability[12].

In the Netherlands, the Court of Appeal, in view of the inhumane conditions endured by asylum seekers who had exhausted all the legal remedies provided for by the law, ruled that the municipality had to offer them overnight stays and meals. In reaching its decision to court also referenced the European Social Charter[13].

A Polish Regional Administrative Court held that the decision of the administrative authority to deny a family allowance for the upbringing of the first child only because the household's income exceeded the statutory ceiling by less than two euros was illegitimate. The refusal was contrary to the purpose of the law and to the principles of social justice pursued by the legal system[14].

---

[10] *N.H.V. v. Minister for Justice and Equality and Ors* [2017] IESC 35, [2018] 1 I.R. 246.

[11] A-2563-502/2015.

[12] Cour adm., 9 janvier 2020, No. 43470C du rôle et Cour adm., 26 Mars 2020, No 43470CA du role.

[13] ECLI:NL:CRVB:2014:4178.

[14] Judgment of the Voivodship (Regional) Administrative Court in Gdańsk of 7 February 2019 (Case No.III SA/Gd 889/16).

In relation to family allowances, a court in Serbia held that parents were entitled to family allowances even if the minor child for reasons of education lived in a different place from the residence of the family. In Sweden, a local administration decided not to grant social assistance to an illegal immigrant because he had not facilitated the authorities to investigate his identity and citizenship. This decision was deemed illegitimate and the man was granted basic support (HFD 2014, ref. 37).

**3.2.**

The second question asked for an outline of a concrete case in which a service or service relating to social rights, recognised by law in favour of nationals of its own country, was considered by the court to be extendable also to foreigners (both EU citizens and non-EU), or in which the court considered the condition of "territorial anchorage" required of foreigners to be unreasonable or not proportionate.

In Austria, the Constitutional Court extended the general principle of equality to foreigners on the basis of Article I of the Federal Constitution on the Elimination of Racial Discrimination. This provision prohibits unequal treatment between foreigners without objective reasons and discrimination on the basis of nationality alone, but the Constitutional Court has further recognised that the difference in treatment of a foreign national is permissible only if it is not disproportionate and justified by a well-founded ground.

In Belgium, the Constitutional Court considered discriminatory a law that excluded foreigners with a legal right of residence from the right to social assistance because urgent medical care is granted only to persons who have no other income or insurance and for whom it is established that the necessary medical treatment is urgent. The deprivation of such assistance, by means of a general and a priori measure addressed to an abstractly defined category of foreigners, cannot be justified by the concern to limit abuses in social matters.

In Cyprus, jurisprudence has stated that there is a right to education for every person. This right is protected by a set of legal instruments and can be enjoyed not only by nationals of the EU State or Member State, but also by recognised refugees, asylum seekers and even irregular immigrants from third countries.

In Estonia, the Supreme Court ruled that where expulsion is impossible, it is essential, in order to respect the principle of human dignity, that the rights established by social law be recognised for the illegal foreigner.

In France, the Constitutional Council ruled that the difference in treatment, for the purpose of obtaining income of active solidarity, between foreigners legally resident in French Guiana and those legally resident in other parts of the territory of the Republic, with the exception of Mayotte, was contrary to the principle of equality.

In Greece, in relation to the benefit of social and family benefits, the Council of State stated that the allowance for the third child must be granted to the spouse of a legally resident EU citizen under the principle of equal treatment of EU citizens in free movement.

In Latvia, the Supreme Administrative Court ruled that it would not guarantee social justice and would be contrary to the principle of a socially responsible State to deny the right to family allowance to the holder of a temporary residence permit as a person who, after reaching the age of majority, continues his studies in the country, on the basis of the lack of the requirement of permanent residence.

In Luxembourg, in several cases, the administrative courts annulled decisions refusing financial aid for higher education because, initially, the law provided for such aid only for resident students (regardless of their nationality). In order to comply with EU law, the law had to extend (under certain conditions) the granting of such aid to students who, while not resident, are nevertheless the children of frontier workers active in Luxembourg.

In the Netherlands, the decision to exclude a Dutch national residing in Belgium from student scholarships (to study abroad) has been criticised by the ECJ. This is because the residence condition did not take into account other factors, such as the nationality of the student, the place where he attended school, his family, language skills or the existence of other social and economic ties.

In Poland, the court recognised the illegality of the refusal of the education allowance to an Indian citizen with long-term resident status in the EU as foreigners with such status are permitted by law to work on the territory of the Republic of Poland and can therefore receive education subsidies in a similar way to foreigners with a residence card with the entry 'Labour Market Access'.

In Spain, the Constitutional Court, after finding that foreigners are entitled to adequate judicial protection under the same conditions as Spanish citizens, declared unconstitutional the rule on free legal assistance, which provided for a limitation of the right for foreigners not resident in the country.

In Serbia, the Court annulled the decision of the administrative authority rejecting the applicant's request for material social security on the grounds that he was not a citizen of the Republic of Serbia, because the legal requirements for exercising this right are residence, not nationality.

In Switzerland, the Federal Court has recognised that the right to adequate and free basic education, enshrined in Article 19 of the Swiss Constitution, is independent of nationality or residence status. According to the Federal Court, even for children who enter the school system late, the goal must be to provide inclusive education, since it is not compatible with the Federal Constitution to provide separate or inferior quality education to foreign children.

**3.3.**

The administrative judges in most of the countries concerned, and within the limits of the jurisdiction described above, have decided on cases in which they were required to recognise, directly to the person who initiated the complaint, some assistance, a benefit or service that the public administration had unlawfully refused it.

These decisions frequently go into the substance of the questions (Austria, France, Spain, Sweden), while in some cases they are merely finding that the administrative measure is unlawful (Belgium, Cyprus, Slovakia).

For example, there are cases where the administrative judge recalculated the amount of the pension, previously calculated incorrectly (Latvia), recognised the entitlement to contributions for a temporary disability (Albania) or calculated the part to be returned to the public administration of a contribution that had previously been paid to a private individual (Netherlands). In other cases, the administrative judge established the relationship between different benefits, ascertaining their cumulation (Estonia, in relation to the subsidies provided for in the case of illness and those provided for as income supplements during the COVID-19 pandemic) or by allowing the beneficiary to choose between two non-cumulative benefits (Poland).

The administrative judge also intervened not directly in favour of the beneficiaries, but for the subjects called upon to provide social benefits (as in Belgium, where the judge recognised the right of a Bar Association to be reimbursed for expenses incurred for the operation of the legal aid service which had been denied by the administration).

One of the areas in which there is frequent litigation is health. In this area, the administrative court established the right of patients to receive reimbursement of healthcare treatments carried out in private facilities (Finland, Greece) or to treat illnesses resulting from work (Portugal), resolved disputes between the health care providers and the public sector that finances the health system (Bulgaria) and established the percentage of a person's disability (Hungary).

In those decisions, the administrative judge has sometimes adopted extensive interpretations of the law in order to adapt its application to the rationale pursued by the legislature (Croatia, Switzerland). In Croatia, for example, the possibility of acquiring benefits related to caregiver status has been extended to children despite being limited by law only to parents and spouses. On the contrary, decisions were also taken that annulled decisions of the administration that had denied some benefits by applying the law extensively. In Serbia, for example, a decision of the public administration was annulled which had denied the right to receive family allowances on the ground that the applicant had the use of a property even though he did not own it. Serbian law, in fact, excludes access to the benefit in question only if the applicant is the owner of property additional to that necessary for family life.

In Sweden, (HFD 2020 ref. 62, only to cite an example) the immigration authority denied a foreigner a certain social benefit because he had got a permanent permit of residence. In all three court-instances, the decision was found to be unlawful and the courts granted the individual the benefit in question.

In the area of social rights, even when the interest in the decision had ceased to exist, the judge considered that the matter was particularly important, and it was therefore appropriate to state a principle in general terms (Ireland).

# GLOSSARY/GLOSSAIRE

| N. | TERM – TERME | DEFINITION |
|---|---|---|
| 1 | **Abuse/misuse of discretionary power**<br><br>**Légalité interne** | Ground of review of administrative acts concerning situations in which administrative authorities have misused their discretionary power either because it has been used for improper purposes (having regard to the proper scope of this legal power) or because the authorities have exceeded the limits of this power or have violated fundamental rights or principles such as equal treatment, reasonableness, proportionality etc.<br><br>Motifs de contrôle des actes administratifs dans des situations où les autorités administratives ont abusé de leur pouvoir discrétionnaire en s'en servant à des fins inappropriées (compte tenu de la portée de ce pouvoir confié par la loi), en outrepassant ses limites ou en violant des droits ou des principes fondamentaux, tels que l'égalité de traitement, la proportionnalité, l'absence d'erreur (manifeste) d'appréciation, etc. |
| 2 | **Access to Documents (administrative procedure)**<br><br>**Accès aux documents (procédure administrative)** | Right granted to the parties to full access to documents, data, and information, while respecting the legitimate interests of confidentiality and of professional and business secrecy. Any limitation to this right shall be duly reasoned.<br><br>Droit des parties d'accéder de manière complète à des documents, données et informations administratifs, dans le respect des intérêts légitimes de confidentialité, et de secret professionnel et des affaires. Toute limitation de ce droit doit être dûment motivée. |
| 3 | **Action for addition of omitted pronouncements**<br><br>**Omission à statuer** | Omission to pass judgment on a claim brought forward by a claimant. Such an omission can be corrected via appeal or through the means of a specific remedy.<br><br>Il y a omission à statuer lorsqu'un juge ne statue pas sur tous les chefs de la demande dont il est saisi. Une telle omission peut être corrigée par la voie de l'appel ou par une voie de recours spécifique. |
| 4 | **Action for annulment**<br><br>**Recours en annulation** | Judicial remedy which enables the Administrative Court to annul an administrative (regulatory or individual) acts, for e.g. violation of the law, incompetence and abuse of power. The action has to be proposed within a time limit.<br><br>Recours juridictionnel permettant au tribunal administratif d'annuler un acte administratif (réglementaire ou individuel), par exemple pour violation de la loi, incompétence et détournement de pouvoir. L'action doit être introduite dans un délai déterminé. |

| | | |
|---|---|---|
| 5 | **Action for clarification of obscure concept**<br><br>**Recours en interprétation (contrôle juridictionnel)** | The parties may request clarification of some obscure concept contained in the judgment, on the understanding that the request for clarification cannot serve to modify the legal statements contained in the judgment or change the meaning of the judgment.<br><br>Lorsqu'une partie considère qu'un jugement n'est pas suffisamment clair, elle peut en demander l'interprétation au tribunal à travers un recours en interprétation; néanmoins cette demande ne peut modifier les déclarations juridiques contenues dans le jugement ou le sens de la décision. |
| 6 | **Action for enforcement proceedings**<br><br>**Demande d'exécution** | Judicial remedy to achieve the implementation of the final judgments of the Administrative Court and of other enforceable measures of the administrative courts.<br>The court, in the event the application is accepted, may order for example enforcement, prescribing the mean; declare null and void any acts in violation or circumvention of the res judicata; appoint, where necessary, an ad acta commissioner; it determines, at the request of one party, the sum of money payable by the defendant for each violation or subsequent non-compliance, or for any delay in the carrying out of the res judicata.<br><br>Recours juridictionnel permettant d'obtenir l'application des jugements définitifs et d'autres mesures exécutoires des tribunaux administratifs.<br>Si la demande est acceptée, le tribunal peut, par exemple, ordonner le respect du jugement, en prescrivant le moyen pour y parvenir; déclarer nul et non avenu tout acte violant ou contournant la chose jugée; désigner, le cas échéant, un fonctionnaire *ad acta* suppléant l'administration défaillante; déterminer, à la demande d'une partie, le montant dont la partie défaillante est redevable pour chaque violation ou manquement ultérieur, ou pour tout retard dans l'exécution de la chose jugée. |
| 7 | **Action for challenging the authenticity of an act**<br><br>**Action en contestation de la véracité d'un acte; inscription de faux** | Judicial remedy which enables the parties to question the authenticity of a written document.<br><br>Recours juridictionnel permettant aux parties de contester la véracité d'un document écrit. |
| 8 | **Action for damages**<br><br>**Recours en responsibilité (extracontractuelle)** | Judicial remedy concerning non contractual liability of the State, which enables the Administrative Court to award compensation for damage arising from the unlawful exercise of an administrative activity or the non-exercise of a mandatory one.<br><br>Recours juridictionnel tendant à engager la responsibilité non contractuelle de l'État, en permettant au tribunal administratif de réparer le préjudice résultant de l'exercice illégal d'une activité administrative ou du non-exercice d'une activité obligatoire. |

| | | |
|---|---|---|
| 9 | **Action for failure to act**<br><br>**Recours en carence** | A judicial remedy which enables the Administrative Court to order the administration, which has remained inert or inactive, to take action within a time limit. (This is known as the remedy of mandamus in common law countries).<br><br>Recours juridictionnel permettant au tribunal administratif d'ordonner à l'administration, coupable d'inertie, d'agir dans un certain délai (aussi connu sous le nom de *mandamus* dans les systèmes de *common law*). |
| 10 | **Action for performance or mandatory injunction**<br><br>**Recours tendant à l'adoption d'une mesure; conclusions à fin d'injonction** | Judicial remedy requiring a public authority to perform a public function. (This is known as the remedy of mandatory injunction in common law countries).<br><br>Recours juridictionnel visant à obtenir la condamnation de l'administration à adopter une mesure déterminée qui lui est demandée (connu sous le nom de « mandatory injunction » dans les systèmes de common law). |
| 11 | **Action for the access to administrative documents**<br><br>**Recours tendant à accéder à des documents administratifs (contrôle juridictionnel)** | Judicial remedy by which the interested party may challenge the decisions (formal or implied) on issues of access to administrative documents and against any other infringement of transparency requirements.<br><br>Recours juridictionnel permettant à la partie intéressée de contester les décisions (explicites ou implicites) relatives aux questions d'accès aux documents administratifs et contre tout autre manquement aux obligations de transparence. |
| 12 | **Administrative Act**<br><br>**Acte administratif** | A binding act by an authority, exercising public power, in an administrative matter.<br><br>Acte contraignant d'une autorité, exerçant des prérogatives de puissance publique, en matière administrative. |
| 13 | **Administrative Act – General**<br><br>**Acte réglementaire** | Binding administrative act which is not addressed to a specific addressee and which, alternatively, regulates defined cases or an undefined number of cases.<br><br>Acte administratif contraignant, sans destinataire spécifique, et réglementant une catégorie de cas déterminés ou un nombre indéterminé de cas. |
| 14 | **Administrative Act -Individual**<br><br>**Acte individual** | A binding administrative act having legal consequences addressed towards one specific addressee or a narrowly defined group of addressees.<br><br>Acte administratif contraignant dont les conséquences juridiques sont tournées vers un destinataire spécifique ou un groupe de destinataires étroitement défini. |

| | | |
|---|---|---|
| 15 | **Administrative activity** | Any kind of activity taken by public administration (e.g. providing administrative measures; material activity of enforcement of administrative acts; providing of public services; etc…). |
| | **Activité administrative** | Toute activité entreprise par une administration (par exemple, adopter des mesures administratives; assurer l'exécution matérielle d'actes administratifs; fournir des services publics; etc.). |
| 16 | **Administrative advice** | Opinion rendered by an administrative authority other than the proceeding one. Depending on the legal context the opinion may be either mandatory (binding) or optional (non-binding). |
| | **Avis** | Avis formulé par une autorité administrative autre que l'autorité prenant la décision. Selon le contexte juridique, l'avis peut être obligatoire (conforme) ou facultatif. |
| 17 | **Administrative complaint/Administrative appeal** | Non-judicial remedy to be filed with same authority which has carried out the challenged measure (objection proceeding) or to be filed with an administrative authority that is hierarchically superior to the one that issued the act or has powers to oversee the respective activities.<br>It may concern the unlawful conduct of a public authority or another entity performing a public administrative duty, or the failure to fulfil an obligation. It may represent a prerequisite for filing a judicial remedy or an optional step. |
| | **Recours administratif** | Recours extrajudiciaire auprès de l'autorité ayant adopté la mesure contestée (recours gracieux) ou auprès d'une autorité administrative hiérarchiquement supérieure à celle dont l'acte émane ou ayant le pouvoir de superviser les activités de cette dernière.<br>Il peut s'agir d'un comportement illégal d'une autorité publique ou d'une autre entité exerçant une fonction administrative publique, ou au non-respect d'une obligation. Il peut s'agir d'une condition préalable à l'introduction d'un recours juridictionnel ou d'une étape facultative. |
| 18 | **Administrative Investigation** | Preparatory phase of administrative procedure aimed at ascertaining all the relevant facts of the matter by means of, *inter alia*, gathering information, carrying out inspections, obtaining documents and any other relevant factors, etc… |
| | **Enquête administrative** | Phase préparatoire de la procédure administrative visant à établir tous les faits pertinents en l'espèce, notamment en recueillant des informations, en effectuant des inspections, en obtenant des documents et tout autre élément pertinent, etc. |

| | | |
|---|---|---|
| 19 | **Administrative Matter**<br><br>**Matière administrative** | A matter dealt with by an authority, exercising public power.<br><br>Questions traitées par une autorité administrative dans l'exercice de ses prérogatives de puissance publique. |
| 20 | **Adversarial procedure**<br><br>**Procédure contradictoire** | An administrative procedure which, in a manner similar to that before a court, grants to each party adversely affected by the intended decision the right to be heard and submit all the relevant evidence and allegations to be considered by the public authority before issuing the decision.<br><br>Procédure administrative qui, comme dans le cadre d'une procédure juridictionnelle, accorde à chaque partie lésée par la décision envisagée le droit d'être entendue et de soumettre tous les éléments de preuve et allégations qu'il importe que l'autorité publique prenne en considération avant de rendre la décision. |
| 21 | ***Affidavit***<br>**Common law**<br><br>***Affidavit* (déclaration sous serment)**<br>**Common law** | In common law, a sworn (or affirmed) document setting out the principal evidence to be adduced by one of the parties.<br><br>En *common law*, un document présenté sous serment (ou une autre déclaration formelle solennelle) exposant les principaux éléments de preuve apportés par l'une des parties. |
| 22 | ***Amicus curiae***<br><br>***Amicus curiae*** | "A friend of the court", typically where a specialist body with expertise in a particular area is appointed by the court to assist in the presentation of the case, generally in a formally neutral or dispassionate manner.<br><br>Personne ou entité disposant d'une expertise dans un domaine particulier, désignée par le tribunal pour contribuer à la mise en état de l'affaire, en général d'une manière neutre ou impartiale. |
| 23 | **Appeal**<br><br>**Appel** | Application to a superior court, which seeks to revise or vary a first-instance judgment.<br>A right to appeal to a higher court, often as of right, but sometimes the permission ("leave") of the court is required. The appeal is often confined to serious errors of law or demonstrating errors in the assessment by the trial court of the evidence.<br><br>Recours auprès d'une juridiction administrative supérieure qui vise à réviser ou à modifier un jugement rendu par un tribunal de première instance.<br>En principe, le justiciable peut introduire de plein droit un appel devant une juridiction supérieure. Parfois l'autorisation de la juridiction est requise («leave»). L'appel peut être limité aux cas dans lesquels de graves erreurs de droit ont été commises, ou lorsque des erreurs dans l'appréciation des preuves par le tribunal de première instance peuvent être dé démontrées. |

| | | |
|---|---|---|
| 24 | **Appeal *de novo***<br><br>**Appeal *de novo*** | In common law, an appeal, which requires the case to be re-heard afresh by the higher court.<br><br>En common law, c'est un appel qui requiert que l'affaire soit intégralement réexaminée par la juridiction supérieure. |
| 25 | **Appeal in cassation/appeal on points of law**<br><br>**Pourvoi en cassation** | Appeal against a decision of an Administrative Court (usually of the court of appeal) which enables the Council of State, or the Supreme Administrative Court to examine errors of law and procedure. In common law countries this is known as an appeal on a point of law.<br><br>Recours contre une décision d'une juridiction administrative (généralement la cour d'appel) qui permet au Conseil d'État ou la cour administrative suprême de contrôler les erreurs de droit et de procédure. Dans les pays de common law, il est connu sous le nom d' « appeal on a point of law». |
| 26 | **Approval**<br><br>**Approbation** | Favourable administrative measure giving enforceability to an act after assessment of its correspondence to public interests.<br><br>Mesure administrative favorable donnant force exécutoire à un acte, par exemple en raison de ce qu'il a été établi qu'il correspondait à l'intérêt public. |
| 27 | **Arbitrariness**<br><br>**Arbitraire** | Ground of review of administrative acts concerning situations in which decision-making is not guided by objectivity and a reasonable application of law.<br><br>Motif de contrôle des actes administratifs dans des situations où la prise de décision n'est pas inspirée par l'objectivité et une application raisonnable de la loi. |
| 28 | **Authorisation**<br><br>**Autorisation** | Favorable administrative measure that removes a restriction on exercising an economic or other activity after a control of requirements and/or assessment of public interests.<br><br>Mesure administrative favorable qui supprime une restriction à l'exercice d'une activité économique ou autre après un contrôle des exigences et/ou évaluation des intérêts publics |

| | | |
|---|---|---|
| 29 | **Authorisation scheme** | Any procedure under which a provider or recipient is in effect required to take steps in order to obtain from a competent authority a formal decision, or an implied decision, concerning access to an economic or other activity. The concept covers, inter alia, the administrative procedures for granting authorizations, licences, approvals, and also the obligation, in order to be eligible to exercise the activity, to be registered as a member of a profession or entered in a register, roll or database, to be officially appointed to a body or to obtain a card attesting to the membership of a particular profession. |
| | **Régime d'autorisation** | Toute procédure ayant pour effet d'obliger un prestataire ou un destinataire à faire une démarche auprès d'une autorité compétente en vue d'obtenir un acte formel ou une décision implicite relative à l'accès à une activité de service ou à son exercice. La notion recouvre notamment les procédures administratives par lesquelles sont octroyés des autorisations, licences, agréments ou concessions mais aussi l'obligation, pour pouvoir exercer l'activité, d'être inscrit à un ordre professionnel ou dans un registre, dans un rôle ou une base de données, d'être conventionné auprès d'un organisme ou d'obtenir une carte professionnelle. |
| 30 | **Automated decision-making** | The use of data, machines and algorithms to make decisions in a range of contexts, including public administration, business, health, education, law, employment, transport, media and entertainment, with varying degrees of human oversight or intervention. |
| | **Prise de decision automatisée** | Utilisation de données, de machines, d'appareils et d'algorithmes pour adopter des décisions dans divers contextes, tels que l'administration publique, les entreprises, la santé, l'éducation, le droit, l'emploi, les transports, les médias et le divertissement, avec différents degrés de supervision ou d'intervention de l'homme |
| 31 | **Automated transcription of hearings** | Automatic speech recognition to provide rough drafts of transcripts in real time. |
| | **Transcription automatisée des audiences** | Processus de reconnaissance vocale automatique permettant de fournir des ébauches de transcriptions en temps réel. |
| 32 | **Burden of proof** | A party's duty to prove a disputed assertion. It includes the burden of production (providing enough evidence on an issue so that the trier-of-fact decides it) and the burden of persuasion (standard of proof such as convincing evidence). |
| | **Charge de la preuve** | Devoir d'une partie de prouver une affirmation contestée. Celui-ci comprend les obligations de production (fournir suffisamment d'éléments prouvant une question, pour que le juge des faits statue à cet égard) et les standards de persuasion (normes de preuve, tels que la preuve convaincante). |

| | | |
|---|---|---|
| 33 | **Cassation**<br><br>**Cassation** | Specific powerof a Supreme Administrative Court to quash a judicial decision against which an appeal in cassation has been lodged, for matters of law and procedure.<br><br>Povoir spécifique, par une Cour suprême administrative, de casser une décision juridictionnelle contre laquelle un pourvoi en cassation a été introduit, pour questions de droit et de procédure; |
| 34 | **Certificate (public)**<br><br>**Certificat** | Document issued by an administration with the function of recognition, reproduction and information to third parties of states, personal qualities and facts contained in public lists and registers or otherwise ascertained by holders of public functions.<br><br>Document délivré par une administration ayant pour finalité de reconnaître ou reproduire des états, qualités personnelles et faits contenus dans des listes et registres publics ou établis d'une autre manière par des titulaires de fonctions publiques, et d'en informer des tiers. |
| 35 | ***Certiorari***<br>**Common law**<br><br>***Certiorari***<br>**Common law** | In common law, the order by a Court to quash an administrative or judicial decision.<br><br>En common law, l'ordre d'un tribunal en vertu de laquelle une décision administrative ou judiciaire doit être annulée. |
| 36 | **Challenge of a judgment by a third-party (judicial review)**<br><br>**Tierce opposition (contrôle juridictionnel)** | A third party may lodge an objection against a judgment even if final, when it affects their rights or legitimate interests.<br><br>Recours permettant à un tiers de contester un jugement, même s'il a autorité de chose jugée, lorsque ce dernier porte atteinte à ses droits ou intérêts légitimes. |
| 37 | **Claimant/Petitioner**<br><br>**Demandeur/Requérant** | Person who initiates a civil or administrative lawsuit.<br><br>La personne qui engage une action contentieuse civile ou administrative. |
| 38 | **(Administrative) Competence**<br><br>**Compétence (administrative)** | Set of faculties, powers and attributions assigned by the law to a particular organ of the administration in relation to the others.<br><br>Ensemble des facultés, pouvoirs et attributions conférée par la loi à un organe déterminé de l'administration par rapport aux autres. |

| | | |
|---|---|---|
| 39 | **Concession (contract of)**<br><br>**Concession (contrat de)** | A contract for pecuniary interest by means of which one or more contracting authorities or contracting entities entrust the provision and the management of services or the execution of works to one or more economic operators, the consideration of which consists either solely in the right to exploit the services that are the subject of the contract or in that right together with payment (in EU law this matter is governed by the Directive 2014/23 of the European Parliament and of the Council).<br>Contrat conclu à titre onéreux par lequel une ou plusieurs autorités concédantes confient la fourniture et la gestion d'un service ou l'exécution de travaux à un ou plusieurs opérateurs économiques, qui sont rémunérés seulement par le droit d'exploiter les services ou de réaliser les travaux ou par ce droit assorti d'un paiement (v., en droit de l'Union, la directive (UE) 2014/23 du Parlement européen et du Conseil). |
| 40 | **Convincing evidence (judicial review)**<br><br>**Preuve suffisante (contrôle juridictionnel)** | Normal standard of credibility of the evidence to be established; conviction is met if there is no plausible reason to believe otherwise. If there is a real doubt, based upon reason and common sense after careful and impartial consideration of all the evidence, or lack of evidence, in a case, then the level of proof has not been met.<br><br>Degré normal de crédibilité auquel la preuve doit satisfaire; une preuve est convaincante s'il n'y a aucune raison plausible de croire le contraire. Ce niveau de preuve n'est pas atteint en cas de doute réel, fondé sur la raison et le bon sens, à la suite d'un examen minutieux et impartial de toutes les preuves, ou en cas de manque de preuves. |
| 41 | **Court officers**<br><br>**Auxiliaires de justice** | Professionals who are designated by a court to undertake a specific mission relating to a case submitted to the court. **(inspector, technical expert, ad acta commissioner)** They may be submitted to obligations similar to that of a judge, for instance impartiality.<br><br>Professionnels désignés par un tribunal pour entreprendre une mission spécifique relative à une affaire soumise à son examen **(inspecteur, expert technique, fonctionnaire *ad acta*)**. Ils peuvent être soumis à des obligations similaires à celles d'un juge, comme l'impartialité. |
| 42 | **Cross-examination**<br><br>**Contre-interrogatoire** | Questioning of one party's witness's evidence by or on behalf of the opposing party. This is often a hostile form of questioning designed to highlight weakness or inconsistencies in that evidence.<br><br>Interrogatoire d'un témoin par la partie adverse. Il vise souvent à révéler les faiblesses ou les incohérences de cette preuve. |

| | | |
|---|---|---|
| 43 | **Decision on lack of competence, *i.e.* territorial jurisdiction (judicial review)**<br><br>**Décision sur la carence du compétence territoriale (contrôle juridictionnel)** | Decision of the administrative court which declares that other administrative court has territorial jurisdiction over the case.<br><br>Décision du tribunal administratif en vertu de laquelle un autre tribunal administratif est déclaré territorialement compétent pour connaître de l'affaire. |
| 44 | **Decision on lack of jurisdiction (judicial review)**<br><br>**Décision d'incompétence (contrôle juridictionnel)** | Decision of the administrative court which declines jurisdiction in favour of another national Court or vice versa.<br><br>Décision du tribunal administratif en vertu de laquelle celui-ci se reconnaît incompétent au profit d'un autre tribunal national, ou ou vice-versa. |
| 45 | **Decision on the merits**<br><br>**Décision sur le fond** | A ruling that determines the substantive claim, be it wholly or partly.<br><br>Décision qui prend parti sur le fond de la demande, en tout ou partie. |
| 46 | **Defendant**<br><br>**Défendeur** | Person or the public body that is sued or has been brought before the Court.<br><br>Personne ou organisme public qui fait l'objet d'une poursuite ou d'une action en justice devant le tribunal. |
| 47 | **Disclosure (judicial review)**<br><br>**Divulgation (contrôle juridictionnel)** | Procedure whereby, generally as a result of a court order, the parties are required to disclose all relevant and necessary documents in their possession relevant to the issues in the trial.<br><br>Procédure par laquelle, généralement à la suite d'une ordonnance du tribunal, les parties sont tenues de divulguer tous les documents pertinents et nécessaires en leur possession concernant les questions litigieuses. |
| 48 | **Discretionary power (Administrative)**<br><br>**Pouvoir discrétionnaire** | Margin of choice conferred by the legal norm to the public administration to act or not act in a given case, and to choose between different consequences, all legal, the most reasonable to best achieve the purpose provided by the law, balancing public interest with other interests involved.<br><br>Liberté d'appréciation conférée par la norme juridique à l'administration publique pour agir ou s'en abstenir dans un cas déterminé, et pour choisir entre diverses conséquences, toutes légales, la plus raisonnable pour atteindre au mieux l'objectif visé par la loi, en équilibrant l'intérêt public et les autres intérêts en jeu. |

| | | |
|---|---|---|
| 49 | **Duty of investigation**<br><br>**Obligation d'enquête** | Duty of Public Administration to take into consideration all the relevant facts by gathering information and evaluating and weighing up the evidence.<br><br>Obligation de l'administration de prendre en considération tous les faits pertinents en recueillant des informations, puis en évaluant et pondérant les éléments de preuve. |
| 50 | **Duty to provide advice**<br><br>**Obligation de conseil** | Duty of Public Administration in its areas of competence to provide assistance and advice and to respond to questions and enquiries of citizens and companies.<br><br>Obligation de l'administration de fournir une assistance et des conseils, et de répondre aux questions et demandes de renseignements des citoyens et des entreprises, dans ses domaines de compétence. |
| 51 | **Electronic application/filing of a claim**<br><br>**Requête eletronique/Introduction d'une action par voie électronique** | Electronic procedure that enables a party to file a claim by exclusively electronic means.<br><br>Moyen de saisine permettant à une partie d'introduire une action devant une juridiction par voie électronique. |
| 52 | **Electronic communication/ e-communication (to open an e-communication channel with the courts)**<br><br>**Communication par voie électronique** | Enables the parties and/or their representatives in cases brought before the court to exchange procedural documents with the registries by exclusively electronic means.<br><br>Permet aux parties ou à leurs représentants d'échanger des pièces de procédure avec les greffes par des moyens exclusivement électroniques dans le cadre des affaires portées devant le tribunal. |
| 53 | **Electronic document/e-document**<br><br>**Document électronique** | Any document in electronic format containing structured data (and possibly also unstructured data) used in the context of an administrative process.<br><br>Tout document au format électronique contenant des données structurées (et éventuellement non structurées) utilisées dans le cadre d'un procès administratif. |

| | | |
|---|---|---|
| 54 | **Electronic file management** | Electronic file management is a document management software solution that allows a party or a court or a judicial officer to capture, store, and manage physical and electronic files. An electronic file management system is specifically designed to replace physical file cabinets and also includes features like search, mobile document access, document distribution, and editing documents. |
| | **Gestion électronique de fichiers** | La gestion électronique de fichiers est un logiciel de traitement de documents qui permet à une partie ou à une juridiction de recueillir, stocker et gérer des fichiers physiques et électroniques. Il est spécifiquement conçu pour remplacer les armoires de fichiers physiques. Il comprend également des fonctionnalités telles que la recherche, l'accès mobile, la distribution et l'édition de documents. |
| 55 | **Electronic file/record** | Administration: data files in a format created by software commonly available to the general public such as Adobe Acrobat, Microsoft Excel or Word, and consumer accounting programs.<br>Judiciary: any text, illustration or other matter supplied or produced by either Party in digitised form on disc, memory stick, via email, online. |
| | **Fichier/Dossier électronique** | Administration: Par opposition aux fichiers papier, les fichiers électroniques sont dématérialisés et créés par des logiciels communément disponibles pour le grand public, tels qu'Adobe Acrobat, Microsoft Excel ou Word, et des programmes de comptabilité grand public.<br>Contrôle juridictionnel: tout document produit par l'une ou l'autre des parties sous forme numérisée, sur un disque, une clé USB, par courrier électronique ou en ligne. |
| 56 | **Electronic signature** | Electronic indication of a person's intent to agree to the content of a document or a set of data to which the signature relates. |
| | **Signature électronique** | Indication électronique de l'intention d'une personne d'accepter le contenu d'un document ou d'un ensemble de données auquel la signature se rapporte. |
| 57 | **Enforcement (judicial review)** | Execution of judgments. |
| | **Exécution (contrôle juridictionnel)** | Exécution des jugements. |

| | | |
|---|---|---|
| 58 | **(Manifest) Error in assessment**<br><br>**Erreur (manifeste) d'appréciation** | Illegality of administrative acts that affected the administrative discretionary measure when the administration grossly and manifestly misunderstood the evaluation of the facts that motivated its decision. This may happen when an element of the legal norm, granting the administrative power, contains an "indefinite legal concept" to be fulfilled by the authority with content and the administration acts taking into account a misrepresentation of the facts.<br><br>Illégalité affectant un acte administratif vicié par une erreur (grossière et manifeste) de l'administration dans l'appréciation des faits ayant motivé sa décision. Cette situation peut survenir lorsqu'un élément de la base légale de la décision comprend une notion dont l'autorité administrative doit apprécier le contenu au cas par cas, et que l'administration agit en tenant compte d'une représentation incorrecte des faits. |
| 59 | **Evidence in chief (judicial review)**<br><br>**Interrogatoire de son propre témoin (contrôle juridictionnel)** | In common law, the leading or adducing of oral evidence from a witness presented by a party as his/her own witness.<br>In civil law, examination in chief is when a witness is asked by the party that has called them. After giving examination in chief, the witnesses are cross-examined by the other party.<br><br>En common law, c'est le fait qu'une partie apporte ou produise une preuve à traves l'interrogatoire d'un témoin qu'elle a convoqué à l'audience.<br>En civil law, l'interrogatoire principal a lieu lorsqu' une partie interroge le témoin qu'elle a convoqué à l'audience. Après l'interrogatoire principal, le témoin est soumis à un contre – interrogatoire par l'autre partie. |
| 60 | ***Ex officio* (judicial review)**<br>**D'office**<br>**(contrôle juridictionnel)** | An issue raised by the court of its own motion.<br>Question soulevée par le juge de sa propre initiative. |
| 61 | ***Ex parte* (judicial review)**<br><br>**Question soulevée par les parties (« *ex parte* »)**<br>**(contrôle juridictionnel)** | A point raised by the claimant or by another party.<br><br>Question soulevée par le demandeur ou par d'autres parties du litige. |
| 62 | ***Inaudita altera parte* hearing (judicial review)**<br><br>***Inaudita altera parte* audience (contrôle juridictionnel)** | A hearing (which is often an urgent one) in which the court hears only one of the parties to the proceedings. In common law it is called: "*ex parte* hearing".<br><br>Audience (souvent urgente) au cours de laquelle le tribunal se limite à écouter une seule des parties. Dans les systèmes de common law on appelle: "*ex parte* hearing". |

| | | |
|---|---|---|
| 63 | ***Inaudita altera parte* order (judicial review)**<br><br>***Inaudita altera parte* ordonnance (contrôle juridictionnel)** | An order made by the court in the absence of one of the parties. In common law it is called: "*ex parte* order".<br><br>Ordonnance du tribunal adoptée en dérogeant au principe du contradictoire. Dans les systèmes de common law elle est appelée: "*ex parte* order". |
| 64 | **Excusable error (judicial review)**<br><br>**Excuse légitime (contrôle juridictionnel)** | Impediments that may justify the non-compliance with time limits.<br><br>Obstacles susceptibles de justifier le non-respect des délais |
| 65 | ***Exhibit* (judicial review)**<br><br>***Exhibit* (contrôle juridictionnel)** | In common law, physical or documentary evidence (such as correspondence between the parties) presented to the court by means either of affidavit or sworn evidence.<br><br>En common law, c'est un élément de preuve phisique ou documentaire (tel que la correspondance entre les parties) présenté au tribunal à travers un affidavit ou une déclaration sous-serment. |
| 66 | **Expert**<br><br>**Expert** | Professional who is designated by a court, on account on his/her expertise in a particular field, to give an opinion on matters of fact relevant to the resolution of a case (e.g., to quantify damages in a complex economic case or to assess causality in a medical case). Experts may also deliver "expert evidence" within the area of their expertise. Their opinion may be rebutted by testimony from other experts or by other evidence or facts. Parties may choose their own experts (referred to as "counsel experts") in order to verify, contradict or confirm the court expert's findings.<br><br>Professionnel désigné par un tribunal, en raison de son expertise dans un domaine particulier, pour donner un avis sur des questions de fait pertinentes pour le règlement d'une affaire (par ex. pour quantifier les dommages-intérêts dans une affaire économique complexe ou pour évaluer le lien de causalité dans une affaire médicale). Les experts peuvent également fournir des « preuves d'experts » dans leur domaine d'expertise. Leur avis peut être réfuté par le témoignage d'autres experts ou au moyen d'autres preuves ou faits. Les parties peuvent choisir leurs propres experts, chargés de vérifier, d'infirmer ou de confirmer les conclusions de l'expert du tribunal. |
| 67 | **Extrajudicial confession (judicial review)**<br><br>**Aveu extrajudiciaire (contrôle juridictionnel)** | Confession made out of court and not as a part of a judicial examination or investigation.<br><br>Aveux faits hors du tribunal, et non pas dans le cadre d'un examen ou d'une enquête judiciaire. |

| | | |
|---|---|---|
| 68 | **Failure to Act** | Factual situation connected to the lack of reaction of the administrative authorities to the claimants' requests.<br>In some legal systems, the law regulating the procedure establishes that this lack of response within the deadline implies a tacit rejection, in such a case the interested parties can challenge judicially the tacit rejection of their application, without having to wait for the issuance of an express resolution. |
| | **Silence de l'administration** | Situation factuelle liée à l'absence de réaction des autorités administratives aux demandes des requérants.<br>Dans certains ordres juridiques, la loi régissant la procédure établit que cette absence de réponse dans le délai imparti implique un rejet tacite. Dans ce cas, les parties intéressées peuvent contester judiciairement le rejet tacite de leur demande, sans devoir attendre l'adoption d'une résolution expresse. |
| 69 | **Final judgement/Res judicata (judicial review)** | Judgment that may no longer be appealed so that the parties are definitively bound by the decision. |
| | **Decisione ayant l'autoriteé de chose jugée (contrôle juridictional)** | Décision juridictionnelle qui ne peut faire l'objet d'aucun recours, et les parties sont définitivement liées par la décision. |
| 70 | **Free assessment of evidence (judicial review)** | The examination of the results of the evidence by the judge. In carrying out this assessment, judges are not bound, in principle, by any statutory rules regarding the evidence but must evaluate in accordance with their personal conviction whether or not the evidence is sufficient. There is no hierarchy applicable to means of proof. |
| | **Libre appréciation de la preuve (contrôle juridictionnel)** | Pouvoir souverain d'appréciation des preuves par le juge. Lorsqu'ils procèdent à cette appréciation, les juges ne sont, en principe, pas liés par la moindre règle impérative concernant les éléments de preuve. Il leur appartient de déterminer s'ils ont la conviction que les éléments de preuve sont suffisants, sans hiérarchie des moyens de preuve. |
| 71 | **Fumus boni iuris** | Criterion used by the jurisprudence (or provided by law) to determine, in interim measures applications, if the claim appears well-founded or there is the likelihood of success of the case on the merits. |
| | **Apparence de bon droit** | Critère utilisé par la jurisprudence (ou prévu par la loi) pour déterminer, dans le cadre d'une demande de mesures provisoires, si la demande paraît fondée ou s'il existe une chance de succès de cette demande au fond. |

| | | |
|---|---|---|
| 72 | **(Oral) Hearing (judicial review)**<br><br>**Audience (orale)** | Part of the judicial proceeding in which the parties can be present and are heard by the judges at their request<br>Partie de la séance de jugement à laquelle assistent les parties et peuvent être écoutes par les juges on leur requête<br><br>Partie de la procédure judiciaire au cours de laquelle les parties peuvent être présentes et demander à être entendues par les juges |
| 73 | **(Oral preparatory)<br>Hearing (judicial review)**<br><br>**Audience orale preparatoire (contrôle juridictionnel)** | Optional oral pre-proceeding set to examine points of disagreement. This procedure does not constitute an exception from the adversarial principle.<br><br>Procédure préliminaire orale facultative qui permet d'examiner oralement certains aspects du litige.<br>Cette procédure ne constitue pas nécessairement une exception au principe du contradictoire. |
| 74 | **Implicit/implied decision ("silent approval", "silent rejection")**<br><br>**Décision implicite (d'acceptation/de rejet)** | Failure on the part of the administrative authorities to respond to claimants' requests corresponding to an implicit/implied decision of approval/rejection.<br><br>Défaut de la part des autorités administratives de répondre aux demandes des requérants, correspondant à une décision implicite d'approbation ou de rejet. |
| 75 | **Inadmissibility (judicial review)**<br><br>**Irrecevabilité et non-lieu (contrôle juridictionnel)** | Judicial decision to be taken:<br>I) to ascertains tardiness in the notification or depositing;<br>II) when there is a lack of interest or standing, or there are other reasons impeding a decision on the merits;<br>I)I) when there are new reasons impeding a decision supervene over the trial (for example: during proceedings arises the lack of interest of the parties in the decision).<br><br>Décision judiciaire rejetant des conclusions:<br>I) en raison du caractère tardif de la notification ou du dépôt de la requête;<br>II) en raison du défaut d'intérêt ou de qualité pour agir, ou lorsque d'autres motifs font obstacle à une décision sur le fond;<br>III) quand un événement faisant perdre son objet au litige intervient en cours d'instance (par exemple: la perte d'intérêt des parties au cours de la procédure) |
| 76 | **Injunction (judicial review)**<br><br>**Décision provisoire (contrôle juridictionnel)** | Procedural order granted by the court, *ex officio* or at the request of the parties, in order to guarantee the effectiveness of the judicial decision, often by preserving, preventing or ensuring the rights and interests are preserved.<br><br>Décision de nature conservatoire adoptée par le tribunal, d'office ou à la demande des parties, afin de garantir le caractère effectif de la décision judiciaire en préservant ou garantissant les droits et intérêts qui doivent faire l'objet d'une décision dans le cadre du procès. |

| | | |
|---|---|---|
| 77 | **Inspection (judicial review)** | Procedure whereby, generally as a result of a court order, one party or the judge him/herself is allowed to visit the premises or property of either the other party or a third party for the purposes of gathering evidence (such as photographs of the scene of an accident). |
| | **Visite des lieux/enquête (contrôle juridictionnel)** | Procédure par laquelle, généralement à la suite d'une ordonnance du tribunal, une partie ou le juge lui-même est autorisé(e) à visiter un lieu afin de recueillir des preuves. |
| 78 | **Failure to fulfil the obligation to state reasons** | Ground of review of administrative acts concerning situations in which administrative authorities breached the principle of grounding in a clear and unequivocal fashion the reasoning followed by the public authority which adopted the decision. |
| | **Méconnaissance de l'obligation de motivation (contrôle juridictionnel)** | Illégalité affectant des actes administratifs dans des situations où les autorités administratives ont violé le principe qui oblige à motiver en fait et en droit le raisonnement suivi par l'autorité publique ayant adopté la décision. |
| 79 | **Internal measures** | Category of administrative measures which, in principle, do not have external effects (e.g. administrative action which manage or direct the affairs of an administrative body and which allocates tasks to specific units; acts guiding civil servants in interpreting the terminology used in a statute for the purpose of applying it to a specific case etc.). |
| | **Mesures d'ordre intérieur** | Catégorie de mesures administratives n'ayant, en principe, pas d'effet externe (par ex. action administrative qui régit ou contrôle les affaires d'un organe administratif et qui attribue des tâches à des unités spécifiques; actes encadrant l'interprétation par les fonctionnaires de la terminologie utilisée dans une loi, aux fins de son application à un cas spécifique, etc.). |
| 80 | **Interrogatories (judicial review)** | Procedure whereby, often pursuant to a court order, one party is required to answer specific questions in writing, under oath or not as the case may require, in advance of the trial |
| | **Interrogatoire (contrôle juridictionnel)** | Procédure en vertu de laquelle une partie est tenue de répondre préalablement à des questions précises par écrit et sous serment ou sans serment au procès, souvent suite à une ordonnance judiciaire. |

| | | |
|---|---|---|
| 81 | **Stay of proceedings** | Suspension of the trial, which implies the temporary halt in proceedings, which may occur for various reasons, such as:<br>- preliminary ruling: when the decision of the disputed issue is conditioned to the prior resolution of another pending question;<br>- a question of unconstitutionality: once the procedure has been completed, the Court appreciates the relevance of raising a question of unconstitutionality before the Constitutional Court, because it considers that there are doubts about the constitutionality of a legal norm relevant to the prosecution of the case;<br>- preliminary ruling CJEU: the Court, also after the conclusion of the proceedings, refers a question to the Court of Justice of the European Union for a preliminary ruling, on the ground that it has doubts as to the interpretation of the rule of EU law or its validity; being essential to resolve these doubts in order to resolve the dispute;<br>- at the request of both parties: If they want a method of settling disputes (arbitration, mediation);<br>- at the request of one party. |
| | **Sursis à statuer** | Suspension du procès, impliquant son arrêt temporaire, qui peut se produire pour divers motifs:<br>une question préjudicielle: lorsque la décision sur la question litigieuse est subordonnée à la résolution d'une question relevant de la compétence d'une autre juridiction;<br>une question d'inconstitutionnalité, en raison de doutes sur la constitutionnalité d'une norme juridique pertinente pour la poursuite de l'affaire;<br>une question préjudicielle à la CJUE: saisine de la Cour de justice de l'Union européenne d'une question préjudicielle en raison de doutes sur l'interprétation de la règle de droit de l'Union européenne ou sa validité, et qu'il est essentiel que ces doutes soient dissipés pour résoudre le litige;<br>à la demande des deux parties: si elles veulent opter pour un mode alternatif de règlement des litiges (arbitrage, médiation);<br>à la demande d'une partie. |
| 82 | **Intervention:**<br>**I) voluntary intervention** | If the ruling has not been brought against one or some of the parties against whom judgment has to be pronounced, they can intervene. |
| | **I) intervention volontaire** | Si la décision n'a pas été rendue contre l'une ou certaines des parties à l'encontre desquelles le jugement doit être prononcé, celles-ci peuvent intervenir. |

| | | |
|---|---|---|
| 83 | **Intervention:**<br>**II) intervention by order of the court**<br><br>**Intervention:**<br>**II) intervention par ordonnance du tribunal** | Order issued by the court, also on the request of one of the parties, when it considers it appropriate that the trial be directed against a third party, orders the intervention.<br><br>Ordonnance rendue par le tribunal, à la demande de l'une des parties, lorsque celle-ci estime opportun qu'un tiers soit mis en cause, dont le tribunal demande l'intervention. |
| 84 | **Joint-consideration**<br><br>**Examen conjoint** | Decision concerning matters pending before different authorities, which have to be jointly examined and decided concurrently by a shared measure.<br><br>Décision concernant des questions pendantes devant différentes autorités qui doivent faire l'objet d'un examen commun et sur lesquelles elles statuent par une seule et même mesure. |
| 85 | **Judicial review**<br><br>**Contrôle juridictionnel** | Review of administrative action by Courts. The term can also be understood as referring to review of the constitutionality of legislation in those legal systems providing for this remedy.<br><br>Décision concernant des questions pendantes devant différentes autorités qui doivent faire l'objet d'un examen commun et sur lesquelles elles statuent par une seule et même mesure. |
| 86 | **Jurisprudence/case law**<br><br>**Jurisprudence** | Set of previous judicial decisions on a particular issue or topic of the Council of State (or SAC) which often serves to the Administrative Courts as an example when a new case is examined, but it is not obligatory for them (or for the Council of State, or SAC, itself) to follow. In common law countries, this often refers to earlier court judgments which should influence the result or outcome of the case ("doctrine of precedent").<br><br>Ensemble de décisions judiciaires antérieures sur une question ou un sujet particulier traités par le Conseil d'État (ou la cour administrative suprême), qui sert d'exemple aux tribunaux administratifs lorsqu'une nouvelle affaire est examinée, sans qu'ils aient d'obligation formelle de les respecter (pas plus que le Conseil d'État ou la cour administrative suprême). Dans les systèmes juridiques de common law, ce terme fait souvent référence aux décisions juridictionnelles antérieures qui devraient avoir une incidence sur la solution du litige («doctrine of precedent»). |
| 87 | **Lack of competence in deciding**<br><br>**Incompétence** | Ground of review of administrative acts concerning situations in which administrative authorities breached the rules establishing the distribution of functions and competences.<br><br>Illégalité affectant un acte administratif dans des situations où les autorités administratives ont enfreint les règles de répartition des compétences. |

| | | |
|---|---|---|
| 88 | **Lack of investigation** | Ground of review of administrative acts concerning situations in which administrative authorities breached the rules related to the investigation to be carried out before the issuance of the decision. |
| | **Manque d'investigation** | Illégalité affectant un acte administratif dans des situations où les autorités administratives ont enfreint les règles de investigation avant de l'emission de la decision. |
| 89 | **Leave to appeal** | Permission to appeal granted by the court of first instance or a higher court to a claimant who wants its decision to be reviewed by a superior court. |
| | **Autorisation d'interjeter appel** | Autorisation de faire appel ou de se pourvoir en cassation accordée par un tribunal de première instance ou d'appel à un requérant qui souhaite faire réexaminer une décision par une cour supérieure. |
| 90 | **Leave to apply** | Procedure whereby a party requiring the prior permission of the court to take a particular step (such as commencing particular types of court proceedings) applies to the court for that permission. |
| | **Autorisation de prendre une mesure** | Procédure par laquelle une partie demande l'autorisation préalable du tribunal afin de prendre une mesure particulière (comme commencer certains types de procédures judiciaires). |
| 91 | **Legal presumption (judicial review)** | Proof of a fact, which is considered established, via proof of another fact and which results directly from the law and has the effect of reversing the burden of proof. The opposing party of the party benefiting from such a presumption must provide evidence to the contrary. It must prove that, despite there being a basis for a legal presumption (the fact provided evidence for), the presumed facts or legal situation do not exist. |
| | **Présomption légale (contrôle juridictionnel)** | Cas où, conformément à une norme supérieure, un fait est considéré comme établi en raison de la preuve d'un autre fait, la charge de la preuve étant ainsi renversée. La partie adverse à celle qui bénéficie de cette présomption doit apporter la preuve du contraire. Elle doit prouver que, même s'il existe une base pour une présomption légale (le fait dont la preuve est apportée), les faits ou la situation juridique présumés n'existent pas. |
| 92 | **Legality (Internal)/(External)** | Substantive conditions to be observed by an administrative decision in order to be legal / Competency, formal and procedural requirements to be observed by an administrative decision in order to be legal. |
| | **Légalité interne/externe** | Conditions de fond qu'une décision administrative doit remplir pour être légale; conditions de compétence, de forme et de procédure que doit remplir une décision administrative pour être légale. |

| | | |
|---|---|---|
| 93 | **Licence** | Favorable administrative measure that allows to perform a particular act or activity after assessment of its correspondence to technical parameters and to public interests. |
| | **Autorisation** | Mesure administrative qui autorise la réalisation d'un acte ou d'une activité suite au contrôle de son opportunité au regard de paramètres techniques et de l'intérêt public (en cause) |
| 94 | ***Locus standi*/legal standing** | Possibility of taking legal action against an administrative act, based on a identification of the (groups of) persons and the conditions they should meet in order to bring a claim before the court (including, e.g. direct and certain concern of the challenged act on the claimant's situation and the concrete and current interest in the judgment of the court). |
| | **Intérêt à agir (*locus standi*)** | Possibilité d'agir en justice contre un acte, sur le fondement de l'identification de la personne ou du groupe de personnes et des conditions qu'elle ou il doit remplir pour introduire une demande devant un tribunal (y compris, par exemple, une atteinte directe et certaine à la situation du requérant et un intérêt à la décision du tribunal). |
| 95 | **Failure to act of the administration** | Failure of the administration to comply with the obligation to provide specific services in favour of those who are holders of benefits provided by a law or by virtue of acts, contracts, or administrative agreements. |
| | **Carence de l'administration** | Manquement de l'administration à l'obligation de fournir des services spécifiques en faveur de personnes beneficiantsd'avantages prévus par la loi ou en vertu d'actes, de contrats ou d'accords administratifs. |
| 96 | **Mistrial** | In common law, where a fresh trial is ordered by a higher court following some material procedural irregularity or serious errors in the admission or handling of the evidence. |
| | **Mistrial** | En common law, situation dans laquelle un nouveau procès est ordonné par une juridiction supérieure à la suite d'une irrégularité substantielle de procédure ou de graves erreurs dans l'admission ou le traitement des éléments de preuve. |
| 97 | **Motion** | Procedural step in the litigation whereby the court is asked to take a particular decision such as, for example, joining a party or dismissing the proceedings. |
| | **Demande préliminaire** | Étape procédurale du litige dans le cadre de laquelle le tribunal est invité à prendre une décision particulière, telle que l'ajout d'une partie ou le rejet de la procédure. |

| | | |
|---|---|---|
| 98 | **Notice of the initiation of an administrative procedure** | Notification to addressees of the intended administrative decision and to any other persons who could be adversely affected by it of the rationale for the initiation of the procedure and of all information referred, inter alia, to the authority competent to adopt the final decision, the responsible official, the time-limit for the adoption of the decision. |
| | **Avis d'ouverture d'une procédure administrative** | Notification, aux destinataires de la décision administrative concernée et à toute autre personne qui pourrait être lésée par celle-ci, des motifs de l'ouverture de la procédure et de toutes les informations communiquées à l'autorité compétente pour adopter la décision finale (dont notamment, le fonctionnaire responsable, le délai pour l'adoption de la décision). |
| 99 | **Notification procedure for service of legal documents (judicial review)** | Communication made in the manner prescribed by law by which the existence of the documents relating to the administrative trial is brought to the legal notice of an individual or entity. |
| | **Notificacion (contrôle juridictionnel)** | Communication faite de la manière prescrite par la loi par laquelle l'existence des documents relatifs au procès administratif est portée à la connaissance d'une personne physique ou morale. |
| 100 | ***Periculum in mora*** | Decisive criterion for the adoption of precautionary measures, consisting in the finding that the execution of the contested act may have an adverse effect on the interests or rights of the appellant, of such an entity or nature that, in the event that the judicial challenge is successful, the procedural result obtained will be useless to make satisfactory reparation for the injury caused.<br>In common law countries, similar criteria are used to determine whether to grant an interim or interlocutory ("holding") injunction. |
| | ***Periculum in mora*** | Critère déterminant pour l'adoption de mesures conservatoires, consistant à constater que l'exécution de l'acte attaqué peut avoir sur les intérêts ou droits du requérant un effet néfaste, d'une nature ou d'un caractère tel(le) que, en cas de succès du recours judiciaire, le résultat procédural obtenu ne saurait réparer de manière satisfaisante le préjudice causé. Dans les systèmes de common law, des critères similaires sont utilisés à la même fin. |
| 101 | **Power of attorney (judicial review)** | Right given to an attorney to act before courts as the representative of a litigant or defendant, or any other party to the case. |
| | **Mandat (contrôle juridictionnel)** | Droit accordé à un avocat d'agir devant les tribunaux en tant que représentant de la partie demanderesse ou défenderesse, ou de toute autre partie à l'affaire. |

| | | |
|---|---|---|
| 102 | **Precautionary suspension (judicial review)** | Judicial decision of a provisional nature adopted in the separate piece of precautionary measures, by which, after weighing the interests in conflict, the enforceability of the act or administrative provision challenged in the process is temporarily annulled, for the duration of the processing of the procedure and until a resolution that puts an end to it. |
| | **Suspension (provisoire) (contrôle juridictionnel)** | Décision judiciaire à caractère provisoire adoptée dans le cadre d'une mesure conservatoire distincte, par laquelle, après avoir pesé les intérêts en conflit, la force exécutoire de l'acte ou de la disposition administrative contesté(e) dans le cadre du procès est temporairement annulée, pendant la durée de la procédure et jusqu'à ce qu'une résolution y mette fin. |
| 103 | **Extincion** | Extinction of the trial because the claim has not been continued or resumed within a period fixed by law or assigned by the Court. |
| | **Forclusion** | Extinction du procès parce que la demande n'a pas été poursuivie ou reprise dans un délai fixé par la loi ou par le tribunal. |
| 104 | **Preventive annotation of demand (judicial review)** | Specific precautionary measure that can be adopted when it comes to ensuring the effectiveness of a judgment issued in the exercise of a real action on assets and rights susceptible to registration. |
| | **Annotation préventive de la demande (contrôle juridictionnel)** | Mesure conservatoire spécifique qui peut être adoptée lorsqu'il s'agit d'assurer l'effectivité d'un jugement rendu dans l'exercice d'une action réelle sur des biens et droits susceptibles d'enregistrement. |
| 105 | **Principle of administrative assistance/mutual assistance** | Obligation for each authority to render assistance in any form to other authorities, when requested to do so. |
| | **Principe d'assistance administrative ou d'assistance mutuelle** | Obligation pour chaque autorité de prêter assistance, sous quelque forme que ce soit, aux autres autorités, lorsque celles-ci lui en font la demande. |
| 106 | **Principle of investigation (judicial review)** | Legal principle imposing the court to investigate the facts *ex officio*, without being limited to the evidence produced by the parties. |
| | **Procédure inquisitoire (contrôle juridictionnel)** | Procédure dans laquelle le tribunal est tenu d'enquêter d'office sur les faits, sans se limiter aux éléments de preuve produits par les parties. |

| | | |
|---|---|---|
| 107 | **Private documents** | Documents produced by a private individual. As long as they are signed, they are full proof of the fact that the statements they contain were made by the person who signed them. Their accuracy is subject to the free assessment of evidence if contested. |
| | **Documents privés** | Documents produits par un particulier. S'ils sont signés ils constituent la preuve complète du fait que les déclarations qu'ils contiennent ont été faites par la personne qui les a signés. Leur exactitude est soumise à la libre appréciation des preuves en cas de contestation. |
| 108 | **Proceedings 'in camera' (judicial review)** | Hearing before the court in which only interested parties' lawyers may participate and which are generally closed to the public and the press. |
| | **Procédures en chambre du conseil ou à huis clos (contrôle juridictionnel)** | Audience devant le tribunal à laquelle seuls les avocats des parties intéressées peuvent participer, et qui sont généralement fermés au public et à la presse. |
| 109 | **Proportionality** | Ground of review usually articulated in three main phases: (1) suitability, (2) necessity, and (3) proportionality in the narrow sense. First, the suitability test requires that the adopted measure be suitable to achieve the stated objectives. Second, the necessity test aims at verifying that the measure was the least restrictive available alternative or that no less drastic means were available. Three, the proportionality test in the narrow sense requires adjudicators to ascertain that the benefit gained from realizing the objective exceeds the harm caused by the adopted measure. |
| | **Proportionnalité** | Fondement de contrôle d'un acte administratif articulé autour de trois tests: le caractère approprié, la nécessité et la proportionnalité au sens strict. Premièrement, le test du caractère approprié demande de vérifier si la mesure est adaptée pour atteindre les objectifs déclaré. Deuxièmement, le test de nécessité vise à vérifier si aucune mesure moins contraignante n'était envisageable. Troisièmement, le test de proportionnalité au sens strict suppose de vérifier que les bénéfices de la mesure sont plus importants que l'atteinte qu'elle porte à des droits ou intérêts protégés. |
| 110 | **Public documents** | Documents produced by a public authority; which are presumed to be authentic, *i.e.* it is assumed that they are indeed attributable to the issuer indicated. They also establish full proof of the truthfulness of the facts represented therein. |
| | **Documents publics (contrôle juridictionnel)** | Documents produits par une autorité publique; ils sont présumés authentiques, c'est-à-dire qu'on suppose qu'ils sont effectivement attribuables à l'émetteur indiqué. Ils établissent également une preuve complète de la véracité des faits qui y sont représentés. |

| | | |
|---|---|---|
| 111 | **Public hearing**<br><br>**Audience publique** | Judicial hearing open to the public and the media.<br><br>Audience judiciaire ouverte au public et aux médias. |
| 112 | **Public participation**<br><br>**Participation du public** | Open invitation to members of the public to submit (within a deadline) comments about a draft of a legally binding general administrative act with a sufficiently determined content to allow input from the interested public and with the aim of gathering suggestions on specific solutions that may lead to adjust the draft in view of the comments received.<br><br>Invitation faite au public à soumettre (dans un certain délai) des observations sur un projet d'acte administratif juridiquement contraignant dont le contenu est suffisamment défini pour que le public intéressé puisse donner son avis, afin de recueillir des suggestions sur des solutions spécifiques qui peuvent conduire à ajuster le projet à la lumière des observations reçues. |
| 113 | **Public procurement**<br><br>**Marchés publics** | Purchases by governments and state-owned enterprises of goods, services and works through public tenders.<br><br>Achats par les administrations et les entreprises publiques de biens, de services et de travaux dans le cadre d'appels d'offres. |
| 114 | **Public service agreement**<br><br>**Contrat portant sur l'exécution du service public** | Contract concerning the performance of a public administrative duty, relating to the field of public services.<br><br>Contrat relatif à l'accomplissement d'une mission d'administration publique, relatif au domaine des services publics (services sociaux, sanitaires, éducatifs, etc.). |
| 115 | **Reasoned decision**<br><br>**Décision motivée** | Administrative act which states factual and legal elements that ground the decision in an appropriate manner by disclosing in a clear and unequivocal fashion the reasoning followed by the public authority which adopted the decision in such a way as to enable the parties to ascertain the reasons for the decision and to enable the competent court to exercise its powers of review.<br><br>Acte administratif énonçant des éléments factuels et juridiques qui motivent la décision de manière appropriée en présentant de façon claire et univoque le raisonnement suivi par l'autorité publique qui a adopté la décision, afin que les parties puissent connaître les motifs de la décision et la juridiction compétente exercer son contrôle. |
| 116 | **Rebuttal evidence (judicial review)**<br><br>**Preuve contraire (contrôle juridictionnel)** | Evidence led by a party to counter a defence adduced by the other party.<br><br>Preuve présentée par une partie pour contrer la ligne de défense de l'autre partie. |

<table>
<tr><td rowspan="2">117</td><td>Recourse of full jurisdiction</td><td>Action which enables the Administrative Courts (of first instance or the courts of appeal) not only to control the errors of law and conclude to its annulment, but also to control the facts of the case and reform the act (in some legal systems, full jurisdiction is provided for all types of litigation).</td></tr>
<tr><td>Recours de pleine juridiction</td><td>Action qui permet aux tribunaux administratifs (de première instance ou d'appel) de contrôler les erreurs de droit et de conclure à l'annulation de l'acte, mais aussi de contrôler les faits de l'affaire et de réformer l'acte (dans certains systèmes juridiques, la pleine juridiction est de mise pour tous les types de litiges).</td></tr>
<tr><td rowspan="2">118</td><td>Rectification of manifest errors (judicial review)</td><td>Rectification of a manifest material and arithmetic errors, by the court or at the request of a party.</td></tr>
<tr><td>Rectification d'erreurs matérielles (contrôle juridictionnel)</td><td>Rectification d'une erreur matérielle ou arithmétique, par la juridiction ou à la demande d'une partie.</td></tr>
<tr><td rowspan="2">119</td><td>Referral to the previous judge</td><td>Judicial decision of the Superior court to refer the case back to the previous judge at first instance where an appeal against that judge's decision has been wholly or partially successful in case of mistrial.</td></tr>
<tr><td>Renvoi</td><td>Décision d'une juridiction supérieure de renvoyer l'affaire devant les juges qui se sont prononcés en première instance ou un appel lorsqu'un recours contre leur décision a été accueilli en tout ou partie dans le cas de mistrial.</td></tr>
<tr><td rowspan="2">120</td><td>Registrar</td><td>Court official tasked with organising the court's diary and drawing up the court's orders and judgments.</td></tr>
<tr><td>Greffier</td><td>Fonctionnaire du tribunal chargé d'organiser l'activité du tribunal et, le cas échéant, de préparer les ordonnances et les jugements du tribunal.</td></tr>
<tr><td rowspan="2">121</td><td>Remote hearing (of a witness for example) by video-conference</td><td>Court hearing where the persons involved are not in the same room and participate via video-conference or on some on-line digital platform.</td></tr>
<tr><td>Audience par visioconférence</td><td>Audience à laquelle les personnes impliquées participent par visioconférence ou sur une plateforme en ligne, sans se trouver dans la même salle.</td></tr>
<tr><td rowspan="2">122</td><td>Renunciation (judicial review)</td><td>Declaration of the claimant to renounce to the claim, which has to be declared extinguished.</td></tr>
<tr><td>Désistement<br>(contrôle juridictionnel)</td><td>Déclaration par la partie demanderesse de sa volonté de renoncer à sa demande.</td></tr>
</table>

| | | |
|---|---|---|
| 123 | **Repeal (also Abrogation) of an administrative act**<br><br>**Abrogation d'un acte administratif** | Power of administrative authority to repeal its (lawful) decision, which means that the legal consequences which have resulted from administrative act, are not nullified, however no further legal consequences may result from such act (*ex nunc*).<br><br>Pouvoir dont dispose l'autorité administrative d'abroger sa décision (légal), ce qui signifie que les conséquences juridiques d'un acte administratif ne sont pas annulées pour le passé, mais qu'aucune autre conséquence juridique ne peut résulter d'un tel acte pour l'avenir. |
| 124 | **Responsible official**<br><br>**Agent chargé d'une affaire** | Official charged by the public authority with managing the administrative procedure.<br><br>Fonctionnaire chargé par l'autorité publique de conduire une procédure administrative. |
| 125 | **Request for revocation of a final judgement**<br><br>**Révision (contrôle juridictionnel)** | Extraordinary remedy enabling the reopening of the proceedings against final judgments delivered by administrative courts in serious cases established by the law such as, for example, if the judgment is the result of the fraud of one of the parties to damage the other; if the judgment was determined on the basis of evidence subsequently declared false; if new facts or essential evidence for the resolution of the case are discovered that were not available to the parties.<br><br>Recours extraordinaire permettant la réouverture de la procédure contre des jugements définitifs rendus par des tribunaux administratifs dans des cas graves prévus par la loi, par exemple si le jugement résulte d'une fraude commise par l'une des parties pour nuire à l'autre; s'il a été rendu sur la base d'éléments de preuve déclarés faux ultérieurement; si des faits nouveaux ou des éléments de preuve essentiels pour la résolution de l'affaire qui n'étaient pas à la disposition des parties sont découverts, etc. |
| 126 | **Right to be heard (administrative procedure)**<br><br>**Droit d'etre entendu (procédure administrative)** | Right granted to the parties to express their views (in writing or orally) to the public authority before a decision which would affect them adversely is taken.<br><br>Droit accordé aux parties de faire valoir leur point de vue (par écrit ou oralement) à l'autorité publique, avant que ne soit adoptée une mesure individuelle qui leur serait défavorable. |
| 127 | **Right to be heard (judicial review)**<br><br>**Droit d'etre entendu (contrôle juridictionnel)** | Right of every person to express his or her reasons in the judicial procedure before any individual measure which would affect him or her adversely is taken.<br><br>Droit de toute personne de faire valoir son point de vue dans le cadre de la procédure judiciaire, avant que ne soit adoptée une décision qui lui serait défavorable. |

| | | |
|---|---|---|
| 128 | **Rules of general experience**<br><br>**Règles d'expérience commune** | Knowledge and experience that every citizen in society has and that can be used by the judge to arrive at a (judicial) presumption on the basis of certain facts that are pleaded before it. In that case, the opposing party does have the possibility of rebutting the presumption. In common law countries this is known as the doctrine of judicial notice.<br><br>Connaissances et expériences que possède tout citoyen au sein de la société et qui peuvent être utilisées par le juge pour dégager une présomption (judiciaire), sur la base de certains faits invoqués devant lui. Dans cette hypothèse, la présomption peut être renversée par la partie adverse. Son équivalent dans les systèmes de common law est la doctrine de la « judicial notice ». |
| 129 | **Sanction (administrative)**<br><br>**Sanction (administrative)** | Unfavorable administrative act provided by the law as a consequence of an offence different from civil or penal sanctions.<br><br>Acte administratif défavorable, prévu par la loi comme la conséquence d'une infraction, distincte des sanctions civiles ou pénales. |
| 130 | **Self-government**<br><br>**Libre administration** | Government under the control and direction of the members of local communities rather than by an outside authority.<br><br>Administration sous le contrôle et la direction des membres de communautés locales, plutôt que par une autorité extérieure. |
| 131 | **Service by publication**<br><br>**Publication** | Service effected by keeping the document available for the people potentially interested on the premises or on the web-sites of the authority for a specified period.<br>A notice of the availability of the document shall be published in the Official Gazette and shall also be published on the official bulletin board of the authority or in a particular newspaper where it can be assumed the addressee will best receive the information.<br><br>La publication consiste à mettre un document à disposition des personnes potentiellement intéressées dans les locaux ou sur les sites web de l'autorité pendant une période déterminée.<br>Un avis de disponibilité du document est publié au Journal officiel ainsi que sur le panneau d'affichage officiel de l'autorité ou dans un journal particulier où l'on peut supposer que le destinataire recevra au mieux l'information. |
| 132 | **Service or notification of administrative acts**<br><br>**Notification des actes administratifs** | Procedure by which a public administration gives appropriate notice of an administrative act to all the interested parties.<br><br>Procédures par lesquelles l'administration publique avise de manière appropriée toutes les parties intéressées de l'adoption d'un acte administratif. |

| | | |
|---|---|---|
| 133 | **Services of general economic interest** | Services provided for economic consideration on a market, which would not be provided without public intervention or would be provided under different conditions in terms of physical and economic accessibility, continuity, non-discrimination, quality and safety. |
| | **Services d'intérêt économique général** | Services économiques fournis sur un marché, qui ne seraient pas assurés sans intervention publique ou qui le seraient dans des conditions différentes en termes d'accès géographique ou économique, de continuité du service, de non-discrimination, de qualité et de sécurité. |
| 134 | **Non-economic services of general interest (or 'non-economic public services')** | Services related to state prerogatives or power (police, justice, legal social security schemes) and those provided without economic considerations (compulsory education and so on). |
| | **Services non-économiques d'intérêt général** | Services relatifs à des prérogatives de puissance publique (police, justice, régimes de sécurité sociale obligatoires) et ceux assurés sans considérations économiques (éducation obligatoire, etc.). |
| 135 | **Standard service or notification** | The standard service is effected by post or e-mail and the addressee is considered to have been informed of the matter after the sending of the letter or e-mail, unless otherwise proven. |
| | **Notification normale** | Normalement, la notification a lieu par voie postale ou par courrier électronique et, sauf preuve contraire, le destinataire est réputé avoir été informé après l'envoi de la lettre ou du courrier électronique. |
| 136 | **Summary judgment (judicial review)** | A judgment entered at an early stage of the litigation where the outcome of the proceedings is clear and the case does not need to proceed to a full hearing. |
| | **Jugement selon une procédure simplifiée (contrôle juridictionnel)** | Décision rendue sans que l'affaire ne doive obligatoirement donner lieu à une audience, lorsque l'issue de la procédure est claire. |
| 137 | **Collateral (judicial review)** | In reference to precautionary measures, a guarantee provided by the appellant in whose favor a precautionary measure is granted, to respond to the opposing litigant for any damages that may arise from the application of the precautionary measure agreed, in the event that the resolution that finally terminates the process finds the cliam inadmissible or rejects it. |
| | **Sûreté (contrôle juridictionnel)** | Il s'agit d'une garantie fournie par le requérant à qui une mesure conservatoire est accordée. L'objectif étant de garantir la partie adversaire contre tout dommage susceptible de résulter de l'application de la mesure conservatoire convenue, dans l'hypothèse où le jugement est irrecevable ou la demande rejetée. |

| | | |
|---|---|---|
| 138 | **Temporary storage of works or items (judicial review)**<br><br>**Stockage temporaire d'œuvres ou d'objets (contrôle juridictionnel)** | Specific precautionary measure that can be adopted when it is alleged that certain works or objects have been produced in violation of the rules on intellectual and/or industrial property.<br><br>Mesure conservatoire spécifique qui peut être adoptée lorsqu'il est allégué que certaines œuvres ou certains objets ont été produits en violation des règles de propriété intellectuelle et/ou industrielle. |
| 139 | **Testimony or viva voce evidence**<br><br>**Témoignage de vive voix** | Oral evidence in court given by witnesses.<br><br>Preuve orale apportée par des témoins devant le tribunal. |
| 140 | **Intervener**<br><br>**Partie intervenante** | A Party added to the proceedings, generally by reason of court order.<br><br>Partie qui vient rejoindre la procédure, généralement en raison d'une ordonnance du tribunal. |
| 141 | **Time-limits for concluding procedures**<br><br>**Délais pour conclure les procédures** | Deadline, provided by sector-specific or general law, for the adoption of the administrative act.<br><br>Délai, prévu par le droit d'un secteur spécifique ou général, pour l'adoption d'un acte administratif. |
| 142 | **Trial court**<br><br>**Tribunal de première instance** | A first instance court which typically hears the relevant evidence and finds facts.<br><br>Tribunal de première instance qui prend en compte les éléments de preuve pertinents et établit les faits. |
| 143 | **Ultra vires**<br><br>**Ultra vires** | A public authority acting or regulating beyond its legal powers.<br><br>Situation dans laquelle une autorité publique agit ou édicte des règles au-delà de ses pouvoirs légaux. |
| 144 | **Unlawfulness**<br><br>**Violation de la loi** | Ground of review of administrative acts concerning situations in which administrative authorities breached the rules on administrative action established by any source of law.<br><br>Motif de contrôle des actes administratifs concernant des situations dans lesquelles les autorités administratives ont enfreint les règles d'action administrative établies par toute source de droit. |
| 145 | **Verifiable service**<br><br>**Notification vérifiable** | The service is verifiable if it is effected by means that provides verification upon delivery (post, or in person against acknowledgement of receipt, or by certified e-mail).<br><br>La notification est vérifiable si elle est effectuée par des moyens qui permettent de vérifier que la livraison a été effectuée (par voie postale, en main propre moyennant accusé de réception, ou par courrier électronique certifié). |

<table>
<tr><td rowspan="2">146</td><td>Very provisional measures (judicial review)</td><td>Emergency precautionary measures that can be requested even before the filing of the lawsuit and without hearing the opposing party, in circumstances that reveal an exceptional or extraordinary urgency, that is, an emergency situation of greater intensity than that normally required for the adoption of precautionary measures. In common law counties this is general done by means of an interim injunction.</td></tr>
<tr><td>Mesures très provisoires (contrôle juridictionnel)</td><td>Mesures conservatoires d'urgence qui peuvent être demandées avant même que des poursuites judiciaires ne soient engagées, et sans que la partie adverse ne soit entendue, dans des circonstances qui révèlent une urgence exceptionnelle ou extraordinaire, c'est-à-dire une situation d'urgence d'une intensité supérieure à celle normalement requise pour l'adoption de mesures conservatoires. Dans les systèmes de common law, des mesures équivalentes sont adoptées par l'équivalent d'un « interim injunction ».</td></tr>
<tr><td rowspan="2">147</td><td>Voidability</td><td>Where administrative act is flawed due to irregularities or illegalities that occurred in the administrative procedure and resulting in the possibility to challenge the decision. Not all of the irregularities affect the legality or correctness of the decision.</td></tr>
<tr><td>Vice susceptible de conduire à l'annulation</td><td>Défaut de l'acte administratif, résultant d'irrégularités ou d'illégalités survenues dans le cadre de la procédure administrative et entraînant la possibilité de contester la décision. Toutes les irrégularités n'ont pas d'incidence sur la légalité ou l'exactitude de la décision.</td></tr>
<tr><td rowspan="2">148</td><td>Voidness</td><td>Fundamental flaw of the administrative act preventing it from becoming final and binding because it contains such a defect that cannot be removed by any legal remedy or by the passage of time can be remedied. Normally voidness must be considered by the authority (or court) ex officio.</td></tr>
<tr><td>Inexistence</td><td>Vice fondamental de l'acte administratif empêchant qu'il devienne définitif et contraignant parce qu'il contient un défaut auquel aucun recours juridique ni le passage du temps ne permet de remédier. Normalement, l'inexistence doit être soulevée par l'autorité (ou le tribunal).</td></tr>
<tr><td rowspan="2">149</td><td>Withdrawal (judicial review)</td><td>Declaration by the plaintiff of his will not to continue the process, without prejudice.</td></tr>
<tr><td>Retrait<br>(contrôle juridictionnel)</td><td>Déclaration de la partie demanderesse de son intention de ne pas poursuivre le procès, sans préjudice.</td></tr>
<tr><td rowspan="2">150</td><td>Written witness statement (judicial review)</td><td>Witness giving their testimony in writing (such as in common law countries by affidavit or written deposition); subject to independent assessment by the court.</td></tr>
<tr><td>Témoignage écrit (contrôle juridictionnel)</td><td>Témoin donnant son témoignage par écrit (par exemple, dans les systèmes de common law, par le biais d'un affidavit ou d'une déposition écrite), sous réserve d'évaluation indépendante par le tribunal.</td></tr>
</table>

Printed in May 2025
by VARIGRAFICA ALTO LAZIO SRL – Via Cassia – 01036 Nepi (VT), Italy
for Merita Edizioni – Torino

*Thanks to the publication of this book,*
*the association Paulownia Piemonte Nazionale*
*will plant a tree in Italy.*
*www.paulowniapiemonte.it*

This book has been produced using FSC-certified paper